# FOUR YEARS

AMONG

# SPANISH-AMERICANS.

By F. HASSAUREK,

LATE UNITED STATES MINISTER RESIDENT TO THE REPUBLIC OF ECUADOR.

NEW YORK:
PUBLISHED BY HURD AND HOUGHTON,
459 Broome Street.
1868.

RIVERSIDE, CAMBRIDGE:
STEREOTYPED AND PRINTED BY
H. O. HOUGHTON AND COMPANY.

# PREFACE.

CONSIDERING the rapid multiplication of books in every branch of science and literature, it has always been my opinion that no new book should be written unless the author has something new to say, or unless he can present something already known in a new and original light.

Of Spanish-America but little is known among us at present. Our reading public probably knows more of China or Japan, than of such countries as the interior of Colombia, Ecuador, Peru, and Bolivia. Scientific men of great celebrity have acquainted us with the geographical and geological features of the Andean valleys and table-lands; but they have told us but little concerning the character, the social and domestic life, the political institutions and troubles of the inhabitants. In this respect, I believe I have had, to a great extent, an unexplored field before me; and I flatter myself that the following pages contain many observations and valuable items of ethnological and historical information which cannot be found in any of the comparatively few English books on Spanish-America.

This is not a book of travels. The impressions of a traveller in a foreign country, who passes from one place to another, taking hasty notes of undigested observations, are often erroneous, and generally unreliable. It is necessary to live among a people, to speak their language, to know their history and literature, to study their customs, and to associate with them continually, in order to be able to write a book about them which those who are thoroughly familiar with the subject will not throw aside as presumptuous and superficial.

I have left many warm friends in South America, friends whose uniform courtesy, attention, and kindness to me, I shall never cease to appreciate. Some of them, I am afraid, will object to certain passages in this book as an uncharitable return of hospitality. But to do good, the truth must be told. Vattel very properly pronounces it to be the duty of every nation to know itself. To acquire a sufficient knowledge of itself, however, a nation should wish occasionally to "see itself as others see it." I have "extenuated nothing," but I have "set down naught in malice." I feel for those unfortunate countries, and the memory of the friends I have left there shall ever be dearly treasured up in my heart. But if the following pages were to have any merit, I had to describe South America as I found it and not as I wished it to be.

THE AUTHOR.

CINCINNATI, *August 23d*, 1867.

# CONTENTS.

CHAPTER I.

PAGE

Arrival in Ecuador. — The City of Guayaquil. — Its Aspect. — North American Enterprise. — Old and New City. — Wooden Buildings. — Palm-trees, Goats, and Gallinazos. — Fortifications and Barracks. — Balsas. — A Floating Population. — Climate and Temperature. — Dry and Rainy Season. — Distant View of Mount Chimborazo . . . . . . . . . . . . . 1

CHAPTER II.

Ancient History of Guayaquil. — Pirates and Buccaneers. — Conflagrations. — Population and Commerce. — Imports and Exports. — Productiveness of the Country. — Want of Roads. — Ida Pfeiffer. — Preparations for the Journey to the Interior. — Trip up the River to Bodegas. — A Tropical Paradise. — Thoughts of Home . 9

CHAPTER III.

Alligators. — The Town of Babahoyo, or Bodegas. — Hiring Horses. — Arrieros. — Galled and Jaded Beasts. — Packing. — Indian Endurance. — The Journey. — The Tropical Forest. — No Great Race has ever sprung from the Tropics. — Savaneta. — Description of Houses on the Road. — Punta Playas. — Camellones or Camels' Backs. — Nights in the Forest. — Mysterious Noises. — Mata Blanca. — Pisagua. — A Horrid Road. — Ascending the Cordillera. — Jorje. — Cuesta de Angas. — Camino Real. — Eating Lice. — Emerging from the Tropics. — Superstition. — View from Mt. Pizcurcu. — A Forgotten Corner of the World. — A Dangerous Descent. — Villages in the Valley of Chimbo. — The Polite "Jefe Politico." — Socabon. — Llamas. — The Town of Guaranda. — Change Horses: — Preparations for passing Chimborazo . . 22

CHAPTER IV.

Passage of Mt. Chimborazo. — A Visit to the Region of Clouds and Storms. — View of the Mountain. — The *Arenal*. — Human Reminiscences and Monuments in the Desert of Sand and Snow. —

PAGE

What a *Paramo* is. — Its Terrors. — Chuquipoyo. — The Hacienda of Chimborazo. — A Dreary Resting-place. — View from Chuquipoyo. — The City of Riobamba in the Distance. — Earthquakes and Volcanoes. — Mt. Sangai. — Rains of Ashes. — Mt. Altar. — Mt. Carguairazo. — The Paramo of Sanancajas. — Descent from the Mountain Heath. — Reappearance of Vegetation. — The Village of Mocha . . . . . . . . . . . . 50

CHAPTER V.

From Mocha to Ambato. — The Volcano Tunguragua. — The Towns of Ambato and Latacunga. — Fleas. — The Volcano Cotopaxi. — Earthquakes and Prophecies. — A Gold Legend. — The Treasure of Atahuallpa. — The Testament of Valverde. — His *Derrotero*. — Mt. Ilinisa. — The Plain and Village of Mulalu. — Description of a Farm-Building. — Signs of General Decay. — The Hill of Callo. — The Footprints of St. Bartholomew the Apostle. — Inca Ruins. — The Paramo of Tiupullo. — The "Accursed Tree." — Rumiñagui and other Mountains. — The Villages of Machachi and Tambillo. — An Ecuadorian Tavern. — End of our Journey . . 68

CHAPTER VI.

Altitude of Quito.— Mt. Pichincha. — Its Height. — The Crater. — The Peaks of Pichincha. — Eruptions. — The French Academicians. — Humboldt, Colonel Hall, and Boussingault. — Dr. Gabriel Garcia Moreno's Three Descents to the Bottom of the Crater. — The Valley and Village of Lloa. — An American Artist in the Crater. — My Visits to it. — View from the Summit of Pichincha. — Pumice-stone. — Temperature. — Approaches to Quito. — Aña-Quito, the Battle-Field. — Turubamba. — Mt. Panecillo. — The City viewed from the Surrounding Hills. — A Retrospect . . 91

CHAPTER VII.

Quito. — Appearance of the City. — Crowds in the Streets. — Streets and Houses. — Queer Mode of Cooking. — Want of Hotels. — A Curate's Idea of the Obligation of Promises. — Traits of Native Character. — Want of Cleanliness. — Incidents. — Excellent Climate. — Mean Temperature. — No Diseases or Insects. — The Rainy Season. — Fruits and Flowers. — Earth's Paradise . . 104

CHAPTER VIII.

Population. — The Whites. — Aristocratic Traditions. — Ancient Nobility. — Prejudice against Labor. — Early Marriages. — Boy-Husbands. — No Spirit of Association. — Mixed Races. — Cholas and Bolziconas. — Servants. — Huasicamas. — Indian Wives. — Laundresses. — Longas, Guambras, and Guiñazhiscas. — Ama de

PAGE

Llaves. — Marketing. — Matrimonial Relations. — An Incident. — Indian Humility. — Other Traits of Indian Character. — Politeness of the Rabble. — Spanish-American Courtesy. — A Lady's Message to a Friend . . . . . . . . . . . . 121

CHAPTER IX.

Spanish Mode of Colonization. — Fortifications and Convents. — Architecture of Quito. — The Moorish Style. — Public Buildings. — Churches. — Nunneries. — The Convent of San Francisco. — Its Painted Miracles. — Interesting Specimens. — The Praying Lamb. — The Chapel of Catuña. — A Romantic Legend. — The Treasures of Rumiñagui. — A Pretended Pact with the Prince of Darkness. — La Capilla del Robo. — Another Legend. — The Parish Church of San Roque. — Flagellation. — The Tejar, or La Recoleta de la Merced. — Religious Exercises in Lent. — Still another Legend. — Indian Reticence. — Burying-places. — How the Poor bury their Children. — Administering the Last Sacraments. — Religious Processions. — Semana Santa. — Holy Thursday and Good Friday. — Splendid Illumination of the Churches. — A Descendimiento. — A Sermon accompanied by a Puppet-show. — Its Effect on the Audience. — A Portable Image of the Lord, and its Travels to the Coast. — Christmas. — Misa de Gallos. — The Clergy. — Ignorance and Immorality of the Monks. — The Curates. — List of Convents and Nunneries. — Fees of Curates. — Divisions of Caste . . 137

CHAPTER X.

Social Life in the Ecuadorian Capital. — The Ladies. — High Opinion of France. — The Populace believes every Foreigner to be a Frenchman. — Female Morality. — The General Prejudice unfounded. — Female Politicians and Conspirators. — Educational. — Literary Dependence of Spain on France. — Want of Newspapers. — Sisters of the "Heart of Jesus." — Music. — The Diplomatic Corps. — Foreigners. — *Exequias*. — *Duelos*. — *Luto*. — Sunday Visits. — Salutations and Etiquette. — Christmas Calls. — *Dar las Pascuas*. — *Cumpleaños*. — Bull-baitings, or *Toros*. — Description of the *Plaza Mayor*. — Cock-fights. — *La Gallera*. — Holidays. — *Inocentes*. — Masquerades between Christmas and New Year. — Fancy Dress Processions. — Carnival. — Queer Observance. — Chicha, the Indian National Beverage. — Indian Degradation, Drunkenness, and Improvidence . . . . . . . . 163

CHAPTER XI.

Agriculture. — Wooden Plows. — Mechanic Arts. — Improvidence of the People. — Beggars. — Commerce of the Interior. — Want of Enterprise. — City lit with Tallow Candles. — Needlework and Embroidery. — Fine Arts. — Painting. — Splendid Copyists. —

PAGE

Cheapness of Paintings. — Saints and Martyrs. — A Scene from Purgatory. — The Liberal Professions. — The Law. — *Tinterillos.* — System of Jurisprudence. — The Country without a Penitentiary. — Physicians. — Drug Stores. — The *Hospicio.* — Leprosy and Elephantiasis. — Female Prison and Lunatic Asylum. — The Hospital. — No Room for Wounded Soldiers. — The Young Men of Quito . . . . . . . . . . . . . 190

CHAPTER XII.

The Political Condition of the South-American Republics. — A Tale of Horror and Misery . . . . . . . . . . 209

CHAPTER XIII.

Trip to the Province of Imbabura. — Descent to the River Guaillabamba. — The Pyramids. — Their History. — The Village of Guaillabamba. — Wild Mountainous Scenery. — The Switzerland of America. — The River Pisque. — A Historical Reminiscence. — Gonzalo Pizarro and the Viceroy Blasco Nuñez Vela. — American Aloe; its Multifarious Uses. — Tabacundo. — *Gente del Pueblo* or Common People. — Alto de Cajas. — Lake St. Pablo. — The Festival of St. John. — Great Indian Celebrations. — The Feast at Otabalo. — Indian Dances and Masquerades. — Gambling. — Ugliness of Indian Women. — The Chapel of Monserate. — Idolatrous Practices. — *Corrida de Gallos.* — San Juan and San Pedro at the Village of Cayambi. — Mt. Cayambi. — Longevity. — Agua Gloriada. — Contra-dances. — *Guarapo.* — Reports of Volcanic Activity. — More Gold Legends. — *Serro Pelado.* — Col. Hall's attempted Ascent of Mt. Cayambi. — Gold Somewhere. — The Napo Province on the Eastern Side of the Cordillera. — Compulsory Sales of Merchandise to Indians by the Governor. — Destruction of Three Cities by the Indians. — No Vestige remains. — Poetic Retribution. — Legends and Traditions. — The Fate of the Captured Women of Golden Sevilla . . . . . . . . . . . 248

CHAPTER XIV.

My Journey to the Northern Province continued. — The Chase. — Esculents. — The Graveyard of Cayambi. — *Doctrina Cristiana.* — Aruchicos. — Speech by an Indian. — Indian Peonage. — Further Peculiarities of Indian Character. — Population and Characteristics of the Town of Otabalo. — The Convent. — Punishment of Indians for neglecting Religious Observances. — *Alcaldes de Doctrina.* — Mt. Cotacachi and Lake Cuicocha. — Dangerous Hunting Parties. — Sunday Markets. — The Village of Cotacachi. — More Remnants of the Inquisition. — *Padronar.* — How Laws and Municipal Ordinances are promulgated in an Illiterate Country. —

PAGE

American Machinery an "Invention of the Devil." — Mt Imbabura. — The Village of Hatuntaqui. — Tolas, or Indian Graves or Mounds. — The City of Ibarra. — Carranqui, the Birthplace of Atahuallpa. — No Vestige left of Indian Civilization. — Digging up Indian Graves. — Strange Discoveries. — Impulse given by the Gold Discoveries at Cuenca. — Lake Yaguarcocha, the Sea of Blood . . . . . . . . . . . . 294

## CHAPTER XV.

Trip to the Province of Imbabura concluded. — A Visit to the Valley of the River Chota. — The Heights of Alaburu. — The Mountain of Pialchan, with its Mysterious Cave. — Another Gold Legend. — Aërial Bridges. — Return to the Tropics. — Sugar Plantations and Negroes. — History of the Abolition of Slavery in Ecuador. — Landslips. — Mass Emigration and Disappearance of Indians. — The Strange Story of Pimampiro. — Geological Catastrophes. — Digging for Treasures. — The Village of Cacha swallowed up by an Earthquake. — Indian Graves. — Ancient Indian Crockery. — Guajara. — The Footpath to Peylon on the Coast. — The English Company. — Negro Dances. — Bomba and Alfandoque. — The Paramo Road to Quito. — Mojanda. — A Farewell to the Fairy Province of Imbabura. — Mountain Lakes. — Return to Quito . 322

## CHAPTER XVI.

### HISTORICAL REVIEW.

Indian Traditions. — Difficulties of Estimating Ancient Indian Civilization. — Scarcity of Materials. — Destruction of Indian Civilization by the Spaniards. — The Religious Element of the Conquest. — Fray Marcos de Niza. — Persecution of the Indian Writer Collahuaso. — The Old Quitu Nation. — Its Conquest by the Carans. — The Giants of Punta Santa Helena. — The Ancient Kings or Scyris of Quito. — Romantic Legend of Condorazo. — Invasion of the Peruvian Incas. — Cacha Duchicela, the last of the Scyris. — His Heroic Resistance against the Inca Huaynacapac. — Battle of Hatuntaqui. — Death of the last of the Scyris. — His Daughter Pacha. — Death of Huaynacapac. — War between his Sons, Huascar and Atahuallpa. — Battle of Quipaypan. — Defeat and Capture of Huascar. — Arrival of the Spaniards under Francisco Pizarro. — Capture and Execution of Atahuallpa. — Downfall of the Peruvian Empire — Usurpation and Cruelty of Rumiñagui at Quito. — Benalcazar's Expedition to Quito. — Genius of Rumiñagui. — Battle of Tiocajas. — Evacuation and Destruction of Quito by Rumiñagui. — The Virgins of the Sun. — Horrid Cruelty of the Spaniards. — Execution of Rumiñagui. — Indian Slavery. — Encomiendas and Repartimientos. — Spanish Colonization. — The Blue

PAGE

Laws of Spanish America. — Protective Legislation. — Pedro de Puelles. — Revolution of the Colonists. — Gonzalo Pizarro. — Battle of Quito. — Death of the Viceroy. — Death of Gonzalo Pizarro. — Revolution and Execution of Hernandez Giron. — The Cause of the Indians Abandoned. — Plan for a Continuation of this History . . . . . . . . . . . . 351

APPENDIX . . . . . . . . . . 399

# FOUR YEARS AMONG SPANISH-AMERICANS.

## CHAPTER I.

Arrival in Ecuador. — The City of Guayaquil. — Its Aspect. — North American Enterprise. — Old and New City. — Wooden Buildings. — Palm-trees, Goats, and Gallinazos. — Fortifications and Barracks. — Balsas. — A Floating Population. — Climate and Temperature. — Dry and Rainy Season. — Distant View of Mount Chimborazo.

GUAYAQUIL is the principal sea-port of the Republic of Ecuador on the Pacific coast of South America. It is situate on the right bank of the river Guayas, about sixty miles above its mouth. I arrived there on the 21st of June, 1861. The city, viewed from the river, presents a lively and business-like appearance, especially at night, when rows of gas-lights are reflected in the waters. There is but little to warn the traveller, at first sight, that it is a town of the present, through which he has to pass into regions still belonging to the past. The principal street, called the "Malecon," extends about a mile and a half along the river; its large frame houses with their curtain-covered porches, some of them strangely dislocated by earthquakes, as if ready to tumble down, without a moment's warning, present a most original and grotesque appearance. The stores are as elegant and tasteful as any of our own stores in a second or third class city could be; gas-light greets us at night, and a lively throng of humanity in the day-time; hundreds of canoes, skiffs, rafts, *balsas*, and small sailing-vessels called *chatas*, come and go with the tide, bringing to town the manifold tropical fruits and vegetables in which the luxuriant country along the Guayas and its affluents abounds. Water-carriers on donkeys, with two barrels on a wooden pack-saddle before them, hurry up and down the streets. At night the air is rent by the lively and sometimes witty exclamations of boys, offering for sale a kind of candy called *caramelo*, tallow-candles, *tamales* (a peculiar dish of the country), ice-cream, if ice happens to be in town, etc., etc. Coaches and carriages, it is true, are not to be seen (there are but two private carriages in town, and these are confined to the Malecon, and a few intersecting streets, because the pavement of the others makes them inaccessible to vehicles), but mule-carts clatter from one end of the landing to the other. A hand railroad-track leads from the wharf to the custom-house, — certainly not suggestive of the fact that we are but one day's journey from regions in which a wagon is never seen. Steamboats like our own (their machinery having been built in the United States) ply up and down the river, reminding us of home; and even a Baltimore steam-engine puffs and snorts through the streets in cases of fire, filling the atmosphere with sounds familiar to an American ear.

In fact, almost all the modern improvements in Guayaquil were introduced by North Americans. An American company has introduced gas into a town to which coal must be brought from abroad. An American company has built the friendly steamboats, which now make their regular trips up and down the Guayas and its tributaries; an iron foundery and machine-shop have been established by Americans, and even the two neat little frame houses on the wharf which are occupied by the officers of the port, were brought from the United States.

The northern part of Guayaquil is called the "Old City," which clusters around the slopes of a hill on which the military hospital is located, and the fresh verdure of which, especially during the rainy season, is pleasing to the eye. The new town, containing all that is business or fashion, occupies a part of the plain or *savana* between the river and a salt-water estuary called the "Estero Salado." It is separated from the old city by several smaller estuaries, over which wooden bridges, always out of repair, keep up the communication. The total absence of brick and stone buildings is striking. The houses are two or three stories high, and built in the southern style, with porches or balconies protruding over the sidewalks and resting on wooden pillars, thus forming piazzas,[1] which afford protection against sun and rain. But few of the streets are properly paved. Some of them have nothing but a bridge of stepping-stones at the crossings as a passage, during the rainy season, from one side to the other. The Malecon, and a few others of the principal streets, are kept tolerably clean, but the by-streets, and the rear part of the city, are shockingly filthy, and disfigured by dilapidated, dingy, and miserable hovels. Stray donkeys and herds of goats roam the streets, and feed on the grass which, in the rainy season, covers the most frequented thoroughfares, giving a melancholy aspect to the place. The palm-tree, the king of tropical vegetation, rises majestically over roofs and garden fences on which the *gallinazo* (turkey-buzzard or carrion-crow) perches, — that silent and greedy companion of death and decay.

[1] Such passages or covered sidewalks are called *portales*.

In the outskirts of the city the houses of the poor are almost as humble as those primitive habitations which we shall meet in the tropical wilderness, on the road to the interior. They have only an upper floor resting on piles, the room below being used for kitchens, or occupied by domestic animals. They are floored and walled with split cane, and thatched with *bijao* leaves, or other dried herbage. The hammock constitutes their principal article of furniture; and thus but a few squares from the splendid residences of the wealthy aristocracy, furnished with Parisian luxury, we find the humble cottage of the poor half-breed, the indolent inhabitant of the tropical forest.

The hill at the foot of which the old city extends, is fortified by batteries commanding the river above and below. Sand batteries, too, dot the landing along the Malecon. They were erected in 1861 and 1862, when war with Peru seemed to be inevitable. [Why batteries should have been planted within the city so as to draw the enemy's fire on a town of wooden buildings, instead of defending it from without, is one of those mysteries of military science which uninitiated civilians are unable to comprehend.] There are three *cuarteles* (military barracks) in the city. The soldiers, especially those from the interior, are generally followed by their wives, who are allowed to live with them. This rather unmilitary indulgence, is believed to prevent the men from deserting; it adds to their comforts, and may be considered an improvement on the morality of camps or barracks. The soldiers are a motley crowd, with and without shoes, and representing all imaginable shades of color. The higher officers are generally white men; but no white men will be found among the rank and file. Indians are exempt from military service on account of their meekness and cowardice.

The market on the landing presents a grotesque and lively sight. The principal food of the poorer classes is the plantain, which is brought to town in canoes or skiffs. It is picturesque to see them come with the tide paddled by one or two half-naked mulattoes, *zambos* or *cholos*, and generally so well filled that the plantain branches overhang the sides and are dragged along in the waters, issuing, as it were, from the very horn of plenty. The principal disadvantage of Guayaquil is the want of sweet water during the dry season, because then the tide runs up to Bodegas, a town about sixty miles above Guayaquil. Hence water has to be brought to the city in casks and barrels on rafts called *balsas*, a most remarkable maritime conveyance invented by the ancient Peruvians. They are made of five, seven, or nine trunks of an exceedingly light tree, called *balsa*. The rafts are made longer or smaller, as they are wanted for fishing, for the coasting-trade, or for the river, and they go with safety as far as Payta in Peru, from Guayaquil. The trunks, or logs of which they are made, are fastened to each other by *bejucos* (a sort of parasite plant) or withies, and have cross-logs lashed so firmly with these pliable plants that they rarely give way, though the sea during their coasting voyages runs very high. Nor does the water rise between the logs, as the whole machine adapts itself to the motion of the waves. Sails, too, are used on *balsas*, and were used by the Indians before the conquest, to the great astonishment of the Spanish discoverers. Houses, with two or three rooms, and kitchens, are generally built on such *balsas;* and thus residences are formed for a literally *floating population*, living on the rivers, and changing about from one part of the country to another as inclination or necessity may dictate. These *balsas* are chiefly inhabited by negroes and mulattoes. Their furniture consists of two or three hammocks, in which they swing in the daytime, and sleep at night. The rivers abound in fish, which they take with a hooked spear, in a very dexterous manner. The plantain-tree, which grows around them in abundance, furnishes them with more vegetable food than they can eat. Clothing they need but little, thanks to the climate, which enables them to go about half-naked. What little fuel they require for cooking purposes, their children will find in the woods along the river banks. They spend nothing for the education of their children, who, like their parents, grow up in ignorance and superstition. To gain a little ready money they take fruits and vegetables to market, and rear fighting-cocks, with which they visit the cockpits in towns or villages. The very bounteousness of Nature has made the poorer classes indolent, lazy, and improvident.

The mean temperature of Guayaquil is about 78° Fahrenheit, in the shade. The dry season lasts from June to December or January, and is exceedingly cool, pleasant, and healthy. The evenings, nights, and mornings are very cool, sometimes even cold. The days are warm, but those whose business does not require strong physical exertion will hardly call the weather hot. At about four or five o'clock in the afternoon, and sometimes much earlier, a cool and strong breeze sets in which is known as the *chánduy*, because it comes over a mountain of that name. It generally blows all night, and sometimes even in the morning, and greatly contributes to the salubrity of the place, although it leads to frequent colds. During the best part of the dry season, there are hardly any mosquitoes, and no epidemics. If it were not for the rainy season, I should say that the reports about the pestiferous climate of Guayaquil are gross exaggerations. The rainy season, however, or "winter," as it is called, is very unpleasant. The sun sends down its burning rays in the day-time, and the heavens open their flood-gates at night. The pleasant *chánduy* ceases to blow, and the atmosphere is hot and oppressive, without a breeze stirring for days and weeks. Mosquitoes cloud the air in dense swarms, and molest the inhabitants in the day-time as well as at night. Puddles are formed in the streets, making many of them impassable from one side to the other. The *savana* (plain) in the rear, and some of the streets in the outskirts of the city, will be under water, owing to the yearly inundation of the low and flat parts of the country. Myriads of little insects will hover around the lights at night, dropping down dead on tables, desks, and other furniture. Fevers and dysenteries make their appearance, and business is suspended on account of the impassable condition of the roads. During this season, Guayaquil must appear gloomy to the foreigner, not on account of the heat, as the mercury never rises as high as during the torrid season of our own country, but on account of its general unpleasantness, and especially the intolerable attacks of mosquitoes and other insects.[1]

[1] Among the insects of Guayaquil, there is one which is not an enemy to man, but to knowledge and science. It is the *polilla* (pronounced *poleelya*), which destroys books and papers by perforating them in a hundred different places, from one end of a volume to the other. The greater part of the old municipality records has thus been destroyed; and to keep up extensive public or private libraries would require the greatest care and incessant watchfulness. Camphor seems to be a safe preventive against the *polilla*; but it evaporates so soon, that its application must be repeated

A great sight for foreigners is a distant view of Mount Chimborazo, which may be seen from the Malecon on clear summer days. On the other side of the river, apparently in the rear of two insignificant hills, rises above the long chain of the Cordillera, the huge mountain covered with masses of snow and ice, the dazzling whiteness of which is intersected by black lines formed by the steep and sharp edges of frightful rocks on which the snow cannot gather. Unpolluted by mortal tread the mountain rears its snowy head. The storms of heaven thunder around its unapproachable peaks; the fleeting clouds are allowed to embrace and to kiss them; the majestic condor alights on them for a short rest after his soaring flight, but no human foot ever profaned them; no human foot ever will. Now you see the mountain before you, as an imposing background to green forests, luxuriant hills, and the undulating chain of the Cordillera; but follow me and you shall soon see it, face to face, and in the loneliness of the desert. You shall see it, yourself, 14,000 feet above the level of the sea, and far away from all human habitations, face to face, amidst the horrors of Nature's solitude. There, where the howling storms sweep over the dreary "Arenal"; there, where the shivering traveller hurries over the lofty pass to avoid the dreadful gusts that may hurl the rider from his horse; there, where the mountain streams separate and rush on, on one side to the Atlantic and on the other to the Pacific; there, if you will follow me, you will bow to Nature's grandeur in the loneliness of altitudes unconquerable by the skill and enterprise of man.

continually. The dampness of the atmosphere, too, (not only in the rainy, but also in the dry season,) is a great enemy to books; but more dangerous still to clothes, silk dresses, kid gloves, and other articles of wearing apparel.

## CHAPTER II.

Ancient History of Guayaquil. — Pirates and Buccaneers. — Conflagrations. — Population and Commerce. — Imports and Exports. — Productiveness of the Country. — Want of Roads. — Ida Pfeiffer. — Preparations for the Journey to the Interior. — Trip up the River to Bodegas. — A Tropical Paradise. — Thoughts of Home.

THE first foundation of Guayaquil took place in the year 1535. Sebastian de Benalcazar, the conqueror of Quito, placed himself at the head of an expedition fitted out at that place, and consisting of one hundred Spaniards, fifty horses, and four thousand friendly, or rather subjugated Indians, who had been impressed for the purpose of carrying the baggage, provisions, and ammunition of their new masters. He made his way to, and through, the valley of Chimbo without difficulty; but when he descended the western branch of the Cordillera, and entered the lowlands, his Indian carriers, unaccustomed to the parching heat and unhealthy climate of the coast, died at the rate of two hundred to three hundred a day. The fame of the Spaniards, however, had already preceded them. The Indian tribes on the River Guayas and its tributaries had heard of the foreign conquerors, before whom the mighty empire of the Incas had fallen, and convinced that, eventually, resistance would prove useless, made their submission to Benalcazar. On the 25th of July, 1535, the latter laid the foundation of the town of Santiago de Guayaquil under the 2° 12′ of south latitude. He appointed Diego de Daza governor of the province, and leaving the greater part of his men in the new colony, returned to Quito to extend his conquests to the north of that capital.

But the Indians of Guayaquil soon repented of their peaceable submission. The Spaniards thirsted for gold, but still more they coveted the wives and daughters of the natives, which so provoked the latter that they rose, and by a bloody massacre destroyed the infant settlement. Of about seventy who had been left by Benalcazar, only the Governor and five others escaped, and after weeks of hardships and dangers succeeded in making their way back to Quito.[1]

The Lieutenant-Governor of that place, Don Juan Diaz de Hidalgo, immediately fitted out a second expedition, which he placed under the command of Daza and another military leader, Pedro de Tapia. Three thousand more Indians were taken along and fell, like their unfortunate predecessors, a helpless prey to the fevers of the lowlands. The Guayas Indians, however, were prepared for resistance, and after many bloody encounters, defeated the Spaniards in a decisive action and compelled them to retreat to Quito.

The news of these disasters reached the newly created Marquis de Pizarro at Lima, and knowing that Benalcazar, engaged in the conquest of the province of Popayan, north of Quito, could not attend to his southern colonies, fitted out an expedition under the command of Francisco de Zaera who, in the following year (1536), after many indecisive actions, concluded a treaty with the Indians, in which these unsophisticated children of nature very ingeniously stipulated that from the countries whence so many Christian *men* had

[1] Herrera's *Historia General de los Hechos de los Castellanos en las Islas y Tierra Firme, del Mar Oceano*, Decada V., lib. 7, cap xv.

come, the Spaniards should also bring Christian *women*, in order that their Indian women might remain unmolested.

To this the Spaniards consented, and so the colony was reëstablished. But shortly afterwards news arrived of the successful rebellion of the Peruvian Indians under the great Manco Inca, who was already besieging Cuzco; and Zaera had to leave Guayaquil with his whole command, and hurry to the assistance of his countrymen. After his departure the settlement remained abandoned, until peace having been restored in Peru, Pizarro sent the notorious Francisco de Or ellana,[1] who founded Guayaquil for the third and last time in the year 1537.[2] It was built on the declivity of a hill called "Cerillo Verde" (Green Hill) on the spot now known as "Old City" (*Ciudad Vieja*).

If we except the distance of Guayaquil from the ocean, its advantages as a port are considerable; and its possession has often been coveted by the ambitious rulers of Peru. The coast of the latter is sterile and sandy; but Guayaquil is the capital and centre of a most fertile province which abounds in timber for ship and house building, and with its exuberant growth of fruit, especially of cacao, plantains, etc., etc., supplies many a foreign market, while the majestic river by which it is irrigated, the most splendid on the Pacific

1 The first European who navigated the Amazon, (from one of its upper tributaries (the Napo) to its mouth,) and published a most exaggerated and improbable account of his discoveries. To this romantic account we owe the story of the Amazons, of cities and villages with golden roofs, etc., etc., and other visionary fabrications.

2 It is stated in the *New American Cyclopædia*, edited by Ripley and Dana, (article "Ecuador,") that Francisco Pizarro landed at Tumbez, now *Guayaquil*, in 1532. This is a mistake, as far as Guayaquil is concerned. Pizarro never was at Guayaquil, nor was Guayaquil formerly called Tumbez. The Tumbez where Pizarro landed is a port in Peru, near the mouth of the river Tumbez, more than a degree south of Guayaquil.

side of Central and South America, forms a secure harbor for vessels of almost every size, at a distance of more than sixty miles from the sea. This distance, although it may have somewhat retarded the progress of Guayaquil as a commercial port, did not prevent the pirates and buccaneers of the seventeenth century from making it one of the many scenes of their atrocities. It was first attacked in 1624 by Jacob H. Clark, who landed with two hundred of his followers, and would have set fire to the town, had it not been for the desperate resistance of the inhabitants. In August of the same year, it was attacked by another party of pirates five hundred strong, who were also repulsed, and on their retreat set fire to the Royal Armory on the Island of Puná, at the mouth of the river.

The French pirates who landed in 1686 were more successful; and took all the treasure they could find in the city. In 1687 the English freebooters, under Edward David, fell unexpectedly upon the town, took $13,400 in treasure, and would have reduced the place to ashes, had not the inhabitants offered them the sum of $40,000 and two hostages for its payment. They withdrew, and killed the hostages after having received the money.[1]

In 1707 William Dampierre took and pillaged the place ; and in 1709, the notorious Clipperton ransacked almost every house in the city. Fortifications were not erected until 1730, because such works could not be undertaken without the sanction and permission of the Spanish Government. Until that express permission could be obtained from the Royal Circumlocution Office, the inhabitants had no right to take the most indispensable measures for their own safety.

[1] See Padre Juan de Velasco's *Historia del Reino de Quito*, vol. iii. p. 115. Also, Manuel Villavicencios's *Geografia de la Republica del Ecuador*, p. 249.

The conflagrations with which the place has been and is still visited from time to time, form another scourge of Guayaquil. In 1707 one hundred and thirty houses were destroyed by fire, and the great conflagration in 1764 destroyed almost the whole city. Fires are very dangerous to a place in which hardly one brick or stone building can be found, especially in the dry season, when months will pass without a drop of rain to moisten the timber parched by a tropical sun. I witnessed a conflagration in November, 1862, and another in August, 1865. In a few hours whole squares were consumed, and only by the greatest exertions could the further spread of the furious element be prevented. There are several voluntary fire companies in Guayaquil, one of which is chiefly composed of foreigners, and comprises many of the most respectable merchants of the town.

The population of Guayaquil is differently estimated. Some place it as high as 24,000, others as low as 20,000, and even 18,000. Ulloa, in 1736, estimated it at 20,000; from which it will appear that the increase, if there has been any, is but very insignificant. Holinski, a Polish traveller, who visited the country in 1851, came to the conclusion that, for twenty years last preceding his visit, immigration from the interior had kept the number of the inhabitants at a figure varying from 20,000 to 25,000.[1] Since 1862 it has been steadily decreasing. I have heard intelligent residents, foreigners as well as natives, assert, that at least eighty per cent. of the population are colored, and my own observations have led me to believe that this estimate is not an exaggeration.

1 *L'Equateur, Scenes de la Vie Sud-Americaine*, par Alexandre Holinski, Paris, 1861, p. 28.

The commerce of Guayaquil is not inconsiderable. On its custom-house receipts the government of Ecuador chiefly depends for its revenue. The interior depends on these imports for the greater part of the commodities and almost all the luxuries of life. There is, proportionately, but little manufacturing industry in the interior, and much less on the coast. The natives of the former can make furniture, saddles, coarse woolen and cotton goods in limited quantities, fine embroidery and needle-work, common rum distilled from the sugar-cane, boots and shoes of a very inferior quality, hats, paintings, etc, etc., but almost every thing else has to be imported from abroad. Common American and English cotton and woolen goods, wines and liquors, cloth, silks, French fancy articles, glass and china-ware, hardware and cutlery, crockery, etc., etc., are important items of importation. Flour, too, has to be imported for the use of the districts on the coast, although in the interior wheat grows in bountiful abundance. But there are no wagon roads, and the mills are very bad; hence the necessity of importation. It is chiefly brought from Chili. Lard is imported from the United States for consumption on the coast.

Guayaquil monopolizes at present the business of importation, because its roads to the interior are mule-paths; while those which lead to the highlands from the ports of Esmeraldas and Peylon are not even accessible to horses or mules, but require merciless foot travelling. It is a common saying in Ecuador, that "*Our roads are roads for birds, but not for men.*"

The principal articles of exportation are the following: —

1st. Cacao (the fruit of the chocolate-tree). The cacao of Guayaquil is famous in the markets of the world. It is raised all along the River Guayas and its tributaries, and brought to Guayaquil in steamboats, *balsas*, canoes, and other conveyances. It being the principal staple of Guayaquil, the good or bad success of the crop generally determines the rate of foreign exchange. Spain receives the largest share of the yearly exportation, if not fully one half.

2d. *Panama hats*, most of which are manufactured in Ecuador, principally at Santa Helena, Montecristi, and other villages on the coast, where it is the only business of the inhabitants. During latter years, however, there has been a great falling off in this article, owing to the introduction of other hats of greater cheapness. This has led to great poverty and distress in the hat-making districts, which, for want of water, are almost without agriculture.

3d. The quina bark of Ecuador (cascarilla) has repeatedly attracted the attention of the scientific as well as the commercial world. In 1859 Mr. Clements R. Markham was appointed by the British Secretary of State for India to superintend the collection of chinchona plants and seeds in South America, and their introduction into India; an experiment which, according to the latest advices from that country, will prove a complete success.[1] While reserving to himself the task of exploring the quina forests of Peru, Mr. Markham secured for the exploration of the Equatorian bark regions the services of Mr. Richard Spruce, a botanist of high standing in the scientific world. The several interesting reports published by the latter contain a great many items of useful information, not only with reference to the botanical but general geographical

[1] See the very interesting work of Mr. Markham, *Travels in Peru and India, while superintending the Collection of Chinchona Plants and Seeds in South America and their introduction into India.* London, 1862.

features of the country, and will frequently be referred to in the course of these pages.[1]

The exports of the country are in no proportion to the richness and fertility of its soil and the variety of its climate. The lowlands of the coast, intersected by navigable rivers in all directions, produce cacao, rice, coffee, sugar, tobacco, cotton, caoutchouc, copal gum, vanilla, sarsaparilla, salt, petroleum, dyewoods, etc., etc., etc. They produce cattle, game, horses, and mules; and a boundless variety of fruits, such as plantains, oranges, lemons, pine-apples (perhaps the best in the world), melons, bananas, limes, nisperos, mangos, cocoa-nuts, mameys, alligator-pears, guavas, guayavas, etc., etc., etc. They also abound in timber for ship and house building, among which the *guachapeli*, said to harden in water and to be almost incorruptible, deserves particular mention. A short distance from the lowlands of the coast — a distance which by the aid of good roads might be reduced to a mere nothing — are the cool and healthy table-lands of the interior, abounding in mineral wealth, and furnishing almost all the products of the temperate zone, such as wheat, barley, indian-corn, pulse, potatoes, European vegetables and fruits, etc., etc. If the resources of the country were properly developed, it would be one of the richest in the world. But there are too many causes at work which prevent its agricultural progress. In the lowlands, the great and almost insurmountable drawback is the want of laborers, owing to the thinness of the popula-

[1] In the province of Loja, the most southern district of Ecuador, the healing virtues of the quinquina bark were first made known to Europeans in the year 1630. In 1638 the wife of the viceroy of Peru, the Countess of Chinchon, was cured by it of an intermittent fever at Lima, for which reason Linnæus, long afterwards, named the whole genus of quinine yielding trees "chinchona."

tion, the enervating effects of the climate, the system of peonage, and the unsettled state of the country with its continual revolutions and impressments. Other dead-weights to agricultural development are the *diezmos* or tithes, the tenth part of all the crops which must be paid for the maintenance of the church establishment, and the *primicias* or first-fruits, a contribution exacted for the benefit of the local curates, and weighing principally upon the small proprietors. But all this will be explained in a more appropriate place.

The roads to the interior, as I have already said, are impassable during the rainy season. Their southern termination is nearly concealed by a rank tropical vegetation, or obstructed by fallen trees undergoing different stages of decay; and thus is bad enough during the dry season. But when the steep ascents and descents of the mountain ranges are made slippery by the incessant showers of winter; when the ravines which must be passed are full of water, mud, and tumbling stones, and the pools and quagmires bottomless, all commercial intercourse between Guayaquil and the interior remains suspended. Should any article in the shape of a bale or box arrive at Guayaquil during the rainy season, the owner, who may be in Quito, must wait for it perhaps six or eight months, or till the roads become naturally passable. With the exception of the letter-carriers, nobody travels during the wet season whose business does not absolutely require it. Poor Ida Pfeiffer, the celebrated Austrian traveller, who thought that she would be able to accomplish what the letter-carriers could do, undertook the journey, against the urgent remonstrances of her friends, in March, 1852. What a horrible time she had, when, poorly prepared, and almost without companions, she climbed over the Andes, more on foot than on horseback, slipping and falling almost at every step, she has described in one of her books, "A Lady's Second Journey round the World."[1]

Before setting out for the interior, — a journey which must be made on horseback or mules, — certain preparations are necessary. An attendant will have to be procured in the first place, to be your servant, guide, and, when necessary, your cook. Saddles and bridles must be purchased, for they cannot be hired with the horses. *Ponchos* for warm and cold weather, and as part of your bedding at night, should be bought, and an indian rubber *poncho*, called *encauchado*, as a protection against the rain. No native ever travels without such an *encauchado* strapped to his saddle, an oil-cloth cover for his straw hat, and trousers made of leather — tiger, dog, or goat skins with the hair left on them — over his pantaloons. These latter are greatly preferable to our leggings, because they keep the knees warm, while they protect the legs against the rain. They are called *zamarros* or *calzones de cuero*. The best *zamarros* are made in the southern province of New Granada, from whence they are imported into Ecuador. I

[1] I cannot judge of other parts of Mrs. Pfeiffer's work; but her two chapters on Ecuador, although they contain a great deal of truth, are full of misconceptions and inaccuracies. As a personal narrative, however, they are very interesting. Her adventures in Ecuador were throughout of an unpleasant character. Her involuntary bath in the River Guayas, her dreadful journey over the mountains during the worst month of the year, and her outrageous reception by the rabble of Quito, were fearful trials for the poor old lady. The scandalous reception she met with on her first appearance in the streets of Quito, must, however, be attributed to the extravagant and ridiculous manner in which she dressed. At a place where foreign ladies are seen but very seldom, the appearance of a strange old woman on a donkey, in a costume exquisitely ridiculous, with a bonnet which everywhere else would have excited merriment, and a butterfly-net now shouldered like a musket, now carried like a lance, could not fail to draw a boisterous crowd around her.

would advise the foreign traveller to adopt the riding costume of the natives. It is very comfortable, and splendidly adapted to the different climates and temperatures through which he will have to pass. In the armor of a fine soft *zamarro*, an oil-cloth cover to my straw hat, and a long *encauchado* protecting my neck and body, and covering even my knees and saddle-bags, I travelled for hours dry and comfortable, in the most drenching rains. The red woolen *poncho* which is generally worn in the interior, the checkered tiger-skin leggings or long-haired goat-skin *zamarros*, the red or yellow oil-cloth cover on the hat (*funda*), and the huge Mexican spurs and brass stirrups in the form of shoes or slippers, and in many cases, the linen or silk masks with or without goggles, worn by gentlemen to protect the face and eyes against the sun, wind, and sand, give the mountaineers a most fantastic appearance, filling the unexperienced foreign traveller with apprehensions of robbers or highwaymen. Such apprehensions, however, are entirely unfounded. There is perhaps no country in the world in which one can travel alone and unarmed with more perfect security than in the interior of Ecuador. A saddle cover (*pellon*) made of cotton, wool, or horse-hair, to give you a soft seat during so long a journey; a little valise (*maletero*) to be strapped to your saddle, containing soap, candles, matches, towels, linen, combs, etc., etc., and two saddle-bags (*alforjas*) with eatables and other comforts, will complete your equipment. I should also advise you to provide yourself with travelling or camp beds, because in many of the miserable hovels in which you may have to pass the night you would not feel inclined to "rough it" on the ground, tormented by fleas and other vermin. Your *ponchos* will be your blankets at night, and the saddle cover (*pellon*) is often used to supply the want of a mattress or pillow.

And now you are ready to start for Bodegas. Formerly you had to go there in canoes, waiting for the tide to carry you up, and exposed to a merciless tropical sun. It took two days, or the greater part of two days, to get there. You had to pass a horrible night at Samborondon, or some other miserable place, consisting of a few bamboo huts on the river bank, and a few houses built on rafts (*balsas*) on the river itself, with alligators all around you and mosquitoes tattooing you all over. But now, thanks to American enterprise, you steam up the majestic river, in neat and commodious steamboats, propelled by American machinery, and giving you the benefit of a delightful draught of air, making you forget how near you are to the equator. The steamers start with the tide and make the trip in from six to eight hours. The trip is very pleasant and interesting. The vegetation on both sides of the river is rich and luxuriant. Forests of plantain trees line the banks. Cacao and coffee plantations arrest the traveller's eye, interchanging with long rows of jungle and impenetrable brushwood. The bread-tree, the mango-tree, the *aguacate*, and the cotton-tree break on your delighted vision. And above all the luxuriant growth and fragrance, the majestic cocoa palm raises its melancholy crown, reminding you that you are in foreign lands, far away from the scenes of your childhood, far away from the beloved ones at home. Oh, how often, when I travelled, surrounded by the richness of a tropical vegetation, did I long for the sight of a winter landscape at home. With the snow that covers the fields and roofs, and beards the branches of the leafless tree; with the icicles hanging down from your windows, and the frozen glass panes forming thousands of fantastic figures and crystallized halls and domes; with the river over which the merry skaters dash, so many of the dearest memories of our childhood are entwined. Think of a merry Christmas night at home; think of the dear old folks gathered around the crackling chimney-fire; listen to the familiar voices that perhaps never, never more will strike your ear; think of the playmates of your childhood, romping with you around the room, and the girls laughing, and the old folks smiling; steal away to the window, and look at the splendid snow-robe covering the garden and the fields outside, with the stars twinkling above, and the calm and blissful rays of the moon resting mildly on the virgin snow. There is home again; there is your father, your mother, your brothers, and sisters; there is the maiden to whom your trembling lips first stammered a confession of your boyish love. But no, — awake: it is the palm-tree that stares at you, the ugly alligator basks in an enervating sun, the parrot whirs shrieking through the air, the monkey chatters on the tree, the *gallinazo* perches silently on the withered branch, the snake steals through the bushes, and you are a lonely traveller in a foreign land.

## CHAPTER III.

Alligators. — The Town of Babahoyo, or Bodegas. — Hiring Horses. — Arrieros. — Galled and Jaded Beasts. — Packing. — Indian Endurance. — The Journey. — The Tropical Forest. — No Great Race has ever sprung from the Tropics. — Savaneta. — Description of Houses on the Road. — Punta Playas. — Camellones or Camels' Backs. — Nights in the Forest. —Mysterious Noises.—Mata Blanca. — Pisagua. —A Horrid Road.—Ascending the Cordillera. — Jorje. — Cuesta de Angas. — Camino Real. — Eating Lice. — Emerging from the Tropics. — Superstition. — View from Mt. Pizcurcu. — A Forgotten Corner of the World. — A Dangerous Descent. — Villages in the Valley of Chimbo. — The Polite "Jefe Politico." — Socabon. — Lamas. — The Town of Guaranda. — Change Horses. — Preparations for passing Chimborazo.

THE number of alligators (*lagartos*) on the river banks between Guayaquil and Bodegas, is legion. They lie on the sand near the water, basking in the sunshine, and presenting the appearance of huge logs of wood. I once counted more than thirty in one group. Sometimes cattle will graze near them, apparently unaware of the dangerous neighborhood. They grow to an astonishing size, and are dangerous, not only to calves and foals, but also to unwary persons, especially children.[1] If an alligator has once tasted human flesh, or cattle, he is said to become

[1] Stuart Cochrane gives the following account of a thrilling incident on the River Magdalena, in New Granada: "A young woman near Narie, escaped the fangs of one of these monsters by an effort of singular presence of mind. She had waded a little way into the water, when the alligator seized her by the thigh, and began to drag her from the shore. She instantly thrust her fingers into his eyes, the anguish of which caused him immediately to let go his prey; and thus she escaped with no other injury than a lacerated limb." — *Journal of a Residence and Travels in Colombia during the years* 1823 *and* 1824.

*bravo* or *cebado*, that is, to conceive such a relish for this kind of food, that he watches every opportunity to gratify this propensity. If it were not for the *gallinazos*, who dig up and devour the eggs which the female alligator has buried in the sand,[1] and for the voracity of the male, who devours as many of his young when they are freshly hatched as the female cannot carry away on her neck and back, they would be, to use the language of Stephenson,[2] "as numerous as flies, and become the proprietors of the surrounding country."

Bodegas, or Babahoyo, the capital of the province De los Rios, consists of a long row of frame houses on the river bank, a plaza, and a few side streets. It is inhabited by a few white store-keepers, sundry government officials, and hacienda-owners; but the overwhelming majority of the population consists of negroes and mulattoes. The melancholy palm-tree overtops the miserable wooden buildings, on the roofs of which innumerable gallinazos perch. Hotels or inns there are none. The strangers, of whom there are always a great many going to or coming from the *sierra* (interior), have to stay on a *balsa*, or to rent rooms at extravagant prices, and take their meals at an eating-house.

One half of the year Bodegas and all the surrounding country is under water. The inundation generally sets in all at once. It begins at Christmas and ends in May. During this time the water reaches nearly the upper stories of the houses, which are built on piles, and the daily intercourse of the inhabitants is carried on in boats and canoes, from one house to another.

1 Ulloa and George Juan, *A Voyage to South America.*
2 *Twenty Years' Residence in South America.*

Travellers bound for the interior must then hire a canoe to Savaneta, whence the journey on horseback becomes possible.

The 24th of June, (when I first arrived at Bodegas,) the festival of St. John Baptist, is a great holiday. It is celebrated by a queer sort of horse-racing. One rider, with a cock in his hand, dashes along the river road, and is followed by the others, who endeavor to snatch the bird from him. If he is skillful, he will evade his pursuers by suddenly wheeling around and darting away in an opposite direction, or he will retain the animal by the rapid motion of his arm. As soon as the bird is taken away from him, his pursuers chase its new possessor, — and so the sport goes on until men and horses are exhausted. The neighborhood of Bodegas is celebrated for breeding good horses, and a great number of foals (*potros*) are annually sold into the interior.

Speaking of horses reminds us that our principal difficulty is about to commence. We must hire horses and mules for our journey. Most of the proprietors of the animals which we now want, live at Guaranda, in the cool and picturesque valley of Chimbo, at the foot of Chimborazo. They come to Bodegas with freight and passengers from the interior, and remain until they get a return load. Our first trouble is to agree with them on a reasonable price. Like all *serranos* (inhabitants of the interior, from *sierra*, mountain-range), they begin by asking an exorbitant sum, and gradually let down. To agree with a *serrano* on any business transaction, is the most difficult task in the world. He haggles without end, and when we believe to be through with him at last, he makes new demands, or invents additional conditions which lead to prolonged discussions. A foreigner visiting Ecuador must arm himself with a good stock of patience. The size and weight of his baggage are another source of difficulties. The *arrieros* (muleteers) will eye it most distrustfully, exchange significant looks with each other, lift it up and set it down again as if to weigh it, then whisper to each other and afterwards return to the baggage to give it another trial. The result of all this will be the expression of an apprehension that your *carga* (baggage) is too heavy for their beasts — the usual load for one of which is ten *arrobas*, or two hundred and fifty pounds. The hire being finally agreed upon, the question, who is to pay the fodder for the beasts, will be raised. It is the custom that the traveller pays the fodder for the saddle-horses, and the arriero, for the beasts of burden. Though this rule is universally recognized, the arriero will always attempt to impose the whole expense on his employer. This part of the business being disposed of, the controversy will turn on how much of the hire is to be paid in advance. The arriero invariably asks for the whole amount ; and it is the custom in the interior of Ecuador to pay something in advance on every contract. But as the beasts may give out, or the arriero himself may prove dishonest, prudence will always dictate to retain as much as possible. But in this the traveller will not succeed without additional quarreling. All these preliminaries being settled at last, the arriero is notified that the beasts must be forthcoming at a certain hour. I should advise always to fix an early hour, as your man hardly ever comes up to time. You want him to be on hand by daybreak, and he will make his appearance by seven or eight o'clock. At last he comes, and presents his beasts to your mortified and astonished gaze. Miserable, thin, and decrepit jades, which threaten to give over after the first half-day's journey, are to carry you over the Andes. In many cases their backs are shockingly galled, and sometimes entirely raw to the whole extent of the saddle. Hideous sores, suppurating and full of crawling worms, offend your sight and nostrils. The stench of these *mataduras* generally penetrates through the sweat-cloth (*sudadero*) which is laid on the animal's back under the saddle, causing nausea to the rider. Nevertheless, such animals are considered fit for service, at least to carry *cargas*, as long as they can move on; this avaricious cruelty being the reason why so many of the narrow mountain defiles are blocked up with the carcasses or skeletons of dead horses, asses, or mules, which nobody thinks of removing.

*Carga suelta* is a term used to denote goods which are sent by merchants on droves of beasts, independent of travellers. The beasts used for this purpose must live on what grass they find on the sides of the road as they go along, or when they are let loose at night. Many of these animals are in a most pitiable condition; some so knock-kneed that by repeatedly striking one against the other the flesh is worn from the bone; and others with their hoofs turned inwards, hobbling on their fetlock joints; yet performing the service of sound animals.

The government experiences much less difficulty in dealing with arrieros. When the President or the General-in-Chief proposes to travel, all the beasts that are within reach are seized and impounded, and the best selected by the managing officer. The compensation paid to the owner, provided he gets any thing, is then determined by the government, and not by the arriero.

Your baggage must now be put on the mules, for which purpose wooden pack-saddles (*albardas*) are used. As deep rivers are to be forded, and on the high *paramos* rains are not unfrequent, even in the dry season, it is customary to wrap trunks or boxes in pieces of strong oil-cloth (*encerrados*), which must be procured at Guayaquil; or to cover them with the dried leaves of the *vijao*, and then to sew them up in common sackcloth. The packing takes its time, as the loads will have to be so distributed as to keep an equal weight on each side of the animal. Every day of your journey the tedious operation of loading the animals, and strapping your *maleteros* (valises), ponchos, and *encauchados* to your saddle has to be repeated, causing such delay that you are forcibly reminded of the truth of the Spanish proverb: "*El salir de la posada la media jornada*" ("To get out of the inn is one half of the journey").

The chief arriero always has two or three servants or *peones* with him, to drive the beasts, load and unload the animals, and push them on or extricate them when necessary. These arrieros and peones, like all other Indians, and a great number of the *Cholos* (half-breeds) go barefoot, their cotton breeches never reaching further than to their knees (only the Indian *alcaldes* or magistrates wear long breeches). They can walk, or rather trot, behind the horses fourteen or fifteen leagues a day, and probably more if required, over rugged mountain roads, through swamps, rivers, and rocky defiles, now ascending steep acclivities, now hurrying down into deep and muddy ravines (*quebradas*). They always sleep in the open air, lying down on the bare ground, and covering themselves with their ragged ponchos, — one night in the damp and miasmatic lowlands of the coast, another, perhaps, on the freezing *paramos* of the high Cordillera. Their food they generally carry with them. It always consists of a quantity of barley-meal, which they eat raw, a few pieces of *agi* (Cayenne pepper), which they take like fruit, and sometimes a bag of toasted indian corn. These provisions maintain them during the day, and in the evening they mostly manage to get, either at the expense of the traveller or the chief arriero, a plate of *locro* (a potato soup, mixed up with cheese, eggs, and Spanish pepper). When eating at somebody else's expense the Indian can devour fabulous quantities; but when faring at his own cost, he is rather parsimonious, and prefers drinking to eating. He likes to take *aguardiente* (rum), but his favorite, and I may say indispensable, drink is *chicha* — a beverage brewed from indian corn in copper kettles. Its taste is rather acid, its color a dirty yellow. He prefers it, not only because it was the beverage of his ancestors, but chiefly on account of its cheapness. The vice of drunkenness does not affect his iron constitution. His powers of endurance are indeed wonderful. The curate of an Indian village once told me that the mortality among Indian children is very great, owing to the recklessness of their parents, and to the prejudice of the Indian against scientific medical treatment; but that having once reached a certain age, the Indian's health becomes almost indestructible — a proof of which is the frequency of remarkable cases of longevity, many of which have come under my own observation.

But it is time to begin our journey. Between Bodegas and Savaneta the flat country extends, which is inundated during five months of the year. It is most unhealthy when it begins to dry, and innumerable swamps and puddles are left exhaling noxious miasmas. The healthiest time is from August to December.

Millions of white butterflies hover around you as you ride along. Sometimes swarms of them are on the ground sucking moisture. When disturbed by the approach of your horses, they fly up, enwrapping you on all sides like the flakes of a snow-storm. Caravans of laden mules and asses, followed by their drivers on foot, pass you during the day. After dark, myriads of fire-flies and lightning-bugs glitter in the jungle and brushwood, appearing and disappearing like fairy gems in the black diadem of night. Swarms of mosquitoes will molest the traveller when he lies down to rest, while his hosts will alarm him with stories of snakes,[1] tigers, or poisonous spiders.

I shall not attempt to describe a tropical country. It has been done by other and abler pens. The luxuriant vegetation, the majestic trees, united by garlands of creepers and overgrown with all sorts of parasites, the impenetrable jungle and brushwood covering treacherous swamps, the boundless variety of fruit and flowers, the shrieks of the parrot, the chattering of the monkey, the cooing of the turtle-dove, and the inexplicable noises of many other inhabitants of the forest, invisible to the bewildered eye, have not that charm for me which they have for other travellers. I do not share the enthusiasm of poets and novelists for the "Sunny South." I feel alarmed at the paleness and sickly appearance of the poor people

[1] The *equis*, a large and deadly snake, is a great pest in the plains of Guayaquil. It takes its name from being marked with crosses (like the letter X) all along the back. — Spruce's *Report on an Expedition to procure Seeds and Plants of the Red Bark Tree*; London: 1861.

who dwell in those regions, where Nature proffers gifts with one hand while she takes health and life with the other. Behind all that glowing verdure and alluring exuberance destruction cowers in boundless variety of form. The appearance is beauty, but troublesome insects and venomous reptiles, fevers and dysenteries, indolence and enervation, the reality. None of the great races of the earth have sprung from the tropics. The nearer we approach the torrid zone, the lower we find man in the scale of civilization. The North, with its ungenial winters, snow-storms and icicles, is, after all, the true home of comfort, progress, and liberty.

The first village of note after leaving Bodegas[1] is La Mona, a group of about twenty houses, on the river of the same name. The river has to be forded, the water reaching to the horse's belly. After passing Palo Largo, a large heath without trees of any kind, Savaneta is reached — a miserable village of hardly twenty houses, but of great importance during the rainy season, as I have already stated. The houses in this part of the country are almost all alike. They rest on piles, only the upper story being inhabited. The room below serves as a shelter for arrieros, hogs, and dogs, and for the baggage of travellers. It is seldom that we find a staircase; generally the ascent must be made on a pole, with notches cut in it for steps. For a person in his riding-dress, or for ladies, this is very inconvenient. The houses scarcely ever have more than one side covered with a wall work of reeds or cane. Many of them are open on all sides. The

[1] There is another road to Guaranda by way of San Antonio and Pucara. It is the one described by Ulloa, and travelled over much less than the Savaneta road. I prefer the latter, not only on account of the scenery, but also because it sooner leads you out of the regions of tropical heat, and has more and better accommodations.

roof is covered with a palm-like leaf called *vijao*, which grows without a stem. The flooring consists of a cane (*caña brava*), which is split open and used, instead of boards. Sometimes a little room is partitioned off by a square inclosure of this *caña brava*, serving as a bedroom for the owner of the building. The hammock is the principal, and in many cases the only, piece of furniture. An empty wine bottle, which you throw away, is picked up by your host as a great treasure. Water is kept in bamboos, or the stems of the *guaduas* tree, corked up at the ends. From these clumsy jars it is poured into calabashes. It is always disgustingly warm.

In such huts I passed many a bad night, with chickens roosting over me, and dogs tearing away at my saddle-bags. These latter animals ascend the notched pole, which serves as a staircase, with remarkable dexterity. A night's lodging is granted to the traveller without charge. He pays only for the fodder of the beasts and the eatables he buys, provided he can get any. It is hardly necessary to ask whether you are allowed to stay. The question "*Hay yerba?*" (whether there is any fodder for the beasts,) is the only important one to be asked. Every house on the public highway is considered a *tambo* or *posada* (resting-place). At one of these wretched hovels I once saw a man cook a soup, which he invited me to buy. I asked him whether it was clean. "Oh, yes," he said, "*es cosa hecha de hombre*" (it is made by a man). The inference to be drawn from this remark as to the cleanliness of the other sex, was certainly not very complimentary. Most of the houses I have now described are inhabited by negroes and mulattoes.

The road from Savaneta to Punta Playas passes through a forest so dense, that the water which remains after the yearly inundation, scarcely ever dries, and you have to travel for many a weary mile through water which splashes you all over. At many places the jungle, which grows with astonishing rapidity, and the branches of bushes and trees, protrude into the road and have to be cut away with a *macheta*, a weapon which many of the arrieros carry. This instrument is of general use and great advantage, the blade resembling that of a ship's cutlass, only broader and curved toward the point, made of wrought iron, which will bend but not break. The handles are usually of wood or horn, riveted to the iron; the back is thick, and the edge kept sharp. It is used for a great many purposes, serving for knife, axe, bill, and sometimes for a sword.

Another feature of the road which considerably retards your progress, is the great number of *camellones* (deep furrows divided by transverse ridges, and named after their resemblance to the humps on a camel's back). These furrows are worn into the soft, loamy soil by the equable step of beasts of burden; they are often two or three feet deep, and filled with mud and water. If they are deep, the horse sinks in up to his breast, dragging his belly and the rider's feet over the ridges which divide the holes, and in its attempts to get out again, flounders and stumbles. Still these *camellones* are of great benefit to the traveller on the steep acclivities and descents of the mountain roads, where they prevent the horse from sliding and falling, and hurling its rider into one of the precipices below. Thus in this neglected country the traveller owes a certain degree of safety to what he feels tempted to curse as an intolerable inconvenience.

When stopping for the night at one of the huts along the road, the first business, as I have already said, is to provide fodder for the horses. On the coast it is *gamalote;*[1] in the interior lucerne, which the natives call *alfalfa*, or simply *yerba*. After this the unsaddling and unpacking of the beasts commences. The baggage remains below, while the saddles, bridles, valises, saddle-bags, etc., are carried up-stairs. Warm water to make coffee or tea will next have to be asked for, and orders must be given for the supper of the servants. To boil water is another very tedious operation with these cottagers, and when it is brought at last, there is almost always too little of it. The delays which beset every, and even the most insignificant, transaction in the interior, already begin to be felt. The saddle-bags must furnish the best part of the supper, unless chickens are to be had, in which case I should always advise to buy another for next day's breakfast. After supper the beds are made. He who carries no mattress or camp-bed with him, must spread some of his ponchos on the floor, for bedsteads there are none in the hovels of the lowlands. At first it is exceedingly hot; the sultry damps of night commence to creep in from three sides, as generally but one side of the house is covered; but little of the surrounding country can be seen, and the clouds come down oppres-

1 "The blade of the *Gamalote* resembles that of barley, but it is longer, broader, thicker, and rougher. The green is deep but lively, and the stalk diversified with knots from which the leaves, which are strong and sometimes two lines in diameter, have their origin. When the gamalote is at its full growth, the height of water during the floods, by rising above its top, presses it down and rots it, so that when the waters ebb away, the earth seems covered with it; but at the first impression of the sun it shoots up again, and in a few days abounds in the same plenty as before. One thing remarkable in it is, that though it proves so nourishing to the cattle of this district, it is very noxious to those from the Cordillera, as has been often experienced." — Ulloa and George Juan, *Voyage to South America.*

sively low. Cats and dogs trip over the sleeper; the inmates of the house tumble about until a late hour of the night; the mosquitoes and beetles do their work, and the *mata blanca*, a small, scarcely perceptible insect of the mosquito tribe, tattoos every spot of the skin which it finds exposed, sometimes causing painful swelling; the toads croak in the neighboring swamps; bats flutter around our heads, and inexplicable sounds of every description frighten us in our sleep, while visions of scorpions and tarantulas haunt our heated imagination. By and by the night air becomes chilly; cold winds pass over the sweating brow of the traveller; every thing is cheerless, dismal, and oppressive, and we rejoice to be able to rise at last and prepare our departure. After such a night at Savaneta, Punta Playas, Las Peñas, or any of the intermediate cottages, it is a great relief to see daylight again, even if a fine rain should trickle down and make the landscape more melancholy, the roads more sloughy, and ourselves more uncomfortable. But when the sun rises on a clear and cloudless day; when we see the outposts of the Cordillera, covered with beautiful green forests, sharply defined in the blue sky, we shake off our fatigue cheerfully, and proceed with new courage on our wearisome journey.

Through cacao and sugar plantations, looking sometimes but little better than a wilderness, our road leads us to Las Peñas. This latter is not the name of a village, although some miserable houses are found at considerable distances from each other, but derives its name from the fact that the swamps are now behind us, and stones and rocks begin to cover the way and annoy the horses. And now we begin, at first almost imperceptibly, to ascend, and a sore trial of patience is in store for us. Little Pisagua and Big

Pisagua have to be passed. Pisagua is the name of a forest through which the road leads from Las Peñas to the *Tambo del Rio Limon.* I am afraid my pen will be inadequate to convey a true idea of the horrible state of that portion of the road, even during the dryest season of the year. Pisagua is a forest — not one of those green and beautiful forests which make us feel well and contented when we travel through them, but a forest like those we should imagine on the dark and gloomy banks of the Stygian river.[1] It is a forest into which a cheering ray of the sun seldom penetrates. No verdure surrounds us excepting the crowns of the trees, which we have no time to contemplate, as our attention must be riveted on the road at our feet. Rocks and mud seem to be the only productions of this dreary region. The atmosphere is damp, and the smell of the long puddles through which we are compelled to wade, mouldy and chilling. Our way can no longer be called a road. It is apparently the rocky bed of a stream, which swells into a torrent when it rains. Trunks of trees have fallen across the miry path, where they are slowly decaying, while nobody thinks of removing them. Through some of the thickest small openings have been hewn, to enable the animals to get through. At other points the fall of these trees has been intercepted by rocks on both sides of the road, so as to form low doorways, through which we must pass stooping. We ascend and descend alternately over rocks and stones, so near each other as to leave scarcely room for the feet of the animals. It is

[1] "Notwithstanding the vast extent of the unreclaimed forests in Ecuador, hardly any part of them is still without an owner, if we except the territory disputed between Peru and Ecuador, on the eastern side of the Cordillera, generally called *Las Montañas del Oriente.*" — Richard Spruce, *Report on the Expedition to procure Seeds and Plants of the Red Bark Tree.*

almost a miracle to see the beasts stumble over them in safety. Where there are no rocks, our progress is embarrassed by the roots of gigantic trees, which rise above the slippery mire. Deep puddles of black loam have to be floundered over. *Camellones* too, out of which it is sometimes exceedingly difficult to extricate the stumbling horses, are not wanting. Rivers and mountain streams in the openings of the forest have to be passed time and again. Some of them are so rapid, not only in the rainy, but also in the early part of the dry season, that the beasts are in danger of being swept away by the current, which would dash them against frightful rocks. The waters rush with such velocity, owing to the great declivity in the course of the streams, that giddiness is produced by looking into the water. Experienced travellers will therefore look upwards while fording such a river. The roaring of the water as it hurries on over rocks and precipices, forming numerous cascades, is so great, that at a distance of ten feet persons cannot understand each other without screaming. This roaring accompanies us through the greater part of Pisagua, and often we hear it without seeing the river by which it is produced. It strikes awe to the soul in the lonely wilderness. Over some of the streams aërial bridges are formed, consisting of one or two trunks of trees, over which the arrieros pass, while their animals ford the river as well as they can, encouraged by the cries and curses of their drivers. Then again defiles will have to be passed, so narrow between dripping rocks, that you must look out how your legs are squeezed against the sides. In these defiles troops of laden mules and asses, which you meet every now and then, will greatly impede and embarrass your progress. It is customary to hail the muleteers at the other outlet, to make them stop their beasts until your cavalcade has passed through.

The absence of all signs of civilization increases the gloom of this dreadful region. It is true there are some miserable huts, even in the heart of Pisagua; but they resemble the crude habitations of savages. Their aspect saddens instead of encouraging. It is a relief to meet with a drove of donkeys and their drivers, and hear their cries: "*Mula! Anda! Burro!*" however unpleasant and dangerous such an encounter may be in the narrow passages or on the precipitous hill-sides of the road.

At last you emerge from gloomy Pisagua, and passing the River Limon or Cristal for the last time, you enter a beautiful valley, with its scenery continually changing, owing to the windings of the road. Some very inconvenient ascents and descents have to be made, sorely trying to an inexperienced horseman. But the beauty of the landscape around La Ceyba indemnifies for this inconvenience. Forests of plantain and coffee trees, on dry ground, greet you with a friendly smile; you behold at least some human habitations and human activity again; you find sugar mills and rum distilleries in operation; beautiful verdure surrounds you on all sides; the atmosphere is fresher and purer, and the road under your feet is a festive walk in comparison with what you have left behind.

When you hear names like "La Ceyba," "Las Peñas," "Jorje," "Pizcurcu," "El Excomulgado," and others with which you will become familiar in the course of these pages, you must not suppose that they belong to any town or village. In Ecuador every lonely house, every characteristic feature of the road, every *hacienda*, and sometimes even a solitary tree, rock, or ravine, has its name. The same mountain or river has different names at different places. The "Pastassa," for instance, a river which takes its rise near Mt. Cotopaxi, is first named "Callo," a little further down "Pumacunchi," afterwards "Cutuchi," still further down "Pillaro," then "Patate," then "Baños," and at last "Pastassa."[1] It will be necessary to bear this strange custom in mind, in order to prevent misconception or confusion.

After continuing our ascent, interrupted by frequent declivities, for a few leagues more, the tambo of Jorje is reached, which, according to Dr. Jameson's measurement, is three thousand and twenty feet above the level of the sea, and commands a delightful view of the valley below. It lies at the foot of the great *Cuesta de Angas* (an uninterrupted ascent to the summit of the first range of the Cordillera), and being out of the swamp region and surrounded by gigantic mountains, its climate is very agreeable, and I have no doubt healthy. The *tambo* is a spacious building, differing from the rest of the houses in this part of the country, by having a staircase, a floor of boards, some furniture, and by being sheltered on three sides — which must be considered a great improvement.

The steep ascent from Jorje to Camino Real is, when it rains, one of the worst break-neck paths in the world. With the exception of Chimborazo, it is the steepest and highest ascent on the whole road, and to scale it, when converted by rain into soft and slippery soap, may be a task of life and death.

There are mules in this part of the country which are trained to slide down slippery declivities. Such ani-

[1] Villavicencio's *Geografia de la Republica del Ecuador*, p. 81.

mals are held in great estimation, and command good prices. They are sensible of the caution required in these descents, for, coming to the top of an eminence, they stop, and having placed their fore legs in a slanting position, they put their hind legs together, drawing them a little forward, as if going to lie down. In this attitude, having, as it were, taken a survey of the road, they slide down with startling velocity. Their dexterity in following the various windings of the road is really astonishing, for by a gentle inclination of the body they turn first to one side and then to another, keeping the most perfect equilibrium, which is the only means of saving themselves and their riders from being hurled headlong forward, or being dashed to pieces by a fall. All the rider has to do is to keep himself fast in the saddle without checking his beast. Any unguarded motion on his part, by disordering the equilibrium of the mule, might lead to fatal consequences.[1]

When the road is dry, the ascent from Jorje to Camino Real may be effected in two or three hours. We are now emerging from the tropics. The fresh mountain air, and the piercing cold mists peculiar to those elevations, announce the change of climate. The plantain, orange, and aguacate trees remain behind us. We have escaped from the fevers, dysenteries, snakes, and mosquitoes of the lowlands. As by a magician's wand, we are transferred from a region of sickening and enervating heat into realms of delightful coolness and salubrity. Beautiful are the towering mountains around us, and beautiful is the scenery at our feet if clouds do not hide it from our view. But generally these clouds cover the entire country from which we

[1] I. Ulloa, 202, English translation, fourth edition. Also II. Stephenson, 260.

have emerged, and form an ocean beneath us so wide, so natural, so real, that ships only are wanted to complete the illusion. No painter could reproduce the wonderful hues of this aërial sea, when lit up by the rays of the rising or the setting sun.

Camino Real, seven thousand eight hundred and fifty-two feet above the level of the sea (Jameson), is a squalid, miserable village, consisting of a few low and dirty huts of reeds, plastered up with mud, no longer resting on piles, but stuck into the ground, and containing but one dark unfloored and unfurnished filthy room, out of the door of which (for windows there are none) the smoke lazily makes its way into the face and eyes of the approaching traveller.

Here it was that I first saw women eat lice. It was a loathsome sight to behold those unwashed and unkempt creatures pick the disgusting vermin from each other's heads, and put them into their mouths, where they crushed them between their teeth.[1]

At Camino Real it becomes necessary to give a short rest to the horses, tired by the long and steep ascent, and to treat them to a repast of lucerne, which, after the southern *gamalote*, they attack with great greedi-

[1] The loathsome practice of eating lice, or crushing them between the teeth, was originally an Indian custom. The ancient Indians seem to have transmitted it to the mixed races and to the white rabble. According to Herrera, the royal historian, who had access to all the original documents, reports, and descriptions of the conquerors, the Indians ate them, not because they liked their taste, but because, having one hand engaged in parting and examining the hair, which is always very long and thick, the other could not dispose of the vermin in a more effective way. The same author says that one of the Inca rulers of Peru had ordered the poor tribes of Pasto, who had nothing else to give, to pay their tribute in lice, not because he wanted them, but to make them acknowledge their vassalage. The Pasto Indians, however, objected to this mode of discharging their tribute, because eating lice was then considered an infallible remedy against sore eyes, and was recommended as such by the Indian doctresses (*curanderas*). — Herrera, dec. v. bk. 4, ch. 2.

ness. The potato, which here takes the place of the plantain, welcomes us as a home-like sight. We are again in a congenial climate. The inhabitants of the village are not pure Indians, but half-breeds, who share with the Indians their ugly faces but beautiful teeth and small feet. Civilized travellers who have to pass a night here cannot sleep inside the huts, which are too filthy and full of fleas. They sleep outside, under the protruding roofs, which protect them from the rain and the dew. A bed may be made on wooden platforms on which *yerba* is piled up during the day ; and the traveller may congratulate himself if he can pass the night without being much troubled by chickens, dogs, cats, or hogs. The nights here are very cold.

Opposite the hut where I used to stop on my journeys to or from Quito, two small niches communicating with each other were dug in the hill-side on the road, in one of which a skull (*calavera*) was placed. In the other candles burned occasionally, and flowers were often laid before the skull. As I had observed this custom frequently, I asked my landlady for an explanation. She told me that a soldier had been slain and buried near the village, in the civil war of 1860, but the dogs dug up the body and scattered the bones. Some pious person then picked up the skull, and placed it in the niche where I saw it. Ever since that time, my landlady informed me, it had been working miracles, and was held in great esteem.

Shortly after passing Camino Real, the descent to the valley of La Chima begins — a romantic and secluded spot, from which a steep, zigzag ascent of about half an hour, leads us to the summit of Pizcurću. And now a most unexpected and most enchanting prospect breaks suddenly upon our view. The valley of Chimbo is at last before us, and we behold a northern home again. We behold another vegetation, another land, another world, differing even in the slightest details from the scenes we left but a few hours ago. Fertile and cultivated fields expand before us, covering hills and plains and mountain slopes with wheat instead of the sugar-cane; potatoes instead of plantains; barley instead of cacao and aguacates; turnips instead of oranges and alligator pears. Villages with houses of stone or adobes, many of them neatly whitewashed, have taken the place of the savage sheds of the low country. Long fences of aloe divide the fields. Indian huts of earth-walls, thatched with gray straw instead of the vijao leaf, are distributed all over the valley and hill-sides. Healthy, ruddy faces meet us on our road, instead of the pale and sickly countenances which frightened us in the lowlands. It is only the active bustle of progressive life and civilization, the merry smoke-stacks and cheerful modern buildings that are wanting, to make us feel as if at home again, and to lessen the awe inspired by the presence of grim Chimborazo, whose hoary dome towers high above the green landscape, and forms an imposing background to the charming, yet melancholy and lifeless scene.

We have now entered one of those forgotten corners of the world which, barricaded against the march of civilization by almost impassable mountains, and inhabited by a thriftless and indifferent race, could not keep pace with the progress of mankind. We are transported into regions which still belong to the past, and whose lifeless quietude strangely contrasts with the enterprise and progress of the present age. Let us not be deceived by the beautiful view which we enjoy from the summit of Pizcurcu. The climate, it is true, is delightful, and all we behold is fertility, but we must not expect comfort and pleasant repose in the villages at our feet. Most of the houses, although they look friendly amidst the green clover-fields and trees, are miserable hovels without windows, and full of dirt, dust, and vermin. The villages, which appear to be at a mere stone's-throw from each other, are separated by roads which one day's rain renders impassable. Nature seems to hold her horn of plenty over the country before us, and yet we shall see but ragged poverty and lazy indolence below. Herds of cattle are grazing on the mountains, and still it will be difficult to procure a drop of milk. Grain of all kinds grows in abundance, and yet there will be no bread. The village of Tumbucu, at the foot of the mountain on which we stand, slumbers in the repose of blessed peace, and yet it was the scene of slaughter and civil war but a few years ago.[1] Everywhere around us, we shall see bountiful nature, derided and counteracted by the inertness and perversity of man.

But let us tear ourselves from the charming view, and descend into the valley. The descent from Pizcurcu to Tumbucu is very steep and precipitous. I remember to have made it once during a heavy rain. My horse slipped and stumbled in such an alarming manner that I deemed it prudent to dismount. My servant had done so before me, and I followed his example with great difficulty, as it was impossible for the horse to steady himself on the slippery declivity. We left the beasts to slide down in their own way, and endeavored to walk, but it was impossible. At every

[1] Battle of Tumbucu, in 1860.

step we fell, and only by throwing ourselves on our backs we escaped a headlong fall down the hill. Our india-rubber ponchos proved a great impediment, and yet we could not do without them, as the rain came down in torrents. Our horses passed their time between falling and scrambling up again, and at last slid down with such frightful rapidity that for a while we lost sight of them. In the mean time our own advance continually grew slower and more difficult. We were thoroughly steeped in mud, and crawled along on hands and feet till a deep hole or series of camellones compelled us to attempt a daring stride. At last my servant devised an expedient. Cautiously he crawled to the hill-side, and with his finger-nails dug out dry earth and threw it on the road before him. Over this improvised path we crept with tolerable safety, until we had passed the steepest places and regained our horses, which were covered all over with mud.

Passing through the small village of Tumbucu, and taking the road to Guaranda, we leave to our left the villages of San José, San Miguel, and Santiago de Chimbo, the inhabitants of which pass their lives in happy ignorance of the outer world and its great events and men. Books and newspapers are unknown, even among the whites who can read and write. They pass the day in stolid indolence, standing listlessly on the *Plaza*, or in front of some public office, staring vacantly into space, or gossiping. Only a cock-fight, or the sight of a good horse, can rouse them from their apathy. They seem to have no purpose in life but to keep themselves warm under their heavy red ponchos, and to eat when they are hungry.

In this connection I must mention a curious incident. On my first journey to Quito, I stopped for the night at the village of San José de Chimbo. The military official who accompanied me, and the government passports and recommendations which he displayed, immediately brought out the *Jefe Politico*, or mayor, who overflowed with the usual Spanish-American assurances of consideration and offers of services. There was no end to the strain of his politeness. He lodged us in the school-house, which contained the only room in the village fit for the reception of strangers. A Quito merchant, who travelled in my company, requested him to have supper prepared. He consented to find a cook, and to give her the necessary instructions. He afterwards informed us that he had given her $1.50, which we paid him. Next morning the cook came in and inquired whether we wanted breakfast. My companion, the merchant, ordered her to prepare it, but to do it well, as she would not have many other chances to charge $1.50 for a meal. It then turned out that the mayor had given her only one dollar putting the additional fifty cents in his own pocket. After breakfast I asked him how much we had to pay for it, offering him the money. He protested that he would take no money from me (forgetting probably that he had done so the day before); that he was sufficiently paid by the honor of extending to such a distinguished gentleman the hospitalities of his humble village; that I would offend him by insisting that he should receive money, etc. At this juncture my travelling companion came in and asked what the matter was. I told him that the mayor would take no money for the breakfast. "Quite natural," he replied, "because I have just paid him for it." Any body else in the place of the *Jefe Politico* would have been shamed to death, but he did not show the slightest embarrassment, and with perfect nonchalance, and the sweetest possible smile, turned the conversation to another subject.

Before reaching Guaranda, a so-called *socabon* has to be passed. A *socabon* is a very ingenious contrivance to avoid the passage of rivers. The Spaniards have learned it from its Indian inventors. When a river is too deep or rapid to be forded conveniently, a bend is selected where the mountainous bank protrudes far into the stream. There the mountain slope is perforated, and a tunnel made, through which the water rushes, forming a new bed and leaving the old bed either dry or easily fordable. Such a tunnel is called a "socabon," and many of them are to be met with in the interior of Ecuador. The socabon at Guaranda, enlarged by the force of the waters in the rainy season, forms a natural arch left hanging in the air, while its foundations are washed away. A strong earthquake will throw it down.

On the table-lands which we have now reached, llamas are occasionally met with. These intelligent animals, with their inquisitive eyes and graceful necks, are very interesting. Their number has been reduced to insignificance by the wantonness of the Spanish conquerors, who killed whole herds of them because they considered the heart and liver of the animal a great delicacy. In Peru and Bolivia llamas are still abundant, but in Ecuador they are nearly extinguished, and no care is taken to propagate the race. The few specimens I saw were used to carry burdens. They are very tame, and take a lively interest in what is going on around them. The female is ripe for copulation at the age of two years. Her pregnancy lasts ten months; but she seldom brings forth more than one young. They need a temperate or cold climate, and sometimes are found in a wild state on the high paramos of Chimborazo. When taken to the hot lowlands they soon die.[1]

Guaranda, nine thousand and sixty feet high, is a poor little town at the foot of Chimborazo. Villavicencio gives its population at eight thousand, which I believe is exaggerated. The houses, as throughout the interior, are built of sun-baked bricks (adobes), or have common earth-walls. The roofs are covered with red tiles, like those of almost all Spanish-American towns. On the Plaza there are several buildings with an upper story, but generally the houses have only a ground-floor. One of the two churches is half in ruins. Most of the buildings present a dilapidated appearance, grass and weeds covering the walls of court-yards and inclosures. The stores, with one or two exceptions, evidence the poverty and parsimony of the inhabitants of the interior, with whom we shall soon become acquainted. The place is rather cold, and very windy, especially during the dry season, owing to the near neighborhood of that Æolus, — Chimborazo. There are two taverns at Guaranda, which also serve as houses of consignment for goods sent to or from the interior. After having passed two nights (an ordinary journey from Bodegas to Guaranda takes two and a half days) in miserable open sheds exposed to the night air, it is a relief to enjoy the luxury of a covered room, chairs, and bedsteads again ; but the rooms of these taverns are sadly neglected, full of cobwebs and fleas ; the furniture is covered with thick layers of dust ; most of the window-glasses are broken, and filth is ac-

[1] I have taken these statements from a *Notice sur le Lama, par S. Wisse. Institut de France. Academie des Science. Extrait des Comptes rendus des Séances de l'Academie, tome* xxix, *séance du* 20 *Août*, 1849.

cumulated in the corners and on the floor. The servants are dirty and slovenly; and were it not for the recollection of past hardships the traveller would feel cheerless and uncomfortable.

In the neighborhood of Guaranda are salt works, where the salt of *Tomabela* is produced.

At Guaranda fresh beasts must be taken for Quito, as the animals which arrive tired from Bodegas would not be able to stand the passage of Chimborazo. Many arrieros live in the neighborhood, and the same trouble about hiring horses which vexed us at Bodegas, has now to be gone through with again. Warm ponchos and clothing have now to be prepared for the passage of Chimborazo, and it is advisable to start early, before daybreak, to avoid the storms on the mountain, which are said to increase in violence as the day advances. Toward noon they are said to be irresistible, and to have hurled many a horse and rider into the yawning precipices along the road. I once passed Chimborazo during so fearful a hurricane (on the 4th of July, 1862), that I was almost blinded by sand and gravel, which were continually blown in my face. At some high and precipitous turning-points in the road, where the rocky path between the mountains on one side and the abyss on the other was hardly two feet wide, the fury of the wind was such that the horses could not or would not advance, until a momentary calm enabled them to pass the dangerous places. These calms, however, are of but very short duration. It happens frequently that persons are thrown from their horses by the wind, or that their clothes and ponchos are torn to pieces. July, August, and September are the windiest months of the year. On the occasion just referred to, one of the mail-carrier's beasts had been thrown into a ravine a few days before my arrival. The animal perished, but its load was recovered.

After these preliminary remarks, I must invite my readers to accompany me on the exciting expedition.

## CHAPTER IV.

Passage of Mt. Chimborazo. — A Visit to the Region of Clouds and Storms. — View of the Mountain. — The *Arenal.* — Human Reminiscences and Monuments in the Desert of Sand and Snow. — What a *Paramo* is. — Its Terrors. — Chuquipoyo. — The Hacienda of Chimborazo. — A Dreary Resting-place. — View from Chuquipoyo. — The City of Riobamba in the Distance. — Earthquakes and Volcanoes. — Mt. Sangai. — Rains of Ashes. — Mt. Altar. — Mt. Carguairazo. — The Paramo of Sanancajas. — Descent from the Mountain Heath. — Reappearance of Vegetation. — The Village of Mocha.

After passing the river of Guaranda, over which, in 1863, a bridge was built, our ascent begins. At first, fields of clover, wheat, and barley, extend around us, but they soon give way to that wild and romantic vegetation which precedes and pleasantly contrasts with the dreary grasses of the highest and coldest region. Alpine flowers and shrubs exhale aromatic perfumes, and legions of birds welcome the rising sun, which richly gilds the highest peaks of the mountains. The road — if road it can be called — now winds itself along precipices which the eye shuns to fathom, now passes through lanes, or rather gulleys, frequently so narrow that it would be impossible for two horses to pass each other. It is here called the "*pongo*," a name of dreadful notoriety in the rainy season, and consists, like most of the mountain and paramo roads of Ecuador, of innumerable ruts, continually crossing and intersecting one another in a most bewildering manner.

The ascent seems endless. One terrace or mountain platform is hardly reached when we discover other and higher ones before us. Vegetation gradually diminishes; crags begin to close upon our narrow path, and over sharp-pointed rocks stumble for a while the panting animals. At last, doubling the mountain amphitheatre which we have slowly ascended to almost its highest point, we lose sight of the valley of Guaranda and its smiling fertility, to find ourselves in a wilderness of dreary mountains, valleys, and precipices covered with the long and cheerless paramo-grass, which for many a weary hour will be our monotonous companion. But the turn of the road has brought us face to face with Chimborazo, whose strange name and enormous height filled us with awe when we first read of it in school histories and geographies. Perhaps only a few of the many strange and difficult names which we then learned, have remained fresh in our memory; but among those few, Chimborazo always held an important place. And now it breaks upon our gaze in its majestic reality and overwhelming grandeur. Of many of the wonders of nature or art, our expectations are wrought to such a pitch that reality will often be fraught with disappointment. Thus Rousseau confesses to have felt disappointed when he first saw the sea, and many other similar instances could be adduced. But I do not believe that any body will be disappointed in the view of Chimborazo, not as it is seen at a distance from the sea, from Guayaquil or the heights of Camino Real, but as it will break upon him in the region of the storms and clouds, and in the fearful solemnity of Nature's solitude.

Fiercer and fiercer grows the wind as we advance; gust after gust comes down from the throne of the king of the Ecuadorian mountains; clouds form and dissolve around its snowy dome, or fleet by it in wild precipitation; carcasses of dead mules or donkeys block up many of the narrow passages of the road; barefooted and shivering arrieros, with their heads and necks bundled up with ponchos or shawls, hurry past us, urging and cursing their jaded animals; from time to time icy mists will hover around us, wetting our hair and ponchos, and hiding the gloomy landscape from our view; and the piercing cold, which many a day freezes the water in these altitudes, mockingly brings to our recollection the tropical scenes which we left but a day or two ago.

Lonely crosses on the roadside, or skulls in niches dug into the mountain, will now be met with, unfolding eloquent tales, in their ghastly silence, of poor travellers whose last journey was brought to an unforeseen end far away from the abodes of man.

At last we reach the Tambo de la Ensillada (saddleback), so called from being built on a saddle-like terrace of a mountain, projecting from the left of our road. It is a poor, dreary, wretched place, consisting of a few low huts of straw, the roofs of which rest on the ground. The inside of these hovels is without flooring; the ground is wet and muddy, notwithstanding the poor roof which covers it, and the inmates are filthy and besotted. These huts are without furniture, and almost always filled with smoke. The open space before them is a deep and muddy pool, worn by the hoofs of mules and horses. At this place a short rest is taken, and hot water procured to make coffee or tea.

Nearer and nearer we now draw to the grim mountain. The inequalities in the road again increase so that it will be a difficult task for an unskillful horseman to keep himself firm in the saddle. Our ascent is sometimes interrupted by almost perpendicular declivities, where the road is hardly two feet wide, with a steep, rocky wall on one side and a yawning precipice on the other. Apprehensive of an increase of the storm, we ask the arrieros whom we meet, "*Como está el cerro?*" ("How is the mountain?") and their shivering reply, "*Savoroso*" ("Savory"), tells us that worse is to follow. The clouds which play around the mountain now cover its upper, now its lower parts; now they hide it completely, now they allow us a full view of its gigantic dimensions, which seem to expand as we approach. A group of solitary trees (*Polylepis*) [1] in a wilderness of rocks, seems to form a landmark of vegetation, which is about to disappear around us. The horses, tired by the long and steep ascent and the wind, require the strong stimulus of our spurs. The fury of the winds increases. Our hats have to be tied to our heads with handkerchiefs or strings. The roaring of the storm often becomes deafening.

But fortunately we are already at the foot of the arenal (the sandy region), which is the highest point of the road. Another steep ascent has to be made, exceedingly tiresome for the horses, which move with great difficulty through the deep sand, strewn with the bones and skeletons of beasts of burden. Reaching

1 "I am inclined to believe that this tree (*Polylepis*) reaches the greatest elevation of any tree on the globe. It occurs on the western descent of Chimborazo at a short distance below the arenal (14,268 feet), constituting a well-defined zone characterized by the absence of any other trees. The trunk, nearly destitute of bark, is gnarled and twisted in the most fanciful manner, and the root penetrates deeply the rocky crevices, thus enabling the tree to resist the violent winds with which it is assailed." [From Dr. Jameson's *Manuscript Notes*, kindly placed at my disposal by the learned author.]. . . . Mr. Spruce says: "The bark of this tree resembles that of the birch in color, and is peeling off in flakes; but if one could suppose an arborescent *Acæna*, it would give a better idea of the pinnate, silvery foliage."

the summit, a sandy plain stretches out before us, which is about the best part of the road between Ambato and Guaranda — wide, smooth, and dry. This is the *Arenal*, 14,268 feet [1] above the level of the sea. It has two divisions — *El Arenal Grande* and *El Arenal Chiquito*, — the one being a continuation of the other.[2] These plains are often covered with sand so as to hide the track which we must follow. Hailstorms, too, are frequent in this windy desert.

To the right of the road we see a heap of stones, which are said to have been piled up to the memory of an Englishman who was murdered at that place by his arriero.[3]

Here, too, is the dividing line of the waters; and Ida Pfeiffer, following the example of Baron von Tschudi on Pasco de Cerro, "climbed down the western side of the mountain till she came to water, drank a little, and poured the rest into a stream that fell down on the eastern side, and then reversing the

1 Hall.

2 "The *Arenal* consists of sand and fine gravel of a pale yellow color. In one place the road, for a considerable distance, resembles a broad, smooth, gravel walk in England. It is scarcely necessary to state that here the wind is always easterly through the day, getting up strong generally about 10 A. M., and rarely continuing to blow with equal force during the night and following morning. Now and then it veers for a moment, and gives the traveller a side blow, which, were he not wary, might unhorse him." — Spruce, *Report of the Expedition*, etc. etc.

3 "He had undertaken to cross the Chimborazo accompanied only by a single arriero. Perhaps he might have done so in safety, had he not had the imprudence, on all occasions when there was any thing to pay, to display a purse well filled with gold. This glittering temptation the guide could not withstand, and when he found himself alone with the unfortunate traveller in this solitary region, he struck him a fatal blow on the back of the head with a great stone wrapped in a cloth, — a common method of murder in this country. He concealed the body in the snow; but both deed and doer were discovered very soon by his offering one of the gold pieces to change." — Ida Pfeiffer, *A Lady's Second Voyage round the World.*

operation, carried some thence to the western, amusing herself with the thought of having sent to the Atlantic some water that was destined to flow into the Pacific, and *vice versa*."[1] A very childish amusement, which I should not have mentioned if in this awful desert, the silence of which is broken only by the roaring storm, and where for leagues around no human habitation can be found, any thing done by, or reminding us of, man, had not a cheering interest for the traveller oppressed by the weight of absolute loneliness.

And now Chimborazo is no longer the background of a distant view; it is our only view to the left of the road, from which it is separated by a broad ravine.[2] From our position near the limit of perpetual snow, perhaps less than an hour's exertion would lead us into the snow-drifts of the mountain. Grand and beautiful

1 Ida Pfeiffer, *A Lady's Second Voyage round the World.*

2 "It is not well settled to how much of the Cordillera the name 'Chimborazo' should be limited. When an Indian speaks of Chimborazo, Tunguragua, etc., he means merely the snowy summit of those mountains, the adjacent paramos having local names according to the streams which traverse them, or the farms and villages adjacent to them. Proceeding from Chimborazo southward we have a lofty ridge, not rising in any part of it to the line of perpetual snow, varied here and there by slight depressions, but whose continuity is nowhere broken by any transversal valley. After forming the western boundary of the elevated plain or valley of Tiocajas, it sinks down abruptly from the heights of San Nicolas to the Valley of Alausi, at the junction of the Puma-cocha and Chauchau. To consider the whole of this ridge as belonging to Chimborazo would necessitate a similar extension of its limits on all sides, and we should have to include in it the adjacent mountain Carguairazo, formerly equally lofty, and separated from it only by a very narrow valley, as also the two 'knots' running eastward across the central valley to the foot of the eastern Cordillera, the one from Sanancajas and the other from the northern shoulder of Chimborazo (*Paramo de Puenevata*), both of which knots include some lofty peaks. I would rather confine the name of Chimborazo to the mighty mass which rises abruptly from the plain of Sanancajas on the east, and reposes to the north and south on Puenevata and the Arenal respectively. On the western side, however, I can find no positive break from the summit down to the plain. There is no intervening salient peak, and no ridge whose origin may not be traced to the peak of Chimborazo." — Spruce, *Report*, etc.

is its majestic dome,[1] and dazzling its whiteness when the sun's rays are reflected from it, as it stands out well defined by the deep azure of the sky. Grim and awful is its appearance when the sky is darkened by clouds, and ghastly vapors are drifting over and around its giant peaks.

Chimborazo rises 21,422 feet (Humboldt) above the level of the sea. No human foot ever reached its summit. The highest point in the world conquered by man, is six thousand and four French metres. It was reached on Chimborazo on the 16th of December, 1831, by the French naturalist Boussingault, and his English friend and companion, Colonel Hall. Humboldt and Bompland, who attempted an ascent on the 23d of June, 1802, reached only five thousand eight hundred and seventy-eight metres.[2] The density of the fog compelled them to return. Difficult as respiration is in those altitudes, climbing is doubly exhausting and often becomes impossible. The heart palpitates alarmingly; a feverish sensation sets in; blood oozes from the lips or the nose, and a propensity to vomit seizes the daring traveller, as was the case with Humboldt and Bompland. Those, however, who are accustomed to live, or are born on the high table-lands

1 "The figure of Chimborazo resembles a truncated cone with a spherical summit. From the foot of the snow its sides are covered with a calcined matter resembling white sand; and although no tradition exists of its active volcanic state, yet the issuing of some streams of hot water from the north side of it, seems to warrant that it is a volcano, or that it possesses volcanic properties." — Stephenson, *Twenty-five Years' Residence in South America.*

2 Humboldt, *Melanges de Geologie et de Physique Generale*, Paris, 1854. See also *Viajes Cientificos a los Andes Ecuatoriales, o Coleccion de Memorias Presentadas a la Academia de Ciencias de Francia, por M. Boussingault i Dr. Roulin, traducidas por J. Acosta*, Paris, 1849. Mr. Boussingault, in his ascents of Chimborazo, Antisana, and other snow-covered mountains, always found it more difficult and exhausting to advance over ground covered with snow than over the bare rock.

of the Andes, are less liable to such attacks than foreigners. The battle of Pichincha, which was fought on an elevation of nearly 11,000 feet above the level of the sea, the life in cities like Bogota, Potosi, La Paz, Micuipampa, and others, which reach a height of two thousand six hundred to four thousand French metres; the strength and agility of the bull-fighters in Quito, and the nights spent by young people in dancing and revelry in places almost as high as Mont Blanc, where the celebrated Saussure had scarcely strength enough to consult his instruments, while his guides, hardy *montagnards*, fainted around him, are unmistakable proofs that man may accustom himself to the rarefied air of the highest mountains.

After passing the arenal, which is about half a league across, our descent commences. At a water-fall (*chorrera*) not very far from the arenal, the road divides, one branch leading to Riobamba, and the other, which we will take, to Mocha and Ambato. We have now fairly entered the region of the paramos. Paramos, properly speaking, are the highest plains or heaths of the Cordillera, covered with high tufts of long and dry grass, which the natives call "*paja*"[1] (straw). A paramo, therefore, is frequently called a "*pajonal.*" Its aspect is dreary and cheerless in the extreme. But paramos may also prove dangerous to

[1] "A species of *Stipa*, with feather-like, silvery panicles, tinged with rose, which forms the mass of the vegetation on the paramo. This grass affords excellent thatch. It is also extensively used in packing, and along all the higher grounds it is almost the only material for fuel. Between the hassocks, especially when there are slight declivities, there is an interesting sub-alpine vegetation. A dense grassy turf is enameled with flowers,— white, yellow, red, and purple, which seem to spring direct from the ground." —Richard Spruce, *Notes of a Visit to the Chinchona Forests, on the Western Slope of the Quitenian Andes.* I may add here that the paramo grass is very good feed for cattle, which stray up into the highest regions, wading up to the knee in the freezing swamps and marshes.

travellers. Winds laden with icy vapors blow over them with tremendous violence, when as the natives call it, the paramo "*se pone bravo*" (gets wild). Dense fogs frequently envelop man and beast; darkness covers the earth and conceals every trace of the road; snow, hail, or sleet comes down unmercifully; and often the traveller loses his way and wanders helplessly over endless heaths. But this is not the worst; when worn out with fatigue and hunger, benumbed with cold and unable to urge on his jaded mules, he dismounts and sits down to recover his exhausted strength, his stomach soon becomes affected as if at sea; his blood ceases to circulate, his muscles grow stiff, and he expires with a ghastly smile upon his features. Travellers thus found dead in these inhospitable regions, are said to be *emparamados*.

Still the Paramo of Chimborazo is not reputed to be very dangerous. The fiercest paramo in Ecuador is that of Azuay, on the road from Riobamba to Cuenca.[1]

[1] "At Sitan, properly speaking, begins the Paramo of Azuay, the tomb of a great number of travellers. When the wind blows there, it brings with it such a quantity of hail and snow that the air is darkened; the traveller, up to his knees in water, is struck with cold; he feels his limbs grow stiff, and often loses the use of them, — if he has the good fortune to escape with life. On the Azuay is a pool of about seventy varas in length (one hundred and eighty feet). The water of this pond is at 9° R. above zero. Further on is another of five or six hundred varas long and from two to three hundred wide. Near these commences the plain of Puyal, dangerous on account of the deep marshes there met with. At the extremity of the Puyal are the ruins of a palace of the Incas. It is built of stone without cement. The Indians evinced a very singular taste in the choice of places where they constructed their pleasure houses, since during eight months of the year there is continued hail and rain here." — Caldas, *Semanario de la Nueva Granada*, Paris, 1849. I do not believe that the ruins to which Caldas refers were those of a palace or pleasure-house. It is more probable that the building was a *tambo*, or resting-place, for the accommodation of royal or noble travellers. The Incas evinced more prudence and humanity by erecting buildings for the use of travellers in the most inhospitable parts of the road, than their Spanish successors, who did not think of building even a common earth hut on such horrible passes as the Paramo of Azuay.

The Paramo of the Puyal, on the direct road from Riobamba to Santiago de Chimbo, is also said to be very dangerous. In October, 1862, I passed it in a perfect calm. I was struck with the great number of condors I saw there.

But let us continue our journey. Beautiful and romantic as the vegetation of Chimborazo is on its western side, so dreary and melancholy does it present itself on the eastern descent. The paramo grass, as I have already said, is our only companion, barren and gloomy mountains our only view. Up one hill-side and down another leads the monotonous road. Many a dreary heath has to be passed, many an icy rivulet has to be forded. No human habitation relieves the eye as far as the horizon extends. Now and then we see a cave or sheltered place under a protruding rock, where the Indian arrieros, when darkness overtakes them on their journeys, pass the night, shivering round a smoky fire of paramo grass, while their beasts are let loose to seek fodder for themselves. But with the exception of the miserable *ensillada*, not a hut or cottage greets us on the long road from the Pongo to Chuquipoyo. We are alone in the wilderness. If but a ruin, a mile-stone, a guide-post or a monument of some kind were to be seen! "Even the record of human vanity," says Bayard Taylor, "is preferable to the absence of any sign of man." In the loneliest prairies of the West we are occasionally gladdened by a sign-post telling us to use "Howe's Cough Candy," or we find "Ayer's Sarsaparilla" painted on a decaying fence-rail; but in this dreadful desert there is nothing to remind us of the cheer and comforts of civilization; nothing to remind us even of the existence of man, except at long intervals droves of mules and asses, followed by barefooted arrieros, gliding along like spectral shadows of the life we left behind us.

At last we reach the tambo, a solitary house called Chuquipoyo, and sometimes undeservedly styled the "Hacienda of Chimborazo." And what a miserable, gloomy, filthy, and cheerless place it is! The Ecuadorian tambos or stopping-places are all bad, but Chuquipoyo deserves the crown of wretchedness. After the hardships of the day, and considering the elevation of this tambo to be 12,540 feet above the level of the sea, one should expect to find at least a warm room with a pleasant chimney fire crackling in the grate, to forget the fatigues of the journey and the freezing paramo outside. But even to the traveller who enters Chuquipoyo without the least expectation of comfort, it will prove a chilling disappointment. The court-yard is a knee-deep pool, steaming with the excrements of horses. No pavement leads through or around the yard. It is necessary to ride to the very door of the principal room to dismount without taking a bath of mud. The room itself is a horrid hole without windows. The country architecture of Ecuador despises ventilation and windows. Two old, dirty, and rickety bedsteads on one side, a stone bench to make beds on on the other, and an old table, constitute the furniture. The flooring of bricks is broken through and rotting away; the atmosphere of the room damp and cold; the first and last coat of whitewash it ever received besmeared all over with inscriptions and obscene drawings, and the plaster crumbling down. Into this room men and women are huddled together to undress and sleep in each other's presence. Those who find it crowded have the choice of a side room about eight by seven feet, also furnished with a bedstead, but with the wall broken through at many places, through which the icy night air blows in unmercifully. The stench of horses and arrieros pervades the whole tambo. One wing of the building is half in ruins, leaving but a kitchen and the sleeping and store rooms of the *mayordomo* (steward). The arrieros and their peones sleep in the court-yard in the open air.

The cooking is done on the ground, in the unhandy, pointed pots of the interior. The only fuel is the grass of the paramo, which makes it necessary for the cook to fan and blow the fire continually. The supply of *yerba* for the horses is always insufficient. To travellers a few eggs and potatoes will sometimes be sold, but in nine cases out of ten, nothing is to be had, either for love or money. In short, a painter who would represent cheerlessness, ought to paint Chuquipoyo. Edgar A. Poe's "House of Usher," or the "Haunted House" of Thomas Hood, are heavens of comfort in comparison with this detestable place.

It was originally built by the government as a resting-place for soldiers, and now belongs to a wealthy citizen of Riobamba, who, with little expense, might not only make it comfortable, but also profitable; for who, in the midst of the cold and lonely desert of Chimborazo, would not gladly pay for a warm and cheerful room? But as it is, it is a disgrace to its proprietor, a disgrace and a reproach to Ecuador.

After what I have said, it would be needless to describe the night to which travellers are condemned. I cannot, however, refrain from relating an incident showing the stolid and uncharitable character of the Ecuadorian Indians. Travelling from Quito to Guayaquil in 1863, I had left Ambato rather late in the day, and it was dark when I came into the neighborhood of

Chuquipoyo. My companions, one of them a member of a Spanish Scientific Commission, who were not familiar with the road, became apprehensive of having passed the tambo without seeing it, and infected me with their doubts. We had already resolved to turn back and proceed in the direction of Ambato until we should meet our arrieros, who were behind with the luggage, when aside from the road we saw a few Indians in the paramo, who had encamped themselves between the high hassocks of grass. We hailed them, telling them that we had lost the way, and asking them for the right direction to Chuquipoyo. But instead of answering us, they ran away, and hid themselves in the high grass of the heath. All our hallooing, all our promises were in vain. The Indians would not come forward. Unwilling to expose ourselves longer than necessary to the chilling night air and increasing darkness, we made after them, found them after a short hunt, and compelled them to give us the right direction.

The view which on fine mornings presents itself from Chuquipoyo, is highly interesting. We descry the sandy valley and city of Riobamba, which name is connected with one of the most frightful geological revolutions known in the annals of mankind. The present city of Riobamba, nine thousand one hundred and eighty-nine feet above the level of the sea, is about three leagues distant from the site where the old city stood, the ruins of which are yet visible among the humble buildings of the two contiguous villages of Cicalpa and Cajabamba. The old city, founded in 1533, by Sebastian Benalcazar, the conqueror of Quito, suffered greatly by the earthquake of 1645; but on the 4th of February, 1797, it was completely destroyed. With the exception of four hundred and eighty who escaped, all the inhabitants perished. The shock was so fearful that the face of the country was entirely changed. A part of the mountain Cicalpa was torn from its base, crushing the city at its foot. "Mountains rose," says Stephenson, "where cultivated valleys had existed; rivers disappeared or changed their course, and plains usurped the place of mountains and ravines." The site of the city was rent asunder, and a rivulet now flows through it which had not existed before. The surviving inhabitants were unable to point out the spots where their houses had stood. Caldas, the Granadian naturalist, who visited the place shortly after the catastrophe, and while the new city was in process of erection in the plain of Tapi, says that many of the survivors still lingered around the ruins, unable to tear themselves from the frightful sepulchre of those they had loved. The new city, according to Villavicencio,[1] contains about 16,000 inhabitants, and several woolen factories. The chief productions of the district are wool, wheat, barley, potatoes, and European culinary vegetables. The streets of the town are broad and the houses low. They are built of adobes, and with the exception of those on the plaza, have but a ground-floor. The number of the churches seems to be in disproportion to the population. The place is very lifeless; the stores are generally attended by saleswomen, and the men pass their time in idleness, gambling, or gossiping.

To the east of Riobamba we discover the smoky summit of Sangai, which is probably the most active volcano on the globe. "Since the day when it was first seen by the Spaniards," says Mr. Spruce, "it has

[1] *Geografia de la Republica del Ecuador.*.

been in continual eruption, whereas other volcanoes have had their periods of repose; but as it stands in the midst of uninhabited forests (for the village of Macas is at least two days' journey away), its eruptions rarely cause any damage to the dwellings of man. Its position is in the Eastern Cordillera, about 2° South, longitude 78° 33′ West. It is crowned by a great breadth of perpetual snow, or rather of alternating layers of snow and ashes, and even (it has been asserted) of modern trachyte. At Bodegas its explosions are often distinctly heard; sometimes also at Guayaquil." On the morning of the 24th of June, 1861, when I first arrived at Bodegas, the little steamer in which I had come had its deck completely covered with ashes, and ashes covered the foliage of the woods between Bodegas and Punta Playas. These ashes, or volcanic dust, had been thrown out by Mt. Sangai. The fall began on the 23d of June, and lasted for five days. On the 18th of July another shower of ashes reached Guayaquil, and fell as thick as drizzling rain. The explosions of the mountain sound like the discharges of cannon. Its height is 17,284 feet.

Nearer to Riobamba is the beautiful Altar, 17,450 feet high. The Indians call it Capac Urcu. There is a tradition that it was once higher than Chimborazo, when after eight years of frightful eruptions, the walls, consumed by the volcanic activity within, could no longer support their own weight, and the top fell in. Since the discovery of the country by the Spaniards, no symptoms of volcanic activity have been observed. On the afternoon of a bright and beautiful October day in 1862, while travelling from Ambato to Riobamba, I had a most perfect view of Altar, Tungurагua, Chimborazo, and other snow peaks. The Altar, however, enraptured me; and for hours as I descended to, and rode through, the sandy plain of Tapi, my eye was fascinated by its wondrous peaks. The two highest peaks at its southern extremity appeared to my excited fancy like a king and queen seated on icy thrones, clad in long snowy robes, and looking down on their hoary court of minor rocks and crags, with calm and melancholy majesty. Sad and sorrowful seemed the queen as the rays of the setting sun lingered on her musing countenance. Perhaps she had come from more genial climes; perhaps birds had caroled and flowers had smiled upon her happy childhood, and now she must pass her dreary life speechless and motionless, as if charmed by an enchanter's spell, at the cold side of her icy consort. There was a melancholy and resigned expression in what I imagined to be her face. Perhaps she was another Blanche de Bourbon, sacrificed to some cruel Don Pedro of those cold and lofty realms, to which even the condor rarely elevates his soaring flight, and where not a leaf, not a flower, not even a vestige of a friendlier world breaks the deathlike loneliness. There all life is extinct; vegetation has ceased; the sweet notes of birds do not penetrate into those unattainable altitudes; and save the storms of heaven, no other sound but the roaring of her fell neighbor Sangai, reaches the ear of the unfortunate queen. In wonderful clearness the mountain rose before me, but soon clouds commenced to circle around it; mists and vapors gradually drew a thin veil over the majestic sight, and at last envious fogs interposed impenetrably between the steady, soft, and melancholy look of the queen on high and the sympathizing wanderer in the plain below. A few minutes more and the apparition was gone, but the impression it left will never fade from my memory.

Will my readers pardon these fantastic digressions? I shall atone for them by at once continuing our journey from Chuquipoyo. Our road now takes a northerly direction, leading us into the dreary Paramo of Sanancajas. The wilderness here seems endless. Again the same monotonous heath, the same gloomy paramo grass, and no human habitation as far as the eye can reach.

We are to make a new acquaintance, however. It is Carguairazo, the northern neighbor of Chimborazo, and so near the latter that the Indians call it "Chimborazo *Embra*," the female Chimborazo. It is 15,664 feet high, and is also said to have been higher than Chimborazo; but on the 19th of June, 1698, its top fell in during a tremendous earthquake, which almost totally destroyed the villages of Mocha, Ambato, and Latacunga. In Ambato sixteen hundred Indians and five hundred and fifty-six Spaniards were crushed by the falling houses, and in Latacunga so many persons perished, that, according to the official records kept in the *escribania de hacienda*, it became necessary to dig ditches for the purpose of burying the dead in heaps.[1] Since that horrible catastrophe, the mountain has given no important signs of volcanic activity.

After passing two gloomy lakes or ponds, which must be of recent formation, as the road which formerly passed over their sites is still visible under the water, we leave the paramo behind us at last. The

[1] Pablo Herrera, *Ensayo sobre la Historia de la Literatura Ecuatoriana.* The author carefully examined the archives of the municipalities of Latacunga and Quito, and extracted from them many valuable items of historical information. See also Zimmermann, *Die Wunder der Urwelt*, Berlin, 1856. Velasco, *Historia del Reino de Quito*, Quito, 1844.

character of the landscape changes as we descend; a friendly vegetation reappears, and our heart rejoices at seeing green bushes, cultivated fields, and human habitations again.

A steep descent to a mountain stream which must be passed, and a short ascent to the other side, leads us to the village of Mocha. In ancient times this was an important Indian town, frequently mentioned in the history of the conquest. Now it is a miserable, filthy, cold, and lifeless village, but greatly welcome after the dreariness of the paramo, and the hospitality of Chuquipoyo.[1] It has a plaza, with an humble church, which is half in ruins ever since the earthquake of 1859. The traces of earthquakes are now bound to haunt us, whithersoever we may go.

1 With regard to taverns along the road, the first white settlers of the country were ahead of their present descendants. According to Herrera, taverns were established along the public highways every five or six leagues. — Dec. v., l. 10, cap. 11. Now the traveller must resort to wretched hovels in which, in many cases, he has to share his lodgings with his filthy hosts. It is fortunate, however, that, especially in the interior, his life and property are perfectly secure, for his hosts are harmless and inoffensive.

## CHAPTER V.

From Mocha to Ambato. — The Volcano Tungaragua. — The Towns of Ambato and Latacunga. — Fleas. — The Volcano Cotopaxi. — Earthquakes and Prophecies. — A Gold Legend. — The Treasure of Atahuallpa. — The Testament of Valverde. — His *Derrotero*. — Mt. Ilinisa. — The Plain and Village of Mulalu. — Description of a Farm-Building. — Signs of General Decay. — The Hill of Callo. — The Footprints of St. Bartholomew the Apostle. — Inca Ruins. — The Paramo of Tiupullo. — The "Accursed Tree." — Rumiñagui and other Mountains. — The Villages of Machachi and Tambillo. — An Ecuadorian Tavern. — End of our Journey.

THE road from Mocha to Ambato leads through long rows and hedges of American Aloe, or *Agava Americana*, one of the most important and useful plants of the interior, of which I shall give a detailed account in a subsequent chapter. The first part of the road leads through a fertile region, producing potatoes, wheat, barley, and other products of the temperate zone. The climate is delightful; neither hot nor cold, though rather cool. The latter half of the road lies through a sandy and sterile country, producing scanty crops of maize, barley, pease, and lupines. The road seems to be buried under deep layers of light sand, and if there is a strong breeze, it drives clouds of unwelcome dust in the eyes of the traveller.

To the southeast of the road, in clear weather, a charming view of Mt. Tungaragua may be enjoyed. This volcano, 16,514 feet high, is one of the most attractive and interesting mountains in Ecuador. Its form is that of a perfect cone, and while its highest parts are covered with a long and splendid robe of snow, the sugar-cane grows at its base in the Valley of Baños. In my opinion, it is the most beautiful of all the snow peaks in the country.

The town of Ambato is not visible from a distance. It lies in a caldron, and does not present itself before you are right above it. It is surrounded by steep and barren sandy mountains, almost without vegetation, but its aspect is very pleasing. It is a friendly green spot — a smiling oasis in a desert, with houses peeping through numberless gardens, orchards, and clover-fields. It is famous for its fruit. Tunas, granadillas, monster strawberries, which the natives call *frutillas*; peaches, apricots, and apples (the three latter species, however, of a very inferior quality); wild cherries (*capulis*), guavas, etc., grow in abundance. Being but 8567 feet above the level of the sea,[1] and protected by high mountains on all sides, its temperature is very agreeable, and a great deal milder than that of Quito. It may, indeed, boast of the climate of an eternal spring. Its population is estimated at eight thousand. It has several plazas and churches; but the houses have seldom more than a ground-floor, with the exception of those on or in the neighborhood of the Plaza Mayor. The buildings are of sun-baked brick, and the better ones neatly whitewashed. The gutters are in the centre of the streets, and through some of them streams of limpid water flow. The only tolerable boots and shoes manufactured in the country are made here. The Cochineal,[2] too, is found in abundance in the

[1] According to the measurement of Mr. Spruce. Dr. Jameson has it at 8540.

[2] "The name given by the Spaniards to this valuable insect is *cochinilla*, signifying a little pig, because it bears a resemblance to one; in the same manner as in some parts of England it is supposed that the wood-louse re-

leaves of the cactus, and collected by the natives for dyeing, although but little or no attention is paid to the cultivation of the cactus, or of the insect. Coarse woollen ponchos are also manufactured at a cheap rate. On market-days, especially on Sundays, the Plaza Mayor, with its motley crowd of Indians, in ponchos of all colors, presents a most lively and grotesque appearance.

The town is situated on the right bank of the river Ambato, along which many friendly haciendas extend. During the fruit season, about Christmas and New Year, Ambato is visited by many of the wealthy residents of Quito, who come to eat fruit and enjoy the mildness of the climate. There is much less rain at Ambato than at Quito and other places of the interior. On clear nights the fiery vapors of Mt. Cotopaxi are visible. The *casa posada* (tavern) which existed there during my time, was a miserable concern, the rooms full of dust, filth, and fleas, and the kitchen abominable. There were, as in all other taverns in the interior, bedsteads in the rooms, but no bedding, as travellers are expected to carry their own bedding with them.

Ascending from the caldron in which Ambato is situate, we reach a broad table-land over which the road leads to Latacunga. The two principal branches

sembles a hog. The cactus on which it feeds is not so prickly as the tuna which in the West Indies is called the prickly pear. The leaves are very green, as well as the rind of the fruit; but the inside is of a most beautiful red color, similar to that of the cochinilla. It is very palatable, and when eaten, communicates its own color to the urine. . . . . Instead of killing the insect, after taking it from the cactus, by placing it in an earthen jar, and exposing it to a heat sufficiently strong to destroy its vitality, and then preserving it in bags, as the Mexican Indians do, it is ground or bruised to the consistency of paste, and often adulterated with the juice of the fruit and flour." — *Stephenson.*

of the Cordillera widen here, and allow us to view the country for miles around. The road lies through an endless prolongation of narrow lanes, formed by interminable hedges of aloes, magueys, and cacti. A beautiful heliotrope which grows among these hedges, casts fragrance on our path. Approaching Latacunga, the country becomes perfectly sterile; the mountains are entirely arid, and dreary plains, covered with volcanic sands and pumice-stone, indicate the neighborhood of the dreadful volcano Cotopaxi, which has caused so much suffering and destruction to this part of the country.

The houses of the town of Latacunga, or as it was originally called *Llactacunga*, are built of pumice-stone, thrown out by the eruptions of Mt. Cotopaxi. They are almost all without an upper story, and present rather a gloomy appearance. The elevation of Latacunga is 9170 feet above the level of the sea,[1] and its climate, cold. It is seldom we see an inhabitant of the place without a cloak or a poncho. There is always a tavern at Latacunga, but naturally, not without the chief production of the place — fleas. In fact, the streets and public squares of the town are filthy *par excellence*. Filth, according to a Spanish-American authority,[2] is a characteristic trait of the province of Quito. Ida Pfeiffer says that after a night's rest in Latacunga, she awoke with her skin marked all over with red spots, as if from an eruptive disease. The place is not one of business or enterprise. It is half in ruins, owing to the many earthquakes with which it has been visited. Some of the churches are down, and in slow process of reconstruction. The town lies at the foot of a little hill on which the old town stood,

1 Jameson. 2 Caldas.

and which is yet covered with ruins. In fact, Latacunga is the very image of decay, and the only celebrity it has acquired, it owes to its earthquakes, and to the pomp of its religious processions. Its population is estimated at 16,000, the great majority of whom are Indians. It was an important Indian town before the arrival of the Spaniards, and temples, palaces, and royal factories are said to have been constructed there by the great Inca Huaynacapac.

After the conquest the Indian population was greatly reduced by the cruelty and avarice of the Spaniards. At present the Indians of Latacunga are famous for their mummeries and dances during *semana santa* (holy week), and between Christmas and New Year's. To do honor to the occasion, they hire fancy dresses and jewels for these dances, at an expense which not only swallows up a whole year's earnings, but generally increases the interminable debt for which they are held to labor. The Indians of Latacunga, especially the women, are very ugly, but have beautiful teeth, of dazzling whiteness.

I have already mentioned what Latacunga suffered from the earthquake which accompanied the falling in of the top of Mt. Carguairazo. Eight thousand persons are said to have perished on that occasion. According to Father Velasco,[1] who carefully compiled and religiously believed in all the miraculous legends he could scrape together, this earthquake had been predicted seven years before it took place, in a sermon preached by Father José de Cases. He announced the catastrophe as a punishment for the immoral amusements, such as masquerades and bull-fights, with which the inhabitants were fond of celebrating the festi-

[1] *History of the Kingdom of Quito.*

val of St. John. Father Velasco quotes from the sermon which the venerable prophet is said to have preached on that occasion. He makes him tell his incredulous congregation that even the temple in which he stood would fall, with the exception of the column that sustained the pulpit. And so, the chronicler assures his readers, it happened. The Carmelite nuns, who had believed in the prophecy, and slept under tents in their garden for seven years after it, to avoid being crushed by the apprehended fall of their convent, were saved.

According to the same credible authority, the earthquake of 1757, by which four hundred lives were destroyed (two hundred persons were killed while listening to a sermon in the Church of the Jesuits), had also been predicted thirteen years before it took place, by a Father Saldaña, a Jesuit. In a country where superstition and fanaticism reign supreme, it is very customary to refer such catastrophes to previous predictions. On the other hand, it requires no prophetic gift to predict calamities which, considering the volcanic nature of the soil, are unfortunately of but too frequent occurrence, and may hourly be apprehended. If the believers in such prophecies are only patient enough to bear them in mind for seven or thirteen years, as in the above cases, it is very probable that they will live to witness their fulfillment.[1]

[1] "The terror which they (earthquakes) cause excites the imagination even to a painful extent, and overbalancing the judgment, predisposes men to superstitious fancies. And what is highly curious is, that repetition, so far from blunting such feelings, strengthens them. In Peru, where earthquakes appear to be more common than in any other country, every succeeding visitation increases the general dismay, so that in some cases the fear becomes almost insupportable. The mind is thus constantly thrown into a timid and anxious state; and men, witnessing the most serious dangers, which they can neither avoid nor understand, become impressed with a

In 1797, many of the churches and convents, rebuilt after former visitations, were thrown down again, and many lives lost. This catastrophe was followed by another in 1802, and still another in 1859, the latter doing considerable damage. These earthquakes (*terremotos*) must be distinguished from those frequent shocks of more or less violence, and doing more or less damage, which the natives call *temblores*. They occur too often to be noticed by the chroniclers;[1] unless we should find a second Santiago Perez Valencia, a New Granadian, who for forty years kept a register of all earthquakes and shocks which took place at Popayan, the city where he resided. According to this register, Popayan experienced one hundred and two earthquakes between the years 1805 and 1841.[2]

But earthquakes were not the only scourge of the town of Latacunga. The eruptions of Mt. Cotopaxi, which is but five leagues distant, formed another source of calamities, alarms, and apprehensions. This

conviction of their own inability, and of the poverty of their own resources. In exactly the same proportion the imagination is aroused, and a belief in supernatural interference actively encouraged. Human power failing, superhuman power is called in, the mysterious and the invisible are believed to be present, and there grow up among the people those feelings of awe and of helplessness on which all superstition is based, and without which no superstition can exist." — Buckle's *History of Civilization in England*, chap. ii.

[1] "In the earthquake of 1743 a Jesuit, Father Vallejo, was in the church when the roof fell in. He remained under the ruins till the third day, when he was taken out unhurt, but his mental faculties were so completely deranged, that he had forgotten his own name, nor did he recollect any of his most particular friends; and although a priest, when his breviary was presented to him, he could not read it, but appeared quite childish. He afterwards resided in the College of Quito, but his memory had so entirely abandoned him that he never could recollect any thing that had occurred to him before the earthquake, not even his studies, and he was afterwards taught to read, and to celebrate a votive mass." — *Stephenson.*

[2] Acosta's Notes to his Spanish Translation of Boussingault's *Scientific Voyages to the Ecuatorian Andes.*

famous mountain (18,890 feet high) is, on clear days, distinctly visible from Latacunga, Mulalu, Machachi, Tambillo, and all the higher points of Quito. Clad in a virgin robe of snow, it presents a most beautiful appearance. Its shape is that of a regular truncated cone, with a flat summit. The crater which opens on the top of the mountain being in uninterrupted activity, dense volumes of white and gray smoke are continually issuing from it, forming themselves into the most fantastic shapes. Generally the smoke assumes the form of an enormous tree with a trunk and branches, until a current of air tears it away from the mountain, and leaves it hovering in the sky, where it remains as a cloud. New formations will then slowly arise from the crater, and are, in their turn, carried away by aërial currents. At night the smoke issuing from the mountain forms a pillar of fire, and fire beams through the clefts and fissures of the summit. The noise produced by the explosions of Cotopaxi resembles the rumbling of thunder, and may frequently be heard at Quito, and sometimes even further to the north. Fine sand and ashes are thrown out almost without intermission, and prove very detrimental to the cattle of the haciendas around the mountain. On its lower declivity, very near the snow limit, is a huge mass of rock called by some *Cabeza del Inca*, (the Inca's head,) according to an ancient tradition that it was the original summit of the mountain torn off and hurled down by an eruption on the day the Inca Atahuallpa was executed by Pizarro at Cajamarca. According to the information collected by Fray Marcos de Niza shortly after the event, that eruption took place the evening before the treacherous capture of Atahuallpa.

Since its second eruption, which is said to have taken place in 1534, Cotopaxi remained quiet for over two hundred years, until in the beginning of 1742 another great eruption took place, throwing out immense quantities of water and mud, and doing great damage to the bridges, fields, and cattle in the neighborhood.[1]

The third eruption took place on the 9th of December, 1742, and was preceded by a rumbling, subterranean noise, which lasted for several days. The roaring by which it was accompanied was heard at a distance of sixty leagues. Its principal feature was a great inundation, which is generally ascribed to the enormous mass of snow which covered the mountain, and was suddenly melted by the heat of the crater and the streams of boiling water it threw out. The flood, breaking over the narrow bed of the river Latacunga, inundated the plain below, destroying many haciendas, a great number of cattle, and a part of the district of Latacunga called "*barrio caliente*." Whether such an inundation can really have proceeded from the melting of the snow-cover of Cotopaxi, may perhaps be doubted. Father Velasco indignantly rejects the hypothesis; but he is no scientific authority. I have often seen the mountain either without snow, or with a part of its snow-cover suddenly missing, — a phenomenon which was almost always accompanied by a sudden rise of the river Latacunga. Whether the snow had melted in consequence of eruptions, or whether it had been completely covered by a layer of brown cinders and scoria, I am unable to say.

On the 4th of November, 1744, the fourth great

1 Dr. Pablo Herrera, the author of *Ensayo sobre la Historia de la Literatura Ecuatoriana*, has corrected the dates of the principal eruptions given by Velasco and adopted by Stephenson. I have adopted these corrections, as they are based on record evidence.

eruption took place. On this occasion the force of the explosion opened a deep cleft or ravine, which now leads from the western side of the crater to the foot of the mountain. The eruption was again accompanied by a most disastrous inundation. The flood reached the Plaza Mayor of Latacunga, filling the streets, court-yards and houses.

February 2d, 1757. This was the third eruption followed by an inundation. Again the plains of Mulalu and Callo, and the town of Latacunga were devastated by a flood, and to increase the general dismay and terror, shocks of earthquake were felt, which threw down the churches of the town, and laid several adjoining villages in ruins.

February 10th, 1766. — There was no earthquake this time, but another inundation, produced by the waters which rushed down from Cotopaxi. The sand and ashes which were thrown out, destroyed the crops for many miles around.

April 4th, 1768. — This explosion was announced by monstrous columns of smoke and fire, which were followed by an earthquake and a rain of ashes, ejected in such quantities that the sun was completely hidden, and for several hours the inhabitants of the neighboring towns and villages were obliged to light candles and use lanterns in the daytime. The thatched roofs of many of the huts were crushed by the weight of the sand and ashes which had fallen on them. The noise of the falling sand resembled that of a heavy shower. The crops were destroyed, and a great number of cattle perished. At the same time the roaring of the volcano was incessant. Such catastrophes always produce the usual manifestations of terror and superstition among the people. Persons rush out on the streets, loudly confessing their sins; the wooden statues of the saints are taken from the churches and carried around in procession; psalms are chanted; and during the earthquake of 1859 at Quito, persons threw themselves at the feet of the archbishop, who was on the Plaza Mayor, and prayed to be absolved from their sins.

January, 1803. — This eruption, too, was followed by a disastrous flood, causing great damage. Humboldt heard the noise of the explosions at Guayaquil, at a distance of fifty-two leagues in a straight line from the crater. It sounded like the continued discharges of a battery.

From that time the mountain remained tolerably quiet until 1851, when the flames went high, and slight eruptions took place, sending sand and ashes to its eastern side.

In 1855 it threw out sand, a great quantity of water, and even stones, which it scattered over the plains of Mulalu and Callo. Since then it has been vomiting forth dense columns of smoke, accompanied now and then by a fine rain of ashes, but has done no damage, if we except the gradual sterilizing of the fields around it, to which the continued eruption of cinders and sand must inevitably lead.

Latacunga is the starting-point of the most romantic gold legend circulating in Ecuador. As it has a better claim to consideration than any other of the many idle gold-stories in which the interior abounds, and as it has led to many adventurous expeditions into the mountains of Llanganati, where the treasure that enriched Valverde is said to be buried, I will give a full account of it, availing myself of the information contained in a pamphlet written by Mr. Spruce, the celebrated botanist, who made a scientific exploration of the wilderness of Llanganati: —[1]

"In the month of July, 1857," says Mr. Spruce, "I reached Baños, where I learned that the snowy points I had observed from Paca-yacu, between Tunguragua and Cotopaxi, were the summits of a group of mountains called Llanganati, from which ran down to the Pastasa the densely wooded ridges I saw to the northward. I was further informed that these mountains abounded in all sorts of metals, and that it was universally believed that the Incas had deposited an immense quantity of gold in an artificial lake on the flanks of one of the peaks, at the time of the Spanish Conquest. They spoke also of one Valverde, a Spaniard, who from being poor, had suddenly become very rich, which was attributed to his having married an Indian girl, whose father showed him where the treasure was hidden, and accompanied him on various occasions to bring away portions of it; and that Valverde returned to Spain, and when on his death-bed, bequeathed the secret of his riches to the King. Many expeditions, public and private, had been made to follow the track indicated by Valverde, but no one had succeeded in reaching its terminus; and I spoke with two men at Baños who had accompanied such expeditions, and had nearly perished with cold and hunger on the paramo of Llanganati, where they had wandered for thirty days. The whole story seemed so impossible that I paid little attention to it, and I set to work to examine the vegetation of the adjacent vol-

[1] Richard Spruce, *On the Mountains of Llanganati in the Eastern Cordillera of the Quitenian Andes, illustrated by a map constructed by the late Don Atanasio Guzman; Read before the Royal Geographical Society of London, on the 12th March*, 1860.

cano Tunguragua, at whose northeastern foot the village of Baños is situated.

"In the summers of the years 1858 and 1859 I visited Quito and various points in the Western Cordillera, and for many months the country was so insecure on account of internal dissensions, that I could not leave Ambato and Riobamba, where my goods were deposited, for more than a few days together. I obtained, however, indisputable evidence that the 'Derrotero,' or guide to Llanganati, of Valverde, had been sent by the King of Spain to the Corregidors of Tacunga and Ambato, along with a '*Cedula Real*,' commanding those functionaries to use every diligence in seeking out the treasure of the Incas. That one expedition had been headed by the Corregidor of Tacunga in person, accompanied by a friar, Padre Longo, of considerable literary reputation. The 'Derrotero' (guide) was found to correspond so exactly with the actual localities, that only a person intimately acquainted with them could have drawn it up; and that it could have been fabricated by any other person who was never out of Spain, was an impossibility. This expedition had nearly reached the end of the route, when one evening the Padre Longo disappeared mysteriously, and no traces of him could be discovered; so that whether he had fallen into a ravine near which they were encamped, or into one of the morasses which abound all over that region, is to this day unknown. After searching in vain for the Padre for some days, the expedition returned, without having accomplished its object.

"The 'Cedula Real' and 'Derrotero' were deposited in the archives of Tacunga, whence they disappeared about twenty years ago. So many people were admitted to copy them, that at last some one, not content with a copy, carried off the original. I have secured a copy of the 'Derrotero,' bearing date August 14, 1827, but I can meet with no one who recollects the date of the original documents.

"I also ascertained that a botanist, Don Atanasio Guzman, who resided some time in the town of Pillaro, and lost his life by an accident near the town of Patate, had headed many expeditions in quest of the gold of Llanganati. He also made the map of the Llanganatis which is prefixed to this sketch. Guzman and his companions, although they found no deposits of gold, came on the mouths of several silver and copper mines which had been worked in the time of the Incas, and ascertained the existence of other metals and minerals. They began to work the mines, at first with ardor, which soon, however, cooled down, partly in consequence of intestine quarrels, but chiefly because they became disgusted with that slow mode of acquiring wealth, when there was molten gold supposed to be hidden close by; and so the mines were at length all abandoned. This is supposed to have taken place in the early part of the present century, but the exact date I can by no means ascertain. Guzman is reported to have met with Humboldt, and to have shown his drawings of plants and animals to that prince of travellers. He died about 1806 or 1808, in the Valley of Seytu, about four leagues distant from Ambato, at a small farm-house now called Seytillo. He was a somnambulist, and having one night walked out of the house while asleep, he fell down a steep place, and so perished."

Mr. Spruce then proceeds to criticise the map of Guzman, and adds a translation of the "Derrotero," which, together with some necessary explanations, will be found in the appendix to this work. After this he gives an account of his own exploration of the road pointed out by the "guide," the description of which perfectly corresponds to the actual locality, until the mountain Margasitas is reached. "Beyond this," he continues, "no one has been able to proceed with certainty. The 'Derrotero' directs it to be left on the left hand, but the explanatory hieroglyph ('and I warn thee that thou must go round it in this fashion ꝺ') puzzles every body, as it seems to leave the mountain on the right. Accordingly, nearly all who have attempted to follow the 'Derrotero,' have gone to the left of Margasitas, and have failed to find any of the remaining marks signalized by Valverde.

"The mines of Llanganati, after having been neglected for nearly half a century, are now being sought out again with the intention of working them; but there is no single person, at the present day, able to employ the labor and capital required for successfully working a silver mine; and mutual confidence is at so low an ebb in this country that companies never hold together long. Beside this, the gold of the Incas never ceases to haunt people's memories. But if the 'Socabon' of Valverde cannot at this day be discovered, it is known to every one that gold exists at a short distance, and possibly in considerable quantity, if the Ecuadorians would only take the trouble to search for it, and not leave that task to the wild Indians, who are content if by scooping up the gravel with their hands, they can get together enough gold to fill the quill which the white man has given them as the measure of the value of the axes and lance-heads he has supplied to them on trust."

Leaving Latacunga on a clear day early in the morning, we have a beautiful view of Cotopaxi in the eastern, and Ilinisa (17,649 feet high) in the western Cordillera, while Tunguragua, Chimborazo, and Carguairazo, remain behind us, and gradually fade from our view. Again the road leads through long rows and hedges of American aloe; but the fields are sandy and somewhat sterile. Cattle-breeding is carried on extensively on the haciendas along the skirts of Cotopaxi. The snows and waters of the mountain form the River Tacunga, which must be passed about two leagues from the town which shares its name. Sudden rises, attributed to the rains and to the melting of snow on Cotopaxi, make it frequently unfordable for several days in succession. Its current is very rapid, and its water sometimes partakes of the brown color which characterizes the volcano whenever it is, or at least seems to be, destitute of snow.

The plains of Mulalu and Callo, to the west of Cotopaxi, present a gloomy aspect. The soil seems to be buried under volcanic sands, and is covered with countless rocks of all dimensions, which tradition attributes to former eruptions of the mountain, although the opinion of scientific men like Wissę, Zimmermann, and other celebrated naturalists, militates against such a hypothesis.

The village of Mulalu is an Indian settlement of no importance. The hacienda on the west side of the road, to which the tambo belongs, is a melancholy picture of sadness and decay. The buildings are designed in a most elegant style, but are now in ruins. The statues in the garden have tumbled from their pedestals. Elegant stone balustrades are crumbling away. The fountains are without water, and their stone basins breaking to pieces. The whole building contains but one habitable and furnished room; the others are miserable, windowless hovels, used for store-rooms or occupied by the family of the mayor-domo. The garden is well laid out, but overgrown with weeds. Every thing betokens the indifference or increasing poverty of the owners. And what I have said of this hacienda is true of most of the farm buildings of the interior; they are all either unfinished or already in ruins, if not both. What the earthquake spares will not escape the sloth and carelessness of the natives. Walls that once tumble down are seldom built up again, or it will take years to repair them. Lifelessness and decay are the characteristic features of the country. If the sins of the fathers were ever avenged in their children and children's children, it has been done in Spanish America. The crimes of the early conquerors have borne their deadly fruits. Ruins and decay, stagnation and indolence, ignorance and superstition, idleness and civil wars, are the causes which blight more than one half of the American continent as far as the Spanish tongue is spoken. There is, indeed, poetic justice in history.

Leaving Mulalu, the aspect of the treeless country increases in dreariness. For miles around, the soil is covered with volcanic sands, rocks, and pumice-stones, allowing only a most scanty vegetation of cacti, mimosa, and spines. In the middle of the plain is a solitary hill about one hundred and fifty feet high — the hill of Callo — from which this part of the plain derives its name. The hill is said to have been piled up by human hands. The ancient inhabitants of the plain are said to have erected it as a shelter against the eruptions of Cotopaxi, a tradition which I am not inclined to believe. Of the Panecillo, at the foot of which the city of Quito extends, the same incredulous story is told.

Opposite the hill, on the other side of the road, is a solitary tree called "*El Arbol de Callo*," overshadowing a huge oblong rock, close to which it grows. This rock is said to be the disguise of a gigantic serpent, keeping watch over a great treasure buried under the tree. There is no want of legends on this sandy, gloomy, lifeless plain. A big rock on the roadside, with a curved line on its upper surface, in which by dint of great imaginative powers we may discover a slight resemblance to the form of a foot or shoe, is said to be the honored spot on which the Apostle St. Bartholomew alighted when he visited this country, leaving the impression of his foot on the rock as a memorial to coming generations. It is customary for the Indians and arrieros who pass this place on foot, to place a pebble or little stone on the rock as a token of their devotion to the saint. Hundreds of these tokens now lie around the rock on all sides.

Near the Cerro de Callo, but not visible from the public highway, are the ruins of an ancient Indian temple, palace, or tambo. But very little is left of them at present, the unreverential owners of the hacienda to which they belong having converted them into a cheap and easy stone-quarry. Ulloa in the last century saw them yet in good condition. The hacienda then belonged to the Augustine monks, whose steward used the ruins as a mansion house. The friars, however, commenced the work of destruction by building dwellings among the ruins, and making alterations in the principal apartments. But now there is little more left than a few walls, enabling us to admire the extreme nicety and exactness with which the stones are joined together. The edifice was built of porphyry, the stones having their exterior surface slightly convex, except at the doors, where the fronts are plain. The dimensions of the stones are unequal, a small one being immediately followed by a large one, while that above is made to fit the inequalities of the other two, and at the same time fill up all the interstices between the projections and irregularity of their faces; and this in such perfection that whatsoever way they are viewed, all parts appear joined with the same exactness. If the work of destruction goes on as hitherto, the last vestige of the ruins will soon disappear. The barbarity of the Roman barons of the Middle Ages, who quarried among their ancient palaces which the Hun and the Visigoth had spared, seems to be destined to repetition as long as monuments of antiquity remain.

After a long and tedious ride through the last and most sterile part of the plain, relieved only by a near view of the smoking crater of Cotopaxi and its craggy neighbors Rumiñagui and Pasachoa to our right, and the snowy crown of Ilinisa to our left, we begin a steep ascent leading us to the paramo of Tiupullo, which in former times was infested with robbers who availed themselves of the *despoblado*,[1] for the purpose of waylaying wealthy travellers. At present, however, the paramo may be passed without the slightest apprehension of danger.

One paramo commonly looks like another, and as the reader is already familiar with the signification of the word, it will be unnecessary to give a description of Tiupullo. I must say, however, that it is infinitely

[1] *Despoblado* means an uninhabited part of the country.

less dreary than Sanancajas and the other paramos of Chimborazo. A solitary tree which attracts our attention at a turn of the road is called "*El Excomulgado*" (the accursed), because a priest is said to have been killed under it by a gang of robbers.

We are now surrounded by mountains on all sides. Pichincha and Cayambi, with their numerous retinue of lesser peaks, rise before us. But nearest of all we draw to Rumiñagui. Rumiñagui, in the Quichua or Inca language, means face or eye of stone. It was the name of an ancient Indian general with whom the reader will become acquainted in another chapter of this book.

Descending from the high paramo region, the beautiful green valley of Machachi and Tambillo opens before us. Its verdure is fresher than that of the plain of Quito, or any other part of the high table-lands. It is a pleasant relief to the traveller, who has left all freshness of vegetation on the western side of the Cordillera. The pastures are exceedingly rich, and the fields well cultivated and fertile. Again we see numberless herds of cattle grazing on the slopes and in the plains. The products of the temperate zone continue around us, in fields fenced in by hedges of aloe. This pleasant impression is disturbed only by the disgusting sight of half-naked and loathsome beggars cowering along the roadside, and pursuing the traveller in a most importunate manner.

From Romerillo, an hacienda and tambo at the foot of Tiupullo, an hour's ride takes us to the tambos of Machachi (9784 feet above the sea), forming two long rows of miserable huts on both sides of the main road. These tambos are detestable hovels, built of earth, thatched with dried grasses, and without windows and floorings. They are notorious for their filth and vermin. In one of them I once passed a horrible night. I was literally lacerated by fleas. Cleanliness is unknown to the inhabitants. Their chief pleasure and passion is *aguardiente* (rum). The nights at Machachi are exceedingly cold, owing chiefly to the near neighborhood of snow-peaks, among which Corazon (the heart) is conspicuous.

Machachi lies at the foot of Mt. Corazon, which is 16,169 feet high, and was ascended and measured by the French academicians in the last century. It looks down on a beautiful valley, destined by nature to be a home of plenty and comfort, but converted by man into a haunt of sloth, filth, idleness, poverty, vice, and ignorance.

Between Machachi and the near village of Tambillo at the foot of Mt. Atacatso (16,168 feet high), were several of the worst passages of the whole road, known as the "*Quebradas de Tambillo.*" They are narrow lanes or defiles, intersected by deep ravines, through which several mountain streams force their way. A paved road formerly led through those gullies; but now the water has broken the pavement, torn up the stones, and washed heavy rocks from the hillside, over which the horses slip and stumble. Fallen trees and big roots obstruct the passages; land-slides have made the paths slippery, and bottomless puddles detain the traveller in the narrow lanes, covered overhead with a dense vegetation which the sun never penetrates, and exhaling the foulest miasmas. The ascents and descents are almost perpendicular. The road breaks off at many places, so that the animal must proceed by springs and jumps. In short, as if to take leave of all that was bad on the road, we had it here combined for a last break-neck farewell. In 1864, however, a road was cut through these *Quebradas*, and bridges were built over the streams.

Tambillo is a little village of about fifty houses. It also has a *casa posada* (tavern), the only room of which is ventilated solely when it is opened for a traveller. The Ecuadorians are very fond of keeping their rooms shut and close, for the better propagation of fleas. The room of the posada was without chairs. One high and unhandy table, two rickety bedsteads, and a few benches four inches wide, formed the furniture. The candles had to be stuck into the walls, as no candlesticks were to be had. The tavern-keeper had no cook of his own, but sent for one to a neighboring house. The cook asked for a few reals in advance to make necessary purchases. Dinner, which I had ordered at half-past three o'clock, was brought in at about seven. The cook brought it in pots, with which she squatted down on the floor, and filled it into the plates with a wooden spoon.

And now but little remains to be told. The road to Quito, which is about five leagues from Tambillo, lies through rich pastures and fertile fields, interspersed with elegant farm-houses and gardens, and countless Indian huts (*huasipongos*). Numbers of Indians carrying loads or driving laden beasts, indicate our approach to a great city. We are surprised by the sight of many an Indian woman, who not only carries a load on her back, with a babe tied to the top of the *carga*, but also spins cotton as she trots along. Other Indian and Cholo women are seen riding astride their beasts, like men.

The Indians carry every thing on their back, the load being tied to their forehead. Their strength lies in the muscles of the neck and not in their arms. They carry stone, brick, sand, lime, furniture, vegetables, meat, etc., and pass along laughing or talking, or in sullen silence, but you never hear them sing. The Indian never sings unless he is drunk, and then his song is an endless repetition of a few monotonous notes. He salutes you submissively as you meet him, but the white man hardly ever deigns to answer his salutation. The laden Indian must make way for the traveller on horseback. A terrible "*lado!*" (aside!) notifies him to get himself and his beasts out of the way. He salutes respectfully and obeys. If he is not quick enough, the whip of the horseman hurries him into compliance. The Indian is like an outlaw, at the mercy of every body, and every body's slave. But his stupefied and beastly nature never revolts. He is the personification of abjectness, beastliness, and servility.

But we have now reached the end of our journey, and passing the ruins of the chapel "*Del Señor del buen pasaje*," we enter the suburbs of Quito over an elegant bridge across the River Machangara.

# CHAPTER VI.

Altitude of Quito. — Mt. Pichincha. — Its Height. — The Crater. — The Peaks of Pichincha. — Eruptions. — The French Academicians. — Humboldt, Colonel Hall, and Boussingault. — Dr. Gabriel Garcia Moreno's Three Descents to the Bottom of the Crater. — The Valley and Village of Lloa. — An American Artist in the Crater. — My Visits to it. — View from the Summit of Pichincha. — Pumice-stone. — Temperature. — Approaches to Quito. — Aña-Quito, the Battle-Field. — Turubamba. — Mt. Panecillo. — The City viewed from the Surrounding Hills. — A Retrospect.

QUITO is built on what may be termed a ledge of the volcanic mountain of Pichincha, at an elevation of 9537 feet above the level of the sea. By some, the altitude of Quito is estimated at over 10,000 feet, but this must be an error. I have followed the measurement of Humboldt. Boussingault gives it at 9525; Dr. Jameson, at 9513 feet.[1] The mountain rises in

[1] Dr. William Jameson, here referred to, is the well-known botanist, whose discoveries in ornithology and botany have made his name familiar to the scieutific world. He is a Scotchman by birth, a graduate of the University of Edinburgh, and came to Ecuador about thirty-seven years ago. He was director of the National Mint at Quito, and is now Professor at the University, where he lectures on chemistry and botany. He is a highly esteemed member of the medical faculty, and as beloved for the qualities of his heart as respected for his mental acquirements. He is in continuous correspondence with several of the scientific societies of Great Britain, besides being the friend and correspondent of such men as the late Sir W. J. Hooker, director of the Royal Gardens of Kew. To Charles Darwin, Esq., author of the celebrated work on the *Origin of the Species*, he furnished items of valuable information. Several interesting Andean plants and birds which Dr. Jameson discovered, have been named after him, and will hand down his memory to scientific posterity. He has made an interesting excursion into the wild country on the River Napo, of which he has given to the world a short but graphic account, which was published by the Royal Geographical Society of London. He also is the author of a Latin work on the

the background to a height of 15,976 feet. (This, too, is according to Humboldt. Boussingault's measurement is 15,676; that of the French Academicians, 15,606; Dr. Jameson's is 15,704.) It is crowned by a wall of trachytic rocks surrounding the crater, the depth of which is 2460 feet, and consequently the bottom, where a volcanic agency is in active operation, is nearly 4000 feet above the level of the city. Snow frequently falls on the sandy desert of the crater, but two or three days of fine weather cause its disappearance, except in some localities where it lies in patches sheltered from the rays of a vertical sun.

The summit of Pichincha barely enters the snow limit, for which reason the congealed water does not assume the compact and crystalline form observed in what is strictly called a glacier. The snow brought down to the city for the preparation of ice-cream has the appearance of a conglomerate of hailstones. On the eastern chain of the Cordillera there are several lofty summits, capped with immense masses of solid ice, reflecting the rays of the setting sun, and presenting to the eye various beautiful prismatic tints, which, so soon as the solar light is withdrawn, assume a pure white color.

The summit of Pichincha, excepting, perhaps, the highest points of some of the peaks, cannot be seen from the city itself. It may, however, be seen from

flora of Ecuador, published in Latin by the Government of that Republic. He is not only the friend and adviser of all the foreigners whom business or scientific curiosity brings to Quito, but his kindness of heart and sterling integrity have endeared him to all classes and parties of the Ecuadorian people. The assistance which he rendered to me in the collection of materials for my work was very valuable; but I am additionally indebted to him for many other acts of friendship and kindness, upon my arrival and during my residence in Ecuador, which shall never be forgotten.

its immediate vicinity. There are three different groups of rocky peaks, which constitute the crown of the mountain. The one which contains the crater is called "Rucu Pichincha," which, in *Quichua*, the language of the Indians, means "old." The other, to the northeast of Rucu, is called "Guagua Pichincha," the word *guagua* meaning "child." Between the two, and so as to form a triangle with them, is the lowest, the middle peak, to which no particular name has been given. Deep valleys and ravines separate the different groups. The snow, which is brought to Quito, as I said, for the purpose of making ice-cream, is taken from Guagua Pichincha.

The view which, on a clear day, presents itself from the summit of the mountain, is one of the most imposing and magnificent perhaps in the whole world. Glaciers show their hoary heads on all sides. Nearly twenty, if not more than twenty, snow-clad mountains rise before you. Imbabura, Cotocachi, Chiles, the grand Cayambi, the majestic Antisana, the venerable Chimborazo and his neighbor Caraguairazo, Ilinisa, the beautiful Altar, Tunguragua, fell Cotopaxi, Sincholagua, Corazon, and a host of others, fill your soul with awe and admiration. You find yourself in the midst of a council of the great patriarchs of the Andes, and you listen amazed to their speaker, Cotopaxi, who every now and then sends his roaring thunders over the land.

Since the conquest of the country by the Spaniards, Pichincha has had several eruptions, of which those in 1575, 1587, and 1660 were the most notable and destructive to Quito. On the 14th of September, 1575, the municipality of Quito resolved that the memory of the eighth of that same month should forever be religiously observed, as only to the intercession of the Holy Virgin it was ascribed that the eruption of Pichincha, which had taken place on that day, did not destroy the whole city. The eruption of 1660 (October 27) was accompanied by a fearful rain of cinders. The ashes are said to have been carried by the winds as far as Popayan to the north and Loja to the south. The volcano is now considered as extinct, although from the cones of eruption at the bottom of the crater smoke and vapors are continually exhaled. It is even said that the mountain's volcanic activity is again on the increase. "In 1845, the chimneys whence the gases arose, formed six groups, only one of which was of somewhat considerable size. Now, the vapors escape through innumerable hollows and interstices, left by the falling away of the stones in each of the craters; and in the principal one a noise is heard similar to that made by the violent bubbling of boiling water in an immense caldron."[1]

The French Academicians Bouguer and Condamine, in 1742, were the first who reached the brink of the crater. Their Spanish colleagues, Ulloa and Jorje Juan, had lived with them in 1737, for twenty-three horrid days, on the rock which crowns Guagua Pichincha, in order to make their measurements; but no expedition to the crater was attempted on that occasion.[2]

[1] See a letter of Mr. Gabriel Garcia Moreno to Dr. Wm. Jameson, dated Quito, January 13, 1858, and published in the Edinburgh *Philosophical Journal.*

[2] Ulloa has left us a graphic description of the sufferings of the Academicians while encamped on the peak of Guagua Pichincha, measuring one of their triangles. "We generally kept within our hut; indeed, we were obliged to do this, both on account of the intenseness of the cold, the violence of the wind, and our being often involved in so thick a fog that an object at six or eight paces was hardly discernible. When the fog cleared up, the

Alexander Humboldt, in 1802, twice surmounted the gigantic wall of trachytic rock which forms the eastern verge of the volcano. About thirty years afterward, Colonel Hall and Boussingault followed in

clouds, by their gravity, moved nearer to the surface of the earth, and on all sides surrounded the mountain to a vast distance, representing the sea, with our rock like an island in the centre of it. . . . . But our circumstances were very different when the clouds rose; their thickness rendered respiration difficult; the snow and hail fell continually, and the wind raged with all its violence, so that it was impossible to overcome the fears of being, together with our hut, blown down the precipice on the edge of which it was built, or of being buried under it by the daily accumulations of ice and snow. . . . . Our fears were also increased by the dreadful concussions of the precipice by the fall of enormous fragments of rock. These crashes were the more alarming, as no other noises are heard in this desert. . . . . The door of our hut was fastened with thongs of leather, and on the inside not the smallest crevice was left unstopped, besides which it was very compactly covered with straw; but, notwithstanding all our care, the wind penetrated through. . . . . Whenever it snowed, we had to sally out with shovels, in spite of the wind, to free the roof of our hut from the masses of snow which were gathering on it; nor would it, without this protection, have been able to support the weight. We were not, indeed, without servants and Indians, but they were so benumbed with the cold, that it was with great difficulty we could get them out of a small tent, where they kept a continual fire. . . . . Our feet were swelled, and so tender that we could not even bear the heat; our hands were covered with chilblains; our lips swelled and chapped, so that every motion in speaking, or the like, drew blood; consequently we were obliged to a strict taciturnity, and but little disposed to laugh, an extension of the lips producing fissures very painful for two or three days together. Our common food in this inhospitable region was a little rice boiled with some meat or fowl, which we procured from Quito, and instead of fluid water, our pot was filled with snow. We had the same resource with regard to what we drank; and while we were eating, every one was required to keep his plate over a chafing-dish of coals to prevent his provisions from freezing. Twenty-three tedious days we spent on this rock, until it became necessary to erect our signals in a lower situation, and in a more favorable region. This, however, did not produce any change in our habitation till December, when, having finished the observations which particularly concerned Pichincha, we proceeded to others, but with no abatement of inconvenience, cold, or fatigue,— the places where we made all our observations being necessarily on the highest parts of the desert; so that the only respite in which we enjoyed some little ease, was during the short interval of passing from one place to another." Thirty-five mountains were thus scaled and inhabited by those heroes of science, who braved more sufferings, dangers, and privations, than many a soldier in a bloody campaign.

the same path ; but the first to descend to its bottom were Mr. Gabriel Garcia Moreno, afterwards President of Ecuador, and Mr. Sebastian Wisse, a French engineer of great scientific acquirements.[1] They went down twice ; the first time in 1844, and the second time in August, 1845. In December, 1857, Mr. Moreno made a third descent, accompanied by a son of Dr. Wm. Jameson, but of this last expedition he has given us no description.

The temperature of the vapors issuing from the cones of eruption, varies much in the different interstices from which they arise. In the southeast crater, the vapors from the highest crevices, when measured by Mr. Garcia Moreno, nearly reached 180° Fahr., whilst in the lower ones the temperature was only 140° Fahr. In the principal crater, the hottest vapors did not come up to 194° Fahr., while in the largest interstice Mr. Moreno examined, and into which a person could easily enter if the thick column of vapor would permit, the temperature was 98° Fahr., at a depth of little more than one (French) metre.

The descent into the crater from the summit of the mountain is very difficult, not only on account of the precipitous rocks over which it must be made, where hands, to use the language of Mr. Moreno, are more useful than feet, but also on account of the rocks and sandy patches which give way under one's foot, and perhaps chiefly on account of the falling stones, which, overcoming the sandy support on which they rest, tumble into the abyss with a deep rumbling noise, shivering at last into a thousand atoms like an exploding bombshell, or striking other rocks and carrying them along with frightful impetuosity.

[1] He died at Quito on the 7th of June, 1863.

In 1862, Mr. Camillus Farrand, an American artist, left Quito for the purpose of descending into, and taking photographic views of, the crater. The journey from Quito to Rucu Pichincha occupies but eight hours. Mr. Farrand, however, remained absent for more than a week, so that I became alarmed for his safety, and accompanied by a son of Dr. Jameson, the same that had accompanied Mr. Garcia Moreno on his last descent, started for the crater to ascertain what had become of him. We left Quito at about one o'clock in the afternoon, and between four and five o'clock we arrived at the village of Lloa, situated in the green and fertile, but nevertheless thinly populated valley at the very foot of what is properly called "Rucu Pichincha." We stopped at an hacienda which formerly belonged to the Jesuits, but is now in ruins, owing to the earthquake of 1859. It is 10,268 feet above the level of the sea. The mornings, evenings, and nights here are very cold. At ten o'clock at night the mercury had fallen to 46° Fahr. Here we learned that Mr. Farrand was safe, and had repeatedly sent down for victuals. He had remained in the crater for over a week, passing some of the nights at its very bottom, others on the ledges near its brink. The weather had been very cloudy; mists and fogs had surrounded him almost continually, frustrating the object of his expedition. He hoped, however, that the weather would clear up, and therefore waited with astonishing perseverance amidst the horrors of Nature's solitude, and almost in the bowels of a slumbering volcano. In the mornings, the tent in which he had passed the night was generally covered with snow, and sometimes to such an extent that the Indians who were with him had to sweep the snow from the door on the outside before it could be opened. Nevertheless, the weather disappointed him; he had succeeded only in taking a few partial views of the inner declivities, and was already on his way home when I met him, about fifteen hundred feet below the summit of the mountain. He immediately proposed to go back with me, insisting that I should not have come so far without seeing what, considering the unfavorable condition of the weather, could be seen. It is possible to reach the brink of the crater on horseback; but, to effect this, the full ascent had better not be made on the same horses. We left our animals about two hundred feet below the crater, where the pumice-stones commence, with which the ground at that distance is literally covered. These stones render it exceedingly difficult to get on. They are so light that they give way under you, and make you stumble and fall continually. This inconvenience, and the great rarefaction of air, which powerfully agitates the respiratory organs, tired us exceedingly, so that it took us almost half an hour to ascend these last two hundred feet. We had to rest every eight or ten paces, to take breath and gather new strength; still, I was so exhausted when I finally reached the summit, that I nearly fainted. Unfortunately, our efforts had been made in vain. Thick clouds and mists hovered over and in the crater, so that not even the opposite side could be seen. It was impossible to see further ahead than about five yards. A wall of snow rose on the brink about four feet high, and of a thickness of about eight or ten feet at the bottom and three or four feet at the top. This wall appeared as regular as if human skill had made it with the greatest care and precision. Mr. Farrand had had a hole cut through it, to get the trunks containing his instruments and chemicals, with less difficulty on the inner side of the crater. When I stood on the brink I smelled, but only for a moment, the sulphur in the vapors arising from below. I soon became accustomed to it, so that it entirely ceased to be perceptible.

On my third visit — I returned to the crater three times after my first visit — these sulphuric vapors were not only very perceptible, but occasionally even oppressive to myself and my companions; another circumstance tending to show that the volcanic activity of the mountain is again increasing.

On the inner declivity of the crater, we were perfectly well protected against the strong east wind which had troubled us so much during our ascent; and while we lay tired and sprawling on some large and smooth rocks imbedded in the sand, the almost perpendicular rays of the sun were burning down upon us in a manner which almost made us forget in what altitude we were. The difference of the temperature between the inner and the outer side of the brink is really astonishing. On my third visit to the crater, the mercury showed, at ten o'clock, A. M., the day being sunny, but 38° Fahr. on the outside; while, at the same elevation on the inside, it rose to 58°, which is but two degrees less than the mean temperature of Quito.

There is no vegetation around the brink of the crater, but Mr. Farrand had brought up a collection of plants from the bottom, which Dr. Jameson afterward classified and prepared for him. They were the same species which Mr. Moreno had found there in 1857. Among the pumice-stones above referred to, I found several specimens of *Frailejon*, the *Calcitium rufescens* of Humboldt and Bonpland, a plant which occurs on almost all the snowy ridges of the Ecuadorian Andes.[1] I also saw a curious flower which the natives call "*chuguiragua*," and which is peculiar to those altitudes.[2] It has a very bitter taste, and is said to be a remedy against indigestion.

There are but three approaches leading to the city of Quito — one from the north and two from the south. On the east and west it is hemmed in by the powerful mountain family of Pichincha; but north and south of it extends that interesting plain known to geographers as the high plateau, or table-land of Quito. The plain at the northern entrance of the city is called "Aña-Quito." It was the scene of the battle fought on the 18th of January, 1546, between Gonzalo Pizarro and Blasco Nuñez Vela, the first Viceroy of Peru, in which the latter was defeated and slain. The plain to the south is called "Turubamba." A traveller approaching the city from any of the above-mentioned roads, can only see a part of it; an isolated mountain called "Panecillo," rising about 700 feet above the town (10,268 feet above the level of the sea), covering it on the south, and ridges coming down from the elevations east and west closing around it on the north. Disappointment, therefore, is the first sensation of the curious traveller. Nevertheless, the city is not a small one, and viewed from one of the surrounding hills, the

[1] "On the mountains beyond the River Chota, there is another plant to which the same name is applied. It is the *Espletia grandiflora* of Humboldt and Bonpland, and yields, by incision, a resinous substance, used externally to relieve rheumatic pains, and known by the name of *resina de frailejon*. Like the former plant, it is enveloped in wool, the color of which approaches to yellow. It makes a comfortable bed for the traveller who happens to be benighted on the lofty region where it grows. Both species grow on the volcano of Pasto, the former, however, reaching the higher elevation." — From Dr. Jameson's *Manuscript Notes.*

[2] *Chuguiragua insignis.*

slopes of which it covers, it presents rather an extensive and interesting appearance, full of significant suggestions to a reflective mind. There it lies at your feet, buried as it were between treeless and melancholy mountains, showing but now and then a spot indicative of cultivation ; isolated from the rest of the world by impassable roads and gigantic Cordilleras. No chimneys overtop its browny roofs; no friendly cloud of smoke curls to the unruffled sky ; no rattling of wagons, no din of machinery strikes your ear; no busy hum emerges from the capital of the Republic. The only noises which ascend from the caldron in which it lies, are the ringing of church-bells, the crow of the cock, or the drums and trumpets of the soldiery.

The lifeless and almost melancholy aspect which the town presents from any of the surrounding elevations, is a true image of its lifeless colonial history, the character of which, firmly impressed as it is upon the commercial and industrial relations and customs of the interior, the almost endless convulsions and revolutions which followed the establishment of independence could not serve to destroy. The dull, gloomy, and spiritless character of that period is so graphically and forcibly described by Villavicencio in his "Geography of Ecuador," that I cannot deny myself the pleasure of translating the passage in question: —

"The foundation of the Presidency of Quito (see pages 8 and 9 of the work referred to) is followed by a cold and monotonous colonial period of 275 years. It was scarcely interrupted by some faint commotions attempted since 1766, by the conquered aborigines, which were promptly and easily suppressed. If we examine Ecuadorian society of those times, we find it tranquil, passive, patriarchal, as it were, but reduced to itself, without knowledge, without communication, without life. The great majority of the people knew nothing of sciences, of events, or of men, and probably did not imagine that there were sciences, events, and men deserving to be known. Their religion consisted of outward observances and an imperfect knowledge of the Papal bulls; their morality, in asceticism and devotion to their king; their history, in the history of the mother-country; their geography, in the maps of Spanish-America and of Spain; their press, in what sufficed to print bill-heads and blank forms; their commerce, in an insignificant coasting trade; their ambition and highest aspirations, in titles of nobility; their amusements, in bull-fights. The arrival of a mail was an event of great moment, and with ringing of bells was received the '*cajon de España*,' which announced the health of the sovereigns. Thus, while Europe was passing through the stormy times of Louis XIV.; while the philosophical writings of the illustrious men of those times found their way into the remotest corners of the globe; while the English colonies of North America conquered their independence; while the Old World was drenched in blood to propagate the ideas which the French Revolution had proclaimed; the Presidency of Quito, walled in by its immense Cordilleras and the ocean, and ruled by monkish ignorance and bigotry, knew as little of men and events as we now know of men and events in the moon."

The churches and convents, which occupy, to be moderate, at least one fourth of the area of Quito, are witnesses, eloquent in their silence, to the justice of Mr. Villavicencio's historical criticism. More than one fourth of the town is covered by convents and their vast but neglected *pateos* (court-yards) and unweeded gardens. If but one tenth of the millions which it cost to build these churches and monasteries — not to speak of the thousands of Indians who perished while being whipped to the unwonted task of carrying on their trembling backs block after block of these edifices — had been applied to the building of roads, this country would long since have taken its rank among civilized nations.

Still, it must be a matter of surprise to the traveller, after passing through primeval forests, crossing bridgeless rivers, floundering over bottomless roads, and ascending and descending immense mountains, to find a city with imposing public buildings, elegant private residences, and a luxury-loving aristocracy, in this almost inaccessible and forgotten corner of the world.

But it is time to effect our entrance.

## CHAPTER VII.

Quito. — Appearance of the City. — Crowds in the Streets. — Streets and Houses. — Queer Mode of Cooking. — Want of Hotels. — A Curate's Idea of the Obligation of Promises. — Traits of Native Character. — Want of Cleanliness. — Incidents. — Excellent Climate. — Mean Temperature. — No Diseases or Insects. — The Rainy Season. — Fruits and Flowers. — Earth's Paradise.

VIEWED from a distance, or from one of the surrounding hills, Quito resembles one of those spell-bound towns in the Arabian Nights, so impressively described by the ingenious Scheherezade. But, as soon as we enter it, it presents a most lively appearance. On the principal streets and plazas hundreds of human beings are continually in motion. It is true, they are chiefly Indians and *Cholos*, and you will meet twenty persons in ponchos and even in rags, barefoot or with *alpargates* (hemp-sandals), before you meet one respectably dressed. But, nevertheless, the motley crowds of men in ponchos of all colors, beggars in rags, vagrants in sackcloth, women with red, green, brown, or blue *pañuelones* and *rebozos*, ladies with gay-colored silk shawls, monks with their immense hats, monks in white, monks in brown, monks in blue, and canons and curates in black, and Indians of a hundred different villages in every variety of costume, not even omitting the naked and painted Indian from the wilderness on the eastern side of the Cordillera, — present a most lively and interesting spectacle. There are but few carts in use, as I have already said; nevertheless, the streets are thronged from morning to evening with mules, horses, oxen, donkeys, and llamas with loads (*cargas*) of every kind and description. Indians, men and women, with loads on their backs, limp to and fro; soldiers in queer clown-caps and with or without shoes, lazily saunter through the crowds; groups of merchants and their friends chat in front of their *tiendas* (stores); *chagras* (country-people) on horseback dash through the streets; ladies will meet their lady friends and embrace and hug them, obstructing the narrow sidewalks; water-carriers with immense jars on their backs, butchers or bakers with meat or bread in troughs on their heads, wend their way to the houses of their customers; children and dogs run about in all directions; mule-drivers swear at their beasts; parrots chatter in the groceries and greenshops; in short, the life within the city favorably contrasts with its melancholy aspect from without.

The city is traversed from west to east by two deep ravines (*quebradas*), through which Pichincha sends down its torrents of melted snow. These *quebradas* are mostly covered with vaults and arches on which the houses rest, but where they are open, they disclose to the eye hideous abysses, the sides of which are overgrown with rank weeds. The territory over which the city extends being exceedingly uneven, as the slopes and spurs of the surrounding hills press down toward the Plaza Mayor from three different sides, a walk through Quito consists of continuous ascents and descents. The course of the streets, however, is generally regular, those running from east to west being intersected at right angles by others running from north to south. The gutters and sewers were formerly in the centre of the streets forming rivulets, through which the water was let down two or three times in twenty-four hours for purposes of public cleanliness; but in 1863 the municipality entered upon an extensive system of re-paving; and the principal streets are now paved in modern style. The streets are not very wide; the sidewalks are exceedingly narrow. The houses are built mostly in the old Spanish or rather Moorish style, with the roofs projecting over the pavements so as to afford a partial protection against the frequent rains. There are but two or three buildings in Quito with two upper stories. Most of the houses have only one. Low and filthy houses of but a ground-floor are found in great numbers, but only in the outskirts and suburbs.

The houses are generally built of adobe (sun-baked brick). The walls are exceedingly thick, forming deep embrasures for doors and windows. There are, strictly speaking, no windows, but glass doors leading to balconies overhanging the sidewalks. The roofs are covered with curved tiles of earthenware; two rows are first placed, the concave side upwards, the joint being covered with a third row reversed, so as to form channels for the water to flow off, which, from the main gutter, is thrown into the streets and court-yards by a number of projecting spouts. These precautions are necessary on account of the heaviness and long duration of the showers in the rainy season. The upper story is the dwelling part of a respectable house. The ground-floor (parterre) is occupied by the servants, or tenanted by poor people who cannot afford to pay high rents. The stores in front have no backdoors, and do not communicate with the interior of the houses to which they belong. They have no windows, and generally but one door, which must serve as entrance, exit, window, show-case, and all. There are but very few shops in Quito which have two doors. The stores consequently are but small; five or six customers, especially of the crinoline gender, will fill them completely. These stores are called *tiendas*, and are closed at early candle-light. They are naturally dark, and most of the business is done at or near the door. The houses have neither fire-places nor chimneys, except in a few buildings of modern construction. The want of fire-places is sometimes severely felt. The smoke arising from kitchen fires must make its way out of the kitchen door, and a few apertures above it. Kitchens, therefore, are black and dark; and as almost nothing but charcoal is used for cooking, they are noisome and uncomfortable. Stoves are not known. There being no flues connected with the hearths, cooking is quite a task, and the cook needs one, two, or more, subordinates to fan the fires; to almost every pot a separate fire, and to two fires, one individual to fan them. Servants, however, are very cheap, although unreliable and lazy; but of this hereafter. The pots used for cooking have not a flat bottom like ours, but are pointed below, so that they cannot stand without being supported by some contrivance, or inserted into the holes which the hearth contains on purpose. The large jars in which water is carried have the same impracticable shape. They are put on wooden trestles, or into holes in a stone bench opposite or at the side of the hearth. The cook generally brings his family with him, allowing his dirty children to romp about the kitchen. A female cook will do her work with the baby tied on to her back, or deposited by her side on the kitchen table. Hair in the meals is of frequent occurrence, without reference to an occasional flea, or a lot of vine-fretters, which have communicated themselves to the soup from the unwashed vegetables.

Most of the houses have one or two spacious square court-yards paved and with drains. In the second, there is generally a covered place for horses, which is paved also. The stables of this country never have boards.

The street entrance is always high enough to admit a horseman with ease. In the upper story there is always a gallery resting on arches or pillars, and leading around the court-yard. All the rooms and galleries are floored with square tiles or bricks, on which mats or carpets are laid. The chinks between the bricks serve as hiding-places for swarms of fleas, particularly troublesome after a room has remained shut up and uninhabited for some time; in which case it is not uncommon, especially on *haciendas* in the country, to drive a sheep through it first, in order to take up as many fleas as possible. The rooms, with the exception of the parlors, or *salas*, are generally but very indifferently furnished, with an incongruous mixture of antique and modern pieces, and kept in a pitiable state of uncleanliness, disorder, and confusion.

The first inconvenience which vexes the traveller on his arrival, is the entire want of hotels. There is not a tavern or inn at Quito, at which a respectable person could stop. The only *casa posada* which existed when I arrived, was not fit to be entered. Black, dirty, and neglected, with but a few dusty rooms, full of fleas, and perhaps other vermin, and without accommodations of any kind, the traveller who is forced into it acquires a valid claim to our commiseration, in spite of the image of the saint in the entrance, before which tallow candles are kept burning almost all the year round. Private hospitality will have to be resorted to, at least until rooms can be rented.[1]

I was rather lucky in making the journey from Guayaquil with a resident of Quito, who had the kindness to make me tarry one day at Ambato, to enable him to go ahead and find a house for me, which he did, to the great astonishment of a native *cura* (curate), who never expected that one of his countrymen should keep a promise which he (the curate) considered to be a mere form of politeness. The curate himself seemed to have no idea of the honorable obligation of promises; nor did he seem to understand that a lie, in such cases, would be ungentlemanly or immoral. I met him at Machachi, where he had awaited me, to make my acquaintance. The officer who accompanied me told him that my mule was very tired, and suggested that he, as the curate of Machachi, would have no difficulty in procuring a horse for me. With usual Spanish politeness, his worship at once offered his own horse, and promised to send it to Tambillo, where I proposed to remain over night. Relying on his promise, I made no further effort to procure another beast; but to my great disappointment, when I had arrived at Tambillo, which is the last station before Quito, the horse arrived, but with the curate on it, who proposed to accompany me to Quito. Taken to task why he had not sent the horse

1 "Houses, completely furnished, with looking-glasses, carpets, lamps, etc., may be hired in Quito; and a very good one, with nine or ten rooms, may be had for fifty dollars a month — a very low price indeed, when the expense is considered, which must be incurred in transporting these things across the Cordilleras." — Ida Pfeiffer, *A Lady's Second Voyage Round the World*, vol. i., p. 215. Fifty dollars a month for a dwelling-house is rather a price for foreigners. Natives seldom pay more than from twenty to forty dollars.

as promised, he made the excuse that he had brought another horse along with him for a part of the way; but overtaking one of my *arrieros*, he was told that I had procured a beast already, and so he sent back the one he had brought along, and came on alone to have the pleasure of travelling to Quito in my company. This excuse was as false as ridiculous. Upon asking the *arriero*, I ascertained at once that the priest had not spoken to him on the road, and that he had no horse but the one he rode. The fact is, that his worship never thought of complying with the promise on which his officious assurances had induced me to rely; and he probably was inwardly amused that I should have looked upon it in any other light than that of a mere *façon de parler*. This custom of making high-sounding promises, which are not intended to be kept, is universal among Ecuadorians of the *Sierra*. If you make the acquaintance of one of them, he will overwhelm you with offers of his services. He will beseech you to "count him as one of the number of your friends" ("*Usted me puede contar en el numero de sus amigos*"); he will place his house, his haciendas, his horses, at your disposal; he will ask you to treat him confidentially, and to speak to him frankly, whenever you should need any thing that he can supply; he will protest his ardent desire to be your friend and to serve you in every possible manner; he will modestly add that unfortunately his friendship may not be worth much ("*yo valgo muy poco; soy muy inutil;*" etc., etc.), and his influence limited, but that he may, nevertheless, find an opportunity of being useful to you in some way, in which case he begs you to rely on him and to apply to him without reserve. All these protestations, which sound very bad in English, but which are delivered by our Spanish neighbors with great eloquence and in the choicest language, are mere conversational phrases, which, from their earliest childhood, they are taught to repeat on every suitable occasion. Should you really apply to them for any of the services so pompously proffered, you must expect, as a general rule, that they will find a well-sounding excuse for refusing. They must not be too rigidly expected to keep a promise when it is inconvenient to keep it, or when it is more advantageous to break it. Good faith is often wanting, especially in money transactions. They lack business habits, especially in the interior of Ecuador, where there is but little commerce. It is very difficult to induce them to do a thing promptly, thoroughly, and at once. They are full of delays and procrastinations.[1] But they are ex-

[1] The lamented Colonel Francis Hall, who lost his life in Quito on the night of the 19th of October, 1833, during one of the many revolutions which have distracted that country ever since the establishment of its independence, comments on the character of Colombians in the following manner: "Long habits of slavery and oppression, partly counteracted by a feverish interval of liberty, ill understood and imperfectly enjoyed; the almost total want of education, and absence of that moral stimulus, which, under the name of *honor* or *character*, forces every respectable individual of European society to a line of conduct conformable with his situation; all these circumstances have produced a negativeness or debility, both in thought and action, which renders them troublesome to deal with, and unfit to be relied on. It is, in fact, impossible to calculate their behavior, except you could be certain of the last idea which has occupied their imagination, for the feeling of interest most immediately present is pretty generally decisive of their conduct. Does a merchant contract with a planter for a quantity of coffee or cacao at a certain rate: in vain would he suppose the bargain concluded should another purchaser appear, and offer the slightest advantage of price. The readiness with which they break a promise or an agreement, can only be equaled by the sophistical ingenuity with which they defend themselves for having done so. In this respect they seem a nation of lawyers, who "with ease twist words and meanings as they please. As the reproach of being a *liar* is the last insult which can be offered or endured among freemen, so is the term *lie* the last to be used in decent conversation; here, on the contrary, not only is the expression a *good one*, and adapted to the meridians of genteelest society, but the re-

ceedingly good-natured, pleasant, and courteous. They are hospitable to a fault. When a respectable stranger arrives, they will overwhelm him with kindness and attentions, especially when he presents letters of introduction. I received presents of sweetmeats, preserves, venison, cakes, pastry, milk, butter, and cheese, almost continually. Many a time I received presents from ladies, even before I had made their acquaintance. These presents are delivered by servants, together with a kind message from the giver. The politeness of the natives is indeed pleasing; they never show the slightest rudeness, and treat even their enemies with distinguished civility. Their manners are exceedingly amiable and cordial, and at the same time dignified. Their language is elegant, and always obliging.

Let us now return to our subject. There is another want still more embarrassing in Quito than the want of hotels: it is the want of water-closets and privies, which are not considered as necessary fixtures of private residences. This inconvenience has undoubtedly contributed a great deal to make Quito what it is — one of the filthiest capitals in Christendom. Men, women, and children, of all ages and colors, may be seen in the middle of the street in broad daylight, making privies of the most public thoroughfares; and while

proach of being a liar may be safely cast on friend or foe with as little offense given or taken, as the term 'rake' or 'prodigal' would cause in a fashionable London circle. It is, indeed, a truth worth a 'thousand homilies' in defense of liberty, that without it there can be no virtue. The most pleasing trait in the character of Colombian Creoles is their good-nature. It is easy to live with them if you require but little of them; they have little or no active benevolence, because such must result from strong powers of imagination and reflection." — *Colombia: Its Present State and Inducements to Emigration*, by Colonel Francis Hall: Philadelphia, 1825.

thus engaged, they will stare into the faces of passers-by with a shamelessness that beggars description. By-streets, especially, are made noisome, and sometimes impassable, by this detestable practice. I know that these statements will offend the delicacy of my readers, but I would leave one of the characteristic features of Quito unnoticed, were I to omit them. Accustomed as we are at home to the utmost cleanliness, it is a difficult task to convey to the minds of an American public an adequate idea of Ecuadorian filthiness. You may enter the most elegant and fashionable parlors, and the dust on tables, chairs, and sofas will, in many cases, be thick enough legibly to write your name on the furniture it covers. And yet parlors are generally kept with greater and better care than other apartments. In the latter, you may discover innumerable cobwebs of venerable age, amidst clouds of dust covering the walls and ceilings, and the incongruent mixture of all possible styles of furniture.

Strong prejudices are entertained by the natives against the use of cold water. On one occasion, a gentleman at Ambato, who saw me wash my face, asked me, with great curiosity, whether I did so every day! In the country, it is generally believed that washing one's face with cold water will produce swelling, fever, or rheumatism. The women, as a general thing, are cleanlier than the men; but of the latter I have known many, of respectable families, who but very seldom washed their faces in the morning. We need not, therefore, be surprised at seeing the Indians bring their vegetables to market bundled up in the same lousy *rebozos* and ponchos with which they cover their unwashed limbs at night. A few incidents, which to many of my readers will appear incredible, may be mentioned in this connection. I had once ordered some flour made of *yuca*, which, for culinary uses, is preferable to the coarse flour of wheat, as ground in the primitive mills of the interior; but I urged upon the woman who had undertaken to furnish it, to keep it clean. She brought it at last, but tied up in a man's shirt, spotted with flea marks. Of course, woman, yuca-flour, and shirt, received a very short but most emphatic notice to quit my premises. On another occasion, I had arrived at Ambato late in the evening, and, disinclined to take any refreshments myself, I asked my *paje* (body-servant) whether he wanted to take any thing. He asked for a cup of coffee, which I ordered to be brought. The boy who attended the bar of the inn seemed to be without a knife to cut a big lump of sugar which he had taken from the shelves, and so he bit off one piece after the other, and taking the pieces out of his mouth, placed them on the saucer on which he intended to serve them. This was too strong, even for an Ecuadorian, and my servant refused to take the coffee after what he had seen. The Indians who sweep the streets of Quito on Sundays have no shovels to take up the dirt. I have seen them, many a time, scrape together the sweepings with their hands and nails, and fill them in their ponchos, which form the most essential part of their wearing apparel in daytime, and serve them as blankets at night. There is nothing more loathsome, however, than to see the common people crush lice between their teeth. In the entrances of houses, on the market-places, in the groceries and green-shops, and in a variety of other places open to the public eye, men, women, and children may be seen picking lice off each other's heads, and crushing them between their teeth. In respectable private residences, I was often obliged to see, at meals, when plates were changed, the marks of fingers on the crockery. Tea and coffee pots were exceedingly dirty; the hands and faces of the servants unwashed, their hair uncombed, their dress slovenly and greasy. If such disregard of cleanliness prevails among the wealthy, one cannot be surprised that the filthiness of the poor beggars description. To see a man pick a flea from behind his necktie, and kill it between his teeth, is not an uncommon sight. I even saw women lick the lice and scab from the combs with which they were combing their children.

These details are certainly disgusting; but the country has its redeeming features: and first of all, the excellence of its climate, which is very agreeable and salubrious, the mean temperature being about 60° Fahr. in the shade. In my library, the mercury never rose above 61°; in my bedroom — which had the morning sun — the mean temperature was 62°. In the shade, the thermometer scarcely ever rises above 70°, nor sinks below 45°. The average range within the twenty-four hours may be stated at about 10°. These observations, of course, apply to Quito and the neighboring plains. A journey of four hours will place the traveller in the region of eternal frost; or in the space of half a day he can descend the deep and sultry valleys that separate the mighty chains of the Andes; or, finally, he may visit the tropical forest extending to the shores of the Pacific. This variation of temperature, dependent on elevation, and occurring within narrow limits, furnishes a daily and diversified supply of vegetable food — from the plantain, which, as a substitute for bread, is largely consumed by the inhabitants of the coast, to the wheat, pulse, maize, *quinoa*, potato, *oca*, cabbage, beets, salads, and pot-herbs, and all sorts of grains and roots, growing luxuriantly on the cool table-lands of the interior. Besides these, the market is furnished with pine-apples, chirimoyas (*Anona chirimoya*), guayavas (*Psidium pomiferum*), guavas (*Inga pachycarpa*), the fruit of different species of passion-flower; oranges and lemons, *camotes*, *yucas*, *arachacas*, *pallemetos*, *citrons*, *granadillas*, and, from January to April, certain European fruits, such as apples, pears, quinces, peaches, apricots, melons, and strawberries — the last-mentioned fruit having been introduced probably from Chili. The quality of European fruit, however, is greatly inferior, there being not the slightest care or cultivation bestowed upon trees.

If it were not for the excellence of its climate, which is never hot and never cold, the prevailing filthiness would make Quito a very sickly place. But, as it is, Quito, with its neighborhood for miles around, may be said to be one of the healthiest localities on the globe. Consumptions and pulmonary diseases are scarcely ever heard of. The fevers peculiar to tropical countries are unknown. Those who get them on the coast will go to Quito and the interior, to get rid of them again. Dysenteries are uncommon. Among the rabble, it is true, cases of tubercular elephantiasis or leprosy,[1] as well as blindness and deafness, will be noted; but there is no doubt that they are brought on by irregular habits and the indescribable filthiness in which these people are brought up and live. As the government has not yet established a department of statistics, I am unable to state the mortality of Quito, although I believe it is considerably less than that of other places of

[1] *Elephantiasis Græcorum.*

an equal number of inhabitants. To judge from the great number of persons of high age I have met with in all ranks and stations, the climate may be said to be favorable to long life. One remarkable observation which I made in this connection, ought to find a place here: corpulency is very frequent among women, but very rare among men. I have found but few corpulent men — I could hardly say ten — among the natives; but I was surprised at the strong disposition to obesity prevailing among women. For this, however, there may be other than climatic causes.

I have already said that the climate of Quito is cool. Persons of sedentary habits will find it cold. I was continually troubled with cold feet, which, in fact, is a very common complaint. Daily and frequent exercise is necessary to prevent it. Those who realize the importance of physical exercise on foot and on horseback, will find the climate delightful. On leaving the city it is difficult to avoid the sun, as trees are scarce. Still, the rays of the sun are not strong enough to do harm. Cases of sunstroke are never heard of. After dinner it is generally advisable to take a moderate walk, for otherwise, one might long for a fireplace, the use of which, in a climate like that of Quito, I should think to be injurious. By neglecting physical exercise, stomach and liver complaints will easily be contracted.

I do not agree with those geographers who have compared the climate of Quito to an eternal spring. I would rather call it an eternal autumn. Between nine to ten thousand feet above the level of the sea, it is nearer the regions of eternal snow than to those of tropical heat. The near neighborhood of so many snow-clad mountains contributes greatly to the coolness of the atmosphere. Cloth, and thick woolen stockings, may be worn all the year round. I almost always wore an overcoat in the evenings, and in the rainy season very often in the daytime also. The rainy season is very unpleasant, on account of its continuous and interminable showers. It rains sometimes several days and nights in succession. The season announces itself by many preliminary showers in October or November, but it does not set in regularly until after the *veranillo* (Indian summer), in December or January. During some parts of it, the mornings are generally clear, and the rains do not commence before midday; but during other parts, it rains almost without intermission. The inhabitants of temperate zones have no idea of the force of equinoctial showers and thunderstorms. The roofs of houses require frequent repairs to keep tight against the masses of water which are continually pouring down from the opened sluices of heaven. When it rains, the natives will generally walk about in *zuecos* (pattens, or rather, wooden overshoes), because the miserable boots and shoes manufactured in the country afford no protection against moisture. The streets of Quito, however, dry very easily. If it ceases to rain for half an hour, they will be crowded as usual with lively throngs of humanity. To the terrible effect the rains produce on the roads of the country, I have already adverted. They have no effect, however, on the climate of the interior, which, occasional colds (*constipaciones, flucciones, i pechugueras*) and catarrhs excepted, remains as healthy in winter as in the dry season.

Not only is Quito a very healthy place, but it is without insects, except those against which cleanliness is a safe preventive, such as fleas and lice. In the country, *niguas* or *piquis* are sometimes, though rarely found; but it is chiefly the Indians, who, on account of going barefoot, are attacked by them.[1] They are very diminutive, and generally introduce themselves into the cuticle below the nails; but the Indians, especially the women, are very skillful in taking them out, which painful operation is performed with a needle. For leagues around Quito, no snake is to be found. Mosquitoes are hardly known; scorpions and tarantulas have never been heard of. Flies, even, are very rare, and do not molest at all. There are mice, but no rats; nor are there bats or lizards, or even bugs or beetles in the grass or on trees. In this respect the near neighborhood of Quito may be said to be a paradise. The coolness of the weather is invigorating and refreshing, and has none of those relaxing and enervating effects which tropical climates produce. But as in the interior of Ecuador you may choose the temperature most suitable to your constitution or taste, so if you are dissatisfied with the autumnal coolness of Quito and its vicinity, a few hours' ride will lead you into regions where an eternal spring prevails, and where the products of all climates cluster around you — potatoes and clover by the side of the orange and

1 "The *nigua*, called *piqui* in Lima and other parts of Peru, is a diminutive insect, in appearance like a small flea. They generally introduce themselves under the cuticle of the feet, which causes a slight itching. When they have established their residence, they deposit a great number of eggs, the whole increasing to the size of a pea. If not carefully taken out, they continue to breed, and, corroding the neighboring parts, they produce malignant ulcers, which sometimes terminate in gangrene. The greatest care is necessary in taking out these diminutive but disagreeable insects: no part should be left behind, and the whole of the bag which contains the ova should be extracted. When they have been suffered to remain several days, they occasion great pain. Negroes are most troubled with them, on account of their going barefoot, and of their inattention to cleanliness." — Stephenson, *Twenty Years' Residence in South America*

the sugar-cane. Indeed, if we may seek anywhere for a land to inaugurate the millennium described in Shelley's "Queen Mab," it is in the highlands of Ecuador. There, neither

—— "The gloom of the long polar night
Lowers o'er the snow-clad rocks and frozen soil;"

nor have —

—— "The tropics bound the realms of day
With a broad belt of mingling cloud and flame,
Where blue mists through the unmoving atmosphere
Scattered the seeds of pestilence, and fed
Unnatural vegetation:"

but —

"Health flows in the gentle atmosphere,
And fruits are ever ripe, and flowers ever fair."

Indeed, the flora of Quito is as beautiful as inexhaustible. Roses bloom all the year round; wild flowers cover the walls of court-yards and ruins; tulips, pinks, and lilies, bloom in the gardens winter and summer, and verdure ever smiles around you on the mountains and in the glens. The sky, when unclouded, is of the purest blue, and the atmosphere as balmy as that of the fabulous Eden — the charming dream of ancient and modern poetry. Here, indeed, we may exclaim with Childe Harold, —

"O, Christ, it is a goodly sight to see
What Heaven has done for this delicious land!
What fruits of fragrance blush on every tree,
What goodly prospects o'er the hills expand:
But man would mar them with an impious hand."

. . . . . . . . . . . .

"For hut and palace show like filthily;
The dingy denizens are rear'd in dirt;
No personage of high or mean degree
Doth care for cleanness of surtout or shirt,
Though shent with Egypt's plague, unkempt, unwashed, unhurt."

## CHAPTER VIII.

Population. — The Whites. — Aristocratic Traditions. — Ancient Nobility. — Prejudice against Labor. — Early Marriages. — Boy - Husbands. — No Spirit of Association — Mixed Races — Cholas and Bolziconas. — Servants. — Huasicamas. — Indian Wives. — Laundresses. — Longas, Guambras, and Guiñazhiscas. — Ama de Llaves. — Marketing. — Matrimonial Relations. — An Incident. — Indian Humility. — Other Traits of Indian Character. — Politeness of the Rabble. — Spanish-American Courtesy. — A Lady's Message to a Friend.

THE population of Quito does not exceed 40,000. On several occasions the government attempted to ascertain the actual number of inhabitants, but failed to arrive at a satisfactory result. The people became alarmed, from an idea that the formation of a census is a preliminary step toward the imposition of a tax, and the information thus obtained was necessarily defective. The census taken in 1861 and 1862, gives but 35,000. The population has undoubtedly decreased. Ulloa, in 1735, estimated it at from 50,000 to 60,000. Stephenson, in 1809, calculated it at 75,000, which is an exaggeration. Caldas, at about the same time, estimated it at 35,000 to 40,000. The "Almanaque Nacional," published in 1845 or 1846, dreams of 80,000. I am satisfied that by adding 5000 to the last official census, to make up for those who were omitted by the census officers, or kept out of their way, or made false statements, I came as near the truth as possible.

Of the elements composing the population, the pure white race does not constitute a majority, although it is, of course, the governing class, consisting of the descendants of Spaniards and other Europeans. They are endowed with a good natural capacity, and quick perception, but lack education, and are without the energy and perseverance necessary to accomplish important undertakings. The want of a road to the coast may be referred to as a standing proof of this assertion.

The descendants of the old wealthy or noble Spanish families, which still form an almost impenetrable aristocracy, have preserved their white blood in tolerable purity, although the black, coarse hair, especially of the women, often reminds us of the Indian *mesalliances* of the first conquerors. In Quito, persons of doubtful color are seldom received in good society, and not even white men of inferior pedigree. The great families do not intermarry with those whom they consider below themselves in rank and dignity, although their equals in color. They still love to hear their old family titles mentioned. The laws, they think, are made for poor people, — Indians and Cholos only, — but not for persons of rank (*de categoria*). These latter, in their opinion, are entitled to make laws without being obliged to obey them. — To the prevailing contempt for labor, I shall refer hereafter.

The custom of marrying very young, and before the bridegroom has secured a position in life, greatly contributes to the poverty of the middle classes. I have seen students marry who had not yet finished their college education, and who, instead of supporting their wives, were supported by them, or rather by their parents and families. Instead of going to their business after breakfast, they went to the University with their books under their arms. The general consequence of this custom is, that after a few months or years, such a child-husband returns his wife to her parents, telling them frankly that he cannot support her! Hence the frequency of husbands not living with their wives, which, in Quitonian phraseology, is called *no hacer vida.* Still, as women in Ecuador are much more numerous than men, the girls prefer this risk to the danger of becoming old maids.

An important trait of Serrano character is their great distrust of each other, which precludes all spirit of association. Partnerships are not customary; corporations are unheard of. Great enterprises therefore, are an impossibility. To this circumstance, more perhaps than to the instability of governments and the frequent recurrence of violent political convulsions, the general decay of the country must be attributed. The colonial period was one of absolute tranquillity and almost undisturbed peace; and yet it was not characterized by important commercial or industrial enterprises. The rich buried their wealth in vaults or walls, instead of investing it in speculations profitable to themselves and the community. The finding of hidden treasures is, therefore, not an uncommon occurrence. During my residence in Ecuador, it happened several times, that the tearing down of old buildings led to the discovery of considerable sums of money buried by their owners, who died without having had time to communicate the secret to their children or relatives.

I have said that the white portion of the population of Quito does not constitute a majority. It is in the aggregate outnumbered by the colored and mixed races Of pure negroes there are but few. Of Zambos[1] (according to Humboldt, the children of mulattoes and

[1] In Quito they are sometimes called *Chinos.*

negroes, or of Indians and negroes), a greater number will be found. The bulk of the population consists of Cholos and pure Indians, especially, however, of the former.[1] Of the Indians, I shall speak hereafter. Cholos or Mestizos are the children of whites and Indians, and their descendants. They are foremost in practical intelligence and enterprise. In their hands are the trades, and a great part of the retail commerce. They are tailors, carpenters, shoemakers, blacksmiths, joiners, etc. The Indians till the soil and do the heavy drudgery, such as working on the roads, and public and private buildings. The Cholos are mechanics and small shop-keepers. They are not as ugly as the great majority of the Indians, especially those of Latacunga and Quito. On the contrary, among the women, we find many of handsome appearance and beautiful eyes. These latter are either *de vestido* or *de centro*, in which case they are also called "*Bolziconas*." The former dress after the Spanish or European fashion; the latter, although gaudily attired, do not wear full dresses, but content themselves with woolen petticoats of lively colors (red, pink, yellow, or

[1] The following is Villavicencio's estimate of the whole population of Ecuador: —

| | |
|---|---|
| Whites descending from Europeans | 601,219 |
| Pure Indians | 462,400 |
| Pure negroes | 7,831 |
| Mixtures of negroes, whites, and Indians | 36,592 |
| | 1,108,042 |
| Add to these the savages east of the Cordillera | 200,000 |
| Total | 1,308,042 |

From attentive observation, I have no doubt that Villavicencio is entirely wrong. His estimate of the pure white population is too high, and that of the mixed races greatly too low. If he had given the number of the latter at 600,000, and the number of the former at 30,000, he would probably have been correct.

pale blue), sometimes ornamented with a profusion of ribbons, lace, fringe, and spangles; white embroidered shawls of cotton, linen, or silk, and *macanas* and *pañuelones*, in which latter great luxury is sometimes displayed. This costume, with the addition of the little straw hat, which such women very frequently wear, is rather gay and piquant. Their shifts are generally embroidered. Over these they wear the light embroidered shawl just referred to; over this the *macana* (or narrow shawl), and over this the *pañuelon* (or wide shawl), with which they cover their heads and shoulders, throwing the right end over the left shoulder. Sometimes the head is uncovered, and the hair hangs in two long tresses down the back. The poor among them are commonly without the light shawl, and go barefooted, or in *alpargates*, a sort of sandals, made of the fibres of the aloe. The *pañuelon* is generally of English flannel, sometimes of cotton, and sometimes of silk. Those who are in better circumstances often wear satin shoes. They all wear bracelets and necklaces of beads or corals, rings of cocoa-shell or galvanized compositions, earrings, etc. They are very fond of jewelry and finery.

But it is time that we should establish ourselves in Quito. We must take a house, and employ servants, who will prove a source of endless trouble and annoyance, for they are generally unreliable, lazy, and filthy, but very good-natured, humble, and submissive. Every respectable family must have at least four or five of them, but in large families from ten to fifteen are sometimes employed. Three or four of them together will not do so much work as is done by one of our good German or Irish servant-girls. They are great on the division of labor. Every one has a certain office, and will hardly do any thing but what he is hired for. Their wages are exceedingly low. A good male cook earned, in 1864, from two dollars and fifty cents to eight dollars per month, which latter wages, however, were paid hardly by any body but foreigners. The natives, accustomed to live cheap, pay their servants but very little. A female cook earned from fifty cents to four dollars a month. But a cook will scarcely ever serve you without an assistant, whose business it is to fan the fires, wash the dishes and vegetables, pare potatoes, carry water, etc. Generally, this work is performed by the *huasicama* or door-keeper, of whom I shall presently speak. Dishes are not exactly washed, but wiped with sawdust kept for the purpose, commonly in an old wine-box. Besides a cook and his assistant or assistants, one or two *pajes*, or body-servants, will have to be kept, who combine the offices of waiter, steward, footman, and chambermaid. Their wages varied from two dollars to six dollars per month.

Another very important personage in the household, is the *huasicama*, or porter, with his wife; for the *huasicama* is always a pure Indian, and the Indian always has a wife, children, and a dog, besides a number of *cuyes*, an animal which seems to form the transition from a Guinea-pig to a rabbit. *Huasicama* is an Indian (Quichua) word, and means door-keeper or turnkey, — literally, "keeper of the house." His room is near the door, which he has to lock at night and to open in the morning. He has to do all the heavy and dirty work, sweep the yards and street in front of the house, to carry water and to take care of the horses, to wash the dishes, and to assist the cook. In every thing he does, he is faithfully assisted by his wife, who is, literally, his helpmate. The affection of Indian women for their husbands, who almost continually ill-treat them, is really remarkable. The Indian wife always carries the baby on her back, in a shawl or poncho tied around her breast or neck. She is generally more industrious and active than her lazy and brutal husband. The huasicama's wages range from one dollar to two dollars a month, in addition to which he gets his food, chiefly *locro* (a potato soup), and a wretched room near the street-door to live in. If he has no room, he sleeps in the entrance. His bedding is a sheep-skin, and his clothes and ponchos are his blankets. His meals he takes cowering on the floor, a custom which is not peculiar to Indians. The poor cholos, negroes, and even the white rabble, especially, however, the *chagras*, or country people, eat their meals on the ground, and in all probability prefer this mode of dining to the use of tables and chairs.

Another indispensable person in the family is the laundress, who washes but for a limited number of persons. If there are three or four ladies in one family, it will be necessary to employ two or more laundresses. There being neither wells nor cisterns in the houses, the washerwomen repair to one of the many streams flowing through the ravines (*quebradas*) by which the city is intersected, and there, tucking up their clothes, go into the water and beat the linen against a rock until it is clean. After this it is spread over rocks or on the lawn, to be dried by the sun. If the weather is unpropitious, this process takes two or three days. While waiting for the clothes to dry, they will usually wash and bathe themselves; and the eye of the passer-by is arrested by innumerable repetitions of the sight for which Diana transformed poor Actæon into a stag, who was torn to pieces by his own hounds. But the

Quito laundresses are no Dianas. Bashfulness is a virtue unknown among the common people of the interior. And even their dogs — for almost every washerwoman has a dog who keeps her company — are not like those of Actæon: they only bark and howl, but do not bite. The dogs of the interior partake of the tameness of their masters. There are dogs in almost every Indian hut, but I never met with a fierce dog. Whether they have no courage, because they get hardly any thing to eat beside the carcasses of mules and donkeys dying on the road, and which not too frequent repast they must share with *gallinazos*, or whether they are affected with the timidity and cowardice of their Indian masters, I am unable to say.

But let us here pass to another class of servants, who are found in every, and even the poorest, native family. I mean the "*Longas*" or "*Guambras*," as they are generally called. They are little Indian, cholo, negro, or mulatto boys or girls, of from five to eight and twelve years of age, who are kept partly as playmates and servants for the children, partly to do as many little things as their age will allow. They are kept with a view of being trained to be regular house-servants when they arrive at a suitable age. They are called "*Guiñazhiscas*" when brought up in the family from their earliest childhood. *Guiñazhisca* and *Guambra* are Indian terms. One of their chief duties is to carry the carpet on which the señora kneels in church during mass. The Quitonian ladies go to mass every day, and sometimes to several masses in one day, but they never go without being accompanied by a little, dirty Indian, cholo, or mulatto boy or girl, carrying the carpet or hassock on the head, and tripping behind his or her mistress. Even when they go out visiting, they are generally followed by a servant, who squats down at the head of the stairs, in the parlor door, or in the room itself, until the lady is ready to leave. The parents of these *longas* or *guambras* are in the habit of selling them for a trifle. It is not a sale in the literal sense of the word; but by paying a few dollars to the parents, you may easily induce them to apprentice their children to you, until they become of age. Many a time such children were offered to me. I recollect one instance in which the mother, an Indian woman, offered me one of her children if I would give her the money to buy a pig. The process of binding out children is simple and cheap. The parties appear before the chief of police, who asks the mother for her name and age (of the latter she is generally ignorant), whether she is married or unmarried, whether the child is legitimate or illegitimate, its name and age, and the name of the father. After answering his questions, the chief of police makes the mother declare her intention to bind out the child, and, as these women are almost always entirely illiterate, one of the witnesses will, at her request and on her behalf, sign the instrument of indenture. The *guambra* or *longa* is fed and clothed (and generally very poorly) by her master, but receives no wages or education. On becoming of age, she may go where she pleases.

In large and wealthy families, there is sometimes an "*ama de llaves*" (literally, a "mistress of the keys"), a kind of female overseer, or stewardess, who has charge of the whole household, with the care of which ladies will have as little to do as possible. Such an *ama de llaves*, however, often increases the peculations to which you are exposed, because she will steal first, and the others will steal after her. Stealing is hardly considered a sin by the common people. I once heard an *ama de llaves* express her abhorrence of Protestantism, because Protestant clergymen had no power to forgive sins; and she thought it horrible that little insignificant thefts, which, in her opinion, every body committed, should, without absolution in this world, be carried to the other side of the grave!

Besides the different classes of servants I have enumerated, there are chamber-maids (if they deserve to be honored with such a name), wet-nurses (*ñuños*, an Indian word), and very frequently two or three supernumeraries, old retainers of the family, who work for their board until they can find more lucrative employment.

Almost all your servants are married, and have families who live with them, early marriages being the custom of the country. The families of servants, however, are not so great an annoyance as the legions of relatives and friends by whom they are continually visited, and who will dine with them, drink with them, and even stay over night with them. Then you will find them huddled together, men and women promiscuously, on the floor of a small room, without windows and ventilation. Such visits sometimes last for a whole week. It is impossible to keep your house clear of people who are not in your employ. At one time I had four persons in my service, and yet I fed fourteen regularly, without counting their occasional visitors. Their appetite is ravenous. They eat, not until they are satisfied, but so long as there is any thing left; and besides what remains of the meals, immense pots of *locro* are cooked for their exclusive benefit.

Fleas are the plague of the interior. I have seen women with perfect collars of flea-bites around their necks. Even in the houses of some of the first native families, fleas are as numerous as in the huts of Indians. These things may appear incredible, but I am satisfied that in many respects my description remains behind the truth.

The cook generally receives a certain sum per day for marketing, for which he furnishes two meals, breakfast and dinner. He is not called to account for what he has expended. Any balance that may remain after he has made his purchases, he keeps for himself. Quito is undoubtedly the cheapest capital in the world. It costs almost nothing to live. For a dollar a day my cook furnished two excellent daily meals. Boarding at the restaurants could be had at from ten dollars to fifteen dollars a month, or twenty-five cents a meal. During the last year of my residence at Quito, there was, however, a steady rise in the price of provisions, which henceforward will never return to their pristine standard.

The mode of marketing is very queer. Of course ladies or gentlemen will not go to market, not even with a servant to carry the basket. This practice, so common with us, would be scandalous and disreputable in Spanish-America. It is the cook, or sometimes the huasicama, who makes the purchases. He will first buy a few breads in a grocery, and with these breads he will buy his vegetables, or other articles worth less than a cuartillo, which is the smallest coin, and the fourth part of a real. One bread represents one fifth of a cuartillo, — twenty common breads being given for one real. The bread thus used consists of small round pieces, weighing but very little, although sufficiently doughy and indigestible. The Indian producers or venders, therefore, receive more bread than money.

The want of copper coin is the cause of this strange custom. Sometimes the cooks will make their purchases by force. They will take what they need, and then throw down not what the Indian seller asks, but what they deem sufficient. Of course the poor Indian never thinks of resisting any body who is not an Indian. Even negroes and cholos he considers superior to himself, and patiently submits to every act of injustice or oppression.

I have said already that almost all the servants are married, and have their families with them. Their standard of morality, however, is rather low. Sometimes they take women on trial, a custom very prevalent among the Indians, who are often compelled by poverty to live with their intended ones, without being married, until they have money enough to pay the fees of the curate, who never trusts. The conduct of the husband *in spe* is, however, almost always characterized by good faith. He seldom rejects the woman with whom he has cohabited with a view to matrimony. The Indian is strongly attached to his wife, and very jealous, although he treats her cruelly ; but the woman does not want to be treated otherwise. If her husband should cease to beat her, she would be convinced that he has ceased to love her. The British Chargé d'Affaires, Mr. Fagan, once protected a woman whom an Indian was beating on the public highway, but she rebuked that gentleman with the remark that the aggressor was her husband, and had a right to wallop her.

I once had a huasicama who formed an exception to the good faith of the Indian toward the other sex. He was a boy of about sixteen or seventeen years of age (according to my calculation, for the Indians hardly ever know how old they are), and lived with two women, with both of whom he seemed to be on terms of great intimacy. One of them I supposed to be his wife; but one day the census-taker came around to add my servants to his list, and asked him the usual question, whether he was married or single. To my great astonishment, he replied that he was unmarried. I then asked him sternly what he kept two women for? He answered very mildly, "*Para casarme*," "for the purpose of getting married," or, "with a view to matrimony." I then informed him that this would not do, and that he had to be one woman's husband, or to discharge them both. He did not like the alternative, and left my employment. About half a year afterward he came back and asked to be reinstated. As he had always been a tolerably good and honest boy, I was not disinclined to take him back, and therefore asked him whether his domestic affairs had remained in the same objectionable shape. "No," he said, "*yo he botado á esa mujer*" ("I have cast that woman away"). Shortly afterward he married another whom his parents had selected for him. The relatives of both parties contributed to deffay the expense of solemnizing the marriage, as bride and bridegroom were penniless.

Lazy and dishonest as the common people of the interior generally are, they are not impertinent or mischievous, but polite and submissive in the extreme. It is seldom that they dare to retort or resent, when insulted by any one who is above them in the social scale. They seem to have learned submissiveness and humility from the Indians, who are perfectly helpless and rightless. Every body kicks them, every body insults them, but they never resent. Indian farm laborers on the haciendas, after having been whipped at the command of their masters, address them, hat in hand,

and as polite and pliable as if nothing had happened. The Indian, trudging along barefoot on the public highway, always takes off his hat to a well-dressed person, giving him the usual salutation, — "*Alabado sea el santisimo sacramento!*" (Blessed be the most holy sacrament!) If you want to light a cigar at one of the Indian huts on the road, the poor man will give you a small firebrand, hat in hand. He is always humble, always submissive in words, but generally very backward in actions. His temper has been soured by long ill-treatment. He will hardly do any thing unless he is compelled to do it. Force is considered to be the only way to succeed with him. I cannot omit, in this connection, to mention an incident which was communicated to me by the British Chargé d'Affaires. On his journey to Quito, he met several Indians on the road who carried fruit to some town near by, for the purpose of selling it there. He offered to buy some, but they refused to sell. He then offered double and treble prices, but the Indians remained stubborn. At last the Chargé was informed by the officer who accompanied him as a guide and guard of honor, that this was not the way to deal with Indians. That gentleman dismounted, and after a few threatening words and gestures, opened the bundles of the Indians, and took out fruit for the whole company. Being asked by the British Chargé what the damage was, they charged the regular low price. They preferred a compulsory sale for the common price to a voluntary sale for a good price. It is true, a decided disinclination to sell any thing on the road before arriving at the place for which they are bound, is universal among them; but on the other hand, it must not be forgotten that experience has taught them to distrust the promises of the white man.

They are accustomed to be wronged and to be cheated, and therefore surrender themselves to an incredulous indifference and stolid unwillingness, which can only be overcome by force. And force they have to experience in every thing. Even the government continually sets the example. When there is danger of a foreign war or revolution, they are compelled to carry loads of muskets, ammunition, or other implements of war, as well as the baggage of officers and privates, or to render other compulsory services.

Notwithstanding their ignorance and filthiness, the manners of the rabble of Quito, if not instigated to some quarrel by rum or chicha, are characterized by the utmost politeness, not only toward their superiors, but also among themselves. The very dregs of the population of Quito, degraded as they may be, are politeness personified; and they will clothe the outbursts of their civility in language, the elegance and correctness of which are really astonishing. The loafing vagabond, who sleeps on the cold, unfloored ground of one of those dreadful hovels which serve as kitchens, bedrooms, chicken-roosts, dog-kennels, and pig-sties, will, when meeting one of his *comadres*, salute her in a manner which we should expect to hear only in drawing-rooms and parlors.

The Spaniards are notorious for politeness, but their South-American descendants have surpassed them. They practice politeness as they do religion. Their set phrases in society are rattled off like their prayers in church. Their civility, like their religious worship, is only an outward observance, which has but little connection with the heart. It is not studied hypocrisy, — it is mere habit and mechanism. With the same thoughtlessness with which they hum and prattle away at their rosaries and litanies, they pour forth their compliments and assurances.

It is amusing to hear a Quitonian lady send one of her servants to deliver a message to another lady. Translated into English, it sounds most ridiculous: "Go to the Señorita Fulana de Tal, and tell her that she is my heart (*que es mi corazon*), and the dear little friend of my soul; tell her that I am dying (*que estoy muriendome por no haberle visto*) for not having seen her, and ask her why she does not come to see me; tell her that I have been awaiting her for more than a week, and that I send her my best respects and considerations; and ask her how she is, and how her husband is, and how her children are, and whether they are all well in the family; and tell her that she is my little love, and whether she will not be kind enough to send me that pattern which she promised me the other day." Now, any body would suppose that the servant intrusted with this highly important message, would forget one half of it, or be unwilling to deliver the long preamble to the short argument; but it is not so. With a conscientiousness that does not distinguish them in other respects, and with a strength of memory that would shame the retentiveness of Sancho Panza, in delivering his master's message from the Sierra Morena to the Dulcinea of his heart, the servants will deliver themselves with a parrot-like fidelity, and in a strange, monotonous, sing-song key of voice, of the complete mass of compliments confided to their charge; they will rather add than omit one; they will rather improve on the original than weaken its effects by giving a synopsis merely, or editing an abridgment.

Having now established ourselves domestically, we may begin to look around in Quito. This shall be done in my next chapter.

## CHAPTER IX.

Spanish Mode of Colonization. — Fortifications and Convents. — Architecture of Quito. — The Moorish Style. — Public Buildings. — Churches. — Nunneries. — The Convent of San Francisco. — Its Painted Miracles. — Interesting Specimens. — The Praying Lamb. — The Chapel of Catuña. — A Romantic Legend. — The Treasures of Rumiñagui. — A Pretended Pact with the Prince of Darkness. — La Capilla del Robo. — Another Legend. — The Parish Church of San Roque. — Flagellation. — The Tejar, or La Recoleta de la Merced. — Religious Exercises in Lent. — Still another Legend. — Indian Reticence. — Burying-places. — How the Poor bury their Children. — Administering the Last Sacraments. — Religious Processions. — Semana Santa. — Holy Thursday and Good Friday. — Splendid Illumination of the Churches. — A Descendimiento. — A Sermon accompanied by a Puppet-show. — Its Effect on the Audience. — A Portable Image of the Lord, and its Travels to the Coast. — Christmas. — Misa de Gallos. — The Clergy. — Ignorance and Immorality of the Monks. — The Curates. — List of Convents and Nunneries. — Fees of Curates. — Divisions of Caste.

The endeavors of Spain with respect to her American colonies, were chiefly directed toward preserving them exclusively to herself, and establishing the authority of the Church of Rome as a means conducive to that object, as well as of government. She studded the coasts with fortifications, and covered the interior with churches and convents. Guns and relics, soldiers and friars, were her instruments and agents; and oppression and superstition, with ignorance, their never-failing attendant, the fruits the colonies reaped from the system. Hence, to understand and appreciate correctly whatever exists at the present day in a Spanish-American republic, whether in politics, morals, or art, Spain and her system must always be borne in mind.

The insalubrity of the Ecuadorian sea-board and the inaccessible nature of the interior, were, perhaps, considered sufficient protection against the intrusion of foreigners, and artificial means to exclude them were not so extensively resorted to as at Havana, Cartagena, Callao, and other sea-ports. Undivided attention could consequently be bestowed on the means of defense against spiritual foes. Thus, though far from having been among the wealthiest of the Spanish colonies, Ecuador, in her capital of Quito, can boast of more extensive convents and costlier churches than many of her richer sisters.

The Spaniards did usually build some secular edifices of a very substantial class in most of their colonial capitals, at least "*la casa de la real audiencia*," and a vice-regal palace, were never wanting, and not unfrequently a theatre was added; but if any of these ever existed in Quito, they must have belonged to a very inferior kind of construction, for none of them are to be found there now. It seems that not even barracks built for such were considered necessary, as the present government is obliged to quarter the small force it supports in portions of some of the old convents. Perhaps the absence of substantial secular edifices is attributable to there having been no employment for military engineers, who generally acted in the other colonies as architects, and understood at least how to build solidly. That the ecclesiastical edifices fared better, may be owing to their always having been a friar or two in each of the convents who took to the study of architecture, as it was practiced in Spain, as a favorite pastime.

Since the establishment of independence, no public building with any pretensions to architecture, except the unfinished Government House, has been attempted; and hence the ecclesiastical edifices are nearly the only ones that are worthy of architectural notice.

Traces of the Moorish style show themselves in almost all the architecture of Spain; and even the buildings belonging to the *renaissance* period are not free of such reminiscences. These, with other peculiarities of Spanish art, were imported into the colonies. The prevailing characteristics are just what might be expected to result from an endeavor on the part of the builder to copy as faithfully as his unaided memory would allow, some favorite model which was the fashion of his day, and which he had seen executed at home in Old Spain.

Not long after the discovery of America, the Gothic style had fallen almost into complete disuse in the mother-country, as it had also throughout the rest of Europe; consequently, excepting here and there a pointed arch standing in startling discord amidst a group of round ones in some of the churches, there is nothing to remind one of that style in Quito.

The fear of earthquakes has led to even a greater degree of massiveness in the style of construction here than at home; and though the extensive use of vaulted coverings and of arches to be observed in Quito does not agree with apprehensions respecting the awful scourge just mentioned, the practice was partly forced on the builders by the scarcity of timber of a proper scantling, of which the vicinity of Quito is bare.

The color of the stone used for building is too dark, yet the material is generally of a good quality, and stone-cutting and carving were brought to a high state of advancement. The lime and sand of the neighborhood afforded excellent mortar, and must have greatly facilitated the practice of vaulted coverings.

With the exception of the Cathedral (the parochial chapels are little better than barns), the principal churches are attached to convents. They therefore rarely present more than the principal façade to the public, and if they happen to stand on one corner of the convents the flanks are left bare of architectural design, to correspond in unsightliness with the rest of the convent walls.

The convents are extensive, covering sometimes as much as eight or nine acres of ground. They generally have one or two spacious arcaded quadrangles, and several smaller ones, but are all more or less in a deplorable state of dilapidation, caused chiefly by the last earthquake and subsequent neglect. Their construction, however, was always of a substantial nature.

Some of the nunneries have large gardens, in which each nun has a little pavilion or bower built for her recreation, and which is her exclusive property. It is her delight to decorate this according to her childish and simple taste, with pictures of saints, trinkets, and embroidery of her own making.

The monastery of San Francisco is one of the largest in Quito, and perhaps one of the most extensive convents in the world. As the number of Franciscans, as well as of monks in general, has greatly diminished, it has lost its ancient importance. A considerable part of it is in ruins, while the southerly wing is used for military barracks. In the arcaded corridors of the courts, numberless oil-paintings adorn the walls, representing incidents in the life of St. Francis, and miracles wrought by him. Each picture is provided with an explanation, in the Spanish language, of what it represents. To give my readers an idea of Quito convents, I shall translate a few of the inscriptions: —

"As the mother of the seraphic father, San Francisco, had despaired of a safe delivery of the fruit of her womb, she followed the advice of an angel who had appeared to her in the form of a pilgrim and told her to await her confinement in a stable. There the birth of the sainted father takes place, in imitation of the birth of Christ; and at his birth, the greatest consternation prevails in hell, and the devil trembles because he foresees the terrible war which the great saint will wage against him."

The painting represents this interesting scene: On one side, the stable and the confinement; and on the other, the infernal legions of horned devils trembling and despairing.

"In Palermo, a city of the kingdom of Sicily, there was a woman who was seized by a most burning desire to eat human flesh. Having no means of satisfying her horrible appetite, she killed, instigated by the devil, her little son. She had already roasted one of his limbs, when her husband came in, and beholding what she had done, was about to kill her. At this moment the sainted father, San Francisco, appeared to them, and commanded them to bring the different parts of the child's body to him, which he put together and blessed, whereupon the child became alive again, and was restored to his parents."

"A monk of a certain order, who would not believe that the wounds of Christ were really impressed on the body of the sainted father, San Francisco, blotted their sacred marks from a portrait of the saint which he had in his possession; when, as a heavenly chastisement, a jet of blood rushed from the picture with such force, that it struck down the monk, and almost killed him."

"The fire of heavenly love which glowed in the breasts

of San Francisco and Santa Clara was so great that their mortal frames could not hold it. It burst its confinement, and filled the whole church of Asei, in which the two were praying, and issued forth from the windows, so that the people believed the church was on fire, and came with buckets and ladders. Thus they were made witnesses of the great miracle which God had wrought through his saints."

"In the convent of Gaeta in Naples, the sainted father was sorely tempted, once upon a time, by the alluring arts of a licentious woman. To preserve his chastity, he threw himself naked into a thorny bush. The spines, bathed by his holy blood, were at once transformed into beautiful and fragrant roses."

"When the holy father, San Francisco, arrived at Arecio, a city in Etruria, he found its inhabitants engaged in a terrible civil war. At the same time, he beheld hovering over the city a number of demons, who fanned the flames of internecine discord. He commanded them to be gone. They had to obey the irresistible power of his voice, and peace was at once restored."

"A lamb which the holy father, San Francisco, kept, worships Jesus Christ during the most holy sacrament."

The lamb is represented standing on its hind legs, in the attitude of prayer. The last painting of this remarkable collection represents the Saint's arrival in heaven, "where the most holy Virgin Mary places the child Christ in his arms." There are at least sixty or seventy of these paintings in the arcades of the convent.

Let us now pass to another legend connected with the convent of San Francisco: On the southeast corner of the immense property, and contiguous to the main church, we find the chapel of Catuña, in the vestry of which a picture of the Virgin is exhibited, with an Indian at her feet, who looks up to her imploringly. This Indian, of whom only the head and neck are represented, is Catuña, the founder of the chapel, and the hero of one of the oldest legends of Quito.

The great treasures which the unfortunate Inca, Atahuallpa, delivered to Pizarro as his ransom, are said to have come from Cuzco and other Peruvian towns. The treasure at Quito is said to have remained intact, and to have been seized upon by Ruminagui, one of the Inca's generals, who, after the capture of his master by the Spaniards, had usurped the government of Quito, and with a view to his own elevation to the throne, had put to death all the members of his master's family whom he could get into his power. On the approach of the victorious Spaniards under Benalcazar, Ruminagui set fire to the town, and evacuated it with the rest of his army. Some say he carried the treasure away with him ; others, that he buried it at Quito before he left the city. And here our legend begins :—

Hualca, a partisan and follower of Ruminagui, was one of the officers who superintended the burying of the treasure. In this he was assisted by his son Catuña, a boy of tender age. After the town had commenced to burn, a wall, near which Hualca's party had been at work, fell in, apparently crushing the child, so that his father left him, supposing him to be dead. Catuña, however, escaped, and was taken care of by one of the Spaniards, who entered Quito immediately after Ruminagui had left it. The boy's injuries were so severe that his features remained distorted and his limbs dislocated, and he became a hunchback of frightful ugliness. He was at last taken into the service of a Captain Hernan Suarez, who took a fancy to the poor cripple, taught him to read and write, and instructed him in the doctrines of the Christian religion. Suarez, having been unfortunate in his speculations, soon afterwards was reduced to great distress, and about to sell his house in order to meet the claims of some of his most pressing creditors, when Catuña told him to have a secret vault constructed under his residence, and to furnish it with all the implements necessary for smelting gold; adding, that he was able and willing to give him enough of the precious metal in bars, but that he would not let him see it in its original form. He also made his master promise never to reveal to any body from whom he had received it. Suarez complied with these instructions, and soon became a rich man. A great part of the wealth which his servant had bestowed on him, he applied to charitable and religious purposes, and when he died, in 1550, leaving neither wife nor children, he made Catuña heir of his real and personal property.

In the mean time, the change in the circumstances of Suarez had aroused suspicion. It was surmised by many that he owed his sudden unaccountable prosperity to Catuña, the ugly Indian imp who served him. This suspicion was confirmed by the great sums of money which Catuña subsequently bestowed on churches and convents, and distributed among the poor. He was taken into custody, and required to declare from what source he had derived his wealth. The Indian knew well enough that, should he declare the truth, his riches would be seized upon by the first conquerors, who considered any part of the treasure of Atahuallpa as their lawful spoils. He, therefore, resorted to a most daring stratagem. He said it was true that he had been the benefactor of Suarez, and a great many others, but that he could have as much gold as he wanted, having made a compact with the Evil One, to whom he had sold his soul. Under other circumstances, this confession would not have improved his case, and he would probably have been dispatched by the tribunals of the Inquisition; but his munificent generosity had gained him the good-will of the priests and rabble, and probably of his own judges, who did not wish to dry up the source from which so much liberality flowed. They affected to pity his misery, and set him free. His statement was the more readily credited, as the Indians were then generally believed to have intercourse with the Prince of Darkness. Many of the priests, and especially the Franciscans, exhorted him to renounce his pact with the Devil and make his peace with the Lord; but he remained unmoved, and insisted that he wanted to have gold as long as he lived. "Secretly," says Father Velasco, the chronicler of Quito, he "laughed at the exhortations of the monks, being at heart a good Christian and extremely devoted to the sufferings of the most holy Virgin" ("Sumamente devoto de los dolores de la Santisima Virgen"). After his death, his premises were searched, and with considerable difficulty the vault was discovered, with a great quantity of gold in ingots, bars, and in vessels, and the tools with which Suarez had provided him. Still the people continued to believe in the story of his pact with the Evil One, "and the truth," adds Father Velasco, "would never have been discovered, if it had not been for a Franciscan monk who had secretly been his confessor, and, on his death, left a written account of what Catuña had confided to him."

One square from the Church of San Francisco is the nunnery of Santa Clara, in the rear of which we find a chapel which bears the significant name, *La Capilla del Robo* (the Chapel of the Robbery), which is said to owe its foundation to the following miracle: —

A great load of valuable merchandise was once on the way to Quito, when, in the outskirts of the city, a band of robbers attacked the caravan, drove away the arrieros and seized the goods, which they hid in a house near the convent of Santa Clara. Some time afterwards, when the mules which had carried the goods were driven past that house, they suddenly fell on their knees and would not move until the stolen articles had been discovered. To commemorate this event, a chapel was built on the spot where it is supposed to have happened.

A few squares west of Santa Clara is the parish church of San Roque, in which flagellation is practiced by the women almost every Tuesday and Friday evening. These performances are exceedingly interesting, although they take place in the dark. Males are not admitted. Through the kindness of the curate, however, with whom I was personally befriended, I was allowed to enter the church unobserved, and to listen to the proceedings, which are as follows: Toward sundown, the curate preaches a short sermon or reads a moral lesson, and then leaves the church in utter darkness. The organist then plays a *Miserere*, the women bare their backs and lash them with cowhides, to which sometimes small pieces of iron or other hard substances are attached. When this discipline is over, they depart in silence. The blood sprinkled over the stone floor and on the walls, betokens the eager earnestness of their devotion. I should endeavor in vain to describe my sensations while, lost in impenetrable darkness, I stood in the old church a silent listener. The solemn tune played by the organist, who chanted the accompaniment in a subdued key of voice, was interrupted only by the dreadful sounds which the lashes produced on the bare backs, and which were reverberated from the high walls of the building, while now and then a sigh would mournfully steal through the darkness.

Similar exercises take place every Lent in the *Tejar*, or *Recoleta de la Merced*, a branch institution of the Order of Mercy. The *Tejar* is situate at a short distance west of the city, which it overlooks. It is the building where the last President of the Royal Audience, Count Ruiz de Castilla, had taken refuge, before he was taken out and murdered by the populace in 1810. It contains a convent, a church, a cemetery, and a number of out-houses for the accommodation of penitents. These out-houses are divided into dark cells — regular prisons — spacious enough for three or four inmates each. During Lent, men and women alternate in the occupation of these buildings. The penitents are required to remain in this retreat nine full days. Ladies and gentlemen of the first families thus deprive themselves of all intercourse with the outer world for more than a week, in order to atone for their shortcomings and frailties. During this voluntary imprisonment, they rise at three o'clock in the morning and go to bed at nine o'clock in the evening; mass is said for them in the adjoining church, from which they return to the *casa de ejercicios*. In the evenings they go to church again to hear sermons preached, after which the process of flagellation begins. I have seen the walls and the stone floor of the church and transepts sprinkled all over with the blood of the disciplinarians. The refectory (dining-hall) is hung with paintings, most of which represent hell with its torments. Men, around whose bodies snakes have coiled, lacerating them with their fangs; dragons tearing the flesh from the bones of the doomed; fiery devils biting and torturing them; rats gnawing away at their legs; demons pinching them with red-hot tongs; and other fearful scenes on the canvas, remind the poor penitents, whose nerves are wrought to the highest possible state of excitement, of what might be in store for them. When they leave the establishment at the expiration of their nine days' retirement, their friends receive them at the door, after which they have to pass through crowds of sight-seers, who have come from the city to gaze at them.

In the neighborhood of the Tejar, the scene of the following romantic legend is laid: —

Many years after the conquest (the exact time, of course, is not stated), a Spaniard made love to a young Indian girl, who was proof against his seductive advances, but told him that if he should marry her, she would make him the richest man in the country. To convince her incredulous lover of the truth of her assertions, she cited him to await her the following night at a certain place in the neighborhood of the Tejar, and made him give her a solemn promise to do nothing but what she would command. The girl made her appearance at the appointed time, and the first thing she required, was that he should submit to be blindfolded. She then led him up the mountain and through several ravines, until they reached the mysterious end of their journey. When the bandage was taken from his eyes, the Spaniard found himself in a cave. "There, behold!" said the girl, who had lighted a torch, "this is the gold I promised thee!"

The Spaniard, amazed and enraptured, beheld an immense quantity of gold in vessels and in bars, — the treasures of Atahuallpa buried by the usurper Ruminagui, before he evacuated Quito.

"All this shall be thine," continued the girl, "if thou wilt marry me. But, silence and good faith!"

The greedy Spaniard attempted to seize some of the pieces that were near him, but the girl warned him off. "Not yet," she said; "if thou attemptest violence, or touchest any of the things around thee, thou leavest not this cave, but thy grave will be with these treasures!"

Cowed by the resolution of the girl, the Spaniard again submitted to be blindfolded, and was led away. Upon his return to Quito, he immediately informed the authorities of his adventure, and an order was issued for the arrest of the girl and all her family. But the eye of love and distrust had watched his steps. The Indians of those days were well aware that the torture and the rack awaited those of their race who should be suspected of knowing the secret of hidden treasures. When the officers of the government entered the humble dwelling of the Indian, the girl, with all her family, had fled, and with their disappearance died the last lingering hope of discovering the great treasures of Atahuallpa. *Relata refero!*

The tenacity with which the Indian can keep a secret, especially when it affects his race, is indeed remarkable. Neither the rack nor fear of death can wring a confession from his sealed lips. Superstitious as he is, he will even be proof against the threats and remonstrances of his confessor. When he is determined not to reveal a secret, he will die protesting his ignorance to the very last. When Tupac Amaru, the great martyr of the Indian race, prepared his rebellion against the Peruvian authorities in 1780, he sent emissaries to all the neighboring provinces. His agents were at work in what now constitutes Ecuador, Peru, and Bolivia. On a given day there was to be a general rising of the Indians throughout the viceroyalty of Peru. But many of his emissaries could neither read nor write, nor had the people he intended to influence any idea of dates. Each of the principal conspirators, therefore, received a bundle of small sticks, of which one was to be taken out and burned every day. When the last stick was burned, the great day had arrived, and the Indians rose in a mass from the southern confines of Peru to the northern frontiers of Tuquerres and Pasto. None had betrayed the secret. Of so many thousand co-conspirators, not one had broken faith. Like a thunderbolt from a cloudless sky, the formidable avalanche of a powerful sublevation broke upon the unsuspecting Spaniards.[1]

But let us return to the Tejar, which is one of the

[1] Ulloa gives an interesting and correct account of the manner in which the Indians go through confession in church: —

"On their coming to the confessor, which is always at his summons, he is obliged to instruct them in what they are going about, and with them repeat the *Confiteor* from one end to the other, for if he stops, the Indian also remains silent. Having gone through this, it is not enough for the priest to ask him whether he has committed this or that fault; but if he be one of the common sort, he must affirm that he has committed it, otherwise the Indian would deny every thing. The priest further is obliged to tell him that he well knows he has committed the sin, and he has proofs of it. Then the Indian, being thus pressed, answers with great astonishment, that it is so; and, imagining the priest really endued with some supernatural knowledge, adds circumstances which had not been asked him. It is not only difficult to bring them to declare their faults, but even to keep them from denying them, though publicly committed, and equally so to prevail on them to determine the number; this being only to be obtained by *finesse;* and then little stress is to be laid on what they say."

two principal burying-places. The other is the *Panteon de San Diego*, most beautifully and picturesquely situated on one of the slopes of Pichincha, at a short distance from the city. Burials do not take place in daytime, but at night. The corpse is accompanied by torch-bearers. The number of torches, however, is now by law limited to twelve. The reason of this limitation was the fearful expense which fashionable burials used to cause. One wealthy family could not bury its dead in a less stylish or pompous manner than other wealthy families, and hence it was customary to employ all the different *hermandades* (burial brotherhoods) to carry tapers, chant *responsos*, and accompany the body to its resting-place. For these services the most exorbitant fees were exacted by the friars. I was assured that thousands were thus squandered on a fashionable funeral.

The Indians and other indigent people bury their children after a very curious fashion. They hire an angel's suit and other ornaments in a church or convent, trick up the dead body, place it on a chair in a sitting posture, and carry it about in procession before they take it to the grave-yard. Before interring the corpse, they take off the gaudy tinsel, which must be returned to its owners. As a general rule, only the poor people are buried in the ground, and without a mound or a cross to indicate their resting-place. The wealthier classes wall up their dead in semicircular niches, constructed for this purpose in brick terraces of several stories, with generally three or four rows of niches in one terrace. As the number of these niches is necessarily limited, the remains, unless an additional payment is made to the "hermandad," are taken out after the lapse of two years, and the bones are thrown into a deep cistern covered with a stone lid, while the coffins are burned. On the walls of the terraces black crosses are painted at short distances from each other, indicative of the sufferings of Christ on his journey to Calvary. Before these crosses the relatives of the dead, especially the women, kneel down and say their prayers on All Souls' Day, when the cemeteries are crowded with men, women, and children.

When the last sacraments are to be administered to a dying person of note, his friends and relatives, carrying lighted tapers, meet at the nearest church, from which they issue in procession, followed by monks chanting hymns. A boy ringing a bell leads the procession; another boy carries the box containing the sacred implements; he is followed by a priest who, sometimes supported by two assistants, carries the *majestad* (a crucifix with the Eucharist). He walks under a baldachin carried by Indians or negroes. The baldachin is sometimes very shabby, and carried by one man, in which case it resembles a big umbrella; but it is very rich and gorgeous, and carried by four men, when one of the high dignitaries of the church marches under it. When the *majestad* appears in the streets, the people kneel down, and generally remain on their knees as long as the procession is in sight.

Funeral processions, however, are not so pompous and attractive as the pageantry of holiday processions. These latter, indeed, are the great sights to be seen at Quito. The greatest extravagance is displayed on such occasions. Wooden or wax figures of the Virgin, the saints, and martyrs, some of which are of frightful ugliness, are carried on heavy platforms, resting on the shoulders of Indians. The windows and balconies before which the procession passes, are hung with costly shawls and drapery, and the ladies who adorn them throw rose leaves on the procession below. Two or three men, with baskets full of rose leaves and flowers, often head the procession, and strew the road before it. Respectable ladies, dressed in black, and carrying tapers, march along with the rabble, which brings up the rear, or crowds around them praying or chanting. Musicians are always engaged for the occasion. At great festivals the procession is enlivened by the military bands, and a turn-out of the military. Banners and flags are displayed, and the eye is dazzled by the immense value of the jewelry which covers the images of the Virgin. Praying and chanting, the procession moves on, while the bells are tolling and guns are firing — praying and chanting, perhaps, the same words and the same tunes with which the victims of the Spanish Inquisition were led out to the terrible wood-pile which was to consume them.

Toward the end of Lent, and especially during *Semana Santa* (Holy Week), the whole female population of Quito is in motion. Swarms of women, with their shawls thrown over their heads, and followed by little girls carrying the carpets on which their mistresses kneel in the benchless churches, are seen going to and from the churches three times a day, if not oftener. There is a sermon at four or five o'clock in the morning, a sermon at two in the afternoon, and another at five or six in the evening. The church of the Jesuits, *La Compañia*, usually draws the largest crowds. It is astonishing to witness the activity which the Jesuits display. At three and four o'clock in the morning they are in the confessional; later in the day they preach sermons or say masses; still later they teach at their college, or receive visitors; and so on until late in the evening.

On Holy Thursday night all the churches in Quito are illuminated. Thousands of candles are lighted around the principal altars. The church and side chapels of St. Francisco blaze in an ocean of light. The convent churches on that occasion vie with each other in luxury and splendor. Dense throngs of humanity, especially women, flock from one church to another to gaze and to pray. According to a pretty general superstition, seven churches must be visited in order to make these pious visits available on high. The women, as soon as they enter, kneel down and commence to rattle off their prayers in a perfectly audible tone of voice, each murmuring away on her own account, and without heeding the devotions of her neighbor. A low humming and buzzing noise, produced by this confused chorus of females, greets you on your entrance, but nothing is intelligible except an occasional "*Santa Maria*," which is pronounced with particular emphasis. — Santa Maria here, Santa Maria there, Santa Maria on all sides, as you squeeze your way through the kneeling multitudes. On these occasions I saw exhibitions of strange devotion. I saw men who knelt with their arms stretched out, as if to receive the Holy Ghost. They remained in this difficult posture until they had murmured off the requisite number of *Paternosters* and *Ave Marias*.

On Good Friday, at twelve o'clock, a sermon of three hours is preached in all the churches, to represent *la agonia de tres horas* (the three hours' agony of the Saviour). It is again attended chiefly by women. In the evening a *descendimiento* is represented in at least one of the principal churches. It consists of a sermon illustrated by a regular puppet-show. I saw one in the Church of San Francisco in 1862, and another at Santa Clara in 1863. On both occasions the same monk, a Franciscan, preached literally the same sermon. On the platform of the altar a wooden image of Christ hung on the cross between the two thieves. Before the cross knelt the Virgin and Mary Magdalen; in the foreground was a painted chest or box with a movable lid, representing the tomb. The monk began by delivering a glowing description *de las siete dolores de la Virgin* (of the seven griefs of the Virgin). He compared the grief of Mary to the grief felt by Abraham when commanded by the Lord to sacrifice his son Isaac. An angel interposed between the victim and the father's knife; but who interposed between the despair of Mary and her bleeding son? The Mother of God anxiously waited for a miracle by which her son might be saved; but no such miracle was wrought. Great, the monk continued, was the grief of Jacob when he was shown the bloody garment of his son Joseph; but greater was the grief of the Virgin, because Jacob had other sons left, while Mary had but one. In this strain he went on, continually quoting the fathers in bad Latin, which the multitude that eagerly hung on his lips was fortunately unable to appreciate. At last the show began. He told the *santos barones* (holy men), who were in attendance, to mount the ladder and take down the holy corpse. This was the signal for such a collective wailing and sobbing of women and children as I never had heard before. They all raised their voices at once, and shrieked and sobbed in a most bewildering manner, while the *santos barones*, a few lay brothers, were taking down the wooden figure, which sunk its arms and hung its head, as if it were a real corpse. The preacher then raised his voice to its highest possible pitch, to be heard above the frantic sobs and groans of the women. He told the actors to turn the corpse around, so as to show its bleeding back. The *santos barones* obeyed, and exhibited the back of Christ, lacerated by the lashes of the Romans. This sight increased the grief of the women and children, whose wailing almost drowned the voice of the preacher. At the same time, the figures which represented the Virgin and Mary Magdalen, which were stuck on pivots and managed from under the stage, commenced to move. Mary Magdalen clasped her hands, while the Virgin was wiping her eyes with a handkerchief. But when the box representing the tomb was opened, and the corpse deposited in it, the two puppets rushed to the grave and fell down before it, while the voice of the preacher was heard roaring above the sobs and shrieks of the audience. The church was so crowded that it was impossible for me to move backward or forward. While the monk told his hearers that for them and for their sins all this had come to pass, somebody abstracted my handkerchief from my pocket, and a simultaneous attempt was made on my watch, which, however, I succeeded in defending.

As soon as the multitude rushed from the church, it became apparent what little moral effect the farce had produced. Men and women elbowed each other with reckless violence; vile curses resounded on the very threshold of the temple; little children were trodden down and trampled upon; old women were pushed from the steps in front of the church; and numberless pockets were picked.

The people of Quito, who have nothing to do, and

nothing to see, look upon the church as on a theatre or a concert room. It is not only their place of religious worship, but the place where they spend most of their leisure time. It furnishes them with amusement and excitement, and breaks the monotony of their daily life. Is it strange, then, that they delight in a religion which gives them images and mimical representations?

Idolatry has been the great offshoot of Spanish Catholicism, and is carried on to a disgusting extent in the countries colonized by Spain. In the Church of San Augustine, at Quito, the image of the Señor de la Porteria is kept and reverently worshiped. To give a literal translation of the "Señor de la Porteria," I would have to say, "the Lord who is carried about." It is a life-sized image of Christ, seated on a chair, in which he is carried about, not only in Quito, but all over the country. In 1863 the Augustine friars were in need of money to repair the cupola of their church, which had been sadly damaged by the earthquake of 1859. The interior being poor, and the faithful heavily taxed by many other ecclesiastical exigencies, the "Señor de la Porteria" was sent to the coast, and re turned after having reaped a golden harvest in the districts of Guayaquil, Bodegas, and Manabi. The cupola was consequently repaired.

On Christmas Eve, at twelve o'clock at night, a mass is chanted in the principal churches, which is called *misa de gallos* (cock-mass), and attended by immense multitudes, especially, however, by young girls and their lovers, whom neither the inclemency of the weather nor the unseasonable hour could induce to forego the excitement of such a mass.

To dwell on the morality of the clergy, especially, however, of the monks, would be a work of supererogation. It is a repetition of the story of the Middle Ages, as the same causes will always produce the same effects. The monks of Quito are ignorant in the extreme. Their knowledge of the Latin, which they are required to study, is exceedingly poor. History or science is unknown to them. Their libraries are in a sad state of desolation. The books are covered with thick layers of dust and cobwebs, or thrown together promiscuously in heaps. They are never consulted by those for whose benefit they were originally collected. The chief occupation of the monks is to visit their friends or relatives; to keep women in the outskirts of the city; to sing, drink, and dance. In 1863 a friar was arrested by the police at one or two o'clock in the morning, for having been concerned in a row in one of the most disreputable streets of the city. He was in plain citizen's dress to disguise his ecclesiastical state. After having passed the remainder of the night in prison, he was taken before the President, who at that time was quarreling with Congress about certain questions of monastic reform. The President immediately sent the poor fellow, dressed as he was, to the senate chamber, as a living illustration of the necessity of conferring additional power on the ecclesiastical tribunals — a proposition which Congress strenuously opposed. The Senate, not knowing what to do with the living document, referred him to the committee on ecclesiastical affairs, who discharged him.

It is a matter of common occurrence to see monks in disguise go "on a spree," and revel for several nights in succession. They frequently select the disguise of a soldier, and often are known to commit violent excesses. I could relate numerous instances to show the vices and immorality of the monks of Quito;

but the subject is only disgusting, and does not present any new feature which could make it interesting.

The curates, especially those in the country, are but little better than the monks. President Garcia Moreno, who, in the beginning of his administration, seriously endeavored to reform the clergy, refused, in 1861, to sanction several archiepiscopal appointments of new curates. He represented to the archbishop that the individuals whom he had selected were notorious gamblers and libertines. The archbishop, however, replied, that all men had their foibles, and that it would be wrong to be too harsh toward an erring brother.

Besides the Cathedral and parish churches, there are the following convents: San Domingo, with a branch institution, or *Recoleta;* San Francisco, with the *Recoleta* of San Diego; San Camilo; San Augustin, with the *Recoleta* of San Juan; and the Convent of the Jesuits.

There are six nunneries, namely: Concepcion, Santa Clara, Carmen-Alto, Carmen-Bajo, Santa Catalina, and the Congregation of the Hearts of Jesus and Mary. The total number of priests, monks, and nuns at Quito exceeds four hundred, which does not include the novices, servants, and familiars.

The convents subsist on the revenues which they derive from their estates; the bishops and chapters of cathedrals are supported by the *diezmos*, or tithes, an unbearable burden resting on the agriculture of the country; while the curates are only entitled to fees and *primicias*, or sevenths.

The amount of the fees which must be paid to the church and curates for solemnizing marriages and performing other religious ceremonies, depends on the color or race of the applicants. For this purpose, the faithful are divided into three classes, as follows: —

First class: the descendants of Spaniards, or white men.

Second class: the Montañeses, Mestizos, or Cholos.

Third class: Indians and Negroes.

For solemnizing marriages the first class pays ten dollars, the second class six dollars, and the third class three dollars. For burials, the first class twenty dollars, the second six dollars, and the third three dollars. *Derechos de acompañamento*, or fees for accompanying the body, are, for persons of the first class, four dollars; of the second class, two dollars; and of the third class, one dollar. In addition to this, there must be *responsos*, or prayers, which are sung over the body, recommending the soul to God. They consist of a Paternoster and an *oracion* (supplication), and cost one real each. If they are not chanted, but simply spoken, four of them are given for one medio (one half of a real). They are either said in the church or at the cemetery. Those who pay twenty dollars get four *responsos*, one *misa cantada* (mass chanted), one *vigilia*, and generally receive their *acompañamento* gratis. Persons of the second and third classes must pay extra for all these services.

These are the fees to which the curate is entitled; but there are additional fees which must be paid to the Church on such occasions. They are called *fabrica de iglesia*, and are applied to the payment of the organist and the singers, for sweeping the building, and for buying wax, wine, and other properties. They are as follows: for burials of the first class, one dollar and fifty cents; of the second class, one dollar; of the third class, four reals. For marriages of the first and second classes, one dollar; of the third class, four reals. For burying children under ten years of age the charges are less. The curate takes for burying children of the first class six dollars; of the second, three dollars; of the third, one dollar. To the Church must be paid, for children of the first class one dollar; of the second class, four reals; and of the third class, two reals. These fees are independent of the charge for the burying place itself, which, in the city of Quito, and to persons of the first class, is an expensive item. Macaulay praises the Catholic Church of the Middle Ages for being adverse to the distinctions of caste. "She compelled the hereditary master to kneel before the spiritual tribunal of the hereditary bondman; and so successfully had she used her formidable machinery, that, before the Reformation came, she had enfranchised almost all the bondsmen of the kingdom except her own, who, to do her justice, seem to have been very tenderly treated." But the Church of Ecuador is not entitled to similar praises. It artificially keeps up and perpetuates, by disgracing classifications and divisions, those distinctions of caste which the progress of time and civilization has done so much to modify and obliterate. It teaches the descendant of the conqueror to shrink contemptuously from the thought of being "buried like an Indian"; and it continually reminds those who once were the lords of the land, that even in death they are inferior to those who have subjected and wronged them.[1]

[1] "On Monday (following Palm Sunday), the Indian procession was to take place; for, though all the inhabitants of the Republic of Ecuador profess alike the Catholic religion, the old Spaniards will by no means allow themselves to be placed on the same footing with the Indians, and, accordingly, the latter have a procession to themselves." — Ida Pfeiffer, *A Lady's Second Voyage Round the World*, vol. ii., p. 217.

Curates receive no salaries. Their income consists of the fees just referred to, and fees for masses, of *fiestas*, and of *primicias*. In every parish the curate has a right to four compulsory feasts (*fiestas forzosas*) per year, which must be paid for by those of his parishioners whom he designates for the purpose. It is his duty to designate others every year. His fee is twelve dollars for every feast. The *fiesta* consists of a chanted mass, sermon, procession, and evening service. One of them is celebrated on the day of the patron saint of the parish or village; another on the day of the patroness; the third on Corpus Christi; and the fourth on All Souls' Day. Sometimes the persons designated by the curate to give the *fiesta* (these persons are called *priostes*), or in other words to pay the twelve dollars, would rather be excused; but the curate may, in case of a refusal, procure their imprisonment until the fee is paid. The *primicias* consist of the seventh part of the fruits of the field. It is only the poor, however, who really give the seventh part. Those whose harvest amounts to less than seven *fanegas* give one seventh. Those who have raised more than seven *fanegas* give only one *fanega*. In addition to this, landowners must pay the regular tithe (*diezmo*), which formerly yielded such enormous revenues to the bishops (the Bishop of Guayaquil alone is said to have made $40,000 a year), that in 1863 Congress ordered the *diezmo* to be collected by the civil authorities, and fixed salaries to be paid to the bishops and canons, the surplus to be paid into the national treasury.

# CHAPTER X.

Social Life in the Ecuadorian Capital. — The Ladies. — High Opinion of France. — The Populace believes every Foreigner to be a Frenchman. — Female Morality. — The General Prejudice unfounded. — Female Politicians and Conspirators. — Educational. — Literary Dependence of Spain on France. — Want of Newspapers. — Sisters of the "Heart of Jesus." — Music. — The Diplomatic Corps. — Foreigners. — *Exequias.* — *Duelos.* — *Luto.* — Sunday Visits. — Salutations and Etiquette. — Christmas Calls. — *Dar las Pascuas.* — *Cumpleaños.* — Bull-baitings, or *Toros.* — Description of the *Plaza Mayor.* — Cock-fights. — *La Gallera.* — Holidays. — *Inocentes.* — Masquerades between Christmas and New Year. — Fancy-Dress Processions. — Carnival. — Queer Observance. — Chicha, the Indian National Beverage. — Indian Degradation, Drunkenness, and Improvidence.

LET us now venture a description of social life in the Ecuadorian capital, beginning with the ladies. There is no lack of beautiful women, especially among the middle classes, though female faces very generally lack that expression which intellectuality alone can give. The appearance of the women is healthy, their faces wear a ruddy aspect, and their feet are exceedingly small and well-shaped; but their features are frequently coarse, and do not betoken refinement. The ladies generally wear their hair braided in two long tresses, dangling down their backs. Their hair is exceedingly thick and coarse; its universal color is black: fair, auburn, or red hair is a great rarity. On that account, red hair is considered a beauty, and I have seen paintings with red-haired madonnas and angels. Sometimes when the ladies return from the baths in the River Machangara, they wear their hair all loose and disheveled, falling over their necks and shoulders. Bonnets are not in use. Some of the ladies of the higher classes occasionally wear them on visits of state, especially to foreign ladies; but this is very seldom. Months and years may pass before you will see a lady with a bonnet; and then she runs the risk of being stared at, if not hooted at in the streets, as a *Francesa* (Frenchwoman); for, in the opinion of the rabble, and many others socially above the rabble, every foreigner is a Frenchman. The common people have no idea that there are other countries in the world than France, Spain, New Granada, Chili, and Peru. Besides, it is easier to them to say *Frances*, than to say *estrangero*. The higher classes are accustomed to look upon Paris as the exclusive seat of civilization. It is the Mecca, the Alpha and Omega of their travelling ambition. If their children are to be educated abroad, it must be in France. If they have seen Paris, they believe, or affect to believe, that they have seen every thing that is worth seeing on this side of the grave.

The ladies go out bareheaded, if they happen to be combed; but generally, they wear the *pañuelon*, which I have already described, and with which they cover the head, and part of the face and shoulders. It gives them rather a nun-like appearance, and although sometimes very rich and gaudy, does not set them off to advantage.

Their taste in dressing is highly primitive. They are fond of gay colors, and gorgeous and ostentatious display. When they are compelled to show themselves in society, they love to wear dresses as at home we should see them only on the stage. For a walk across the street, to the bath, or to church, they will not doff their *negligé*, but wrap themselves up in the *pañuelon*, with which, when they wish to remain unknown, they can hide their faces completely, leaving but one eye uncovered. At home the *pañuelon* is more than ever their inseparable companion. It saves them the trouble of combing and dressing their hair, and the vexation of having their bodice laced. Those who paint their faces — and a great many do it — (*tout comme chez nous*) — have an unfortunate habit of overdoing it. Meeting them in the streets of New York, Boston, or Philadelphia, we would mistake them for females of easy virtue, — an impression to which their gaudy dresses would greatly contribute. Notwithstanding this unnatural custom, we would not be entitled to draw inferences disparaging to their morality. A great many things have been said about the conduct of South American women, which I have found to be either grossly exaggerated, or entirely false. I cannot say whether they deserve their reputation in Lima; in Quito and Guayaquil they certainly do not. I am convinced that there is less immorality in Quito than in any other capital. I do not believe that the women are very sensual or passionate. They seem to be incapable both of great vices and of great virtues. Their hearts are like the atmosphere they live in, of a mean temperature. It will be remembered that Quito is nearer the regions of perpetual snow than those of tropical heat. The violent changes of winter and summer, and their exciting influence on the human system, are unknown there. The temperature is nearly the same all the year round. The disposition of the women, whether the result of the climate or not, seems to be lazy and indolent. They pass the day cowering on their window-seats (*estrados*), gossiping. They generally sit with their legs crossed like Turks. In some of their private rooms there are low benches, like tailors' benches, for them to squat on. In this position they seem to be more at ease than on chairs or sofas. Even in church, when they get tired of kneeling, they will drop down and sit on their legs.

The church is their daily amusement. In political affairs they take a very lively, active, and even passionate interest; but as Ecuadorian politics mainly consist of personalities in which but very seldom an important principle is involved, their political excitements may be considered as a part of their daily gossiping and intriguing.

The chief aspiration of a young lady in Quito, the chief object of her intrigues and anxieties, is to find a husband as soon as possible. That object attained, she resigns herself to indifference. The cares of the household trouble her but little. Brooms but very seldom wend their way through the neglected rooms of houses in the interior. She resigns herself to fleas as well as to social apathy. She no longer cares to appear in society, nor is she very ambitious to receive company at her own house, as she is scarcely ever dressed or combed, and shuns the trouble of passing through those operations unnecessarily. She is generally very careful of her conduct, because she knows the tongues of her friends and acquaintances, who would interpret the most innocent step in the most uncharitable manner.

When the Señoras have put themselves in a fit state for the reception of visitors, or when they have overcome their first timidity and receive a new acquaintance, although they may not be combed or dressed, they are generally very kind and very amiable. Their manners are excellent. Their natural dignity, gracefulness, and politeness, their entire self-possession, their elegant but unaffected bearing, and the choiceness of their language, would enable them to make a creditable appearance in any foreign drawing-room. It would also be unjust to say that the women of Quito are without natural talents. On the contrary, they possess a great deal of common sense, quickness of perception, and ready wit. They are prompt at repartee, and full of pleasant good humor. Their natural talents are very great, but their education is sadly neglected. They are like the soil of their native country — fertile but uncultivated. They have learned to read, but they hardly ever read any thing but their prayer-books. Those who aspire to a slight literary knowledge, have read such French novels as the Church has not prohibited. In this they follow the example of the mother-country, which, for its scanty literary food, must depend on its French neighbors. What little there is known in Spain of English and German literature, is only known through French translations. Even her printing and publishing Spain must do in France. Most of the Spanish books which have come to my hands were printed in Paris or Besançon. Fernan Caballero, the celebrated modern Spanish novelist, could not find a bookseller in all Castile to venture on the expensive enterprise of publishing her works It had, at last, to be done at the expense of the Queen. And this in the face of the many sensation articles we are, of late, accustomed to see in reviews and newspapers on the "revival of Spain."

But to return to our subject. The ladies of Quito can hardly be blamed for their ignorance. It is the monkish system which keeps them down, because it does not deem it convenient to awaken a taste in them for intellectual enjoyments. Their husbands, too, rather discourage any incipient movement of their wives in the direction of self-instruction. They would not like them to know more than they do themselves. The average Quitonian does not read nor desire to read himself; why should he encourage his wife to become his intellectual superior? The game of *tresillo* or *rocambur*, an insipid chat with his friends on the plaza, or at some street corner, if not in a grog-shop, and above all, the training of fine horses, are subjects of infinitely greater importance to him than such trifles as science or literature. Of course I speak of the average Quitonians, which does not preclude the existence of many highly honorable exceptions, who sincerely deplore the intellectual lethargy of their countrymen, and especially of the rising generation. In 1862, a number of French or Alsatian nuns were imported by the government to take charge of the education of young ladies; but, being ignorant and bigoted themselves, these "Sisters of the Heart of Jesus" will not work important educational reforms.

In spite of the difficulty of transportation, there are about one hundred and twenty pianos in Quito, very indifferently tuned; but there are only very few ladies who play well. The guitar and the harp are great favorites, especially with the middle and lower classes; but a woman who plays either of these instruments, scarcely ever knows a note. Her stock of music is therefore very easily exhausted, whenever she is called upon for songs. Moreover, they sing chiefly through the nose, especially when they sing one of their national tunes (*tonos*). In jewelry, great luxury is displayed. There are ladies at Quito who have invested quite a fortune in diamonds, pearls, emeralds, bracelets, necklaces, etc.

In almost every Spanish country the spirit of provincialism reigns supreme. So it does in Ecuador, much more, however, on the coast than in the interior. The inhabitants of the former most cordially hate and despise the *Serranos*, as the inhabitants of the interior are called, from *Sierra* (mountainous country). The Guayaquil ladies are full of these provincial prejudices. The *Serranos* are charged with falseness and treachery, stinginess and want of cleanliness. At Guayaquil they are the butt of popular witticisms. They do not, however, retaliate in kind. On the contrary, when Guayaquilians visit the interior, they are generally treated with great kindness and attention. Other provincial jealousies exist between different parts of the interior. The inhabitants of Cuenca, for instance, who are nicknamed *Morlacos*, are very freely ridiculed at Quito.

There is no foreign society in Quito with the exception of the foreign diplomatic representatives. There are almost always French, English, and Spanish Charges d'Affaires, and a Minister Resident of the United States. New Granada, too, is generally represented; Peru and Chili occasionally. Other foreign residents there are but few. Their number in my time hardly ever averaged a dozen. It is true there are always a great many New Granadians in Ecuador who profit by the inferior education and enterprise of the Ecuadorians, but they can hardly be called foreigners. The necessity of foreign immigration is universally admitted, and the wish for a large influx of industrious and enterprising foreigners generally expressed. But what the feelings of the natives would be if such an influx should really take place, I shall not venture to predict.[1]

[1] I am greatly inclined to coincide with the following observation of

There is but very little social life in Quito. In former times, the place is said to have been more lively and attractive; but the civil war of 1860, and the bitter animosities it produced, are said to have broken up society. Besides, a certain vanity and love of ostentation prevent the upper ten from inaugurating social pleasures. They would not give a party, a dinner, or a ball, if they were not sure to outshine every thing that had ever been done by others. As,

Colonel Hall, in the pamphlet to which I have already referred: "One of the facts," he says, "which most agreeably presents itself to the mind of the European traveller in almost every part of Colombia, is the opinion which seems universally felt, and is universally avowed, of the necessity of a larger influx of foreign settlers. Everywhere he hears an outcry for foreigners; everywhere lamentations over the ignorance and indolence of the present inhabitants. All this is pretty much as it seems: the necessity of a foreign population, that is, of an increase of population, which can only be obtained from foreign countries, is obvious to the dullest capacity; nor is the fact of the inability of the present inhabitants to profit by the immense advantages of their own soil, less irresistibly clear. Foreigners have won its independence; foreigners have created its commerce; its marine has been furnished, armed, manned, and commanded by foreigners; its soldiers have been disciplined, and are still armed, clothed, and in a great measure fed, by foreign capital; yet all this mass of opinion and circumstance by no means proves that foreign settlers would meet with that active and benevolent assistance from the inhabitants, which gratitude, as well as interest, would dictate, and which their own opinions seem to promise. It is uncertain how far they might view with philosophic good-will, a foreigner taking advantage of circumstances which, though their indolence had neglected, their cupidity might prompt them to lament. Let us suppose a foreigner to discover a mine or a lucrative branch of commerce, or by some invention or improvement to create a new, and consequently to dry up an old, channel of profit, would the real and imaginary sufferers in this case — those who had missed the discovery or were sharers in the loss — be likely to regard the intruder with particular favor or satisfaction?" — *Colombia, its Present State, in Respect of Climate, Soil, Productions, Population, Government, Commerce, etc., etc., and Inducements to Emigration with Itineraries.* By Colonel Francis Hall, Philadelphia, 1825.

I may add here, that although the natives admit the superiority of foreigners in mechanic arts and spirit of enterprise, there lingers, nevertheless, a hidden conviction in their minds, that foreigners are inferior to them in manners, social refinement, and intelligence. As far as manners are concerned, they may perhaps be right.

however, their wealth consists chiefly in real property (*haciendas*), and not in ready money, they find it too expensive to gratify this vanity.

One of the principal features of social life in Quito, is the unpleasant recurrence of invitations to funeral honors. Burials, as I have already said, take place in the night time. But a few days after a fashionable death, printed invitations are sent, not only to the acquaintances and friends, but to all persons of note, to attend *las exequias*, a grand requiem chanted, generally in the Church of San Francisco, for the soul of the deceased. Two long rows of seats facing each other, and leading from the door to the altar, are prepared for the reception of the invited guests. For two or three mortal hours the ears of these are torn by the music of a very bad organ, and the worse chant and cracked voices of a choir of hoarse and ugly friars and their assistants. The Franciscans of Quito are proverbial for their ugliness. A mass, not commendable for its shortness, concludes the performance. Fortunately, however, it is not obligatory to be present all the time. Most of the condolers, with the exception of those more immediately interested in the deceased, remain in their seats for a short time only, and then retire to the great court-yard (*pateo*) of the convent, where they walk to and fro and chat with their friends in the long corridors, until it is time to return to the church, in order to be present at the exit, and to be seen by the family and friends, who, posting themselves at the door of the temple, let the invited guests pass by in procession, giving them solemn nods of recognition.

There is another form of *duelo* (manifestation of condolence), which, although gradually falling into disuse, is still practiced to some extent. On the death of a member of the family, the friends call at the house in the evening, or if his house is not suitable to the purpose, at the house of some other member of the family, and sit down in the parlor, where chairs ranged along the walls are prepared for their reception. There they sit, the men on one side, the women on the other, without saying a word, and without looking at each other, for a half hour or more. In silence they enter, in silence they remain seated in the dimly lighted room, and in silence, one by one, they drop off again. This dreary performance is repeated every night for about a week. The survivors remain in mourning one year, if the deceased was a parent, consort, brother, or sister, and six months for other relatives. During this time they cannot take part in any amusement; they cannot show themselves on public occasions ; nor can they allow pianos or guitars to be played at their houses. The *luto* must be rigidly observed. These austere customs greatly interfere with the most innocent pleasures of social life ; for, as in a small place like Quito, the principal families are almost always, in a more or less remote degree, related to one another, one half of society is continually in mourning.

Sunday is general visiting day ; that is to say, visits of etiquette are made on Sunday, between twelve and three o'clock. You will be called upon by gentlemen whom you do not know, and who do not bring any body to introduce them ; but their winning manners, courtesy, and cordiality soon set you at ease.

Married ladies who want to assure a respectable foreigner or new-comer of their hospitality, send him their cards shortly after his arrival. The cards of married women contain both their maiden and their husbands' names. They are not known, however, by their husbands' names. If, for instance, Mercedes Fulana marries Mr. Sutano, her friends, acquaintances, and the public in general, will continue to call her Mercedes Fulana, although her name is Mercedes Fulana de Sutano. You will never hear any body speak of Mrs. Sutano.

An Ecuadorian lady does not rise when you enter, nor does she rise when you depart. It is considered good breeding in Spanish-America for a lady to remain as motionless as possible. She will be seated on a sofa, and you sit down on a chair opposite. The conversation begins and ends with the customary quantity of compliments, or offers of services, protestations of friendship, etc.

Calls must be made at Christmas and Easter. This is called *dar las pascuas*, and is obligatory on friends and relatives. You must also visit your friends on the days of their patron saints (*cumpleaños*) ; but in most of the houses you find a table with paper and ink on the staircase, so that you may write down your name, or leave your card.

Public amusements there are almost none, except at certain times of the year. There are no theatres, no concerts, no lectures, or public meetings. There are, however, on certain occasions, other amusements which, as they are characteristic of the country, and most of them unknown among us, I shall endeavor to describe.

The first and most popular of all is bull-baiting. It is called *toros*. Between Christmas and New Year; on the 10th of August, which is the anniversary of Ecuadorian independence; at the inauguration of a new President, and on many other solemn or festive occasions, this amusement is indulged in by all classes of the population. The performances generally commence at three o'clock in the afternoon and last until dark. They are not confined to an exclusive set of performers, but every body is allowed, and even desired, to take an active part. One of the public squares, or *plazas*, is the scene of action. The *Plaza Mayor* of Quito is decidedly the handsomest part of the town. It will compare favorably with any other South American plaza. It is seamed by handsome buildings, and has a fountain in the centre. The west side is occupied by the Government Palace, a tolerably respectable structure. It contains the offices of the President and the Ministers; the office of the Governor of the Province, the Supreme and Superior Courts, and the Post-office. The rear of the northwestern part of the building was destroyed by the earthquake of March, 1859, and is now in ruins, which, however, cannot be noticed from the plaza. The south side of the plaza is wholly occupied by the Cathedral, with a very handsome terrace before it, which, in the afternoon, is generally crowded by persons in search of fresh air and exercise. Opposite the Cathedral are the Archbishop's Palace and two or three private mansions, which are built in the same style, and seem to belong to it. On the east side stand the House of the Municipality, and a few of the most elegant private residences of Quito, one of which, in the middle of the block, has two upper stories. All the buildings on the plaza are most symmetrically arranged. The structures on the east and north sides rest on rows of columns, and afford a covered passage or arcade, which is called the *portal.* In these passages there are not only a great many stores, but also the stands of the *cajoneras,*—women who sell notions, such as buttons, ribbons, scissors, soap, matches, pencils, slates, catechisms, needles, pins, knives and forks, hatchets, combs and brushes, etc. They unpack their goods early in the morning, and at about six o'clock in the evening they pack them up again and retire for the night. Between their stands are the stools of women who make and sell lace.

In the windows and on the balconies of the public palaces and private residences of the plaza, the *elite* or *haute volée* of Quito used to assemble on the great occasion of a bull-baiting. Ladies in their richest and gaudiest apparel, and covered all over with dazzling jewelry, adorned three sides of the square, manifesting the liveliest interest in the barbarous proceedings. The terrace before the Cathedral and the Government Palace, the *portales* on the east and north sides, as well as the fountain in the centre of the square, and even the roof of the Cathedral, were densely crowded by the common people, — men, women, and children, whites, Indians, cholos, zambos, mulattoes, and negroes. It was a most picturesque sight. The men in jackets, ponchos, and hats of every style and color; the women in their *macanas*, *rebozos*, and shawls, of every possible variety; the many different complexions of the motley crowd, the swaying to and fro, and the cheering and huzzaing of the populace; the luxury and splendor in the windows and on the balconies; the young *caballeros* dashing or prancing from one end of the plaza to the other on beautiful fiery steeds; the soldiers in their Sunday uniforms mixing with the crowd below; the boys whistling and the dogs barking at the approaching bull; flags streaming from roofs and windows; a brass band pouring forth exciting strains; rockets and fire-crackers exploding; and the bull wildly running up and down, with the rabble scampering and screaming before him; all this presented a grotesque and fascinating sight to the unaccustomed eye of the foreign traveller. But you must not suppose that —

> "In costly sheen and gaudy cloak array'd,
> But all afoot, the light-limbed matador
> Stands in the centre, eager to invade
> The lord of lowing herds."

Nor must you suppose that, —

> "Foiled, bleeding, and breathless, furious, to the last,
> Full in the centre stands the bull at bay,
> 'Mid wounds, and clinging darts, and lances brast,
> And foes disabled in the brutal 'fray."

The performances are of a widely different character. The outlets of the plaza are barricaded to prevent the escape of the maddened animals into any of the neighboring streets. In one of the latter a temporary inclosure is put up, in which the bulls are kept during the three days the festival generally lasts. As soon as it is time to commence, a bull is brought out, and the sport begins. Men and boys, the majority of them in a high state of intoxication, tease the bull by displaying ponchos, coats, hats, cloths, and rags before his eyes, poking wooden lances into his sides, throwing stones at him, and even pulling him by the tail. The spectators below accompany these experiments by whistling, yelling, and hissing, for the purpose of still more enraging and bewildering the animal. If the bull charges, every body runs away from him; the more skillful *toreros* will spring to one side, throwing the poncho or cloth with which they incited him, over his head. I have witnessed some very narrow escapes at such performances. If the animal stands still, his tormentors will approach him again. Sometimes they will put up scarecrows for him, and lustily rejoice when he knocks them down. The object of those who plume themselves on being good *toreadores* is to goad him to make desperate charges on them, and then earn the applause of the spectators by skillful dodging. I once saw a negro who performed wonderful feats of agility, and at last tired out the bull instead of getting tired himself. Generally, however, there is a want of good *toreros*. The rabble teases the bull, but runs as soon as he gives a threatening start. Nevertheless, serious accidents are not wanting. A fierce bull (*toro bravo*) will generally knock down or gore a few of the sportsmen who are too slow or too drunk to effect a timely escape. But this is a necessary part of the performance ; it makes the sport interesting and exciting to the multitude. A bull-day without several persons wounded or even killed, would be considered rather insipid. The more accidents on the preceding day, the larger will be the crowd on the next. One afternoon, I saw three fellows carried off insensible. One of them afterwards died. I have seen others who jumped up immediately after being knocked down, and waved their hats to show that their limbs and spirits were unbroken. Sometimes an obstinate bull is brought in, who absolutely refuses to gratify the public, or to get excited. He is at once laughed and hooted at by the crowd, and driven off to make room for another. For every bull that gets tired or flags, another is substituted. Sometimes a bull will be astute and wily. He will not move at first, and make the crowd believe that he is very tame, when, all on a sudden, he will make an unexpected and terrible charge. The general practice is to throw fire-crackers and rockets at the head or between the legs of the animal to increase its fury. Salutes, too, are fired at suitable intervals. I was told that in many cases, especially at the festivals in the country, utter recklessness and audacity are displayed by the *toreros*. They do not constitute a regular class like the professional bull-fighters of Spain, Mexico, or Peru. They are only amateurs; but they will jump sometimes, so I was told, on the bull's back, and maintain themselves on it, riding, while the animal dashes along with furious speed; or taking refuge on a table, they will jump over the bull's whole length while he makes an attempt to gore them. In the country, where fiercer bulls are kept than those used for the sports in the city, such feats are said to be common. I never saw them myself. I did, however, see feats performed by mounted *toreros*, which did great credit to their horsemanship.

Perhaps no act of President Moreno gave greater dissatisfaction than his making a park of the plaza, by sodding it and planting avenues of trees, for the purpose of putting an end to bull-baiting. He had to desist from the attempt to abolish this cherished sport; but as he had made the Plaza Mayor unfit for it, bull-baitings now take place on the plaza of San Francisco. Whenever apprehensions of a revolutionary outbreak are entertained, the government considers it good policy to give bull-baitings, in order to divert the people, and make it forget its insurrectionary whims. The philosophy of the old cry of "*Panem et Circenses*" is not yet obsolete.

Next to bull-baiting in popularity, especially with the gambling portion of the population (and that portion is very large, and not at all confined to the lower classes), are cock-fights. They take place every Sunday and Thursday, in the afternoons, in the spacious court of an old building opposite the Church of Santa

**Catalina.** This place is called *La Gallera*, from *gallo* (rooster). The admission fee which visitors are required to pay is half a real. It is collected by an agent of the municipality to which it belongs, and which has prescribed rules and regulations for the management of the sport. This small admission fee yields a monthly revenue to the city of over a hundred dollars. The municipality appoints a judge, who presides over the proceedings, maintains order, and in doubtful cases decides which party has been victorious. With him the stakes must be deposited, and he gets a percentage on the wagers. The cocks are set to fight either with their natural or with artificial spurs. The latter consist of sharp little steel blades (*navajas*), which are tied to the natural spurs of the poor fowls, and with which they cut each other up terribly. With these artificial spurs the fight is but very short. It hardly lasts a minute. Sometimes both the combatants remain dead, or mortally wounded, in the ring; then it becomes an important question which of the two gave out first. This, of course, it is for the judge to decide, from whose decision an appeal lies to the municipal tribunals. As soon as one of the cocks is down, the owner of the victor rushes in to take him away, and prevent him from being hurt by his wounded or dying enemy. Most of the spectators bet on the issue of the combats. Considerable sums of money are won or lost, and many a lazy loafer does nothing else but rear fighting-cocks, with which he supports his miserable existence. The noise and excitement during a combat is very great. It is heightened by an array of cocks tied to stakes in the rear of the spectators, and crowing incessantly. There are seats around the ring for the visitors. The judge has an elevated seat, from which he can overlook every thing, and to which he ascends with great dignity when the owners of the cocks and the betters are ready for the fray. Each owner generally holds his own rooster until the judge gives the sign with a bell. Sometimes they first poke the roosters against each other, to excite them to greater fury. Upon the sign of the judge they set them down and let them loose. What then follows I shall not describe. I do not know whom to pity more — the cocks, who rise to the level of heroes, or the men, who sink to the level of beasts.

The rules by which cock-fights must be governed, are prescribed by the municipality, and printed. The judge has a right to fine persons who disobey his orders or resist his authority, from one to twenty-five dollars, or to send them to prison for twenty-four hours. Bets are valid in law, if the stakes are deposited with the judge. His fees are two per cent. on the money passing through his hands.[1]

Let us now pass to another popular, and less barbarous amusement — the masquerades which take place between Christmas and New Year, which period is called *el tiempo de los inocentes*, literally, "the time of the innocents." During this time, in addition to masquerades, all those jokes are practiced, which among us are confined to the first of April. To "fool one," is called *hacerle una pegadura.* The *inocentes* begin with the masquerades of the children, who run about in the disguise of monkeys, with tails of formidable length, and perpetrating hideous noises. On the second or third day, the common people begin to haunt

[1] See *Tabla que rije en el Establecimiento de la Gallera en la Ciudad de Quito; May* 1, 1860; *signed, J. M. Cardenas, Chief of Police.*

the streets in different mummeries, chiefly, however, in the disguise of monkeys, or of old men and women with ridiculous hats or bonnets, flaxen wigs, and very ugly masks. They dance through the streets, screaming and cheering, and good-humoredly striking the people whom they meet, especially the Indians. Their rambles are continued day and night until the holidays are over. The masquerades of the higher classes are of a different character. They are generally carried on after the style of our surprise-parties. The programme is as follows: Several friends, generally the younger members of two or three families, agree upon a fancy-dress expedition for a certain night. Word is then sent to another family who is not of the party, that an expedition of masks will "wind up" (*rematar*) at their house that night. This, of course, is an intimation to the family to prepare for their reception. But before repairing to the final rendezvous, the party will call at the houses of all their other friends, acquaintances, and relations, to take them by surprise. Boisterous laughter, and a wild confusion of dissembled voices on the staircase, announce their arrival. They swarm into the parlor, laughing and chatting, saluting and asking unintelligible questions, all at the same time. They dance around their victim, bantering him to identify them, and enjoying his mistaken guesses. Some will pull him to one side and trumpet into his ears, while others will pull him to the other side, inviting him to a dance; until after a wild, hoydenish scene, they rush away as rapidly as they came, many a time making room for another party, which follows in their wake. It happens very often that four or five different parties will call at the same house during one evening. When they meet at the street door, in the hall, or on the stairs, the noise and laughter become deafening. But I never saw or heard of any impropriety, violence, or indecency, either in the streets or in the houses, except perhaps the diabolical noise with which they move along.

After having visited all their friends, they hasten to the place where they are expected for the rest of the night. There they "wind up." This "winding up" almost always lasts till daylight, and consists of an improvised ball. If there is no piano at the house, one or two musicians are generally brought along by the party. Sometimes a harp or a few guitars compose the orchestra, and the night is spent in dancing and revelry. The different calls which they made, and the fun enjoyed during the expedition, furnish them with an interesting subject of conversation and merriment for the many long and dull weeks and months that follow the holidays. The costumes paraded on such occasions are sometimes very elegant and well-devised; sometimes, of course, very silly and tasteless. Sometimes they will mimic well-known characters in a very ingenious manner. In 1863, one mask mimicked the Apostolic Delegate and his foreign accent, voice, and peculiar mode of speaking so well, that the police felt itself obliged to put a stop to it. I have also seen torchlight processions of masked parties, in splendid costumes, and preceded by bands of music, — a highly romantic spectacle, reminding us of the golden times of the Roman and Venetian Carnival.

On the nights when processions of masks are expected, the streets, and especially the *portales* of the plaza, are crowded with dense throngs of men, women, and children, anxious to see the sights. Chairs and tables will be carried under the *portales* for the women to sit down, and masked as well as unmasked passers-by will have to squeeze their way through the multitude. All this is very interesting, and presents a very lively and grotesque appearance; but there are considerations which make it disgusting to come into too close a contact with the populace of Quito. I was perfectly horrified one night when coming home from a stroll through the densely crowded *portales*, I discovered on my overcoat two of those detestable animals so abundant among the people of the interior. Let us drop the curtain on this last part of the picture, and pass to the regular Carnival, which, strange to say, is not the time of masquerades in Quito.

The manner in which Carnival is observed by the populace is as barbarous as bull-baiting. Groups of men and boys gather on the corners of the streets, or in the low shops and groggeries, and throw eggs, mud, and water at one another or at the passers-by. Servant girls in the windows and balconies enjoy the discharge of water-pots at the heads of persons below. The Indians and the rabble in general, besmear each other's faces with eggs, soot, paint, or mud, and drink until they are hardly able to maintain themselves on their legs. Their unwashed and ugly faces, with an additional layer of soot or paint, distorted by excitement and drunkenness, present a hideous appearance. The Indians of Quito and the neighborhood are distinguished by their ugliness, to which they ought not to contribute by artificial means. This observance of Carnival is carried on for almost a week, the last days being, of course, the worst. The streets are everywhere covered with egg-shells and made slippery with their contents. Even respectable ladies in the balconies, seized by the general excitement, pelt their friends with egg-shells filled with corn meal or flour, and other playful missiles. The Carnival now is not so offensive as it was in former times. I was informed by old residents that in former years persons were seized by the mob, (headed but too frequently by young men of the best families,) and ducked in the sewers, or forcibly painted and besmeared in a most shocking manner. Serious frays and fights used to be the consequence of these abominable practices, and the police was at last compelled to check them. Still, what has remained of them is vexatious enough, although I never heard of excesses. As the populace does not know to fight at fisticuffs, knock-downs scarcely ever take place; knives are drawn but very seldom; and murders or the inflicting of wounds belong to the rarest occurrences. I cannot recollect more than one case of murder, and but two cases of manslaughter committed in the city of Quito during the time I resided there. Even assaults and batteries are very rare. Drunkenness, petit larceny, and vagrancy are the most common offenses. I cannot pass over the chapter of drunkenness without alluding to the beverages in use among the masses. They are rum and *chicha*. The *aguardiente del pais* is distilled from the sugar-cane, and has, to me at least, a very repugnant taste. From it, by the addition of aniseseed, another kind of liquor is prepared, which is much in vogue; it is called *anisada*. But the Indian's national beverage is *chicha*. It was the beverage of the natives when the Spaniards took possession of the country; and although most of their ancient traditions were lost in the course of three hundred years, *chicha* has maintained itself to this day. It is brewed from indian corn, in large copper kettles, and accessible to the poorest on account of its great cheapness. Its color is a dirty yellow, and, the dregs being continually stirred up in the kettle, it has no clearness or transparency. Its taste is slightly acid, and not altogether unpleasant. The better families sometimes partake of it, sweetened with sugar or sirup, and mixed with other ingredients. It is brewed in a great many Indian habitations, in cities as well as in the country. Considering the extreme filthiness of its manufacturers, and of the localities in which it is made, it will not be very palatable to a foreign taste. Those who make it, and their friends or relatives, together with their children, often sit around the kettle, like witches around a caldron, uncombed, half-naked, and unwashed, on the floorless ground of their dark, smoke-blackened, windowless, filthy rooms, which pigs, dogs, and chickens share with their human masters. There they sit, men and women, and sot, and dote upon one another, and grin and simper, or sleep in each others arms or laps, or dance, and sing, and revel, until they sink to the dirty ground, overcome and exhausted, not to awake till the next morning, when they rise to repeat the scenes of the previous day. As long as there is *chicha* in the kettle, or a little money in their pockets to buy it somewhere else, this revelry will be carried on. This is the manner in which the Ecuadorian Indian has been civilized by his Spanish conquerors.

The police never take cognizance of cases of drunkenness, either because they are not considered dangerous to the public peace, or because they are of hourly occurrence. The white portion of the community never make any serious efforts to raise the Indian from his abject condition. On the contrary, the general tendency among his superiors is to oppress and degrade him still more. Labor being considered disreputable by the white gentleman, what would become of the country if the Indians were to be enlightened and educated, and should take it into their heads occasionally to be something better than mere drudges? They are now considered as little better than beasts of burden, and even nicknamed accordingly. While horses and mules are called *bagages mayores*, asses and Indians are called *bagages menores;* that is to say, as a beast of burden, the Indian is considered below the horse and the mule, and on a level with the donkey. Kicks and brutal words are the only encouragement he receives from his betters, before whom he crouches in abject servility and cowardice. In former times there were many wealthy Indians in Ecuador, now I know of but very few. The Indian has no chance to make his way in life, except as a beast of burden and a drudge. It is neither in him, nor in the circumstances in which he lives, to be any thing else. He is destitute of all ambition, of all energy, of all industry, of all spirit of enterprise. He is accustomed to be a slave, and to be kicked and brutally treated, all his lifetime. He does not aspire to be any thing else. If he has enough to give some money to the priest, and to buy his raw food (corn or barley meal, agi, and potatoes), and rum and *chicha* for what remains, he is perfectly satisfied. Like children, the Indians live for the moment only. They never think of the morrow, they never think of old age. Their improvidence knows no bounds. Their women are almost entirely destitute of that little vanity with which the women of all other nations attend to their dress and appearance. It is much if they bedeck themselves with a necklace or bracelet of beads or false corals. To eat to excess and to get intoxicated, are their chief wants and their only tastes. A few rags to hang around their bodies and to cover themselves with at night, will answer their purposes. The Indians need no bed, for they sleep on lousy sheep-skins spread on the unfloored ground of the hovels in which they live. They need no books, for they cannot read; they need no furniture, for they cower on the ground. All their money that does not find its way into the bottomless pockets of the Church, is sacrificed to satisfy their greedy appetites. They are strangers to the higher emotions of human nature. Bashfulness, hospitality, magnanimity, compassion, gratitude, and all the other virtues by which good men excel, are unknown among them. They are completely imbruted; completely stupefied. They have forgotten the ancient glorious traditions of their race. The great names of Huaynacapac and Atahuallpa are meaningless sounds to their ears. The most that can be said in their favor is that they are not savages; they are humble and submissive, docile and obedient, abject and timid; and if we except the ill-treatment of their wives, they scarcely ever commit acts of violence. They will go to mass with the utmost regularity; they will go to confession as often as the Church prescribes; they will give to the Church more than they should, in justice to their own wants; they will kneel down before the image of every saint, and prostrate themselves before the image of the Holy Virgin; they will say their prayers many times a day, and will punctually comply with all the outward observances of their religion; they will carry the heavy statues of the saints at the many processions gotten up by the Church during the year, and they will carefully attend their own separate religious festivals and processions; but they know nothing of religion except its outward forms and ceremonies. That He who dined with publicans and sinners, and selected his Apostles from among fishermen and peasants, would also have extended his kind hand to the rightless Indian, is a thought foreign to their ignorant minds. And yet these poor creatures are, after all, the most useful members of Ecuadorian society. The Indian does more work than all the other races together. He tills the soil, builds houses and roads, carries heavy loads, and performs all that hard and heavy work which nobody else could be hired to do. He is harmless and inoffensive, good-natured, and easily manageable. But his position in the social scale is in an inverse proportion to his usefulness. He is far below the North American negro. The word *Indian* is a term of contempt, even among Indians themselves, who cannot offer a greater insult to one another than by the epithet "*Indio* bruto" (Indian brute). They will never call one another bad names without strengthening their vocabulary by the term "Indian," which is the most effective and most expressive of all.

Filthy, servile, superstitious, drunken, indolent, as they are, they claim our sympathy and commiseration. These poor and degraded beings were once the owners and masters of the country, and the subjects of a powerful empire. The ancestors of those who now dwell in miserable huts, had built stately palaces and magnificent temples, and vast treasures belonged to the race that now bends its weary neck to carry the burdens of their conquerors. It is true the ancient Indians were slaves also, but they obeyed masters of their own race. Under the sway of a patriarchal government which provided for all its children, they knew at least no poverty; and whatever hard work they were compelled to do, they did cheerfully, because their rulers were the embodiment of their religion. At their revels nowadays, they sing and dance to the tune of a drum and fife, or the harp, or an instrument resembling the ancient rebeck. It is but one and the same sad and monotonous tune they play, and to which they sing and dance for hours and days. The same tune that enlivens them at their festivals, resounds at their funerals; but that tune is full of the deepest significance. It is slow and plaintive, like the mourning of a subjected race, bewailing the loss of its ancient greatness, and its present misery and degradation.

## CHAPTER XI.

Agriculture. — Wooden Plows. — Mechanic Arts. — Improvidence of the People. — Beggars. — Commerce of the Interior. — Want of Enterprise. — City lit with Tallow Candles. — Needlework and Embroidery. — Fine Arts. — Painting. — Splendid Copyists. — Cheapness of Paintings. — Saints and Martyrs. — A Scene from Purgatory. — The Liberal Professions. — The Law. — *Tinterillos.* — System of Jurisprudence. — The Country without a Penitentiary. — Physicians. — Drug Stores. — The *Hospicio.* — Leprosy and Elephantiasis. — Female Prison and Lunatic Asylum. — The Hospital. — No Room for Wounded Soldiers. — The Young Men of Quito.

In one of the preceding chapters, I referred to the melancholy fact, that in agriculture almost no progress has been made since the conquest. Wooden plows are still in use. The Indian who tills the soil, trained to a blind routine and as thoughtless as a child, is averse to all improvement. The process of threshing is performed by horses, which are driven over the wheat to stamp out the grain with their hoofs. Butter churns, as I have already said, are unknown. To separate the corn from the cob, in some parts of the country, for instance in the valleys of Puembo and Yaruqui, heavy wooden shoes are used, with which an Indian dances on the spikes, until the work is accomplished. Hogs are singed, not with hot water, but with burning straw placed on their bodies. Spades I never saw. Hoes are of the most awkward and impracticable construction. Modern machinery for other agricultural purposes is not dreamed of. Every thing is done by hand, and as slowly as possible.

The same helplessness prevails with reference to mechanic arts. There is not a good shoemaker in Quito. The native shoemakers do not know how to take the measure of a foot. If you have no lasts to give them, your boots will be guess-work. The process of tanning is equally unknown. The leather is beaten against a stone until it becomes pliable. Boots and shoes, therefore, will pinch until they commence to tear. To shoe a horse, takes almost a whole day, and square nails of about one third of an inch in thickness are driven into the hoof. But the ugliest feature of transactions with mechanics is their asking for money in advance, either to buy the stuff or material on which they are to work, or to have something to live on while engaged in the task. They will beg as long as you are willing to give. If you give much, the probability is that they will spend the money without doing the work. In many cases recourse must be had to the police, in order to compel a dishonest artisan to perform an obligation for which he has been paid in advance. In this respect the character of the people has not changed since Ulloa complained of their unreliability and bad faith. As he described them in 1739, so I found them in 1864.

Upon one occasion, I wanted two book-cases made. I sent for a cabinet maker, and showed him an old case, after the model of which I wanted the new ones made. He had no measure or inch-rod, but measured the case with little pieces of wood and straw, which he cut so as to suit the required dimensions. After a long consultation with a partner, or workman, whom he had brought along, he asked two months' time to finish the cases; but, yielding to my remonstrances, he finally agreed to have them ready in six weeks.

During this time he returned frequently to measure the old case over and over again, and always in the same tedious and awkward manner, — sometimes spending half an hour in measuring and deliberating with his companion. Of course, he asked for money incessantly. First, he wanted it to buy boards, which he said were very dear. Next he wanted money to buy locks. Then, again, he protested that he had nothing to live on; but I remained inflexible, and owing probably to my stern refusals, the cases were ready shortly after the required time.

Still, it is generally indispensable to pay a part of the price in advance, for even master mechanics are almost always without the funds to buy the necessary materials. These cholos live like the Indians, from one day to the other. To the improvidence of the people, the great number of beggars must chiefly be ascribed. My servants used to spend their monthly wages as soon as they received them, if they had not already spent them in advance. Give one of these careless creatures ten dollars to-day, and he will ask you for a real to-morrow. I often told them that their fate would be that of those hundreds of beggars who, on Saturdays, crowded the palace of the archbishop and the houses of the principal inhabitants; but my exhortations produced no effect.

There are several trades in which considerable cleverness is displayed. Silver and gold smiths and wood-carvers especially, deserve to be mentioned for their skill. But in almost all other mechanic arts the people of Ecuador are centuries behind the age. The crudest tools and implements are used, and weeks and months are required for what, in other countries, would be accomplished in a few days.

In 1862, President Garcia Moreno commenced the construction of a wagon-road from Quito to Guayaquil. The necessity of the work had always been felt and admitted, and many a congress had decreed that it should be done, prefixing long strings of pompous whereases to its resolutions; but, instead of building new roads, the old ones were suffered to become entirely impassable. At last Mr. Moreno undertook the task. But it was a lamentable sight to see how it had to be carried on. Heavy excavations had to be made through the high hills on both sides of the old mule-path. There were no instruments except crowbars and shovels. There were no spades and pickaxes to dig with, nor carts or wheelbarrows to haul away the earth. It had to be filled in sheep-skins and ponchos, which the Indians carried on their backs, and with which they climbed up the hills where they deposited their scanty contents. Two foot-paths were made, leading to the summit. One of them the carriers ascended with their loads, to return by the other. Paving-stones, lime and bricks for the construction of bridges, as well as the necessary tools and instruments, were carried in the same manner on human backs. Sometimes beasts of burden were used; but the principal and cheapest beast of burden is the Indian. He does not work voluntarily, not even when paid for his labor, but is pressed into the service of the government for a certain length of time, at the expiration of which he is discharged and another forced into his place. He works unwillingly, and is kept to his task by the whip of the overseer. It is evident that but little progress could be made under these circumstances. But slowness is one of the chief features of the country. To build houses is an equally helpless task. The timber required for building purposes is brought to Quito with oxen. Generally but one or two beams are tied with a long rope to a yoke of oxen, and thus dragged along on the ground; and this in an age of steam and electricity.

The commerce of the interior corresponds with the deplorable condition of its agriculture and industry. Commodities and luxuries of life which have to be imported are very expensive, and at certain seasons, not to be had at all. Excepting the high districts around Pichincha, Cotopaxi, Chimborazo, and Tulcan, coffee grows in every province of the republic; and yet it happens sometimes that the supply of coffee at Quito gives out entirely. I remember one occasion when not a pound could be procured in the capital. The merchants of Quito are without enterprise. Indolence and inactivity pervade all classes of the people. A shopkeeper opens his store at about seven o'clock in the morning, or later, and shuts it at nine to go to breakfast. At ten or half past ten he returns. At two or three he shuts up again to go to dinner, after which he saunters back to the shop at about four or half past four. At six or half past six in the evening he closes up for good, there being no business done after dark. It is only a few cigar stores that are kept open after nightfall, lighted by one or two melancholy tallow candles. The streets are lit in the same way. Every householder is obliged to hang out a tallow candle in a lantern at seven P. M., provided there is no moonshine. At ten o'clock the candle ends have generally burnt down, and darkness reigns.

To get any thing done, is certainly a difficult task in Ecuador. Nobody is in a hurry. Nobody can get ready. Every step is beset with difficulties, delays, procrastinations, and disappointments. Every thing is troublesome. The simplest transactions of daily life are full of impediments, obstacles, and vexations. It requires endless talk to make a bargain with a salesman, *arriero*, or mechanic; but the bargain is hardly made when the other party will want to have it changed again, and ask for more favorable conditions. But few persons can be met with whose word or promise can be relied on. Mechanics will work for three or four days, and then suddenly stay away, especially when they have succeeded in getting some money in advance. To move from one house to another, — there being no carts or wagons, — the services of about a dozen Indians will be required, whom it will not always be easy to find. They will groan and chatter incessantly; it will be necessary to spur them on and watch them continually; and after you have paid them their own price, they will commence to bother you for an additional sum to buy *chicha* or *aguardiente*. I have already said that the Indian does not care to earn money. As long as absolute necessity does not compel him to do a little work, he will not look out for employment, nor accept it when it is tendered to him. It is necessary to coax him to carry a load or a message. I once met one of the public water-carriers on the street, and asked him whether he would not bring a jar of water to my house. He replied in the blandest and most submissive manner, "No, *mi amo* (my master), I 'd rather not."

There are some branches, however, in which the natives of Quito manifest considerable proficiency. Among these, ornamental needlework deserves to be honorably mentioned. Handkerchiefs, collars, chemises, petticoats, bed-sheets,[1] towels, etc., are embroidered in the most beautiful manner. This kind of work requires extraordinary patience and perseverance, and is comparatively but poorly paid. Lace, too, is manufactured in great quantities, and without machinery, and although not so tasteful, is much more durable than European lace. The embroidery and lace of Quito are well known, and in considerable demand at Guayaquil and Lima.

Of the fine arts, painting is greatly cultivated. The number of painters is very great, and some of them are men of talent, and even genius. But their defect is want of originality. They can copy from other paintings, but they cannot copy from nature, or conceive an idea of their own. It was only at my suggestion that Rafael Salas, one of the best painters in Quito, left the beaten track, and undertook to paint Ecuadorian scenery and *costumbres* (customs). But the prices paid for paintings are too miserable to encourage artists. Copies from Horace Vernet, Correggio, and others, for which, on my return home, I was offered $200 apiece, I had bought for $30 or $40. Still, I always paid more than a native would have given. Mr. Salas often told me

[1] The bed is one of the principal objects of the care and expense of old-fashioned Quitonians. It is generally in an alcove, the framework of which is sculptured, richly gilt, and hung with damask or velvet. The bedstead is finely carved, the sheets and pillow-cases are beautifully embroidered and trimmed with home-made lace. During the day the curtains are undrawn, that the bed may be seen. Much less, if any, care is bestowed upon the extermination of fleas, with which the rooms of the rich as well as the poor are infested. The rooms are generally shut. Fresh air is excluded with great care. Even on haciendas in the country it is sometimes deadening to enter the well-furnished but unventilated rooms, the pent-up atmosphere of which reminds us of a sepulchre rather than a dwelling-house This custom of keeping every thing closed is but too favorable to the propagation of fleas.

that his principal supporters were the foreigners who came to Quito from time to time. The natives seldom pay more than $16 or $20 for a large-sized portrait. Other pictures of merit are sold from $4 to $20, according to their size — prices that are hardly sufficient to pay for the canvas and colors. Painters, therefore, instead of endeavoring to study and to improve, have to daub off saints and Virgins to earn their daily bread. Superstition must support them. The painted saints and Virgins of Quito are not only sold all over the country, but exported to other parts of South and Central America. They are as bad as cheap. Martyrology, hell, and purgatory, are frequently drawn upon for subjects. Such pieces are always conceived in a loathsome spirit of butchery and extravagance, to awe the vulgar. I cannot refrain from describing one of them as characteristic of Spanish civilization. It was a view of purgatory. The lower part represented the fiery pit in which the poor souls were suffering. Men and women, old and young, handsome and ugly, kings, knights, and bishops, were huddled together in agony. Even a pope, with a tiara on his head, was among the rueful company. They were all cutting dreadful faces, some expressive of repentance, others of despair. Some were praying with uplifted arms and clasped hands, others bowed down their heads in utter dejection. The negro element, too, was represented by one or two specimens. A little above this lowest and largest group, the tortures which the inhabitants of that unhappy place are believed to undergo, were represented. Two poor fellows were hanging on a gibbet, where they had to endure continual agonies without being able to die. To their right hand was a large, fiery oven, with two apertures to it. Through one of them a caldron was visible, in which a select company of five or six sinners were boiling or roasting. On the top of the fiery furnace knelt five or six souls that were already purged of their sins. They were painted white, and lifted their arms toward heaven. Two or three others were seen flying up to heaven, at the entrance of which they were received by a negro bishop, who kindly helped them in. But the ugliest contrivance below was a large wheel, to which the naked bodies of several unfortunate sinners were tied. This wheel revolved so near to a heavy post from which two or three sharp-pointed iron hooks protruded, that they tore up the breast and entrails of the wretched sufferers. Within the wheel there were other penitents enwrapped in flames. Near by, a man was fixed upon a stake, which ran through his body and came out of his head. Other sufferers were swimming promiscuously in a lake of fire. A little further up there was a large basin of water in which souls were bathing, but for what purpose I do not know. Some said it represented a bath of ice, destined to make the sinner change from the pangs of parching heat to the pains of freezing cold. Close to this bath was a crowded prison with a small door in its upper corner, which an angel, with a chalice in one hand and a key in the other, had come to open. Just above this prison, and apparently a part of the same building, was a chapel, in which a priest was saying mass for the souls below. To this happy circumstance they owed their deliverance by the angel. This part of the picture was the "*argumentum ad hominem*," advertising the great advantage of having masses said for the souls of deceased relatives. It was supported by another device: a bridge in the form of an arch was spanned from the land of death to the gate of paradise, just in the rear of the altar before which the priest was officiating. This bridge, like the one leading to the paradise of the Mohammedans, seemed to be thin as a hair and sharp as a sword. Some souls passed over it in safety, while others tumbled down into the fiery abyss below. Angels hovered over the bridge, encouraging the righteous, or throwing morsels of heavenly bread into the pool for the relief of the sufferers. A saintly woman knelt on an elevation above the chapel just described, with a basket of bread in one hand. She distributed the bread among the angels, who threw or took it to the wretches in the pit. On high there was the Virgin Mary with the Christ-child on her lap, and surrounded on both sides by an ugly company of shabby monks and nuns, who were praying for the penitents below. Some of these monks had wings like angels; every one of them had a broad tonsure on his head; and one of the female saints held a child in her arms. The whole party knelt, with the exception of the Virgin, who looked down mercifully on the suppliants in purgatory. As the negro element was represented above and below, my eye searched for Indians, but in vain. For them there seems to be no place either in heaven or in purgatory. Even the pious brush of the artist dooms them to that third place, from which there is no escape. This picture, thoroughly Spanish in its conception and execution, is a favorite piece with the rabble of Quito, and copies of it are continually being made for chapels and private oratories.

From the arts let us turn to the liberal professions. A young man of good family, who has nothing to do except to assist in the superintendence of the family estate, will always be sent to college, or to the University,[1] for the purpose of acquiring the title of "Doctor." That title is as common in Quito, as the decoration of the "*legion d'honneur*" in France. Every white person respectably dressed, may safely be presumed to hold it. The proverb *non omnes doctores*, says Caldas, the Granadian naturalist, does not apply to Quito. Honorable and flattering as the title may be, I do not believe it is very profitable. Lawyers, for instance, innumerable as they are, have nothing to do. They do not even keep offices, but are consulted at their residences. There is but very little law business. Of criminal practice it would be unnecessary to speak. I have already said that but very few crimes are committed. Only cases of petty larceny or cattle stealing are of frequent occurrence, and the usual plea or excuse is the temptation of poverty, the usual defense a recommendation to the

1 "Education has never been patronized by the Government or Congress; for which reason the system at present pursued must be considered objectionable, inasmuch as attention is principally devoted to the study of law, medicine, and theology, to the neglect of practical science. From my connection with the University, I am enabled to subjoin a statement of the branches of knowledge taught in that institution, with the annual salary paid to each professor: —

| | |
|---|---|
| Latin and Spanish Grammar | $450 00 |
| Canonical Law | 300 00 |
| Civil Law | 300 00 |
| Economical and Political Legislation | 300 00 |
| Natural Law, administrative and Constitutional Science | 300 00 |
| Anatomy | 300 00 |
| Physiology | 300 00 |
| Pathology, Medical Jurisprudence, and Midwifery | 300 00 |
| Clinical Medicine, Materia Medica, and Pharmacy | 300 00 |
| Chemistry and Botany (Dr. Jameson) | 300 00 |
| Literature | 300 00 |
| Secretary of University receives salary of | 300 00 |
| Vice-Secretary | 200 00 |
| Total | $3,950 00 |

"The receipts of the University amount annually to the sum of from $4000 to $4500. No fees are paid by the students to the Professors." — *From Dr. Jameson's Manuscript Notes.*

mercy of the court. Such practice, of course, cannot be very lucrative. For a defendant who has no means, the court appoints an attorney, who is bound to serve without compensation. Civil practice is but little better. Quito is not a mercantile town. But few commercial questions arise which cannot be disposed of without the intervention of lawyers, by the "*juez de comercio*" (commercial judge), an inferior tribunal. The only important questions that arise, are questions of inheritance, involving the title to large estates. But these are too few and far between to support an independent legal profession. In civil cases of less importance, attorneys are not expected to ask for a compensation. The principal families are always, in some degree, related to each other, and two or three lawyers are always to be found within the family circle. Hence, the cousin, the nephew, the brother-in-law, will have to take charge of the current court business of the family, in consideration of love and affection. It would be preposterous on their part, to suggest the idea of payment. A plate of fresh bread, a box of preserves, a dish of sweetmeats, or a few bottles of wine, are considered a sufficient recompense for the successful attorney. It requires an established reputation and a good practice, to arrive at a yearly income of from $200 to $600. Hence, gentlemen of the bar will pay but little attention to the business which they may have in court, if they have haciendas which require their superintendence. It is their property and not their profession, on which they depend for subsistence. Their profession pays only when they are lucky enough to secure a judgeship or other judicial appointment. Nevertheless, the town is infested with a number of pettifogging scribes, not admitted to the bar, who are continually stirring up litigation, or volunteering their advice and assistance. They are called *tinterillos*, or inkworms, a class well known to Spanish caricaturists and playwrights.

The Ecuadorian system of jurisprudence is based on the Code Napoleon, the Roman Law, and the Spanish Institutes. Criminal cases are tried by jury. In civil cases juries are not admissible. There are parochial judges, corresponding to our justices of the peace; commercial judges, and *alcaldes municipales*, corresponding to our courts of common pleas. Then there are superior courts and a supreme court. From the commercial courts of Guayaquil there is no appeal to the supreme court. Capital punishment is inflicted by shooting. Penitentiaries there are none; offenders are condemned to perform public works, such as sweeping or repairing streets — a punishment which but very seldom reaches criminals belonging to the higher classes. These are either allowed to escape, or they are not prosecuted at all.

In jury trials the attorneys are not allowed to appeal to the sympathies or feelings of the jurors. Their eloquence is restricted by the narrowest and most jealous rules. Witnesses are not examined by the attorneys, but by the judge. If an attorney wants to ask the witness a question, he submits it to the judge, who repeats it to the witness, thus giving the latter time to prepare his answer. If a witness fails to appear, his original deposition may be read, even in criminal cases. The number of petit jurors is nine. There is a *jurado de acusacion*, which resembles our grand jury. The system of new trials is unknown.

Physicians are paid much better than attorneys; but the number of those who enjoy a good practice can be but small. The population of Quito is not much more than 40,000. Of these, probably two fifths are pure Indians, who never submit to scientific medical treatment. Two fifths are cholos, mestizos, and negroes, too poor to pay a physician. Medical men must depend, therefore, on the last fifth, consisting of white men and the wealthier portion of the mixed races. But physicians, as a general rule, are not very fond of their practice. If they have haciendas in the country, the superintendence of these will be more important to the doctor than his sick list. Every now and then he goes to the country, leaving his patients to take care of themselves. And even while in town he forgets his medical calls but too willingly. If the patient is not in danger, he visits him as seldom as possible. He promises to come, but either neglects or forgets it, and finally stays away whether the man is well or not. A patient who wishes to pass through a thorough medical treatment must run after his physician continually. He must visit the doctor instead of being visited by him. In this the physician follows but the general custom of the country. I never saw a people who cared so little for "making money" as the *serranos* of Ecuador. Time, as I have already said, has no value. Nobody is in a hurry; nobody seems to be busy. There is no occupation so pressing as not to bear postponement. *Vuelva V. mañana* (come back to-morrow), the great motto of Spain, has been fully naturalized in her former American colonies.

Drug-stores (there are but three of them in Quito) are kept in a manner corresponding to the general want of activity and enterprise. The apothecary does not furnish the bottles or boxes for the medicines which he compounds. If the remedy you require is a liquid, you must send a bottle, a cup, or a glass with the prescription, to fill it in. Sometimes the simplest and most necessary remedies are not to be had. I remember that on one occasion, only with great difficulty, four ounces of castor-oil could be obtained; and this in a country where the castor-plant grows wild, and in the woods of which the most precious balsams and medicinal herbs abound. But the medicinal plants which are found in the mountains, in the valleys, and in the forests of Ecuador, on both sides of the Cordillera, are waste treasures. No drugs are extracted from them, and their very existence is better known to scientific foreigners than to the natives of the country. Some most valuable specifics are known to the Indians, especially to those of the Napo wilderness; but the chemists and physicians of the country do not take much trouble to ascertain their medicinal properties.

On the northern slope of Mount Panecillo, overlooking the city, and commanding a very fine view, is the *Hospicio*, a cluster of buildings devoted to three very incongruous purposes. It is used as a prison for the female convicts, a lunatic asylum, and a hospital for the *elephantiacos* or *leperos*. The insane are not subjected to a methodical, scientific treatment. They run about in the corridors and *pateos* as they please, and are locked up only when they are considered dangerous. I noted more cases of idiocy than of insanity. The *elephantiasis*, or leprosy, is a horrible disease, which has hitherto been considered incurable and contagious.[1] It very often causes a swelling of the face or limbs, and manifests itself in horrible sores, which eat off the noses, fingers, lips, or cheeks of the

[1] Tubercular Elephantiasis.

patients. It is of comparatively recent appearance, for when the *hospicio* was built, it was not yet known in Quito. In Cuenca it is of more frequent occurrence than in other parts of the republic. The number of patients in the *hospicio* of Quito approaches one hundred. The disease in its manifestations bears a resemblance to the ravages of secondary and tertiary syphilis. The poor victims live together in the upper part of the *hospicio*, where they have their gardens, and are even allowed to intermarry. Their fate is dreadful. They are excluded from all intercourse with their fellow-men, while certain and inevitable destruction carries them slowly but irresistibly to an untimely grave. They can daily watch the steady progress of the horrid affliction, conscious that there is no remedy by which their doom might be averted. There is a chapel in the *hospicio*, where mass is said every Sunday and holy day, and other religious exercises take place. On such occasions the female prisoners and the lunatics assemble in the hall below, and the lepers in the choir above. I once saw them all assembled — a frightful spectacle of decomposition of living beings. I listened to their singing, monotonous and plaintive, and it rang in my ears long after I had left the place.

The street running down from the *hospicio* leads to the hospital maintained by the municipality. After having read Mrs. Ida Pfeiffer's description of that institution, I felt loth to enter it. From my knowledge of the country, however, I am inclined to believe that Mrs. Pfeiffer did not exaggerate. The funds of the hospital are very scanty. In 1864, a number of patients had to be turned out, because there was no money to provide for more than the number allowed by law. Those poor helpless creatures crept from house to house, appealing to the charity of the inhabitants. Among the victims that were thus cast upon the streets, were many wounded soldiers, who had shed their blood at Cuaspud, in the war with New Granada, — poor wretches whom the government had impressed into the army, and afterwards allowed to be driven from their miserable pallets to perish in the streets. In any other country, or among any other race of men, steps would have been taken immediately to relieve the sufferings of those unfortunate beings. Committees would have been formed, money would have been contributed and placed at the disposal of the directors of the hospital. Not so among the *serranos* of Ecuador. They are good-natured, affable, polite, attentive, hospitable, and kind, but they lack the spirit of charity. They pity the sufferers, but do nothing to *relieve* them. In this respect the want of a spirit of association is sadly felt. They have no idea of acting together, not even for a benevolent purpose.

Considering the low state of the liberal professions, and the want of commercial and industrial enterprise, it is not to be wondered at that the young men of the better families of Quito do not know what to do, but pass their time in idleness and frivolity. The great questions and events which agitate our age trouble them but little. They are not fond of reading or study. They are thoughtless, and without much moral or physical courage. When General Mosquera, after having routed the Ecuadorian army at Cuaspud, was expected to march upon Quito, not a dozen of them stirred to defend their native city. In their opinion, the defense of the country is the business and duty of the poor man, who is forcibly impressed into the army, and sacrificed to the ambition of his rulers, although he has no interest whatever in the questions for which they go to war. When these poor recruits are brought to Quito, they are received in silence. Not a handkerchief waves; not a friendly voice is raised to welcome them. When the war is over they are dismissed without the money to return to their villages. Thus, frequently, hordes of beggars are let loose upon the country; and yet there is, as I said already, but very little crime. This, however, must not be attributed to education. There are no common or free schools in the capital. Colleges and universities are liberally endowed; but very little attention has been bestowed upon elementary education. In 1861, French friars were imported to teach boys the rudiments of knowledge; but the education of poor girls is still left to private charity. The number of those who cannot read or write must be enormous. Parents are not required to send their children to school; on the contrary, illegitimate children were excluded, by an order of President Garcia Moreno, from the schools of the French friars. Besides, the system of education which now prevails is very bad. In the elementary schools nothing is taught but reading, writing, religion, and a little arithmetic. In the higher schools, Latin, and perhaps Greek, monopolize the time of the student. Geography is taught without maps; the natural and mathematical sciences are neglected, and every deference is paid to religious intolerance. As a proof of this, I shall refer to but one instance. For many years, Vattel's "Law of Nations" was a text-book at the University. Several years ago, however, the Archbishop remonstrated against the use of it as heretical, because it advocates religious toleration. It was immediately prohibited, and Bello's meagre essay substituted in its place.

## CHAPTER XII.

The Political Condition of the South-American Republics.—A Tale of Horror and Misery.

About one month before his death, General Bolivar, the so-called "Liberator" of South America, wrote a letter to the late General Flores, of Ecuador, in which the following remarkable passages occur, which have never before been published in the English language:—

"I have been in power (*yo he mandado*) for nearly twenty years, from which I have gathered only a few definite results:—

"1. America, for us, is ungovernable.

"2. He who dedicates his services to a revolution, plows the sea.

"3. The only thing that can be done in America, is to emigrate.

"4. This country will inevitably fall into the hands of the unbridled rabble, and little by little become a prey to petty tyrants of all colors and races.

"5. Devoured as we shall be by all possible crimes, and ruined by our ferociousness, the Europeans will not deem it worth while to conquer us.

"6. If it were possible for any part of the world to return to a state of primitive chaos, that would be the last stage of Spanish America."

Thus, almost with his dying breath, wrote Simon Bolivar, the man to whom admiring congresses had voted the title of "Liberator," and whom his friends and partisans, very improperly in my opinion, have called the "Washington of South America." Thus he wrote on the 9th of November, 1830. He died on the 10th of December of the same year. His constant and well-grounded fears of conspiracies against his life, had greatly accelerated his end.

We shall see now, whether time and experience have verified his predictions. Our Spanish-American neighbors have had a trial of forty years of republican institutions, and, I am sorry to say, the result is all but encouraging. From the very beginning of their national existence, they have been in a state of chronic anarchy and interminable convulsion. Their little republics have either been at war with each other, or a prey to internecine strife, or both at the same time. With them a state of war is the rule, and peace the exception. Their administrations are not changed by elections, but by revolutions. Plots and conspiracies take the place of political campaigns. An election is a farce, as it is almost always controlled and carried by the government. The opposition has generally but one chance, that of insurrection, revolution, and war.

Chili is the most prosperous and respectable of the South American republics. She has built roads over the Andes, not only wagon-roads, but also a railroad. She has had less revolutionary troubles than her neighbors. Her white population is not so prejudiced against labor as Spanish-Americans in general. The Chilians are more enterprising than their neighbors. Chilian commerce is flourishing. It is true, that an important share of their prosperity is owing to the large number of foreigners who have settled in Chili; nevertheless, the superiority of the native Chilians over their Spanish brethren must not be underrated.

Bolivia is probably the most wretched of the South

Pacific republics. It has but one sea-port, the town of Cobijas; but there is no communication whatever between that port and the interior. Hence, all the imports and exports of the republic have to pass through Peru, on the good-will of which the commerce of Bolivia depends. Bolivia owes its independence to the military skill and valor of General Sucre, one of the most meritorious generals of the revolutionary war. It owes its name to General Bolivar, the Liberator, who made a constitution for it, which the Bolivians, with more courtesy than discretion, accepted. It was so visionary and impracticable an instrument, that it had to be discarded in less than a year. It was a compound of all possible political institutions, ancient and modern. Bolivar very modestly said of it, that it combined the political wisdom of all ages and nations. It provided for the election by the legislature of a president, who was to hold his office for life, with power to appoint his successor, the vice-president. It provided for a legislature of three houses, — tribunes, senators, and censors. It teemed with visionary crotchets, and contained but one sound principle — that of religious toleration — which was subsequently abandoned. That constitution was probably the greatest weakness of Bolivar's life. He clung to it with incredible tenacity, after its impracticability had been fully exposed. He would not be convinced that it was unsuitable to the spirit of his or any other age and people. A practical trial had led to its rejection in Bolivia; nevertheless, the "Liberator" untiringly strove to effect its adoption in Colombia, the domestic tranquillity of which he sacrificed by encouraging *pronunciamentos* in favor of the Bolivian Constitution, with General Bolivar as president for life. A belief that he plotted to make himself dictator and destroy the liberties of the country, rapidly spread, and led to a conspiracy, and an attempt to assassinate him, the terrors of which haunted him ever afterwards. Bolivia fared as badly under a constitution of her own as under that with which General Bolivar had presented her. For the frequency of her revolutions and civil wars, for the violence and vindictiveness of her party leaders, and the sanguinary spirit of their followers, she is almost without a rival among her sister states.

Peru is the wealthiest of the republics on the Pacific coast, being the owner of the celebrated Chincha, or Guano Islands, and by economical and prudent management might have subsisted almost without taxation. But her resources were most recklessly squandered by her rulers. Money is thrown away most wantonly and extravagantly. To satisfy the claims of hungry aspirants who would conspire against the government if not pensioned off, useless offices must be created continually. During my residence in the South, the Peruvian Government sent ministers to every possible foreign country, with which Peru had no relations whatever, merely for the purpose of providing for political camp-followers. Even a mission to China was created, with a large outfit and liberal salaries for the minister, his secretaries, and attachés. With all its guano wealth, Peru has not yet built a road to the highlands of the interior, and the capital of the ancient Incas. The populace of Lima generally dictates the foreign and domestic policy of the administration. Revolutions and civil wars are very seldom terminated by fighting, but by bribery, treachery, and intrigue. The ladies of Lima are famous for their zeal and skill in plotting the overthrow of governments. I may be warranted in saying that the very wealth of Peru has proved a great source of its political misery.

New Granada (now the United States of Colombia) has just emerged from a bloody and most cruel civil war of about five years' duration, and bids fair to plunge into another. It took over four years of bloodshed to establish religious freedom there, a principle which no other Spanish-American republic has established. Protestantism is freely tolerated in Buenos Ayres; but freedom of conscience is not a constitutional right. Not even Chili has done away with the institution of a State Church; and the toleration it accords to foreigners and dissenters is measured most scantily. In 1865 a concession was made in this respect to the spirit of the age, by the Congress of Chili, after long and excited debates, but it was done after a most determined opposition, and in a most chary and unsatisfactory manner. The Constitution of the United States of Colombia is a great failure. It attempts to base a union and national government on the fundamental principle of secession. It dooms the country to confusion, weakness, and impotence. It recognizes the right of each individual state to secede from the United States whenever it pleases. It creates a federal executive, but leaves the execution of the federal decrees and enactments to the executives of the different states. If these should refuse to execute them, the whole machinery would be brought to a dead-lock. The most notable feature of its Congress is a house of plenipotentiaries, appointed by the different states. The latter have no governors, but presidents, with cabinets and cabinet-ministers, and all the pomp and circumstance of sovereignty. The federal executive is elected for only two years. Such a government will not stand the test of time. It affords no security, and creates no confidence. The first strong blast will bring it down.

Venezuela, the birthplace of Simon Bolivar, has enjoyed hardly a moment of repose since the beginning of the war of independence. History visits the sins of the fathers on their children and children's children; and the execution, by command of Bolivar, of several hundred Spanish non-combatants at Caraccas, in 1814, including many inoffensive old men who had never sided with either party, seems to have borne its bitter fruits. Venezuela formed a part of the old Republic of Colombia, which could not hold together because it contained too many generals who were anxious to preside over governments of their own. Thus Paez detached Venezuela, and Flores, Ecuador. Many attempts have since been made to unite the three republics, but failed.

But it is unnecessary to continue this general review. The array of specific facts which I shall lay before my readers, is chiefly taken from my Ecuadorian experience, but will, *mutatis mutandis*, apply to almost any other Spanish-American republic. Change the names and the cast, and the tragedy remains the same. Those countries, I am sorry to say, are republics in name, but despotisms in fact. Their constitutions are generally liberal, but laws and constitutions are made to be disregarded. They all establish the system of three coördinate powers of government, but, in point of fact, there is but *one* power — the will of the man who, for the time being, has secured the obedience of the soldiery.[1]

[1] The last Constitution of Ecuador was adopted in 1861. With the exception of the article establishing the Catholic religion as the state church,

For this reason, a Spanish-American revolution, to be successful, must originate with, or be supported by, the soldiery. The conspirators begin with bribing a portion of the garrison of an important post. Military barracks (*cuarteles*), will never be attacked without a previous secret understanding with some of the officers and men who are in charge of the post. In the negotiations for such purposes the ladies take a most active part. They are passionate politicians, and very energetic secret agents. They carry letters and despatches,

and excluding every other, its provisions are sufficiently liberal. The legislative power is vested in a Congress, consisting of a Senate and House of Representatives. Every province elects two senators, and one representative for every thirty thousand inhabitants, or every fraction over fifteen thousand. Senators and representatives are elected for two years. The sessions are biennial. Every two years the term of one half of the members expires. The President is elected for four years, and has a veto. He cannot exercise his functions at a distance of more than eight leagues from the capital. He is not allowed to deprive an Ecuadorian of his liberty, or banish him the country. He must not interfere with the course of justice or the liberty of the press. The elections are direct and by secret ballot. Every Ecuadorian, without distinction of color, who can read and write, has a vote, and may be elected to office. The cabinet consists of three members — one for the Interior and Foreign Relations, the other for Financial affairs, and the third, a Minister of War and the Navy. In certain cases, the concurrence of a council of state is necessary to authorize executive acts. This body consists of the vice-president, the cabinet, one member of the supreme court, one representative of the clergy, and one representative of the landed interest. The last three are elected by Congress for four years. The president cannot be reëlected. The judges of the supreme and superior courts are elected by Congress. Slavery is abolished. Every Ecuadorian is allowed to emigrate with his property whenever he chooses, and to return to the country whenever he desires. Arbitrary arrests are prohibited. Persons can only be arrested according to law, and must be notified by the proper tribunal within twenty-four hours after their arrest, of the nature of the accusation against them. They can be tried only by a court of competent jurisdiction, and cannot be compelled to testify against their accomplices or near relations. In case public necessity shall make it indispensable to take private property, the value thereof must first be paid to the owner. Taxes and contributions can only be imposed according to law. The liberty of the press is guaranteed. Soldiers cannot be quartered upon private citizens without indemnity to the latter. All foreigners are permitted to come to the country, engage in business, etc.

excite discontent, conceal political refugees and facilitate their escape, and keep their banished friends posted as to the state of affairs at home. During my residence in Ecuador, several of these female agitators were banished the country by President Garcia Moreno. They went, hurling defiance into his teeth. He could imprison or shoot the men, who trembled before him, but he could not break the spirit of the women.

The moment a revolutionary party has secured a foothold somewhere, they resort to the customary mode of Spanish-American warfare. Its principal features are, forcible impressments, and forced loans and contributions, in addition to which they seize all the horses, mules, cattle, provisions, Indians, and other property they can lay hands on. The government does the same. There is no legal or equitable system of conscription or draft. By common consent, "gentlemen" (that is to say, white men of good families) are exempt from it; but the poor, the half or cross-breeds, the journeymen, mechanics, and farm-laborers, are seized and impressed wherever found, and without reference to age, condition, disability, or the time they may have served already. The appearance of the recruiting officers on the street always creates a panic among those liable to be "recruited." It is a pitiful spectacle to see those poor fellows run away in all directions, wildly chased by the officers and their men. Compulsory service in the army is a calamity greatly dreaded by the populace, and from which they try to escape in a thousand different ways. They will flee to the mountains, and hide themselves in forests or deserts (*despoblados*); they will take refuge in churches or convents, or in the houses of foreign representatives or residents, and they will not show themselves on the streets or public highways until the danger is over. When they are near enough to the frontier, they will leave the country in order to avoid impressment. In Peru alone there are over ten thousand Ecuadorians who left their own country to avoid impressment. Ecuadorian soldiers are but poorly clad and poorly paid. Many of them have to go barefoot. When their services are no longer required, they are discharged without the means to return to their homes. Under these circumstances, it cannot appear strange that such soldiers should revenge themselves on society whenever an opportunity offers. When marching from one place to another, they will take from the poor people living along the public highways whatever they can find. Hence, when it becomes known that a regiment or company of soldiers will march through a certain district, the people living along the road, even in times of profound peace, will hide their valuables, drive away their horses, mules, cattle, or sheep, take their provisions, chickens, etc., to some out-of-the-way place in the mountains or forests, and make preparations as if they expected the arrival of a savage enemy. The houses along the road will be deserted; the men will carefully keep out of the way of the marching columns; and only now and then an old woman will be found to tell the soldiers how poor she is. Many a time when, during my travels in the Cordillera, I stopped at a hut to buy eggs or other provisions, the people told me with a sigh: "We have nothing to sell, sir; the soldiers were here and took all we had."

I have said that "gentlemen" are exempt from military impressment. As a general rule, laws and customs are only enforced against the common people. Our neighbors have established a republican form of government without being republicans. They still cling to their aristocratic traditions, and virtually maintain distinctions of class and caste. The descendants of the old noble families still cherish their ancient titles of nobility. They look with great veneration on the pomp and splendor of European monarchies, and distinguish those of their own number who can boast of a count or a knight among their ancestors. Labor is disreputable in their eyes, and even on commerce they look down as not altogether respectable. Commerce, under the old Spanish law, was considered incompatible with nobility. The cream of the aristocracy consists of those who live on what their landed property produces, and therefore can afford to do nothing at all. The *caballero* would rather starve than perform manual labor, which, in his opinion, would be degrading, and which becomes only an Indian or Cholo. No white man will condescend to menial offices. White servants or laborers cannot be found in the interior of Ecuador, unless they be foreigners. Poor as the white native may be, he will generally manage to maintain himself without working. How a great many succeed in this, is a mystery to the uninitiated observer; but I believe that gambling and borrowing are freely resorted to. President Garcia Moreno once told me of a young man of genteel family who had asked him for an office, representing that he had a wife and six children, without any means to support them. The president told him that, for the present, he could not give him a better place than that of overseer on the new road from Quito to the coast, which was then in process of construction. The young man accepted the position. He remained at his post for two days, but on the third he told the president to appoint somebody else, as such employment was unworthy of his family and standing in society.

Another incident will illustrate the prejudice which our Spanish neighbors entertain against labor. A Scotchman, a very intelligent and well-educated man, and an excellent machinist, had been brought to Ecuador by a Mr. Carlos Aguirre, a wealthy land-owner, to fit up and carry on a factory of woolen goods, at the village of Chillo, about ten miles from Quito. The Scotchman, of course, went to work practically, and finding no one to rely on, did as much of the work himself as was necessary. This greatly astonished the natives who visited Chillo in order to see the new machinery, and many of them returned to Quito in a state of amazement at having seen a "*white man who worked like an Indian.*" But still more astonished were the poor Indians themselves, who told him, quite naively, that "*there could certainly be no Indians in the country he came from!*"

The first measures of a party which succeeds in a revolution or civil war, are generally acts of retaliation or revenge on the vanquished, who may congratulate themselves if only forced contributions are resorted to. The wealthy members of the losing party are notified by the new "government," that within a certain number of days or hours they must pay a certain sum of money. If they refuse, the amount is sometimes raised, and even doubled, and the victims are imprisoned, either in their own houses, or in the military barracks, until they "pay up." If they are storekeepers, their goods are seized as security. If they are hacienda-owners, their cattle or horses are taken in lieu of money. If they are women, they are placed under a military guard, and not allowed to leave their rooms, or to consult with their friends, until they comply with the arbitrary edict of the despot of the day. I shall relate but one instance of the many that came to my knowledge. In 1860 a contribution of several hundred dollars (I do not recollect the exact amount) was imposed upon a gentleman who had held office under the government that had just been overthrown. He being absent from Quito on his hacienda in Esmeraldas, on the coast, a detachment of soldiers was sent to his house with a command to his wife to pay the money. The lady protested that her husband had left her no money, and that she was unable to pay the required amount. Her answer was deemed unsatisfactory, and her house was surrounded by soldiers, who did not allow any body to enter or to leave it. She was not permitted to send for victuals or for water, nor was she allowed to employ counsel or to see her friends. For three days and nights she was kept a prisoner, until, coerced by starvation, she yielded at last, and paid the amount which had been assessed without warrant of law by the caprice of the victorious party.

A political adversary is considered an outlaw, who may with impunity be treated in the most arbitrary and cruel manner by those in power. His haciendas are laid waste by soldiers quartered on them; his cattle and horses are at the mercy of a reckless government. The greatest sufferers, however, are the owners of beasts of burden, whether they take part in political affairs or not. Their horses and mules are taken whenever they are needed for the transportation of military stores. They are used generally without compensation to the owner, who may congratulate himself if they are at last restored to him. Their galled backs and emaciated bodies are the pay he gets, all constitutional and legal provisions to the contrary notwithstanding. Those who own mules or donkeys which they hire out to travellers, or on which they bring their vegetables to market, keep away from cities in times of war or civil commotion, for fear of being robbed of their means of subsistence. Their beasts they send to the fastnesses of the mountains until the danger is over. Thus the city markets will be but scantily supplied, merchants cannot ship their goods, travellers find no means of transportation, and the whole country suffers and decays because governments will not respect individual rights and private property.

When the country is threatened with war, foreign invasion, or revolution, or when a violent change of government has taken place, the houses of foreign ministers, consuls, and other foreigners, are eagerly resorted to by all classes of the population. Not only will ladies and gentlemen take refuge there, but such houses will be depositories for all sorts of valuables, — goods, trunks, and boxes, belonging to merchants, mechanics, private citizens, and even the government. During the war with New Granada, in 1862, when it was feared that General Arboleda, after his victory at Tulcan, would march to Quito and occupy the town, the government made arrangements to deposit the silver bars belonging to the mint in the house of one of the foreign ministers. The houses of foreigners are respected, not only because the governments to which they belong are expected to shield them with a strong arm, but also because even the victorious or ruling party are interested in maintaining the sacredness of asylums to which, perhaps to-morrow, it may be their turn to resort as the vanquished. In Ecuador, foreigners alone enjoy the rights and privileges which the constitution, on paper, guarantees to the citizen. The persons of foreigners are secure; their servants are not taken away from them; their beasts are never interfered with; their property is respected; and if they have a diplomatic representative in the country, they are favored in a thousand different ways. They are the only class of persons who can carry on business in safety. Of course, they will suffer from bad times, when the country is desolated by revolutions or civil war, but they have little to fear from the government and party leaders; and while forced contributions of money or goods will be exacted from the native capitalists; while their servants and laborers, horses and cattle, will be taken away from them; the person, property, laborers, and servants of a foreigner will be secure. No wonder, therefore, that every extensive land-owner, every wealthy merchant in the country, wants to make himself a foreigner. I was almost continually troubled by persons who wanted to know how to make themselves North-American citizens. Every body, almost, who has any thing to lose, is anxious to abjure his nationality, and place himself under the protection of a foreign flag. Many went to the United States for the sole purpose of taking out first papers, which, as they believed, would protect them against forced contributions and other losses. Others go abroad to make themselves foreign subjects, and then return to carry on their business as before. I have heard hundreds who protested their anxiety to clothe themselves with a foreign nationality, in which case alone they considered their property secure. Mr. Buckalew, the American minister under Buchanan, once saved a man from a loss which, according to the Ecuadorian himself, would have amounted to at least $10,000, simply by allowing him to hoist the American flag over his farm buildings.

Whenever, even in times of profound peace, the government desires to erect a structure, or to repair a building, a road, or a bridge, orders are given to the police to seize all the masons and carpenters that can be found. From the number thus arrested, the directors will select the ablest, and compel them to work for such wages as it may be convenient to pay them. Political adversaries, who are suspected of revolutionary intentions, are arrested and detained in prison for months, without a charge against them, and without the benefit of a trial before the proper tribunals. Political prisoners are generally treated in a cruel and barbarous manner. I know of many who were kept in heavy irons for weeks and months, during which time their relatives had to feed them, as the government was not in the habit of furnishing meals to prisoners of state. They were generally banished to the unredeemed wilderness on the eastern side of the Cordillera, commonly called the "Napo Country," from the Napo River, — one of the affluents of the Amazon, — or to Brazil, by way of the Napo. To understand fully the inhuman nature of this punishment, it must be borne in mind that the road to the Napo, beginning at the village of Papallacta, — about two days' journey from Quito,—is a mere foot-path, inaccessible to horses or mules. The prisoners, with their limbs sore from the irons in which they had been kept, had to walk over rocks, and scramble through bogs and woods; now descending the cold and snowy summits of the Cordillera, then wading through deep and rapid streams; now exposed to the almost incessant and drenching rains of those regions, then again to the burning sun of the equator; with no provisions but those they carried with them, with no bed but the wet earth, and no cover but the sky, until they reached their inhospitable destination, where only the painted Indian's humble hut afforded them shelter, without protection from wild beasts, poisonous snakes, and tropical fevers. If such cruelties were committed in Turkey or Russia, they would not astonish us, but in countries styling themselves "republics," they must provoke our indignation and abhorrence.

Another shocking practice was the flogging of men by order of the president, and without process or warrant of law, the number of lashes varying from twenty-five to six hundred. In 1860, an old general, a mulatto, who is said to have creditably served in the wars of independence, was seized by order of Mr. Garcia Moreno, — then chief of the so-called provisional government, — and received five hundred lashes, in presence of the garrison, and probably at the hands of the very soldiers who had been under his command. He died a short time after this punishment. He had not been convicted by a court of competent jurisdiction, civil or military. No charges had been preferred against him. He was not allowed to make a defense, but the punishment was inflicted at the command of one man, who had no constitutional or legal right to judge or punish him.

An unguarded expression sufficed to condemn the suspected. In 1861 a certain Viteri had a christening at his house. Among the guests was a military officer of the president's party. Viteri, heated by wine and the merriment of the occasion, pointed to the officer's epaulettes, and told him that they would soon be torn from his shoulders. On the following day he was arrested, kept in prison for some time, and at last banished to the Napo wilderness, in direct violation of the constitution, which expressly prohibits such banishments.

The president loved to deal his blows in all directions. His lashes not only tamed his political opponents, but also interfered with the course of justice. In 1861, a fellow who had been arrested and indicted for manslaughter, escaped from custody before the day fixed for his trial. He was recaptured, and the president ordered four hundred lashes to be given him, and then handed him over to the civil tribunals. At the trial, this circumstance was commented upon by his attorney, who urged that a man ought not to be punished twice for the same offense; that the man had already been whipped to the very point of death, and ought not to suffer more. In this connection the lawyer was imprudent enough to hint that it was improper for the executive to interfere with the administration of justice. He had hardly left the court-room when he was arrested and banished to New Granada.

In 1863, a French druggist had furnished drugs to the garrison at Guayaquil, for which the government refused to pay. The case came before the Supreme Court, by which judgment was rendered in favor of the claimant. The president, highly indignant at this decision, ordered the judgment to be paid out of the amount due the judges for salaries.

When Mosquera, President of the United States of Colombia (New Granada), had defeated the Ecuadorians under General Flores, at Cuaspud, and subsequently taken military possession of the province of Imbabura, several individuals attempted a *pronunciamento* in favor of General Mosquera. They were arrested, and on the restoration of peace, handed over to the civil tribunals. The judge of the criminal court found them guilty of treason, from which decision they appealed. Suddenly the president was pleased to interfere, and ordered them to be put in "*la vara*," which is an instrument of torture similar to the English stocks, with the difference only that the prisoner is laid on his back, which position it is almost impossible for him to change, because his legs are fast in the stocks. The judge who had convicted them, remonstrated against this torture, as unconstitutional and illegal; stating, at the same time, that the prison in which the defendants were kept was perfectly secure, and that there was no danger of an escape, and no necessity for such cruelty. The president, enraged by this remonstrance, hinted to the judge that he would enable him to satisfy himself by personal experience that the "*vara*" was not an instrument of torture. In other words, he threatened to put the judge in the stocks. The judge withdrew, and sent in his resignation, which was not accepted. The men, however, remained in the stocks until it pleased the president to release them.

In 1864, General Maldonado had made himself conspicuous as the leader of a conspiracy, the object of which was to rid the country of the tyranny of Garcia Moreno. The plot was discovered, and many of the conspirators were sent to the Napo wilderness. General Maldonado succeeded in making his escape to the mountains, where, after an exciting pursuit of several weeks, he was captured on his way to Peru, and taken to Guayaquil. President Garcia, who was then at Quito, immediately gave orders to the general commanding at Guayaquil, to send the prisoner to the capital. The poor fellow knew that this would be his last journey, and begged hard to be allowed to leave the country. The general commanding declared his willingness to let him go in case $30,000 should be deposited in the bank of Guayaquil as security for his future good behavior. This sum the friends of the prisoner were either unwilling or unable to make up. They knew very well that the amount, if deposited by them, would immediately be seized and expended by the government. Thus Maldonado was sent to Quito. On his arrival there, he was at once taken before the president, who upbraided him for his conduct, and ordered him to be led out to the Plaza in front of the government palace, for immediate execution. The whole town was amazed, and many a hasty effort was made to save the victim, but the president was inexorable. The sympathies of the people were with Maldonado; even the soldiers who were commanded to shoot him could hardly repress their tears. If Maldonado had snatched the sword from the hands of the officer who commanded the troops on the Plaza, he might have made a successful revolution, and turned the tables on his enemy. The soldiers would have cheered and obeyed him, and the people would have welcomed him as their deliverer. But his spirit was broken. His wife arrived, and a scene took place on the Plaza which those who witnessed it will remember to their dying day. The last farewell of the consorts was heart-rending. Mrs. Maldonado had to be torn from her husband's embrace, and was led away almost insensible. She could hardly have walked one square, when she heard the discharge of the muskets which took her husband's life. She fell on the pavement with a frantic shriek. President Garcia was at his office in the palace, and may have witnessed, and probably did witness the execution, which took place under his very windows. This horrible event cast a gloom over the whole country. It was but the forerunner of more appalling deeds.

In 1865 another attempt was made by the Urbina party to overthrow Garcia Moreno. About thirty resolute men seized the river steamer *Washington*, during one of her regular trips from Bodegas to Guayaquil, and arriving on board of her at the latter place, brought her alongside the only man-of-war the Ecuadorian government then had, and which was lying quietly at anchor in the middle of the stream. The captain and crew of the man-of-war, who had suspected nothing of the kind, allowed themselves to be taken by surprise. The captain was killed, his men were overpowered, and the man-of-war, after having her cables slipped, was towed down the river by the other steamer. The whole thing was done so noiselessly and quickly, that both vessels were out of sight before the batteries on shore could get their guns in readiness. The blow was struck so suddenly and so well, that, had the revolutionary party followed it up immediately by an attack on Guayaquil with what few men they had, they might have succeeded in taking the place, which has always been considered the military and political key to the whole republic. But they allowed the precious opportunity to slip away. They wasted almost a month in inactivity, hovering around the mouth of the river with a little squadron which they had formed, and waiting for reinforcements and aid from their friends in Peru. In the mean time Garcia Moreno, whose tremendous energy and undaunted bravery challenged the admiration even of his enemies, had hastened to Guayaquil, put it in a state of defense, and immediately prepared for taking the offensive. By dint of great exertions he raised a large sum of money, with which he bought a merchant steamer from the agents of the British Pacific Steam Navigation Company, at an enormous price, and overcoming numberless obstacles, fitted her out and armed her in a few days. In this steamer he sailed to attack the enemy's squadron, consisting of two ocean steamers, one river steamer, and two sailing vessels. All the probabilities were against him, but he succeeded in taking his careless enemies completely by surprise. One of their big vessels had not even steam up when Garcia hove in sight. He attacked them at once, ran into the man-of-war they had carried away, and sunk her after an engagement of about half an hour. All the other vessels he captured, together with a number of prisoners, who had no time to gain the shore and to effect their escape to Peru. And now the executions commenced. Two of the prisoners he shot immediately, on board of his own vessel. Twelve or fifteen he shot in the afternoon of the same bloody day, and about six or ten on the next day, before his return to Guayaquil. He was in such a hurry to execute, that two men were shot whom the successful party had not even taken the trouble of asking for their names. These victims, it must be remembered, were not killed during the heat of the combat, but they were prisoners whose execution was ordered after the battle. No court-martial had sentenced them to death. The president himself interrogated them, and selected his victims from their number. A list of them was afterwards published in Guayaquil, which wound up with the following characteristic statement: "*and two more, whose names are unknown!*" Still, these men had been taken while in arms against a *de facto* government; and though many of them may have been forcibly impressed by the chiefs of the rebellion, in the districts along the coast which their squadron commanded, the circumstances under which they were taken may have served as an excuse for their execution in an unsettled and anarchical Spanish-American country. But the deed which I am now going to relate is inexcusable. It is a cold-blooded murder, which stands almost unparalleled in the history of civil commotions.

Dr. Viola, a lawyer at Guayaquil, a scholar and a gentleman, was known to sympathize with the opposition. It was known that he disapproved of the high-handed, illegal, and unconstitutional measures of President Garcia Moreno. This was his only crime. Nothing else could have been proved against him. On the day of the president's successful return to Guayaquil, after his naval victory at Jambeli, Garcia Moreno issued a decree of banishment against Dr. Viola, and ordered him to leave the country by the next steamer. That very same night, the president, while perusing the papers found on board the vessels captured by him, discovered a letter addressed by Dr. Viola to a Mr. Yerobi, an Ecuadorian exile in Peru, who, although the brother-in-law of General Urbina, the chief of the revolutionary party, had not taken part in his expedition, but, as was subsequently ascertained, had quietly remained at Lima while the events above narrated took place. His family had remained in Ecuador, and as Yerobi was very poor, his relatives occasionally sent him some money to Peru, to enable him to live in his expensive exile. For the transmission of these amounts to Peru, they availed themselves of the services of Dr. Viola, their attorney at Guayaquil. Dr. Viola also transmitted their private correspondence. But as it was generally believed in the country that letters directed to any of the Ecuadorian refugees in Peru, would be detained or opened by the Ecuadorian post-office authorities, it was the general practice to direct such letters to fictitious names, previously agreed upon. Dr. Viola, following this precaution, notified Yerobi in a short note, of the pseudonym to which he would send his letters. This note never reached Yerobi. His brother-in-law, General Urbina, received it for him at Paita, and took it with him unopened when he started on his expedition. Thus it fell into Garcia Moreno's hands, after the engagement at Jambeli. It hardly filled one page of note paper. I saw and read it with my own eyes, and I recollect its contents distinctly. It proved nothing; it raised no presumption. The jealousy of a despot might have looked upon it as a suspicious circumstance, but it admitted of a satisfactory explanation. At all events, it was not sufficient to overcome, unsupported by other evidence, the legal presumption of the man's innocence. No civilized tribunal would have convicted him on such a document. Not even a court-martial of Garcia Moreno's own selection would have found him guilty. The president's principal officers, with only one exception, were opposed to the execution; but such considerations had no weight with Garcia. Early in the morning of the day following his return from Jambeli, he sent for Viola. He showed him the letter, and asked him whether he had written it. "Is this your signature?" "Yes, sir; it is." "Then you are a traitor, and as such, you will be shot this evening at five o'clock!"

The horrible news spread like wild-fire over Guayaquil, and created universal consternation and horror. Every body felt that the sword of Damocles was suspended over his own head. Capital punishment was prohibited by the constitution in political cases. According to another provision of that same instrument, the president, when beyond a certain distance from the capital, became a mere private citizen, while the executive power remained temporarily vested in the vice-president. And yet Mr. Garcia undertook to take the life of an innocent man, without warrant or authority of law, and without any cause or excuse. Every body interceded for his life. The bishop, the clergy, the president's aged mother, — a venerable old lady, who had to be carried to the government building in a sedan-chair, — the principal merchants and bankers, the president's personal and political friends, the foreign consuls and residents, pleaded for Viola's life, but Garcia was inexorable. When somebody suggested that it would be much better to send Viola out of the country, he sneeringly answered, "he goes to the other world!" ("*al otro mundo se va!*") Viola was, personally, very popular. Every body knew him, and every body liked him. The president was besought during the whole day to spare his life, but in vain. No other declaration could be wrung from his lips but the stern sentence: "He will be shot this evening at five o'clock!" When the bishop suggested that such an execution would be a violation of law and an infraction of the constitution, the president replied that, it being impossible to save the country from anarchy by attempting to govern it according to the constitution, he had taken the responsibility to govern it according to his own views of right and public necessity. He said that an example had to be set, and he was determined to set it.

While the whole town were thus besieging the president for a commutation of the dreadful sentence, Viola was kept in irons until the fatal hour arrived. He was not allowed to see or take leave of any of his friends. Only one of them was admitted to his prison, and to him he dictated his last will, and a few private letters. No one else was permitted to see him, and he refused to see the priest who was sent to him by the government. He was kept in chains until he was led out to execution. When he asked that his manacles be taken off but for a few minutes, so that he might write a letter to a lady friend, his keepers said that they had no authority to comply with his request. At five o'clock he was led to the *savana* or *pampa*, in the rear of the city. Here his chains were taken from him, and he was shot in the back as a traitor. Inadvertently his executioners had made him kneel down near a nest of black ants, which covered his body as soon as he fell, and before life was extinct. A second volley had to be fired, as the first had failed to kill him. Nobody was allowed to attend his funeral. He was even denied a Christian burial. Such is republicanism in Spanish-America!

But I cannot finish this tale of horrors without relating another deed, still more revolting in its details than the murder of Viola. A short time after the incident just related, the president returned to Quito to open the regular session of Congress. At Bodegas, while on his way to the capital, he demanded a list of those who had been imprisoned by order of the local authorities. This list contained, among others, the name of a poor old man, a resident of the village of Pimoche, in the neighborhood of Bodegas, who, while in a state of intoxication, had hurrahed for General Urbina, the leader of the revolutionary party. The president ordered him to be sent to Pimoche in a canoe, to be executed there on that very day. Immediately after the canoe had left with the victim on board, the governor and principal citizens of Bodegas called on the president, and assured him that the man he had just sentenced to death was entirely innocent. They proved to Mr. Garcia Moreno's fullest satisfaction that the poor old man had always been known as a staunch supporter of the government, and that only on one occasion, and while under the influence of liquor, and not knowing what he said, he had made a few drunken remarks in favor of General Urbina. The president saw that he had committed a sad mistake, and dispatched a second canoe to Pimoche, with an order countermanding the execution. But the messenger of grace arrived too late. When his canoe came in sight of the village, he heard the reports of the muskets which had just done their bloody work.

The majority of both houses of Congress was opposed to Garcia Moreno and his policy, and might have become troublesome. But Garcia was not the man to allow himself to be thwarted or molested by the representatives of the people. He at once banished a number of the opposition members to Peru and New Granada, and thus intimidated the few whom he allowed to remain. Hence, when the widow of General Maldonado charged the president with the murder of her husband, and demanded an investigation, Congress refused to consider the accusation, and voted the thanks of the nation to Garcia for the energy and promptness with which he had repelled Urbina's invasion, and defeated the revolutionary party at Jambeli.

In this connection, I must state that Garcia Moreno

himself owed his elevation to power to a revolution against a legitimate government. General Robles was the constitutional president of Ecuador in 1860, when complications arose with Peru which led to a declaration of hostilities. General Urbina, who was commander-in-chief of the army, had marched against the Peruvians, and left the capital almost without a garrison. This auspicious moment was seized by Garcia Moreno and his followers, who rose against the administration, organized a provisional government, and with an extemporized army marched south in pursuit of Urbina. The latter, on hearing of their movements, at once suspended his march to the Peruvian frontier, and marched back in the direction of the capital. He defeated Garcia Moreno at the village of Tumbucu, near Guaranda, reëstablished his authority at Quito, and drove the scattered remnants of the "Provisionals" into New Granada, after which he again set out to fight the Peruvians. But, aided by the conservatives of New Granada, the Provisionals again invaded the country, and took possession of the capital. In the mean time, General Franco, at Guayaquil, had pronounced against Robles and Urbina, and proclaimed himself dictator. Thus Robles and Urbina were compelled to give up the struggle, and fled to Peru. Franco, after a protracted civil war, was in his turn driven out of the country by Garcia Moreno, who thus secured his own elevation to power.[1]

[1] In justice to Mr. Garcia Moreno, I must add here that he was not without redeeming qualities. He was entirely disinterested in money matters, and expended all his salary for public purposes. When not blinded by passion and prejudice, he was fair-minded, and even distinguished by a high sense of justice; which, however, he marred by his endeavors to meddle with every thing, and to regulate every thing. He was undoubtedly the bravest man in Ecuador, and probably in Spanish-America, and ever ready to sacrifice his life, of which he was as reckless as of the lives of others.

That under such circumstances there can be no liberty of the press, can easily be imagined. Indeed, it can hardly be said that there is a press in Ecuador. No political papers were regularly published at Quito during my residence there, with the exception of one or two semi-official organs, established for temporary purposes, — such as to harangue the people when war was apprehended, and to be discontinued as soon as the danger was over. Peruvian papers were not allowed to circulate in the country. Other foreign papers were virtually excluded by the exorbitant postal charges established by the president. The regular official paper — "El Nacional" — came out once a week, with occasional interruptions and irregularities, and contained nothing but official notices and correspondence, new laws and decrees, the decisions of the auditor's office (*tribunal de cuentas*), and now and then an abusive editorial. Violent and abusive language, and a pompous and almost oriental style, full of exaggerations and hifalutin, characterize the great bulk of Spanish-American journalism. Even governments will not require their organs to employ calm and dignified language; and the editorial productions of cabinet members themselves are as abusive and unmeasured as the secret publications of their persecuted, outlawed, and embittered antagonists.

In the beginning of Mr. Moreno's administration, a poor devil, a Mr. Riofrio, relying on the professions which the successful party had made before their acces-

He was endowed with wonderful energy and restless activity; neutralized, however, by his heedless precipitation and lack of judgment. He was well-meaning and sincere in his fanaticism, and, I have no doubt, really had the good of his country at heart; but Torquemada, too, was a sincerer man than Talleyrand, for example, and yet he was a curse to Spain, and unproductive of any good to his country or race.

sion to power, attempted to publish an opposition paper in Quito, but was immediately set upon by the authorities, and saved himself only by a rapid flight over the most unfrequented paths and by-ways of the Cordillera. I saw him when he arrived at Tumaco, New Granada, sore-footed, and worn out by hardships and fatigue, a melancholy illustration of South-American liberty.

There is, however, no special desire to read newspapers among the people in the interior of Ecuador, where we find convents instead of printing-presses, and military barracks instead of school-houses. Street talk is the means of circulating home news, and about events in foreign countries the people care but little.

In 1862, a dentist came to Quito — a native of Venezuela, and a man of some intelligence — who had travelled for years through Ecuador, Venezuela, New Granada, and Peru; still he did not know that there was war in the United States. He was but one of many. I have even found men of great positive knowledge, and important public positions, who spent years of their lives without reading a newspaper, and who knew of current political events in the outer world only from hearsay. For the political affairs of their own country, it is true, a press is hardly needed. They scarcely ever rise above the level of mere personalities. I often listened to political discussions between men belonging to different political parties, and heard a great deal of personal criticism, but it was very seldom that I heard an abstract principle discussed, or a question of statecraft or political economy argued. One party vilified the other; one party charged the other with the very same crimes and acts of tyranny with which it was itself charged in return. When I objected to this mode of political discussion I was told that persons were the representatives of principles, and that by promoting the political claims of certain persons, the principles which they advocated would be furthered. Hence we see these partisans faithfully follow the standard of a favorite leader, no matter how often he changes his principles or belies his professions.

Yet it would be unjust to speak of the tyrannical and arbitrary spirit and practices of South American governments, without considering the great disadvantages at which they are placed. Nothing, of course, could extenuate crimes and outrages like those I have related, yet from what I know of Spanish-American character, I cannot believe that a government, which should endeavor to keep itself strictly and conscientiously within the bounds of legal and constitutional obligations, would be able to maintain itself for a single week against the anarchical and revolutionary tendencies of the opponents with whom it has to deal. We must likewise consider the peculiar disadvantages under which the political existence of our Latin neighbors began. We must consider the colonial system and policy of Spain, which had unfitted them for constitutional self-government, instead of preparing them for it.

From a centralized, meddling, and relentless despotism, the Spanish-American colonies passed to a state of unbridled licentiousness. They were not prepared for liberty, which they did not understand. With their education sadly neglected, and their minds perverted by monkish superstition on one side, and the extravagance of the first French Revolution on the other, and without any political or parliamentary experience or training, they were called upon to lay the foundations of a new system of government and society. Their impulses were good and generous, but the vices inherent to Spanish civilization got the better of minds ill-regulated and entirely unfitted for the great task which they were called upon to undertake.

When the North American colonies first gave vent to their just grievances, they asked only for their rights as Britons. No new theories were advanced, no innovations were attempted. Free utterance of opinion was not a novelty to the Anglo-Saxon; and to the principle of self-taxation even the arbitrary Tudors had been constrained to defer. The American Revolution was not so much of a change as a vindication of principle. British-Americans were accustomed to local and municipal self-government, and to the utmost freedom of individual locomotion and enterprise. Not so our Spanish neighbors. They had no ancient rights to vindicate, for the king was absolute in both hemispheres. They had never known colonial legislatures, for most of their laws were made in Spain. They had no parliamentary or representative experience, and were unacquainted with the institutions and experience of the only European nation that had a constitutional history. Heretical England was a sealed book to them, which the Inquisition did not allow them to read. The fountain-head of all power over the colonies was the "*Consejo de Indias*," a tribunal which sat in Spain, and the members of which, appointed by the crown, were mostly Spaniards, many of whom had never seen America. The viceroys of the colonies were Spaniards who came to the new world for the purpose only of enriching themselves and their minions. The ports of the colonies were closed to immigration. Even to the visits of foreigners they were almost hermetically sealed. The inhabitants enjoyed no freedom of locomotion, no freedom of commerce and trade, no liberty of the press or political discussion, no liberty of conscience. They were not even the masters of their own property. What they should plant or sow in this or in that colony; what branch of industry should be cultivated in this or in that district; where they should buy, and where and what they should be allowed to sell; with what ports they should trade, and whither they should go or not go; how much they should be allowed to import or export; when and where they should get married, and when and where, not; and how long they should be allowed to stay away from their wives; all this and a great deal more was regulated and prescribed by law. Nothing was allowed to regulate itself. The government provided for every thing, and carried on all sorts of commercial, agricultural, or industrial business. There was no relation of private and every-day life with which the government did not interfere, and which it did not attempt to regulate. Like children, the colonies had allowed themselves to be ruled. They had been kept in darkness and ignorance by the Inquisition, and were corrupted by the baleful influences of Indian and negro slavery. Titles of nobility constituted their only object of ambition; and though the American Spaniards hated the European Spaniards, whom they nicknamed "*Chapetones*," they vied with the latter in loyalty and obedience to their king. They would never have dared to take charge of their own affairs, had not Ferdinand VII. been captured by Napoleon. The first revolutionary steps in Spanish-America were taken in the name of "our beloved and worshiped king," and avowedly for the purpose of maintaining his divine authority against the agents and emissaries of the

French intruder. The faithful colonies would never have entertained the idea of independence, at first suggested only by a few extreme radicals, had not Ferdinand VII. recklessly, foolishly, and brutally driven — I may even be allowed the expression — kicked, them away.

When the chains fell at last, all restraint was broken through ; and ambitious generals, rapacious demagogues, and well-meaning but unenlightened, inexperienced, and violent enthusiasts, every one of them jealous and distrustful of the other, with an ignorant and imbruted mass to build upon, were to reorganize society. Is it to be wondered at that they failed?

Their war of independence lasted very long, and was carried on in a most unrelenting and barbarous manner on both sides. Prisoners were massacred, and non-combatants were executed without mercy. The civil wars of the old conquerors were repeated by their descendants. The Spaniard was not yet expelled from the soil of America when the Republicans themselves turned their bloody weapons against each other's breasts. Endless civil wars followed the establishment of Spanish-American independence. Political ambition, personal jealousies, impracticable theories, official venality, reckless disregard of individual rights and legal obligations, foolish, meddling, and empirical legislation, and an absolute want of political morality, formed the principal features of their republican history. Contempt for labor — that fatal Spanish inheritance — and an intolerant, bigoted, and rapacious state church, sucked at the vitals of the young republics. Such causes could not fail to produce the effects we have seen.

The Spanish-American did not know, and has not

learned, to abide by majority decisions, or to redress wrongs by legal and constitutional remedies. From the ballot-box he invariably appeals to the sword. The restlessness and jealousy of his political leaders are unbounded, the ignorance of the masses is extreme. Those in power will not voluntarily surrender it. Those out of power will strain every nerve to oust their lucky rivals. Bloody executions, forced loans and contributions, tyrannical confiscations and arbitrary banishments, reckless issues of worthless paper money, unjust impressments, and willful destruction of property, mark the path of the victorious party; in all of which outrages, as a general rule, it only follows the previous examples of its vanquished predecessors. The latter, defeated on the field of battle, will resort to plotting and conspiracy, in which arts they are masters. They will conspire as long as their enemies remain in power. Baffled in one plot, they will immediately concoct another, and, in their own opinion, they are always sure to succeed. Having hardly any thing else to do, and hardly ever wishing or intending to do any thing else, they can devote the best part of their time to intriguing and fomenting discontent and rebellion. No great commercial schemes or industrial enterprises engage their attention. The business of a Spanish-American republic is periodically paralyzed by war or revolution. Its agriculture is continually interfered with by the recruiting officers, who carry away farm-laborers and beasts of burden. The middle classes always become poorer, the poor remain poor, and the number of wealthy families is continually diminishing. Men whose ancestors belonged to the richest of the land, will be found struggling with misery and privation. They can leave nothing to their children but prejudices and aristocratic pride. They may be graduates of colleges or universities, but almost every white man of good family is, and hence liberal professions do not pay. How, then, are these gentlemen to live? It does not become their dignity to stoop to the level of an Indian or half-breed by performing common labor, and they have no capital or energy to engage in commercial enterprises, nor could the anarchical condition of the country encourage them to do so. They are bound, therefore, to live on political employments; and the overthrow of a government that does not provide for them will be their chief object and occupation. They are revolutionists from necessity, and are ready to do the bidding of those who are revolutionists from ambition or idleness.

It will now be understood why a government, instead of endeavoring to promote the general welfare and develop the resources of the country, must strain every nerve to maintain its bare existence against the restless and unremitting efforts of its enemies. To detect conspiracies, to prevent insurrection, to watch suspected characters, and to rid itself, by whatever means, of its declared enemies, must be the principal and almost exclusive care of an administration so placed. To this object every other consideration will be sacrificed. Individual rights will be trampled upon, depredations without end will be committed, and the soldiery will have to be kept in good humor, at whatever cost. Hence it is that in a country which bountiful Nature has intended for a paradise, crumbling ruins and tottering walls, impassable roads and miserable hovels, neglected fields and uninhabited wastes, lazy vagabonds and filthy beggars, cry out against the depravity and culpable incapacity of man.

Shall we be surprised, therefore, if monarchical ideas are gaining ground in those countries? The advocates of a monarchical system of government are more numerous than is generally supposed. They often speak without reserve. They argue in the following manner: "Experience has taught us that our race is not fit for republican self-government. The principal purpose of all government is the security of person and property — the protection of individual rights. This purpose our institutions have failed to accomplish. Our lives and liberties are at the mercy of every political adventurer who succeeds to power. Our property is continually being pillaged or destroyed by those who ought to protect it. We cannot maintain order at home; we cannot remain at peace with our neighbors. Our agriculture has not advanced beyond what it was at the time of the conquest. Our commerce is languishing; manufacturing industry we have almost none. We have no roads. Our cities decay; the condition of our finances is hopeless; we are poor in the lap of boundless natural wealth. Is this state of affairs to last forever? We cannot exist as republics, and we cannot establish a monarchy of our own; for without foreign aid it would not maintain itself for a single day. Still we admit the almost unconquerable difficulties of establishing a strong government or a monarchy by the aid of foreign intervention. The traditions of our war of independence are still dear to the people. They dislike foreigners, and still cling to the republican name. And yet we have no alternative left. We must either submit to be swallowed up in the end by the Anglo-Saxon race, or follow the example of the French party of Mexico. The former would be preferable to our present miserable existence; but we naturally cling to our nationality, our religion, and our language, and should not like so radical a change. Moreover, we cannot afford to wait until, in the natural course of time and events, the Anglo-Saxon extends his dominion over South America. Bad, therefore, as foreign intervention may be, it is our last and our only hope. And yet what foreign power would undertake the hopeless and unprofitable task of saving us from ourselves?"

To such reasoning I was often compelled to listen. There are points in it which cannot be answered. The present condition of the Spanish-American republics is indeed very discouraging. The infusion of fresh blood — a mass immigration of a vigorous and enterprising foreign element, might perhaps save them. But where is that immigration to come from? As long as our immense territory west of the Mississippi; as long as British Columbia and the young giant Australia promise a vast and fertile field of enterprise to European immigration, — a field where every thing is ready for its reception, and where religious toleration, constitutional liberty, and security of person and property are really guaranteed to the settler, — who would bury himself, however splendid the climate, and however rich the soil, in the inaccessible highlands of the Andes, with their impassable roads, their earthquakes, the religious fanaticism of the inhabitants, their want of schools, and their endless foreign wars and revolutionary convulsions? Who would seek a home in the lowlands on the sea-board, under the burning sun of the tropics, with their fevers and dysenteries, and other climatic diseases, as long as there are room and prospects for him in the cradle of future Empire States between the Mississippi and the Pacific Ocean? who would prefer Spanish indolence and poverty to Saxon enterprise and prosperity?

There is no hope for the present that Spanish America — perhaps Chili and Buenos Ayres excepted — will be rejuvenated by a large and civilizing foreign immigration. A remote future may realize this expectation, but it is too far in the distance. When the hand that writes these lines has long moldered in the grave, and generations upon generations have passed away, then perhaps will the area of Saxon civilization extend from Hudson's Bay and New Cornwall to Patagonia and Cape Horn. Then, perhaps, will the world see a new conquest effected, not by the prowess of military heroes or savage filibusterism, but by modern genius and the blissful arts of peace. Then, perhaps, will prosperous empires stretch over this western hemisphere, based not on the "manifest-destiny" programme of an insatiable slave power, but on the rights of man, the triumph of modern civilization, and the blessings of real liberty and law. Then will the crimes of Negro slavery in the North, and Indian slavery in the South, be atoned for; and peace and prosperity will reign at last over the graves of Montezuma and Atahuallpa. The vision is beautiful, but, alas, it is yet a dream!

In the mean time, it becomes our most imperative duty to counteract by our own example the pernicious effects which the example of Spanish America continually produces in the Old World. It becomes our duty to prove to the nations of the earth, that republican constitutional self-government is not a vision or a dream, but a living reality; so that when the enemies of liberty and republicanism point to Spanish America in order to prove the correctness of their reactionary views, the friends of liberty may be able to point to North America for a triumphant refutation. This is a duty we owe to ourselves and to humanity. We cannot force other nations to be like ourselves; we cannot force other nations to be virtuous and wise. We cannot compel our Spanish neighbors to abide by the laws of their own making, and to love peace, order, and liberty as we do. But we can prove to them, by our own increasing prosperity, intelligence, and happiness, what a blessing it is to be law-abiding and tolerant; to preserve order and domestic tranquillity without sacrificing liberty, and to maintain liberty without endangering order and peace. North America may lean on its past, and its short but glorious political history, and thus be truly progressive while truly conservative; but Spanish America must bury the institutions, customs, prejudices, and idiosyncrasies of the past, beyond the possibility of resurrection. She must drain the swamp of stagnation, indolence, and thriftlessness, and pile mountains of solid rock and fresh earth on the grave of the Middle Ages, before she can hope to see, instead of the *ignes fatui* and fungi of the swamp, the healthy foliage of modern civilization.

## CHAPTER XIII.

Trip to the Province of Imbabura. — Descent to the River Guaillabamba. — The Pyramids. — Their History. — The Village of Guaillabamba. — Wild Mountainous Scenery. — The Switzerland of America. — The River Pisque. — A Historical Reminiscence. — Gonzalo Pizarro and the Viceroy Blasco Nuñez Vela. — American Aloe; its Multifarious Uses. — Tabacundo. — *Gente del Pueblo* or Common People. — Alto de Cajas. — Lake St. Pablo. — The Festival of St. John. — Great Indian Celebrations. — The Feast at Otabalo. — Indian Dances and Masquerades. — Gambling. — Ugliness of Indian Women. — The Chapel of Monserate. — Idolatrous Practices. — *Corrida de Gallos.* — San Juan and San Pedro at the Village of Cayambi. — Mt. Cayambi. — Longevity. — Agua Gloriada. — Contra-dances. — *Guarapo.* — Reports of Volcanic Activity. — More Gold Legends. — *Serro Pelado.* — Col. Hall's attempted Ascent of Mt. Cayambi. — Gold Somewhere. — The Napo Province on the Eastern Side of the Cordillera. — Compulsory Sales of Merchandise to Indians by the Governor. — Destruction of Three Cities by the Indians. — No Vestige remains. — Poetic Retribution. — Legends and Traditions. — The Fate of the Captured Women of Golden Sevilla.

Desirous of acquainting myself with the country to the north of the capital, and especially the province of Imbabura, of whose beauty and fertility I had heard so much, I left Quito on the 24th of June, 1863. There are two roads leading to the northern province. The one crossing the paramo of Mojanda is considerably shorter, but impassable in rainy weather. The other, through the village of Guaillabamba turns the mountain chain that separates the provinces of Pichincha and Imbabura, and traversing a ridge by which that chain is connected with the folds of Mt. Imbabura, descends to the lake of San Pablo. To know both I took the latter, resolving to return by the former

For several leagues to the northeast of Quito, and

before reaching the sandy deserts of Pomasqui and San Antonio, the country is nearly level, and clothed with an ever-verdant growth of native grass, sparingly dotted with trees of wild cherries (*capuli*) and myrtle.

At a point called "Chaupicruz," the Camino Real separates from the road to Cotocollao and Pomasqui, which we now leave to the left, and descend into a sandy plain called "Carretas," from which we have a view of the valley of Tumbaco and Puembo to our right. Passing through an insignificant village called Chingletina, we arrive at the brow of a steep hill, from which the descent to the tortuous Guaillabamba commences. This river takes its rise at the head of the valley of Chillo, and is augmented by several streams coming principally from the eastern Cordillera. It finally unites its waters with those of the Esmeraldas in its course to the Pacific.

A yawning *quebrada* (defile or ravine) now opens at our feet. The mountain is so steep and precipitous that we must wend our way down in a continuous zigzag. The different paths, or rather ruts, which we follow, are generally narrow, and sometimes so near the precipice that the eye involuntarily shrinks from the contemplation of the depth over which we seem to hover. This, however, is nothing uncommon on South-American roads. It is a sensation to which the traveller will have to get accustomed on his way from Chingletina to Tabacundo.

The descent from the table-land to the bottom of the valley, measuring a perpendicular height of nearly three thousand feet, can hardly be achieved in less than two hours, during which the traveller is incommoded by the heat of the sun reflected from the bare rocks and sand, to avoid which he prefers, if possible, to start with the early dawn.

The upper part of the mountain on which we now stand is bleak and barren, particularly when viewed from a distance. Nevertheless, upon beginning our descent, we meet with an abundance of wild flowers, relieving the monotony of a scarce and stunted vegetation and a parched and dreary soil. But dreary and barren beyond conception, and almost repulsive to behold, are the hills to the right of the quebrada, and in the direction of Puembo and Pifo. Intersected by innumerable ravines, they seem to form a mass-meeting of independent paupers, stripped of every thing like dress or vegetation, except an almost imperceptible threadbare coat of faded yellow green, insufficient to hide their nakedness. In the rear of the plain resting on these hills, rise the mountains on which the plateau of Quito rests, and in the rear of all, Pichincha raises its rocky head. To the east of Pichincha, the Corazón, the Ilinisa, Rumiñagui, Pasachoa, Cotopaxi, Sincholagua, and Antisana range in an imposing semicircle, from which they look down into the valleys of Chillo and Puembo, which are separated from each other, by an isolated mountain called "Ilalu."

We are so high now that we cannot hear the wild rushing of the waters below. In front of us, on the other side of the river, we see the village of Guaillabamba in the distance; a fresh green spot, pleasing to the eye, and relieving the barren monotony that surrounds us. It rests on a pedestal of bald hills, and is surrounded by a second and higher range of bleak and sandy mountains. To our right, on the other side of an abyss, the bottom of which we cannot descry from our present stand-point, is the pyramid of Caraburu, one of the points of the triangle selected by the French Academicians and two Spanish mathematicians, in 1736, for the purpose of measuring a degree of the meridian under the equator. Two pyramids were intended to commemorate their labors, the one just referred to, and another at a point called Oyambaro, near the village of Yaruqui; the summit of Mt. Pambamarca, having been selected for the vertex of the triangle. The pyramids now existing are not the same, however, that were erected by the French Academicians in the year 1736; these latter having been demolished by order of the Royal Council of the Indies. M. de la Condamine, one of the French Academicians, it seems, had proceeded with their construction without having consulted his Spanish colleagues, Don Antonio Ulloa and Don Jorje Juan, who had been appointed by the King of Spain to assist in the arduous and important enterprise of ascertaining the true shape of the earth by the above-mentioned measurement. Condamine had not even consulted his French colleague, M. Godin, who seems to have been his superior in the expedition; and in the tablets which the former inserted in the pyramids, the names of the Spanish mathematicians had not been mentioned. This want of courtesy, however, did not create so much indignation among the inhabitants of the province of Quito, as the French arms, the lilies, with which Condamine had adorned the pyramids. This act was considered by the populace as equivalent to an assertion by France, of a right to the possession of the colony, and a universal outcry was raised, which led to judicial proceedings against the pyramids before the *Real Audiencia* of Quito. The suit was instituted at the complaint of the Spanish mathematicians, and defended by Monsieur de la Condamine with great vigor and ingenuity. He said that the lilies, being the arms of the house of Bourbon, could not be derogatory to the dignity of Spain, as branches of the same family ruled over both countries. He further said that those very lilies were sculptured on the façades of several of the churches of Quito, without giving umbrage to anybody. With regard to the omission of the names of the Spanish mathematicians, he was willing to insert them in the inscription, and to place them above and before the names of the Frenchmen. To some such arrangement the *Real Audiencia* of Quito consented, and ordered the obnoxious features of the pyramids to be changed; but the Council of the Indies was dissatisfied with this moderation, and in conformity with instructions received from the Court, commanded their demolition, and the erection in their stead of other suitable monuments. The Marquis de la Ensenada, by whom this order was given, however, as if ashamed of its barbarity, modified it by a second order issued two months later (Oct. 17, 1746), in which he instructed the Audiencia of Quito to spare the pyramids if the obnoxious inscriptions could be removed without injury to the structures; but the work of destruction had already been accomplished, and during the century following their demolition, not a vestige of them remained. In November, 1836, President Rocafuerte rebuilt them, depositing under their foundations an urn containing a tablet with a Spanish inscription, of which the following is a translation: —

"The French Academicians, Messrs. Louis Godin, Peter Bouguer, and Charles Maria de la Condamine, sent by Louis XV., King of France, and under the ministry of M. Maurepas, erected these pyramids in the month of November, 1736; they were destroyed by command of the kings of Spain, and rebuilt one hundred years afterwards, in November, 1836 (on the exact points determined by the French Academicians), by order of his Excellency Vicente Rocafuerte, President of the Republic, the Hon. Antonio Morales being Minister of Foreign Affairs. At that time the throne of France was occupied by Louis Philippe, the president of his council of ministers being M. Thiers, and John Baptist W. De Mendeville consul of France to the Republic of Ecuador. This tablet was made and engraved in the mint of Quito, November 20th, 1836, M. Alberto Zalazza being first director of the establishment, and it was deposited under the base of this pyramid on the 25th of the same month of November, of the same year 1836."

In 1841 the French Academy presented to the Ecuadorian government an inscription which they desired to have engraved on the pyramids,[1] but it has not yet been done, and probably never will be. The structures themselves are pyramids only in name. They are low, square piles of bricks, whitewashed, and covered with a pyramidal roof of tiles. At a distance, if it were not for their coat of whitewash, they could not be distinguished from common Indian huts, which they resemble in appearance.

But it is time to commence our descent into the yawning *quebrada* of Guaillabamba.

With our descent, vegetation increases, but it is a quaint, cheerless, withering vegetation. The stunted trees of the *Mimosa* or *Espino* (*spine*), as the natives call them, flattened on top in a most curious manner, are covered with a parasitical vegetation — resembling long, gray beards — floating from their branches, and giving them, as they stand between the rocks, and

[1] Geminam pyramidem, Monumentum doctrinæ simul et grande adjumentum, olim injuria temporum eversam, Vicentius Rocafuerte Reipublicæ Æquatorialis præses restituit, gloriosæque instaurationis litteris consignandæ Annuente consortium Ludovico Philippo I. Rege Francorum, ornari conjunctis utriusque gentis insignibus jussit curavit. Anno MDCCCXXXVI.

queer and fantastic formations of cacti and pencos,[1] the appearance of old wizards haunting this enchanted scene.[2] A stone bridge is thrown across the river, the bed of which is about six thousand three hundred feet above the level of the sea, and the deafening noise of the rushing waters follows us long after we have passed it.

The ascent on the other side of the river is less steep and precipitous, and we soon reach the small villages of Cuchupango, Cachipamba, and Guaillabamba, which seem to form one continuous population. The village of Guaillabamba is situated about a mile farther to the east of the bridge, and but six hundred and forty-six feet above the bed of the river. The character of the scenery now changes. As if by enchantment, we are transported into a semi-tropical region. Here grow the coffee-tree, the sugar-cane,[3] and many of the rank creepers peculiar to southern climes. The houses, or rather huts, are no longer of earth or *adobe*, like those around Quito, but of a species of wild cane which the natives call *cariso*, interwoven with twigs. They are low, having merely a ground-floor, and are thatched with the straw (dried leaves) of the sugar-cane. The

1 *Penco*, the *Cereus sepinus*, D. C. V. iii., p. 467; *Cactus sepinus* H. B. K., Syn. Pl., vol. iii., p. 370, to which is appended the following remark : "Ad sepes construendas inservit et baccæ contra colicam biliosam feliciter adhibentur." The whole plant abounds in mucilage, which, mixed with gypsum, or powdered lime, is used economically in whitewashing. It is perhaps the only species which reaches the elevation of 10,600 feet. — *From Dr. Wm. Jameson's Manuscript Notes.*

2 This profuse, beard-like growth, is the *Tillandsia usneoides*, a widely distributed species, occurring in the hot valleys of the Andes, in some parts of the country near Guayaquil, in the woods near Rio Janeiro, and even in some districts of the United States. Among the natives it is known by the name of *Salvage*, or *Barba de Salvage*, and is used as an ordinary article for stuffing mattresses, sofas, and other furniture. — *Ibid.*

3 At the village of Guaillabamba, the sugar-cane requires a period of eighteen months to arrive at a state of maturity. — *Ibid.*

inhabitants no longer present that ruddy and healthy appearance which cheers the heart in the Ecuadorian highlands, but are pale, sickly, and haggard. A plat of marshy ground, on the left side of the village, fills the atmosphere with miasmatic exhalations. Intermittent fevers are prevalent. A single night's sojourn will frequently communicate the germ of the malady, which may, after several days, be developed in another place, far removed from its influence.

I left Guaillabamba between one and two o'clock in the afternoon. A short ride up the mountain side, and I had again left every thing behind that reminded me of the tropics. I now rode along the slopes, and over the ridges of sandy mountains, forming deep and narrow defiles, through which murmuring and rushing rivers wind their tortuous course. I was in the Switzerland of America again. The same scarcity of trees that characterizes other parts of the interior strikes us here. But here the mountains are covered with green shrubs rising to the height of little trees, and enameled with wild flowers, so that they are not so saddening to the eye as those that cluster around the entrance of the *quebrada* of Guaillabamba. Our path leads us along precipices for several leagues. The rocks through which passages have been hewn, and which sometimes overhang the road in a most threatening manner; the quaint and curious vegetation with which these rocks are covered; the height in which we toil along; the foaming rivers below, impatient of their confinement; the almost perpendicular mountain sides down which one false step of the horse or mule would inevitably hurl us into the deeper abyss of death; the mountains themselves towering around and above us, now and then crowned with trachytic rocks of queer formation;

the loose stones with which our path is frequently covered, if not obstructed; and the setting sun casting a last smile on the wild scene, present a highly picturesque and romantic aspect, and fill the soul with the grandest emotions. Now we pass over the lofty mountain ridges, with nothing but the sky above us, and that singular vegetation around us which precedes the monotonous grass of the paramo; now we descend into the deepest recesses of hidden defiles, in which the majestic *aguacate* tree, with its beautiful dark-green foliage, affords a pleasant relief to the wandering eye; now we have to descend to a river and ford it, then again to ascend the highest ridges on the other side.

One of the rivers I had to cross, was the Pisque, which takes its rise on Mt. Cayambi, and flows through these narrow valleys over huge masses of basalt, detached from its banks, which latter reach an elevation of nearly fifteen hundred feet. A narrow path ascends from the other side of the bridge, cut with infinite labor through the basalt, and paved with the same material. Here it was, according to an unsupported account of Father Velasco, that in 1546, Gonzalo Pizarro awaited the arrival of the Viceroy Blasco Nuñez Vela, who, falling into the snare prepared for him by the former, had left his safe retreat at Popayan, and, reinforced by Sebastian Benalcazar, marched on Quito, having falsely been made to believe that Pizarro had gone south with his forces, leaving only a small garrison under Pedro de Puelles to protect the town. Father Velasco then goes on to state that the Viceroy, in the disguise of an Indian, reconnoitered in person the position of Gonzalo, and finding it impregnable, determined to go to Quito by another route. The Father also speaks of a tradition that Gonzalo Pizarro reconnoitered the position of the Viceroy on that very same day, and also in the disguise of an Indian. These stories, however, must have originated in the over-fruitful imagination of Father Velasco, who is continually carried away by his love for the marvelous and romantic. None of the contemporary authors whom I have consulted on the subject, mentions them, even as legends. On the contrary, according to Zarate, the armies were so near each other that such dangerous reconnoitering was entirely unnecessary. The Viceroy's camp was on the steep hill-side forming the opposite bank of the river, and the voices of the sentinels could be distinctly heard in the opposite camps, and "they did not fail to salute one another with the epithet of 'traitors.'"[1] Finding that Pizarro's position was such as to enable him to hold his own against superior forces, the Viceroy, whose forces were considerably inferior, did not dare to attack him, but by a night march, attempted to get into his rear. Leaving his camp-fires burning to deceive the enemy, he began his circuitous march in the direction of Quito. But from the description of this part of the country, and its roads, which I have just given, my readers will be able to judge of the hardships which he had to suffer. Unfortunately it began to rain. Rivers and defiles had to be crossed, and precipitous mountains to be ascended and descended, in the darkness of a tempestuous, cheerless night. Many horses fell on the slippery ground, and rolled into abysses; and, losing his way, instead of falling upon the rear of Pizarro's position, which he could not reach, the Viceroy had to lead his exhausted and discouraged troops to Quito, near which,

[1] Zarate, *Conq. del Peru*, lib. v. chap. 34.

a day or two after this fatal march, the decisive battle was fought (January 18, 1546).

Wending our way through a labyrinth of narrow valleys, rivers, and defiles, we at last reached the Chorrera, a cascade through which the waters gathering on the table-lands above, are discharged into the rivers, the course of which we had followed for the last two or three hours. A few miserable huts are built around it. Orange and aguacate[1] trees are planted around some habitations below the waterfall. But the regular tambo is about two hundred feet above it. It is built of reeds brought up from Guaillabamba, but it is the last building of that kind on our onward march to Ibarra. It may be considered a landmark of the semi-tropical region which we have just left; for now the houses which we pass on the road are made of adobes, as around Quito. The tambo belongs to a little hacienda, occupying the narrow ridge of a mountain projecting into and forming a bend in the stream. It contained two unfloored rooms, if they may be called so, — one for the accommodation of travellers, with four platforms of reeds fastened to the sides of the building, and serving as bedsteads; and another, a smaller one, in which the landlord slept, with his numerous family; and which, at the same time, served as kitchen, the smoke finding its way out of the hut as well as it could, through the door, and the chinks in the side-walls. Windows there were none. There was an opening for the door, which served as an entrance, but there was no door to it, and the cold night air poured in unmercifully. But travelling in Ecuador is a campaign life. For whatever enjoyment the scenery

[1] *Aguacate* is the alligator pear, this being the English name by which it is known in Jamaica. In Peru it is called *palta*.

affords to the traveller, he must dearly pay with vexations and hardships, produced by the total want of all those accommodations and comforts to which civilization has accustomed us. One who cannot make up his mind to "rough it," had better not visit this country.

On the morning of the 25th, a little before sunrise, I continued my journey. I soon reached the table-land extending to the base of the eastern Andes. The first village I arrived at, after a ride of about an hour and a half, was Cachiguango. It consists of two rows of Indian huts, built of earth or adobes (sun-baked bricks), the region of the reeds being fortunately behind us. At the same time the mountains seemed to have disappeared from beneath our feet, and removed far away into the distance. The sight of wheat and barley greeted us, instead of the sugar-cane, orange, and aguacate. It is wonderful with what rapidity we pass in these highlands from one climate to another. The fields, as well as the sides of the roads, are inclosed by long hedges of *cabulla* (American aloe), the pointed blades of which, in many a narrow passage, threaten the eyes and face of the unwary traveller. The aloe is one of the most important and useful plants of the country. So manifold are the useful purposes for which it is employed, and so frequently is it found in the Ecuadorian highlands, that I must give it a better introduction to my readers. *Maguey*, or *cabulla*, is the "*Metl*" of the Mexicans, the *Maguey de Cocuyza* of the inhabitants of Venezuela. It is the *Agava Americana* of botanists, and the American aloe of plain English parlance. According to a vulgar but erroneous idea, it flowers only once in a hundred years. In Mexico, *Pulque*, the national beverage, is extracted from it by incisions made in the stem. In Ecuador there is no end to its uses. In the neighborhood which I am now describing, the Indians thatch their huts with its leaves. The leaves, when tapped, yield a large quantity of syrup, called "*miel de cabulla.*" The fibrous portions of the same organs are woven into sacks (*costales*), of which large quantities are manufactured in Ambato and the neighborhood, and in Hatuntaqui and Ibarra. From the same fibre ropes are made, and a very important article called "*alpargates*," a species of sandal worn by the common people all over the country.[1] Those who travel to the Napo, as the eastern province is generally called, or to Esmeraldas by land, or through other mountainous districts where mule-paths are still unknown, must wear *alpargates*, because no other kind of boots or shoes would last them longer than a day. *Alpargates*, however, are strong, light, and durable; although it takes some time to accustom a civilized foot to the burning sensation which they at first produce. The broad leaves of the agave are used in schools (of the poorer classes) instead of paper, to teach the rudiments of writing. The flower stalks constitute a light and indestructible material, of which ladders are made, besides being applied to other domestic purposes. The flowers boiled, with the addition of vinegar, make an agreeable pickle called "*alcaparras.*" The roofs of huts, as I have just said, are sometimes covered with the leaves, and I have

[1] "To make these sandals, the fibre is first formed into a braid nearly half an inch wide, which is tightly coiled and stitched together to form the sole. A fore-part is then woven to contain the point of the foot, with merely a band behind to secure the sandal to the heel. . . . . . The pulp of the leaves of which this fibre is made, is a very good substitute for soap; and the porous wood of the stem, when dried, forms an excellent strap for sharpening cutting instruments, on account of the fine grit it contains." — *Notes on Colombia, taken in the years* 1822 *and* 1823, *by an Officer of the U. S. Army*. Philadelphia, 1827.

also seen the side-walls of Indian *chozas* patched up with them. The common people use the leaves as soap to wash with. In some districts, where great scarcity of fuel prevails, the poor people supply with them the place of firewood, for which they are, however, but a poor and smoky substitute; and the Indians cut off the spines, and use them in the place of pins.[1] Hedges, in the Ecuadorian highlands, are scarcely ever any thing else than living fences of aloes or *lecheros*, a tree of which I shall soon have occasion to speak. There is another plant which greatly resembles the aloe, it is the *Maguey verde* (green maguey), with which the long rows of *cabulla* are not only frequently, but almost invariably interspersed. Its color is greener and lighter, but in form it somewhat resembles the same, although it belongs to a totally different genus. It is, in fact, a species of *Yucca*, and yields a large quantity of fibre, used for domestic purposes.[2]

At about 10 o'clock, A. M., I reached Tabacundo, a considerable village, inhabited, however, only by *gente del pueblo* (common people) ; and I have already explained that between these and the higher classes the lines of demarcation are strongly drawn. The barriers which divide them are impassable. In a country where governing is the exclusive province and privilege of the upper ten, if not of certain families in which all polit-

[1] From the long leaves of this plant, by bruising and beating, a thick juice is expressed; this is mixed with water, boiled and kept skimmed, until reduced to the consistence of honey; it is then fit for use. In cases of cuts, when severe and dangerous, if applied, it cures in three days, and never permits gangrene to take place. The most inveterate ulcers are not known to resist its sanative powers more than fifteen days." — *Journal of a Residence and Travel in Colombia during the years* 1823 *and* 1824, *by Captain Charles Stuart Cochrane, of the Royal Navy.* In two volumes; London, 1825.

[2] From Dr. Jameson's manuscript notes.

ical influence seems to be concentrated, the favor of the common people needs not be courted. It is true, the common man has a vote, if he can read and write; but very little does he care for voting, and very few opportunities are given him to decide any thing by his vote.

At Tabacundo I stopped for breakfast at a house which an unorthographical inscription on the wall announced to be a *casa posada*, although at such places almost every house is considered to be a *tambo*. The landlady got through her preparations uncommonly quick. Generally, it takes them a couple of hours to prepare the most indifferent meal. The cause of this slowness is the clumsiness of their cooking utensils and fire-places, if a few stones piled up against a few smoking sticks of wood can be called a fire-place. I was led into a large room, which at the same time served as a dining-room, laundry, tailor's shop, gambling saloon, and bedroom. The breakfast consisted, as usual, of *locro de queso* (a potato soup with cheese and *agi*), fried eggs, with baked plantain slices and toasted bread, some meat, and, to my utter astonishment, chocolate, — a luxury which I had not expected at Tabacundo, and which placed the establishment, however modest in its appearance, far above the common level of *tambos*. When I asked the landlady what my bill was, she gave me the very common and always unpleasant answer, "*Lo que V. guste*," ("what you please.") I could not induce her to name the amount, and had to give her what I thought would be fair.

The women whom I saw at Tabacundo were not handsome. Their faces betrayed more or less their ruling passion — drink — the chief and almost only amusement of the common people of the country. These women can swallow fabulous quantities of strong liquor, and are passionately fond of bacchanalian orgies. Tabacundo is chiefly an agricultural population, but I saw many weaving looms in the houses, on which coarse cotton and woolen goods are made. The number of the inhabitants is estimated at two thousand, which I believe to be overrated.

After having proceeded from Tabacundo in a north-easterly direction for some time, I reached the north-western end of the plain, which is here hemmed in by a prolongation of Mt. Imbabura. The road now suddenly turns to the west, ascending the Alto de Cajas, a ridge by which the folds of Mt. Imbabura are connected with the opposite mountain range of Mojanda. This time our ascent led through rich pastures, on which herds of cattle and sheep were grazing. The meadows and mountains on the sides of the road were treeless again, but the verdure with which this alpine region was covered was fresh and pleasing, and the slopes were dotted with clusters of Indian huts, with their quaint pyramidal roofs, thatched with gray straw or dried weeds. Upon reaching the summit of the Alto, which is covered with a vegetation of shrubs and wild flowers, such as generally precede the dry grass (*paja*) of the paramo, the lake of San Pablo lay at my feet, serenely calm in the valley below. Its shores are covered with haciendas, fields, and Indian habitations called "*huasipongos*," and rise slowly and gradually to the mountains in the rear. On the right of the lake is the village of San Pablo, covering a considerable area of ground, and having its *plaza*, like every Spanish village, however small and miserable it may be. The lake is encompassed by mountains, but above them all rises the beautiful snow-clad Cotacachi, forming an appropriate background to this most charming scene. Imbabura, a volcano, but only occasionally covered with snow, rises to the right of our position; the gloomy Mojanda, with its horns of trachytic rocks, to the left. The view which I now enjoyed was different from any thing I had hitherto seen in Ecuador, but, nevertheless, unmistakably impressed upon it was that indescribable air of sadness and melancholy, that stillness and death-like repose, which are inseparable from a Quitonian landscape. The houses are without chimneys, from which a cheerful cloud of smoke might lustily curl up into the air. If smoke can be seen at all, it lazily and timidly clings to the roofs, and seems incapable of separating itself from the cottage from which it issues. No grove, no forest, relieves the wandering eye. The noises of railroads, saw-mills, or steam-boats are listened for in vain. All is silence below. Not a boat, not a sail, not even a canoe, ruffles the waters of the melancholy lake; not a coach, not a cart or wagon, enlivens the deserted highways. The cattle slowly moving along the shores or on the hills are the only evidence of life the scenery presents. But it is the gloomy life of the brute; and there are no vestiges of the active, struggling, intelligent life of enterprising man.

The lake is about a league and a half in circumference; its waters are exceedingly cold; its depth is very great. A small species of fish which the Spaniards call "*preñadilla*," and the Indians "*imba*," is to be found in the shallow water near the shore. The Indians, when they want to cross from one side to the other, construct of reeds, which grow along the shore, a kind of *balsa*, on which they ride astraddle up to their hips in water, and paddle themselves across. But even this primitive system of navigation is but little in use. It is perhaps less troublesome to walk around the lake than to construct a *balsa* of reeds.

My descent into the valley was soon effected. The road leads through the village of San Pablo, which I found in a great state of excitement on account of the festivals of *San Juan*, which in this province are always celebrated with great pomp and enthusiasm. For the Indians especially, this is a time of great rejoicing. It is their happiest week in the year. What St. John has done to befriend the poor Indians more than any other of his heavenly colleagues, I am unable to say. The truth is, probably, that they merely want a pretext for following their ancient custom of carousing and dancing to their hearts' content, once or twice a year. I had heard so much of the strange and curious manner in which the Indians of Otabalo, Cotacachi, Peguchi, Hatuntaqui, etc., celebrate the feast of St. John, that I had hastened my trip to the province of Imbabura in order to be in time to see the sights.

Being tired, rider as well as horse, I wanted to arrive at a resting-place as soon as possible, and therefore did not stop to see that day's performances. Nevertheless, I shall note what I saw while riding through the village. In one of the streets I met a group of men in strange array. Some of them had crowns of high feathers on their heads, after the ancient Indian fashion. They were clad in long robes, with handkerchiefs, or a kind of apron (our regular aprons are never worn in this country), tied to their shoulders and floating down their backs. They were faced by an equal number of men disguised as females, and gorgeously attired. The whole company held wooden arches in their hands, covered over with ribbons, and ornamented with flowers. A very crude sort of violins and guitars constituted the orchestra, which accompanied them. They went through a sort of contra-dance, consisting of a variety of figures. They first danced in the streets, and then in the Plaza. The whole week of San Juan is dedicated to amusements and revelry. The Indians commence their performances early in the morning, and hardly rest at night. Three days are devoted to the real feasts and public amusements; the remainder to private revelry. Sometimes a few days of bull-fighting, accompanied by endless drunken sprees, are added to the programme. The Indians of the village through which I now passed, as well as those of the neighborhood, have a curious mode of prolonging their orgies. When they see a passer-by, they hail him, and offer him a cup of rum. If he takes it, it is understood that he must give them a *medio* (half a real), if he does not want to arouse their indignation, and to expose himself to their gibes and sneers. If he gives them money, they say, "*Dios se lo pague, niño!*" or, "*Dios se lo pague, mi amo!*" ("God pay you for it, master!") and immediately invest it in strong drink. Humble and submissive as they may be all the year round, on these occasions they lose their natural timidity, and beg with an importunity which it is difficult to shake off.

I left the *dansantes* (dancing party), and crossing the Plaza, pursued my way, which lay through the whole length of the village. In the outskirts I saw groups of Indians amusing themselves in small squads. They were most ludicrously attired. They danced continually, and only stopped to drink. Even those who played their poor flutes danced along, turning slowly around, bowing to one side, and stamping on the ground to keep time, without end. Others accompanied the performance with monotonous, pitiable songs. Others again were dancing alone, all by themselves, on the highway. It was extremely ludicrous to see a solitary Indian on the road, in his senseless masquerade, sing and dance without companions to see or accompany him.

I soon had the village of San Pablo behind me, and passing along the northern shore of the lake, left that behind me also. A *rumipamba* (field of stones), such as are almost always found in the neighborhood of Quitonian volcanoes, reached down the hill-slope to the northwestern end of the lake. The waters of the lake find their outlet through a river at this place, called the Peguchi, which, forming a handsome cascade a few squares from the woolen factory of the same name, throws itself down into the green valley of Otabalo, which it irrigates. Uniting itself with the river Mojanda, it forms the Rio Blanco, which further down, after its union with the Tauhando, is called the Ambi, and disembogues into the Chota or Mira.

Peguchi is the name of the factory and beautiful country residence of Don Manuel Jijon, one of the most pleasant and enterprising gentlemen in the Republic. At this place, where I was fully undisturbed and independent, with a beautiful garden and shade-trees before my window (the former a sight so rare and welcome in this country), I proposed to establish my head-quarters for a few days, to facilitate my visits to the most important points of the neighborhood. It must always be borne in mind that in a country where there are no inns or taverns, and scarcely any accommodations for the traveller, it is of the highest importance to one who wishes to study and to observe, to be near a civilized place, upon which he may easily fall back for a friendly roof and a clean covered room — a place where he may find respite from the fleas and dirt of *tambos* and *posadas*.

In the factory of Peguchi coarse woolen goods are made, such as *bayetas* for ponchos, *jergas* for the Indians, and shawls for their women (these shawls are dyed red, yellow, blue or brown, but the red color is most in demand) ; cloth for coats, vests, pantaloons, carpets, etc. These goods are exported chiefly to New Granada, as far as Pasto and Popayan in the interior, and Barbacoas on the coast. The laborers employed in the factory are almost all Indians. They are *concertados*, or *peones*. The factory yields about thirty pieces of cloth per month, which in 1863 was sold at two dollars a yard, double-width.

The great Indian festivals of San Juan had already been going on for two days when I arrived. On the 26th of June, early in the forenoon, I rode over to the ground where the dances take place. The ground to which I refer is nearly opposite Peguchi, on the other side of the beautiful valley of Otabalo. This latter is the name of a very ancient town, which claims to be the second in the province. It has two well-built churches, and a large plaza, lined with two-story houses ; but the great mass of the buildings of which the town consists, have but one floor. There are mineral springs in the outskirts and immediate neighborhood. The chapel of San Juan, around which the Indians celebrated their feast, lies at a short distance, about half a mile west of Otabalo.

It was a pleasant, level greensward on one of the lower platforms of the mountains on the south side of the valley. A most picturesque view presented itself from this elevation. Almost opposite to the fair-ground rose Mt. Imbabura in its lofty majesty. To the right, the town of Otabalo; to the left, majestic Cotacachi, with its snowy peaks; to our rear, the towering Cordillera, and at our feet the fertile plain, dotted with friendly villas and haciendas, and now and then interrupted by isolated hills, covered with corn fields and Indian *huasipongos*. But far more picturesque and surprising was the view which the ground itself presented. For a moment I was overcome with the novelty of the scene, to which no description will be able to do justice. At a distance, one would have supposed that an English army had encamped on the ground, for hundreds of Indian women, in their favorite red shawls, sat in long rows on the greensward, on which the feast took place, and on the rising ground at its western extremity. On this latter acclivity stood the chapel of San Juan, which is now in ruins, destroyed by the great earthquake of 1859. Weeds, shrubs, and wild flowers had taken possession of the interior of the temple, and a rank but interesting vegetation had overgrown its roofless walls. At the foot of these ruins the slope was covered with dense groups of Indian women, and rows of them were ranged along the sides of the dancing place below. They all dress after the same fashion; but the leading feature of their dress is the coarse woolen shawl with which they cover their breast and shoulders. This shawl, as I have already said, is almost always red. You may judge of the impression produced by six or seven hundred red-shawled women, sitting in a large semicircle around almost as many Indian men, in all sorts of masquerades, and forming a striking contrast to the ruins above, and the melancholy verdure in the valley below.

While the women were thus ranged about as spectators, and enjoying themselves with food and drink, the men went through the dances, of which the festival principally consists. The Indian wife accompanies her liege lord to the festive scene, but her province is not the dance. Her business is to watch the movements of her husband, and to take care of him as soon as he gets unmanageably or helplessly drunk. Faithfully to comply with this duty is considered highly honorable to a wife. As soon as her spouse commences to be overpowered by the immense quantities of rum or *chicha* which he consumes, she is at his side, and remains with him. A woman who would fail to comply with this most important of her marital duties on a great occasion like this, would be despised by the whole Indian community, if not abandoned by her own husband. I do not propose to say that she does not get drunk too; but never so drunk as to become unable to manage him. She clings to him with the utmost tenacity. She holds him back and rolls him off when his intoxication assumes a belligerous character; she prevents him from committing excesses; she makes him sleep on her lap, and finally leads him to his home.

Two long rows of booths running to the foot of the acclivity on which the old chapel stood, from the entrance of the fair-ground, lined it on the north and south. In the booths on the left side of the entrance only liquors and candies were sold. The stock offered for sale consisted of the common rum of the country (*aguardiente*), distilled from the sugar-cane of the province, and preserved in hides; of *anisadas* (rum seasoned with anise-seed), and of *mistelas* (sweetened liquors). The booths were constructed of poles driven into the ground, with staves nailed to them transversely. Their tops and sides were covered with dried hides. In the liquor booths I saw spectators belonging to the half-white or cholo rabble, huddled together on the ground, men and women promiscuously, sleeping in one another's laps, beastly drunk. In the booths on the right hand of the entrance, meals were prepared. They were the cook-shops, and *agi de cuy*, *agi de queso*, *agi de lobrillo*, *locro*, *cariucho*, and other national dishes, were prepared for those who had money to pay for them. As potatoes form the principal ingredient of all these dishes, but very little money was required. No crockery was used. The eatables (*comida*) were filled from the pots (*ollas*) into calabashes. Ladles were generally wanting, smaller calabashes supplying their places. Only wooden spoons were used. At a distance of a few feet from the cook-shops, and in front of them, was another row of saleswomen, but without booths. They were the *fruteras*, who, squatting on the ground, sold fruit, which in this neighborhood is very cheap. Around these three rows of stands crowds were continually thronging, as the eating and drinking went on incessantly. Hundreds of besotted Indians, simpering and reeling, and supported by their faithful wives, were drinking to the health of their *compadres* and *commadres*, now embracing and hugging one another, now bickering and tearing about, to their hearts' content. Others were singing, with hoarse drunken voices, to the tune of the harp or guitar, or even without accompaniment, while still others lay stretched out on the ground, fast asleep. Yet they were all harmless and inoffensive, and committed no excesses whatever.

The Indian men were most quaintly attired. Of

course, all of them went barefoot, men as well as women. Some of the dancers had curious caps on, meant to represent certain incomprehensible characters. Others wore straw hats of ludicrous dimensions. But most of them wore the gray woolen hats, which are very common among the Indians of the interior, where they are made. Tied around their chins, and over their hats, they almost universally wore a cotton handkerchief of lively colors, which they consider a great ornament on such occasions. Some of them wore it hanging down over their faces like a vail; others had it floating over their neck and shoulders. Most of the participators wore white goat-skin trousers (*zamarros*), such as I had already noticed at San Pablo. Their light-colored ponchos, expressly purchased for the occasion, or recently washed, were yet clean; and in connection with the red shawls of the women, which I have already described, gave a most lively appearance to the scene. It is very customary among the aborigines to hire dress-coats or hats, or other incongruous articles of costume, for the three days of the feast. All sorts of coats were represented on the ground. Some wore black dress-coats, others frock-coats, which formed a most ludicrous contrast to their bare feet and goat-skin trousers. One wore a military coat; another a red coat with great yellow buttons. Jackets, too, of various sizes and colors, were worn in great numbers. Others appeared in light red shirts, which they wore over their trousers. Some had their faces painted with an ugly brown-red color; others were painted black to represent negroes, which seems to be a favorite mummery among the Indians. In short, it was the queerest mixture of incoherent and detached articles of costume I ever saw. Persons who have offended an Indian, are very frequently mimicked by the injured party on such occasions; and it is only to be regretted that besides the unsophisticated mimicker himself and a few of his initiated friends, nobody will suspect or be able to understand the object of his disguise. I once heard of a poor stupid Indian who, having been struck by a soldier, threatened him with his revenge. "Just wait," he said, "on San Juan I shall mimic you!" ("*Aguardate, en San Juan te he de remedar!*") Poor, childish, down-trodden race!

Innumerable were the musical instruments on the ground. The most common of all was the *rondador*, a most primitive instrument, consisting of a number of reeds shortening gradually toward one end, such as Pan, the god of the shepherds, is represented with. This instrument is a great favorite with the Indian. It accompanies the herdsman as well as the arriero, and simple, few, and melancholy, are the tunes it yields. Flutes and violins, such as we would give to our little boys, I saw in great numbers. Others had guitars of a very common and indifferent make. There were also several harps and one or two horns, which sounded like the trumpets of our American firemen. I saw no drums, which, however, may have been accidental. With the Indians of Quito the drum is highly popular. With a boy's drum and fife they can amuse themselves for days, in their monotonous, melancholy way. The instruments just described were not united in an orchestra, but each of the many different parties who marched up and down or around the grounds, had at least two or three of them. They played but one solitary tune. It was the same from morning to night, without variation or intermission.

Most of the men I saw on the ground had very long and thick hair. It was like the hair of all the Ecuadorian Indians, — of a deep black color, and very coarse and smooth. The Indians of Otabalo, Hatuntaqui, Cotacachi, etc., look upon it as a great ornament, and never cut it. With some of them it reached down to their waists. They either wore it loose, or had one little thin braid twisted on top of it. The men wore no jewelry. The women, however, are very fond of bracelets and collars of red beads, to some of which numbers of reals or half reals were suspended.

Of their dances, in which they are untiring, I noticed three different figures. About twelve or fifteen dancers, more or less, form a procession, somewhat irregular, with little boys among them, in fancy dresses like their seniors, and march up and down the fair-ground to its whole length, wheeling around at one end to return to the other. While marching, some of them will play their crude flutes or guitars. Even harps will be carried along in the procession, with their bottoms resting on the back of a little boy, while the musician harps away at the strings, and one of his companions beats the time on the side of the instrument. The marchers trip to the tune of the music, making one long and two short steps. In fact, this peculiar step, with which they march and countermarch, and wheel about, constitutes the whole of the dance. From time to time they will form a circle with one or two of the musicians in the centre, and then they will march around them, always with the step just described, until the leader of the party commands "*Damos una vuelta! Damos una vuelta!*" when they all turn about and trip away in the opposite direction of the same circle. This figure is repeated until they get tired of it, and form a procession again. The third figure which I observed is one of less activity. The members of the party cluster around one another, and then each man turns round, beating time with his feet, in slow but continuous rotation. The musicians do the same, marking time with their heads and the upper part of their bodies. The musicians are amateurs, and enjoy the double pleasure of playing and dancing. While engaged in the dance the faces of the participants will be as serious and dignified as if they were performing a task of awful solemnity. Their countenances, as well as their indefatigable perseverance, indicate that they are pleased, but no smile betrays it. They never get wildly excited, they quicken their step but very seldom; they never run or romp, however drunk they may be. As long as they are in the dance they do as their fellows do. Sometimes the leader of the party, or one of his followers, utters a deep, guttural, and almost ghastly laugh, but this is a part of the performance, and sounds strained and unnatural. Sometimes, they join in a hearty cheer; but it is only done at the command of the leader. Each party seems to have its leader. The dancers only stop to eat and to drink, and then fall into the line of procession again.

Behind the booths to the right of the entrance several gambling establishments were kept up, patronized, to the honor of the Indians it must be said, exclusively by white persons of the lower classes, and cholos. One was a *rueda de fortuna* (wheel of fortune), consisting of a long iron needle, turning round on a pivot, over a board on which numbers are painted, and set in motion by a jerk. The other was a game well known to our children. It consisted of a round board with little holes, and numbers in them. A ball running into one of the holes from out of a winding chimney, decides the victory. This game is called *cachito.* But another game, which attracted the greatest number of participants and spectators, and which they called *bolichi*, was something new to me. It consisted of a large round pit dug in the ground, about forty feet in circumference and twelve in diameter, in the shape of the inside of the lower half of a hollow globe. Into this pit the player throws an even number of little wooden balls. They roll to the bottom, where there are two small receptacles, the larger one of a round form, the smaller one, an oblong square. If the number of balls that run into the latter is even, or if they all run into the round hole, the player wins; if not, those who bet against him. Most of the spectators join in the bets. Even women and little boys throw down their reals, carried away by the excitement of the game. The pit is covered with a shed, to protect the company from sun and rain.

While going over the ground, I was again struck by the repulsive ugliness of the Indian women. Whether it is their habit of beastly drinking that produces this ugliness, or the hard work which they are compelled to perform, I am unable to say. There is a general belief at Quito that the Indians of Otabalo, and especially the women, are handsomer, and cleaner than those of Pichincha, Latacunga, etc., but I have been unable to discover the slightest foundation for such an opinion. It is the same national type, and the same ugly, stupid, simpering look that distinguish them all. As far as cleanliness is concerned, the difference, if it exists, is imperceptible to a foreign eye. The only thing in which the Otabalo Indian excels is his long hair, which, of course, he never cuts, and, I may add, but very seldom combs.

On my return from the festive grounds to Peguchi, I passed the chapel of Monserate, where another Indian feast was going on. This chapel, too, was in ruins, having been destroyed by the earthquake of 1859; and the rule outside of Quito seems to be that if a building once tumbles down, it is not to be built up again. Ruins, as I have already said, are a characteristic feature of Spanish-American civilization.

The chapel of Monserate is about half-way between Otabalo and Peguchi. It is at the foot of that almost circular mountain chain which seams the pleasant and friendly plain of Otabalo. As the Indians who had assembled to celebrate their *San Juan* on this spot belonged to the immediate neighborhood only, their number was but small. One fellow, with his face painted black to represent a negro, acted the part of a clown, and by his pranks and capers imparted life to the scene. His companions, too, seemed to be much gayer and livelier than those I had just left. As I distributed some money among them, the arrival of our party was greeted with great rejoicing, and the Indians hastened to go through their whole programme for our especial benefit. They had a wooden image of St. John with them, which stood on a portable platform, and was nicely dressed and bedecked with tinsel and finery. As soon as the dance commenced, two of the men took the apostle on their shoulders, and made him join in the dance, passing through all its figures and variations. Even in the circle-dance the saint merrily participated; and when the word was given to wheel about (*damos una vuelta*), his carriers, who could not turn round with their load without breaking up the circle, danced backwards. What a queer spectacle it was! These dances were the principal enjoyment of the Indians under their heathen Incas and Scyris. The Spanish conquerors, seeing no reason for suppressing them, accommodated them to Christian instead of pagan holidays. And now we see the Indians, in their quaint mummeries, and covered all over with floating handkerchiefs, dance the same dances around the Christian cross that they formerly danced in honor of the sun, the moon, or Pachacamac; and in the midst of their pagan revelry, carried in the same manner in which formerly some old Peruvian high-priest or idol was carried, hops about the gayly dressed wooden image of the Catholic saint. The ceremonies have remained the same; the ignorance and superstition of the Indians have remained the same; it is only the name of the idol that has changed. Formerly it was called Pachacamac, now it is called St. John.

But the dancing saint was not the only mixture of Catholicism and heathenism. There were sacrifices, too, live sacrifices of cocks and other birds, because it is believed by the Indians that the blood of the victim is a pleasant offering to the Christianized Pachacamac. This barbarous custom, which I shall now describe, is called "*Arrancar los gallos.*" A rope was tied to a tree on one side, and run through a pole driven into the earth on the other. To this rope, the end of which remained in the hands of some of the company, a live cock was tied by his feet, and tossed up and down by those who held the rope, while a number of others performed a circle dance under him. These latter finally seized the poor animal, one of the dancers after the other, and plucked off his feathers, throwing them into the crowd. It is a barbarous, horrible sight, to behold the agony of the poor, helpless bird. After continuing the dance a little longer, they seized the victim again, one by the leg, another by the head, others taking the wings, and unmercifully tore him asunder. And now another senseless part of the performance begins. Those who have succeeded in getting hold of a part of the animal, make a general attack on their friends, striking them with the bloody remains in the face, over the head, on the neck, etc., without minding the clean handkerchiefs and ponchos with which they have ornamented their dress, or the fancy articles of costume expressly hired for the occasion. The others in their turn, attempt to snatch the pieces of the sacrificed bird from the hands of their assailants, and so a general scuffle follows, which, although carried on amid great laughter and shouting, very frequently leads to serious blows. Two cocks were thus sacrificed in my presence, and as no greater supply was at hand, the boys hung up little birds, several at a time, and disposed of them in the same manner. During the main festival in front of the chapel of San Juan, twelve cocks were sacrificed that day, as I was afterwards informed.

I returned to Peguchi at about five o'clock in the afternoon. There I learned from the director of the factory and haciendas of Mr. Jijon that at Cayambi, a village at the foot of the mountain of the same name, and belonging to the neighboring province of Pichincha, the great feasts of San Juan and San Pedro would begin on the following Sunday, and continue for several days. On the first day the celebrated contradances of the "San Juanes" were to take place, — a spectacle given by two or four dozen whites and cholos, one half of them in female dresses, and all of them in fancy costumes. On the second day the Indian dances would take place, and end, as they always did, in great and serious pitched battles between the Indians of the different haciendas, — the Indians of the neighborhood of Cayambi being much more pugnacious and violent than their countrymen in general. The festival was to conclude with bull-teasings, the interest of which was said to be considerably enhanced by the ferocity of the *toros* (bulls) brought down from the paramos. These announcements promised a rich field of observation; and on the 28th of June, 1863, at about eight o'clock in the morning, I started from Peguchi, which is about five leagues from Cayambi. I again passed by the lake of San Pablo, and rode through the village of that name. I reascended the heights of Cajas from which I had come down a few days ago, and descending on the other side into the fertile plain of Tabacundo, intersected in the direction of my destination by several streams, — one of which, the San José de Cayambi, is exceedingly noisy and rapid, — I reached the village of Cayambi at about twelve o'clock meridian.

Mt. Cayambi, from which the village derives its name, is one of the highest mountains in the world, and the second highest in Ecuador. Its majestic dome, covered with a robe of perpetual snow, rises to a height of 19,813 feet. The village is 9724 feet above the level of the sea. Humboldt pronounces the mountain to be one of the most beautiful he saw; and in fact there is no sight more imposing than its masses of snow and ice glowing with crimson splendor in the rays of the setting sun. As Cayambi, in clear weather, can be seen from Quito, I frequently went to see it. It shines forth like a fairy dome as long as the sun's farewell rays are reflected upon it. No mortal painter's brush could do justice to the brilliancy of its prismatic tints. But as soon as the sun begins to hide his face behind the western Cordillera, the lower buttresses of the mountain assume a pure white color, leaving only the higher peaks in all the splendor and brilliancy of a short but enchanting refulgence, which is followed by the pure whiteness of death. Like a gigantic ghost, shrouded in sepulchral sheets, the mountain now hovers in the background of the landscape, towering ghastly through the twilight until darkness closes upon the scene. It is a sight which richly indemnifies the foreign traveller for his hardships in floundering over wretched roads, sleeping in miserable hovels, and scrambling over the roadless Cordillera; for nowhere in the wide world could he enjoy such a view again.

The village of Cayambi is a cold, windy, unfriendly, and dirty place, with narrow streets and mean little houses of earth or *adobes*. There are but two two-story buildings, and these are on the Plaza. The church is almost entirely in ruins, having been destroyed by the earthquake of 1859. I was very hospitably received by the curate, who lives in a large but neglected and uncomfortable building in the rear of the church. The houses have no glass windows, but only wooden shutters, which, in a cold place like Cayambi, makes them doubly uncomfortable. The cold climate of the place is attributable, not so much to its elevation, which is but two hundred feet higher than that of Quito, as to the immediate neighborhood of the mountain, which, in my opinion, makes it one of the coldest inhabited places in the province of Pichincha, although it is almost directly under the line, — Mt. Cayambi being, according to Humboldt, the only snowy place in the world over which the equator passes. Cold and uncomfortable as the valley may be, it is, nevertheless, very healthy. The curate told me that the inhabitants attained a very high age, and that persons who lived a hundred or more years, did not at all constitute exceptional cases. The streets of the place —or rather lanes, for they hardly deserve the name of streets—are long and tortuous, but its population is not in proportion to its extent, as the houses are generally built at a considerable distance from one another, separated by intervening courts, gardens, and fields. A river called the Rio Blanco (White River), passes by the village at its northern extremity, and is formed, like so many others which irrigate the plain of Tabacundo, by the melting snows of Mt. Cayambi.

It was a dull, cloudy, gloomy day, with every now and then one of those slow and piercing mists or rains which, in these regions, are called "*paramos*," and very frequently develop into regular showers. They owe their origin to the nearness of the clouds lowering from the mountains, and to the mists in which the real *paramos* (high plains or heaths) are almost continually enveloped. The natives have a welcome-drink which they always prepare for arriving travellers, and which they call "*agua gloriada*," or "*aguita de azucar*." It consists of sugar dissolved in boiling water, with a strong addition of that detestable rum which the sugar-cane districts of the province of Imbabura pour over the land. This beverage was inflicted on me with the urgent recommendation that it was the *aguita del pais* (the water of the country), and I had to struggle hard to ward it off as much as possible. After I had rested a little, I went to the Plaza, where the dances of the "San Juanes" had already commenced.

The spectacle that now presented itself to my view was entirely novel, not only on account of the fantastic and not at all unbecoming dresses of the performers, but also of the skill and promptitude with which they went through the most difficult figures of their dance. The latter somewhat resembled our cotillons. There were twenty-four dancers on the ground, twelve of whom were in female attire. These latter wore little black felt hats, ornamented with waving black plumes, and little vails attached to the rims. They also wore long locks of false hair. Their dresses were white and neat, and over their shoulders they wore little silk shawls of gay colors. The men wore little caps, with tinsel and plumage of all colors, silk jackets or vests, silk shawls or handkerchiefs over their shoulders, and clean white pantaloons. Every one of the party carried an arch in his hands, covered with ribbons, cockades, and flowers. These arches played a prominent part in the formation of the figures of the dance. To complete the costume, the company wore yellow dancing-shoes, made of the coarse and heavy leather of the country. The orchestra consisted of a trumpet, a big drum, two flutes, and a horn. They played the same tune, consisting of only a few notes, during the whole of the mortal two hours that the dance lasted. This tune is also called "San Juan."

A fellow with his face painted black to represent a negro, and with a red soldier-jacket and white pantaloons, and a little drum at his side, performed the part of the leader, and, at the same time, clown of the party, delivering funny addresses to the audience, ordering groups of the spectators to sit down, or to withdraw to the houses, so as not to obstruct the view of those behind them, and threatening to stop the dance in case of disobedience. His imperious requests were always complied with. He was assisted by his counterpart, — a fellow in the disguise of a negress, — who whipped the boys away and did other funny things. She and her pretended husband or master danced around the other dancers in comic style. There also was a fellow in the popular disguise of a monkey, with a long tail, who, by his independent pranks, entirely unconnected with the other proceedings, greatly amused the junior part of the audience. On one occasion, he snatched a bag from an old Indian woman, opened it, and in regular monkey fashion examined its contents, throwing at the boys the few pieces of *agi* it contained. The dancing took place in the middle of the Plaza. The spectators (all the men in ponchos) occupied the windows, porches, and house-tops of the square, and the ruins of the old church, or were seated on the ground around the dancers. It was a grotesque sight, and I only regretted that Mt. Cayambi was concealed from our view by mists and clouds. Its snowy dome would have formed a strange contrast to the fantastic dancers, and the motley crowd of spectators below.

As I have already said, the great dance lasted about two hours, at the end of which the negro leader proposed *vivas* (cheers) for the President of the Republic, for the curate of the village and his coadjutor, for the dancers (*los Sanjuanes*), and for himself. All these cheers were given, not by the multitude in attendance, but by the dancers themselves. After this, single dances were performed, one pair at a time. They consisted of the slow and easy *alza que te han visto*, to which I have already alluded.

As soon as this performance was over, the dancers, and a great number of the spectators in their wake, adjourned to the residence of the curate, in whose large court-yard they repeated some of the figures of the cotillon, and refreshed themselves with *chicha*, *aguardiente* (rum), and a smoke, in all of which those disguised as females heartily participated. The negro leader then made his appearance on the curate's porch, and compelled some of the gentlemen present to pass through an *alza que te han visto* with the pseudo-damsels below. In the same manner some of the lady guests were prevailed upon to dance a round with the indefatigable *Sanjuanes*, who afterward formed a procession and marched through several of the streets of the place. The liquor-shops were crowded until a late hour of the night. Besides chicha and aguardiente, great quantities of *guarapo* were consumed. *Guarapo* is the juice of the sugar-cane boiled and partly fermented. Its taste is acid, and it is very intoxicating. It is not necessary to boil the juice. Simple fermentation suffices to produce a very popular beverage. But the guarapo of the boiled juice tastes better, and is therefore preferred.

Early in the morning next day I took a stroll around the village, but the weather continued unfavorable, and Mt. Cayambi could not be seen. Having seen it very often from Quito and other places from which it is visible, I was very anxious to see it near by. But Andean scenery is continually fraught with disappointments, and weeks will sometimes pass away before the envious clouds lift their vail from a mountain whose fame has excited the curiosity of a nature-loving traveller. While conversing with the natives, a report was mentioned to me which, if true, would prove highly interesting to geographers.[1] I was told that Cayambi is a volcano, which is still in activity; that on its eastern side it has two craters, from which frequent eruptions are said to have taken place, witnessed by the *mayordomos* (superintendents or stewards) of neighboring haciendas who had penetrated into the wilderness in the rear of the mountain in search of stray cattle. Sportsmen who followed game into those lonely deserts, are said to have made the same observation. The craters are not on the summit, but on the east side of the mountain, and throw their ashes and water (for South-American volcanoes do not throw out lava) in the direction of the wilderness on the Napo, one of the

[1] Dr. William Jameson, to whose valuable manuscript notes I have repeatedly referred, undertook an ascent of Cayambi in December, 1859, of which he gave me a most interesting narrative. I subjoin the following extract: "The village of Cayambi is situated on a gentle declivity, forming the base of the mountain bearing the same name. The latter is situated east-northeast of Quito, and according to Humboldt, directly under the equator.. The flora of the village is in every respect similar to that of the last-named city. The soil is remarkably fertile, and watered by numerous streams that derive their origin from the snow. The system of irrigation is extensively practiced by the proprietors of cattle estates, who derive a liberal emolument from the productions of the dairy, particularly from cheese, which, in this country, is consumed in enormous quantities. The number of cattle distributed over the different farms of Cayambi, cannot be less than thirty thousand. There is one estate, that of Guachala, where thirty thousand sheep are reared, furnishing a proportional quantity of wool for the manufacture of a coarse cloth, connected with the establishment. This article is purchased at the price of two reals a yard, and sold in the mining districts of Barbacoas at rather more than double its original price. December 23d, being close on Christmas, to persuade any one to accompany me to the snowy region, was not to be thought of. I had to wait three days, and on the 26th set out, accompanied by an Indian. Our ascent on the northern side was an easy task, and occupied us about six hours. Toward the afternoon, we had attained an elevation of about 14,000 feet, and my guide pointed out to me a forest of *Polylepis*, which I ascertained to be identical with that growing on Chimborazo at nearly the same height. In the midst of this forest we found a couple of huts, well covered with straw, and abundance of material for fuel. Botany being my principal object, I cannot say I found any material difference between the flora of Cayambi and that of Pichincha, with which I am well acquainted."

most memorable tributaries of the Amazons. At present the impression prevalent in scientific circles is, that Cayambi, if it ever was a volcano, has become dormant. This belief is supported by the fact that, from its western, southern, and northern sides, which present themselves to the inhabited parts of Ecuador, no eruptions have ever been noticed. It seems strange that none of the scientific travellers who examined the mountain and its botany and geology, should ever have gone behind it. Colonel Hall, to whose exploring expeditions I have already referred, and who died a lamentable death before he had published his most valuable scientific observations, made an attempt to scale the mountain from its western (the village) side; in what year I am unable to state. He had already reached a considerable height, when he found himself unable to proceed any further, on account of the steepness of the rocks, and the snow-drifts, in which he was continually losing himself. Having also been abandoned by the Indians whom he had hired to accompany him, he was compelled to return before having accomplished the object of his expedition. Dr. Jameson, who ascended the mountain from its northern side, went a little beyond the snow limit, but confined himself to botanical observations, not having heard the report I just mentioned. My curiosity, therefore, was greatly excited by what I had heard, and I concluded to attempt the ascent from the eastern side. Preparations, however, being necessary for such an expedition, and the object of my present journey being the province of Imbabura, I resolved to postpone the exploration of the rear of Cayambi till the month of December (the Indian summer), when the storms on the paramos would have subsided, and the weather would be clear. Subsequent events, however, prevented me from carrying out my intention.

Many other stories are told about the unexplored country in the rear of Cayambi, and around its southern neighbor, Sara Urcu.[1] One of the villagers informed me that his father, while on an expedition in search of the probably fabulous Serro Pelado, discovered a silver mine in one of the upper rocks of Sara Urcu, but that he lacked either the means or the necessary energy to work it. In speaking of those regions, it must always be borne in mind that they are complete deserts, without roads or paths, without huts or habitations, without a nourishing vegetation; and that while it is impossible to penetrate into them on horseback, sharp rocks, frightful abysses, deep ravines, and the frosts and snows of the paramos, will soon arrest the sore foot of the weary pedestrian. The mists and fogs in which the paramos are enveloped, sometimes whole weeks without intermission, will make him lose his way. The streams which he passes will rise behind him and prevent his regress, perhaps for days, during which his supply of provisions will give out, exposing him to the danger of starvation. All these obstacles are well calculated to dampen the ardor of races more energetic than Spanish-Americans. The

[1] *Sara Urcu* or *Supai Urcu*. This volcano is of little consideration, and situate in the chain of Guamani, which is detached from the great Cordillera. According to Father Velasco's *History of Quito*, this volcano had two eruptions of fire; but lately it ejected great quantities of volcanic ashes, first in December, 1843, and then in December, 1856. The first of these eruptions lasted two days, and produced the greatest consternation among the inhabitants of Quito and the neighborhood. The elevation of this mountain is 6210 yards (*varas*) above the level of the sea. It is situate thirty-five miles to the east of Quito. The mountain-chain of Pesambillo, and others of less importance, are also known by the name of Sara Urcu." — *Translated from Manuel Villavicencio's Geography of the Republic of Ecuador*, published in New York in the year 1858.

Pizarros, Almagros, Alvarados, Benalcazars, and Quesadas are no more. That iron energy and perseverance with which they braved the perils of the unexplored wilderness, and endured incredible hardships in search of the Eldorado of their dreams, do not distinguish their descendants. Too indolent to develop the resources before their own doors, how can it be expected that they should set out to conquer an unknown wilderness?

The story of the *Serro Pelado*, just referred to, is differently told. Many are the legends in which it figures. Most of them locate it somewhere in the rear of Cayambi, between that mountain and Sara Urcu. According to others, it is believed to be in the rear of Cotopaxi. It is said to be on the other side of a stream, impassable partly on account of the perpendicular height of its rocky banks, partly on account of the rapidity and depth of its waters. The signification of the word *pelado*, is *shorn*, or *bald*. The mountain is said to be entirely barren, and its large and fabulous veins of gold are reported to have been seen from this side of the fatal river. There is one point, however, in that Cordillera, as the story runs, where the river is easily fordable. That point, so difficult to find on account of the mists and clouds hovering over the paramos, was accidentally discovered by an Indian of the neighborhood of Cayambi. He had run away from his master, by whom he had been harshly treated, and losing his way in the wilderness, he suddenly found himself opposite the Serro Pelado at a fordable point of the stream. He saw the veins of pure gold from his side of the river, crossed the stream, and with no other instrument but his hands, dug out a large lump of gold, a part of which, on his return home, he gave to a white *com-*

*padre*. He is even said to have returned to the mountain for fresh supplies of the precious metal. The sudden change in his circumstances, as well as in those of his *compadre*, — who seems to have played some unexplained part in the drama, — excited public attention, and the Indian was arrested and compelled to confess. Great excitement followed the discovery, and an expedition was immediately fitted out to explore Serro Pelado; but before it got ready to start, a revolution broke out, like a *deus ex machina*, and so convulsed the country for some time afterwards, that the enterprise was abandoned. Meanwhile the Indian died, and expeditions that afterwards went out in search of the fabulous mountain, returned without results. This is the least mythical of the different versions of the story that have come to my knowledge. Others, to give it a romantic touch, let the expedition be interrupted, not by the breaking out of a revolution, but by the sudden death of the unfortunate Indian, who had been impressed as guide. He died mysteriously the very day before the intended departure of the expedition; and with him the secret of the locality of Serro Pelado was sunk into the grave.

Whether such a mountain has really been seen by somebody, is a matter of great doubt, and perhaps improbability. The fact is, that many expeditions went out in search of it, and that it was not discovered.

Improbable, and vastly exaggerated as most of these gold-stories appear, they are excusable in a country whose immense richness in precious metals, under its ancient native rulers, are historical facts of unquestionable certainty. "There must be gold in our country, for otherwise, where should the Incas have taken it from?" This is the argument with which the natives generally conclude the relation of the above and similar legends. It is, however, too vague and too general to prove the point in question; for the Incas may have found their precious metals anywhere in the countries now known as Ecuador, Peru, and Bolivia, on the eastern or on the western side of the great Cordillera, if not in the mountains themselves, in mines which have become inaccessible by the destruction of Indian civilization. Another argument, however, which I heard frequently, ought to be mentioned in this connection. That part of the tropical wilderness beyond the Cordillera east of Quito, which is generally designated by the name of the "Napo country" (its official name is *Provincia del Oriente*), furnishes the Ecuadorian market with a yearly quantity of gold-dust. However limited this quantity may be, it fully corresponds to the value of the articles which the Napo Indians purchase during the year, at fabulous prices, from the governor of the province or his partners in trade. Those functionaries, in spite of all legal prohibitions, still follow the ancient practice of *repartimientos* (compulsory sales). They unite the Indians on certain days of the year, distribute a certain quantity of baize and other articles among them, which the savages are compelled to take, and then command them to pay in gold-dust for the debts thus forced upon them, within six months. Naturally, the Indians do not wash more gold than necessary to discharge their obligations to the governor or his favorites. The gold-dust which they furnish is washed in the streams having their origin in that part of the Cordillera to which the Cayambi, Sara Urcu, Cotopaxi, and other Quitonian mountains belong. It is, as the natives say, *oro arrastrado*, gold washed away from its original layers by the force of the current. Hence it is argued, why should there not be gold in the mountains themselves, when there is gold-dust in their streams. I repeat this argument without, of course, indorsing it. Scientific explorations alone will be able to determine the truth. Had it not been for Spanish avarice and cruelty, the country on the head-waters of the Amazons would not be what it now is — a roving place for unconquered savage tribes. The district of Macas, to the east of Riobamba, on the other side of the Cordillera, was the richest in precious metals at the time of the Spanish conquest. Its boundless treasures attracted a great number of adventurers and colonists, who founded three flourishing cities — Mendoza, Sevilla de Oro (the Golden Sevilla), and Logroño, the fame of which soon rivaled that of Cuzco and Lima. Forty-seven years of progress had cleared the impenetrable forests on the rivers Palora, Upano, and Paute, and roads were cut through the rocky deserts of the Cordillera. But the Indians of the Orient were not so meek and timid as their brethren of Cuzco and Quito. The warlike Jivaros, who had defeated the conquering schemes of the great Inca Huaynacapac, were not the men to bend their necks to the rapacious tyranny and cruelty of Spanish adventurers. Under the leadership of the valiant and cunning Quirruba, — of whom we must regret not to know more, for he deserves a place in history as the liberator of his race, — they flew to arms, and in a short and terrible conflict wiped from their virgin soil the colonies of the European intruder.

A few miserable huts, now constituting the village of Macas, are said to indicate the place where the golden Sevilla once stood, but of Mendoza and Logroño not a vestige has remained. The impenetrable density of the tropical forest again closed upon the scene, and the poisoned arrow of the savage threatens with death and destruction the intruder whose daring foot should have escaped the sting of the serpent or the fang of the wild beast.

There is a legend that the Jivaros, after taking Logroño, killed the Spanish governor by pouring down his throat a quantity of molten gold. But there is no historical evidence whatever to warrant a belief in this piece of poetic justice. It is true, however, that no men were made prisoners. Those who did not escape in time were mercilessly butchered by the exasperated Indians. The young women alone were spared, and carried off as the wives or slaves of their barbarous conquerors. To this catastrophe it is to be ascribed that in the features of a whole tribe of unredeemed Jivaros there is yet traceable the blood of Castile. What a life of horror and despair those woe-begone women must have led in the hands of their Indian masters, only the pen of a Shakespeare or Goethe, Byron or Schiller, could describe. An ocean between them and the land of their childhood; an impenetrable wilderness of forests and mountains between the place of their captivity and the settlements of their countrymen; and the embrace of a savage heathen between their despairing hearts and their Church!

## CHAPTER XIV.

My Journey to the Northern Province continued. — The Chase. — Esculents. — The Graveyard of Cayambi. —*Doctrina Cristiana.* — Aruchicos. — Speech by an Indian. — Indian Peonage. — Further Peculiarities of Indian Character. — Population and Characteristics of the Town of Otabalo. — The Convent. — Punishment of Indians for neglecting Religious Observances. — *Alcaldes de Doctrina.* — Mt. Cotacachi and Lake Cuicocha. — Dangerous Hunting Parties. — Sunday Markets. — The Village of Cotacachi. — More Remnants of the Inquisition. — *Padronar.* — How Laws and Municipal Ordinances are promulgated in an Illiterate Country. — American Machinery an "Invention of the Devil." — Mt. Imbabura. — The Village of Hatuntaqui. — Tolas, or Indian Graves or Mounds. — The City of Ibarra. — Carranqui, the Birthplace of Atahuallpa. — No Vestige left of Indian Civilization. — Digging up Indian Graves. — Strange Discoveries. — Impulse given by the Gold Discoveries at Cuenca. — Lake Yaguarcocha, the Sea of Blood.

LET us return to Cayambi.

Friends of the chase will find an abundance of deer on the slopes, and in the valleys formed by the great mountain. The deer are hunted with dogs, the sportsmen following wildly on horseback. The sport is very popular among the natives, and called "*corrida de venados.*" Many a time the deer are followed up to the snow limit. Rabbits, too, are found in great abundance; so are wild ducks and pigeons, and a species of partridges.

Numberless herds of cattle are kept around Cayambi, as well as around Cotopaxi, Antisana, and other giants of the Cordillera. The cheese of Cayambi is most favorably known in Quito and the neighborhood, although its preparation is carried on with the usual disregard of cleanliness. The milk in these alpine regions is exceedingly rich; nevertheless, neither on the rich man's nor the poor man's table is butter to be found as a common esculent. The natives do not seem to like it much. As a general thing, they do not care for enjoying what a plentiful Nature proffers. Meat, for instance, is very good, but they do not know how to prepare it. They always manage to get it on the table in a tough and unsavory state. Their notions of cooking do not advance beyond two or three kinds of potato soup, which constitute their chief nourishment.

On the south side of the village church is the cemetery. I found but two monuments under which persons of note had been buried. Excepting these, there was not a cross nor an inscription in the graveyard, nor were the graves made prominent by mounds. They are trodden upon indifferently by those who visit the burying-place. But what, after all, would be the use of sepulchral inscriptions among a people who cannot read?

On this cemetery the Indians of the parish assemble twice a week to recite the *Doctrina Cristiana*, consisting of the Paternoster, ave, credo, the commandments, and an abbreviated catechism. An experienced Indian, who knows the *Doctrina* by heart, recites it sentence by sentence, and the others repeat it. Those who neglect to attend these meetings are whipped for their dereliction, as I shall afterwards describe.

The inhabitants of almost all of the towns in the cold regions of the interior, with the exception of the capital, go about all day wrapped up in double ponchos of *bayeta* (a kind of coarse wool), to which they frequently add a shawl worn around the neck, which is called "*bufanda*." To a cold and unfriendly place like Cayambi, the shivering appearance of these lazy loiterers gives a still colder and gloomier aspect. The total want of fire-places contributes to the general cheerlessness.

The day (June 29th) had opened very windy. Fearful gusts blew down from Mt. Cayambi, banging against the houses, or rather huts, of the village, and driving clouds of dust into the eyes of those who had come out to see the mummeries of the Indians. At about mid-day the *Aruchicos* (this is the name by which Indians in masquerade are designated) commenced to march into the Plaza. Besides the fantastic attire which the great occasion required, they came armed with tremendous clubs and sticks, to be prepared for the fight which in former years was the solemn order of the day. I could see at once that they were descendants of tribes entirely different from those of Otabalo. Their movements were quicker, their songs more savage, and a certain boldness and determination seemed to animate their faces. Their dances consisted of a wild running around in rings, and of a fussy advancing and retreating in long files, instead of the slow, measured step of the Otabalo Indians. There were two or three parties on the ground before I left it. They differed from each other in their costumes, as well as in their manner of dancing. The first party wore black *zamarros* (goat-skin trousers) with very long hair on them, little straw hats with white covers, a handkerchief around their head, and another over their shoulders, and under it a vest-like garment of an iron-colored woolen stuff, in folds, called "*cushma.*" But the most remarkable part of their attire consisted of two or three cow-bells fastened to a strap of leather, which they wore over one shoulder like a scarf. In imitation of the Cholo performance of the previous day, the leader of the party had his face painted black, while his costume was intended to be soldier-like. He was also assisted by a pretended negro woman cutting all sorts of capers. His men endeavored throughout to keep up an appearance of military discipline and bravery. Judging from my riding-dress and poncho that I was somewhat above the rank of the crowd of mounted men around me, he singled me out from among the rest, and taking a position at the right of my horse, delivered himself of a speech, one third in Quichua and two thirds in Spanish, in which he assured me that his forces were always at my disposal, and that whether in daytime or at night, he and his men would be ready whenever I should need them. Of course he called me *amo mio* (my master), which is the usual Indian allocution; and after saying a great many things which hardly any body could understand, he wound up by asking me for a *peseta* (two reals). Upon my giving it without hesitation, he ordered his men to dance for my especial edification. They were drawn up in a line, and hurriedly swayed backward and forward, until he ordered them to form a ring, not, however, with their faces towards the centre, but following one another in Indian file, and going through the same *Damos una vuelta* that I had already seen at Otabalo. While the dance was going on, the leader continually made exclamations consisting of incoherent words in Quichua and Spanish, to which the others replied in a monotonous chorus. But what he said and what they answered I could not make out. Bystanders, however, who were familiar with the Quichua language, assured me that it was sheer nonsense — words thrown together higgledy-piggledy, and intermingled with meaningless sounds; their chief object being to keep time to their step. I soon afterwards had an opportunity to observe that the Indians on such occasions sing any thing that flashes through their minds, accommodating the words to the melody. At the *Hacienda* of San José, for instance, at which, after leaving Cayambi, I stopped for about an hour, a drunken Indian came up to me while I was speaking with the mayordomo, and told us in a song of great length, as he had to repeat many of the words to keep up the tune, that he was a faithful old Indian, who did his duty at all times of the year, and who was fond of his work; but that for the present he must be excused, for this was a time of holidays, which he wanted to enjoy like his brethren. The mayordomo told him it was all right, and he went away contented.

The second party of Aruchicos that attracted my attention on the Plaza, wore white cotton pantaloons, cotton handkerchiefs around their heads, and instead of the *cushma*, handkerchiefs over their arms and shoulders. Some wore an embroidered shirt over their trousers, while others had handkerchiefs suspended from their hats, like vails. They were accompanied by demons with horns, monkeys, and other fancy masks. There were little boys among them, but no women. They all carried cow-bells, and the leaders had their faces blackened, and were assisted by men in the disguise of negresses. Some of them wore formidable wigs of flax or wool, which gave them quite a savage appearance. I also noticed that the Cayambi Indians wear their hair shorter than those of Otabalo and Cotacachi.

I have already said that they were all armed with clubs and truncheons, to be ready in case of a battle. This, however, did not take place, as the enemy had been detained at home. The Indians belonging to several of the neighboring haciendas, and especially to that of San José, are the old enemies of those whom I saw on the Plaza. From time immemorial regular yearly battles had been fought between them on these holidays. All their mutual animosities and resentments, all the spite and grudges that had accumulated during the year, were fought out on these occasions. From two to three men were killed every year, and an equal or greater number badly wounded, until at last efforts were made to check this barbarous custom. Parties of citizens placed themselves at the four entrances of the Plaza, and took the clubs from the Indians as they came in. This precaution, however, proved ineffectual, and other measures had to be adopted. Separate festivals were organized at San José and other neighboring haciendas, and free rum, chicha, and bull-teasings given to the Indians to keep them at home. The mayordomo of San José afterwards told me quite naively, that these expenses had become necessary to prevent the killing of Indians, whose death, as they always were in a manner purchased by the land-owners and constituted their laboring capital, would be a great pecuniary loss to the parties interested. Not for the sake of humanity and civilization, therefore, but from considerations of interest merely, had a stop been put to this time-honored barbarity.

In this connection it becomes necessary to explain the system of Indian servitude prevailing on the haciendas of the interior. The Indian farm laborers — and it is only the Indians and negroes who work on farms, and by the sweat of their brows maintain the white population by whom they are oppressed — are called *gañanes*, or *concertados*, or *peones*. Their wages do not exceed a *medio* (half a real) per day, which would amount to about twenty-three dollars per year.

In addition to this, the land-owner is obliged to give to each man a suit of coarse common cloth, and a hat, every year. He also gives them a small piece of ground which they may cultivate for themselves, and on which they may build their huts, called *huasipongos*. For this miserable allowance they are compelled to work from early dawn till five or six o'clock in the evening. Before beginning their regular work they are obliged to perform an extra task, such as gathering fuel, repairing the roads, carrying bricks, etc. This extra task is called *faena*. If they absent themselves from their work, the days they lost to their masters are deducted from their scanty wages, and they are in most cases punished for their dereliction.[1] Besides the labor which they must perform for their masters, they are also compelled to do a thousand little things for their curates, who are generally more despotic and cruel than the land-owners. Their wives and children must cultivate the land of the curate, if he has any, and furnish him with servants in addition. Under these circumstances but little time remains to the Indian for the cultivation of his own piece of ground, but his faithful, industrious, and untiring wife steps in and does what her husband cannot do. The Indian women, however, are not exempt from labor for the land-owners. They must perform their *faenas* like the men, although they are not paid for it. It is evi-

[1] It cannot be said, however, that the Indians alone are liable to be whipped by order of their masters. Negro and colored *peons* are generally treated in the same manner, especially on haciendas remote from cities where they have no opportunity of preferring a complaint. The hacienda proprietor is often as arbitrary and despotic as an ancient feudal lord. On an hacienda on the river Guaillabamba, a zambo peon had run away from his master to try his fortune somewhere else. He was captured before he reached Quito, and his master immediately ordered him to be put in irons, and to receive one hundred lashes Happening to be present, I interceded, and obtained the master's promise that at least one half of the sentence should be remitted.

dent that however cheap living may be in the interior, and however limited an Indian's wants may be, half a real per day is insufficient to maintain him and his family. (I have already said that the Indian never is without a family. He marries at an early age, and generally rears a great number of children, who, like their parents, grow up in benighted ignorance and superstition.) He needs a hog, or a calf, or a sheep, a *tercio* of barley or corn to grind his raw meal for *mashca;* his wife wants a piece of *bayeta* for a shawl or a petticoat; his children must be baptized, and no credit is given by the curates, who inflexibly adhere to the cash system; a festival takes place in the neighborhood for which a little money is required: the land-owner therefore advances the money or furnishes the necessary articles, and he does so willingly, because it is his interest to keep the Indian in debt. An account is kept of all these transactions; but the poor *gañan*, to whom the art of reading or writing is a mystery, is at the mercy of the mayordomo or *escribiente* (the clerk who keeps the books of the hacienda). At the end of the year, the Indian not only remains in debt to his master, but the debt for which he was originally purchased has generally increased. It is not usual to settle accounts every year. In many cases it is done only when the Indian, tired of his master, asks for a settlement. He is then taken before a justice, or if it is in a city, to the police station, a balance is struck, and the debtor imprisoned, as imprisonment for debt has not yet been abolished in Ecuador. His *huasipongo*, and the little piece of ground around it, now revert to his master, and the Indian remains in jail until somebody else pays his debt, and thereby purchases his services. It is true he might make an assignment of his property, or, as we should call it, take the benefit of the insolvent act ; but these are rights which he does not know, and how should he get the money to buy *papel sellado* (stamp-paper), and pass through complicated legal proceedings ? Moreover, the courts would hold that by entering on a new year he made an implied contract to serve during that year, and specific performance would at once be decreed. His new master is generally on hand ; laborers are in great demand ; the Indian himself perhaps has already made an arrangement with his new master before he left the old one (and some Indians are shrewd enough to do this to their advantage) ; and so he passes from one master to another, a slave in fact, though not in name.

It is considered a great piece of perfidy and bad faith on the part of the Indian if, in consideration of some promise or present, he thus changes his master ; but what is it to him for whom he works ? It being the only right he has, to ask for a settlement and be transferred to another owner, why should he not avail himself of it if he can turn it to some account ? But the Spaniards are so accustomed to a dog-like servility and submissiveness on the part of the Indian, that the least symptom of a distant refractoriness, fills them with wrath and indignation. Do they really suppose that it will be possible forever to retain thousands of human beings, on whose hard and unrequited labor the whole country lives, in a state of abject servitude and oppression ? The Indians of Ecuadorian hacienda-owners are their working capital, the same as negro slaves in other countries. Great sums of money are invested in their acquisition. An hacienda-owner once told me that his Indians owed him $13,000. Another assured me that his capital invested in Indian labor amounted to $15,000. There are haciendas to which whole colonies of Indian families belong. The debts for which they are generally sold, vary from fifty to one hundred dollars. At the police court of Quito, many such transactions took place during my residence at the capital. Many a time I was informed by acquaintances that they had just bought a number of *peones.* Their maintenance costs but little. The land-owner manages to keep the Indians in debt, but he does not allow them to get into it too deep. Their necessities, as I have already said, are very limited. Medical attendance, for instance, they do not require at all. But very few Indians would submit to scientific medical treatment. They have no confidence in white physicians, but cling to the ancient traditions of their race. When they are taken sick they apply to some old woman of their own race who has the reputation of being a *curandera* (one who cures), and subject themselves to her treatment. Fortunately, the constitution of the Indian is strong, and his health, in spite of all his filthiness and intemperance, remarkably good. His death is a double loss to his owner, who loses the man's services and the debt he owed. My readers will now understand the motives of interest as well as humanity by which the land-owners around Cayambi were actuated in putting an end to the customary yearly battles of their Indians.

I did not wait for the *toros* (bull-fights) which were to commence on the following day, and to occupy the remainder of the week, inclusive of Sunday; but returned to my head-quarters at Peguchi. The hacienda and *quinta* (villa) of Peguchi are situate at the foot of a mountain which separates the plain of Otabalo from the valley of San Pablo. I left the *quinta* with regret, after having stayed there about a week, and proceeded to Otabalo, where I proposed to stay a few days. I have no reliable data by which to estimate the population of that town, to the extent of which the number of its inhabitants does not seem to correspond. But when the ancient Spaniards founded a town or village, they divided the soil among the settlers, allotting generally but four proprietors to one square, so as to enable them to have kitchen-gardens, court-yards, or orchards around their houses. Their settlements, therefore, always extended over a considerable area, and as the country progressed but very little, the results of this system still present themselves to our view. Many a time we find but two or three houses in one square. Long walls, covered with that dense vegetation which clings to ruins, roofs, and walls, line the streets, and protect the unweeded and neglected gardens and court-yards behind them. In some of them cabbage or clovet is raised; in others, fruit-trees, to which the climate is very favorable, have been planted; but most of these gardens are neglected, or used as *corales* (pens or pounds).

The situation of Otabalo is friendlier than that of Quito, because cultivated fields and meadows expand over the surrounding hills and plains, and the welcome sight of trees in a country where there is such a scarcity of them, produces an agreeable impression. The streets are laid out in the usual Spanish-American style, intersecting each other at right angles, and having the gutters in the centre. They are overgrown with grass, and without life or animation. Stores there are but few, as the town has no commerce. The windows are without glass-panes, as at Cayambi, which is very disagreeable on account of the near neighborhood of Mts.

Imbabura and Cotacachi. The weather is sometimes very cold and stormy, especially at the beginning of the dry season. I may add here that glass is not manufactured in the country, and is therefore high in price.

The elevation of Otabalo, according to Dr. Jameson's measurement, is 8470 feet above the level of the sea. The *naranja agria* (sour orange), the lemon, and even an occasional upstart of sugar-cane, grow in the gardens, but the fruit on which the inhabitants plume themselves most, is a kind of raspberry (*mora*), from which a very pleasant beverage is prepared. The people are very hospitable and courteous to strangers.

There is no want of ruins at Otabalo, for otherwise it would be untrue to its Spanish-American character. In the interior it takes very long to erect or repair a building. Not only does the work progress slowly, but the owner has generally begun it without a previous calculation of the probable expense. In this case the work will be abandoned for months, and sometimes for years. The general practice is to cover the walls with tiles, so as to protect the bricks or *adobes* of which they are made against the rain, and then leave them until the work can be resumed. In the mean time weeds grow up in the intended rooms, and hogs will establish their quarters within the inclosures.

The whites and Cholos of Otabalo all speak the *Quichua*, or Indian language. They learn it from their earliest childhood, and speak it with great ease and perfection. To the owners of haciendas in this neighborhood, a knowledge of the Quichua is indispensable, for there are hundreds of Indian farm laborers who cannot speak a word of Spanish.

There is a convent at Otabalo, but its corridors and cells are in ruins, and its court-yards overgrown with wild weeds. The monks to whom the building belongs do not live in it. They live with their families or mistresses outside. The practice of keeping women is carried on by them without shame or apprehension. They beget children and own them; they even show themselves in public at the side of their concubines. They lead such a lazy and easy life that the mayordomos of haciendas, who cannot provide a better lot for their sons, generally destine them for the Church, which supports them without requiring them to work. All the convents in the country own great haciendas, from which rich revenues are derived, to be swallowed up by vicious, lazy, and ignorant monks.

Happening to be at Otabalo on a Sunday, curiosity impelled me to go to mass. Standing on the open square in front of the church, my attention was attracted by about two dozen Indians, most of them women, brought up by a few Indian *alcaldes*, who led them tied to one another with a long rope, probably in the same manner in which the king of Dahomey would chain together the slaves intended for the foreign market. Their offense consisted in having failed to attend religious service, especially the *doctrina*, for which they are compelled to meet twice a week. They were driven up and cuffed by the *alcaldes*, who for this purpose are intrusted with a little despotic authority, which they are delighted to exercise. These *alcaldes* are appointed by the curates, and are called "*Alcaldes de Doctrina.*" (The Indians are afflicted with three classes of regular oppressors — the government, the hacienda-owners, and the curates; but the last are said to be the worst of all.) Other *alcaldes* are appointed by the government. Their business is to procure Indian laborers or carriers for the public service whenever they are wanted. It is the duty of these officers to furnish slaves whenever slave labor is required by the fountain-head of iniquity—a South-American government. The twenty-four offenders of whom I just spoke, were made to kneel down in front of the church, and exposed to public view — a punishment which is intended to shame them. Disgusted with this spectacle, I entered the crowded church, and witnessed the saying of mass. But here the devotion of the congregation was continually disturbed by an unwashed dirty fellow in a red poncho, who went up and down with — not exactly a plate, but some other begging utensil, apparently of silver, calling out every now and then, "*Para la cera del santisimo sacramento*" ("for the wax of the most holy sacrament").

About ten miles from Otabalo, in the lap of Mt. Cotacachi, on its southern side, is Lake Cuicocha, 10,200 feet above the level of the sea, a very romantic little lake, with two islands, or rather hills, in the centre, which seem to have remained after the falling in of that part of the mountain, to the disappearance of which the lake probably owes its origin. The hills or islands are covered with dense green shrubs and little trees, which give them a very pleasant, although melancholy appearance. No human habitation, except two or three Indian huts, are visible from the shore. Pleasure parties, I was told, will sometimes build provisional cottages on the ridges of the steep banks by which the lake is hemmed in, and embark on frail *balsas* constructed of reeds growing in or near the water along the shores. As the lake is in a hollow, it cannot be seen from a distance. The view breaks upon you suddenly, and not before you approach the brink. There is but one practicable path to descend to it. It leads to a little opening among the shrubs, which is called the *embarcadero*. Lovers of the chase will hunt deer on the surrounding hills, and drive it into the lake, which it will swim, crossing to one of the two islands, where it may be taken without difficulty by the dogs. Hunting in this vicinity constitutes a most dangerous amusement. Through a dense growth of spines (*mimosa*), which tear the rider's face and hands, the sportsmen follow their prey, preceded by a pack of hounds, who are the chief actors in the play. I was shown a narrow track which the deer usually takes, and which consists of a steep and narrow path leading to the *embarcadero*, exceedingly slippery in rainy weather, with a precipice on each side. To the north, one false step or slide of the horse will precipitate its rider into the lake, while to the south it would throw him into a wilderness of spiny shrubs and thorns. Accidents are very frequent, and sometimes fatal, but they are unable to dampen the ardor of hunting parties who, from time to time, resort to this place. When I visited Cuicocha the weather was very favorable, and while ascending the slopes of Cotacachi I found myself in a circle of majestic mountains. There was Cayambi, after a cold night, with a long white robe which reached far below the usual snow limit; there was Imbabura, its trachytic cupola sprinkled all over with snow; there was Cotacachi, with the lake in its lap, and its hoary peaks frowning down upon the intruders; there was Chiles, visible in an uncertain distance to the north, struggling with the clouds that hung around it; while to the south the peaks of Cotopaxi and Pichincha peeped over the range of the Cordillera, which divides the plain of Otabalo from the plain of Aña Quito.

At Otabalo, Cotacachi, and all such country places,

more business is done on Sunday than on any other day. In fact, whatever purchases or sales the Indians have to make, are made on Sunday. These Sunday markets are called "*ferias*." The sellers squat on the ground, sometimes under little screens of baize or sack-cloth nailed to a clumsy wooden contrivance supported by a pole which is driven into the ground. Here they sell *macañas* (a sort of narrow cotton shawls), ponchos, wool, cotton, beads, rosaries, leaden crosses, strings of glass pearls, collars and bracelets of false corals, and other cheap ornaments; meat, fruit, vegetables, salt, agi, barley-meal, and such popular dishes ready made, as *cariucho*, *locro*, *chocllos*, *mashca*, toasted corn, etc.

It was on a Sunday when I rode over to the village of Cotacachi, which is about an hour's ride from Otabalo. I saw many Indian graves (mounds), some of them very high, along the road. Cotacachi is the village which suffered most from the earthquake of 1859, yet I noticed less ruins there than anywhere else in the country. Cotacachi, Hatuntaqui, and Guano, near Riobamba, are the most industrious villages of the Republic, and the natural effect of labor is prosperity. Cotacachi, therefore, presents a friendly appearance. New houses greet you on all sides, and buildings are everywhere in process of construction. The chief article of manufacture is ponchos, which are exported to Quito, Guayaquil, and New Granada. It is calculated that about six thousand cotton ponchos of all colors are manufactured monthly. The cotton thus consumed is raised in the hotter parts of the province. Woolen stuffs for ponchos, coats, and pantaloons, and silks for vests, cravats, etc., are also manufactured. The silk used is imported from abroad. Efforts are making to introduce the silk-worm in Ecuador, but as yet nothing can be said as to the result. The instruments used for these manufactures belong to a bygone age. Every thing is done by hand, and in a slow but steady manner. Modern improvements and machinery, although known in the neighborhood, have not yet found their way into the patriarchal community of Cotacachi.

When I arrived, throngs of Indians were just leaving the church and assembling on the graveyard, where they sat down on the ground — the men on one side, the women on the other. And here I witnessed another of those scenes so revolting to human dignity and self-respect. It began with a roll-call, which is called "*Padronar.*" The names of the Indians, men and women, of the parish, are inscribed on three or four wooden tablets, with a handle to each. In front of each name is a small hole, through which a string is drawn, with a knot at each end. The names on the tablets are read off by an alcalde, and each individual meekly responds, "*Aqui estoy, mi amo*" (" here I am, my master"). If the knot attached to a name is found hanging outside, it is a sign that its owner failed to attend the last rehearsal of the *doctrina cristiana.* These rehearsals, as I have already said, take place twice a week. As soon as the name of the offender is called, he is required to step forward and to lie down flat on the ground, where he receives three lashes, which are given with a long cowhide doubled for the purpose. The women only kneel down, and, taking off their shawls, receive the lashes on the back. The poor creatures submit to this indignity with the utmost humility and patience, although many of them know that such treatment is prohibited by law.

There were cock-fights on the plaza — a usual Sunday amusement. When these were over, the *pelota* was played, a ball game that requires considerable physical exertion. At the same time a music band was playing to convoke the residents to listen to the reading of a new municipal ordinance. In a country without newspapers, such means must be resorted to to give publicity to laws and ordinances.

Between Otabalo and Cotacachi is the *quinta* of Mr. Pedro Perez Pareja, with an important cotton factory, the machinery of which is perfect, and was made in Patterson, New Jersey. The cost of transportation amounted to over $40,000, and many pieces were lost or broken ; nevertheless, it works well, and the owner sells all he can make. But the expense of establishing the factory was so great, that the speculation turned out unprofitable. When the native weavers first saw the machinery in motion, in its most ingenious complexity, and saw that it did in an hour what they could not do in days and weeks, they thought that it was an invention of the devil, or rather that the Prince of Darkness himself was the power which set it in motion.

The road from Otabalo to Ibarra is very good in summer, and cannot be very bad in winter. It is remarkably level, gently declining toward Ibarra, and passes along and across the western slope of Mt. Imbabura. This interesting volcano does not enter the line of perpetual snow, and derives its name from *imba*, which in Quichua means " little fish," and *bura*, that which produces ; because in its eruptions of water it threw out great quantities of those little fishes, which the Spaniards call *preñadillos*, and which, as I have already remarked, are found in the shallow water along the shores of Lake San Pablo.

Hatuntaqui, which is about a league from Cotacachi,

and two leagues from Ibarra, is the place where the great Indian battle was fought which terminated in the defeat and death of Cacha, the last Scyri or King of Quito. This unfortunate monarch was the descendant of an ancient and powerful dynasty of rulers, who, though inferior in arts and civilization to the Peruvians, were greatly superior to the Indian tribes of New Granada. Their language was a dialect of Peruvian Quichua, from which the common origin of both nations is inferred. They had arrived at that period of civilization which archæologists call the period of bronze. Their kingdom consisted of a great number of Indian tribes, among which the Caranquis were the most warlike. For many years the Scyris had fought against the slowly but irresistibly advancing power of the Incas, by whom they were at last driven from their capital, and overwhelmed in a decisive battle on the plain of Hatuntaqui. There it was that the Inca Huaynacapac, the victorious invader, added to the *borla* the emblem of Peruvian royalty, the emerald of the Scyris of Quito. Hatuntaqui was afterwards transformed into a fortified camp of the Incas. There the great drum is said to have been kept, the sound of which could be heard for many miles around, and from which the present village derives its name; for Hatuntaqui, in Quichua, means *gran tambor*, or the big drum of war.

The village of Hatuntaqui, as I said above, is one of the most industrious and enterprising of the Republic. There, straw hats are made in considerable quantities; sacks or bags in still greater quantities are manufactured from the fibre of the American aloe; but the most important business of the place is the hiring out of beasts of burden, on which the products of the province, its woolen and cotton goods, its sugar and rum, its salt and grain, are transported to Quito and New Granada. The village is inhabited by a great number of arrieros, who are doing a lively business in all directions. Like Cotacachi, it does not present that gloomy aspect which characterizes other Ecuadorian towns. New houses are in process of erection in almost every street; schools are being built, streets are repaired, and gardens laid out, pleasantly contrasting with the decay of other and more renowned places.

Hatuntaqui is about half a league to the west of the main road from Otabalo to Ibarra, in a plain dotted with an immense number of *tolas* or Indian graves. Many of them arose after the great battle to which I have just alluded, and after which the corpses of thousands of the victors and vanquished covered the bloody ground. Many of these tolas are ploughed over, and the corn of the conqueror now grows on the graves of the ancient lords of the land. The country around Cotacachi and Hatuntaqui is chiefly a grain region. indian-corn, barley, wheat, and potatoes grow in unlimited abundance. All the grains and fruits of the temperate zone could be introduced here. In the gardens and orchards, the peach, the fig-tree, and the wild grape grow by the side of the chirimoya, the aguacate, and the raspberry. The climate is delightful. It is the same all the year round: no torrid season enervates the inhabitant of this favored realm; no icy winter sends him shivering to the chimney fire. In fact, stoves and chimneys are unknown; and to know what heat is, one would have to descend to the sultry valley of the Chota, where the negro hums his merry tunes among coffee and plantain-trees, and the sugar-cane. There is no starvation in this neighborhood; nobody dies from cold; nobody sinks sun-struck to the ground; no troublesome insects molest the inhabitants; epidemics are unknown; healthy faces peep at you through the long hedges of aloes; healthy faces stare at you from every Indian cottage. It is not sickness, it is foreign war and internecine strife and perpetual convulsions, that decimate the population and scatter death and decay where wealth and bliss should smile.

> "The golden harvests spring; the unfailing sun
> Sheds light and life; the fruits, the flowers, the trees,
> Arise in due succession; all things speak
> Peace, and harmony, and love. The Universe,
> In Nature's silent eloquence, declares
> That all fulfill the works of love and joy.
> All but the outcast Man! He fabricates
> The sword which stabs his peace; he cherisheth
> The snakes that gnaw his heart."

There is but little traffic between Ibarra and Otabalo. The Ecuadorians are not a migrating or travelling people. Weeks will pass before some resident of the former place will visit the latter, or *vice versa*, although the distance is but inconsiderable. Only occasionally the traveller meets a few *cargas* of sugar, *rapadura*, or rum, going to Quito, or a solitary New Granadian going to or coming from Pasto or Popayan.

The plain of Ibarra presents a most friendly aspect; for although the mountains by which it is bounded on the north, and at the foot of which Ibarra seems to rest, are arid and monotonous, like the Cordillera in general, our sight is gladdened by trees around the habitations on the road from San Antonio to Ibarra. Ibarra itself is almost hidden among orchards, kitchen gardens, clover fields, and rows of willows (*sauces*), and only the cupolas and steeples of its churches remind us of its dignity as the capital of the province. To our right, as we descend into the plain, lies the friendly village of Carranqui, where Atahuallpa was born, in happy ignorance of those who were to take his crown and life.

Ibarra occupies the lowest part of the plain now before us. Its situation is somewhat damp and swampy, for which reason it is occasionally visited with intermittent fevers, which, however, never assume a malignant character. The town extends along the left bank of the river Tauhando, an affluent of the Ambi, which the queer poetry of the common people has immortalized by the following stanza, sung all over the country by arrieros and *chagras* (churls): —

"En el rio de Tauhando
  Mi sombrero va nadando,
Y con la copa me dice
  Que mi amor se va acabando."[1]

The town of Ibarra is said to contain from 7000 to 8000 inhabitants, which I am satisfied is an exaggeration. The inhabitants are very social and hospitable. This latter virtue is one of great importance to the traveller, because the place has no tavern or *casa posada*. The stranger who arrives without knowing any body is compelled to thrust himself on private hospitality without preliminaries, which to a person of delicacy is very embarrassing. I was, however, most hospitably received by the worthy governor, Don Luciano de la Sala, and his amiable family, at whose house I remained for over a week.

Ibarra is neither an industrial nor a commercial place. In thrift and enterprise it is far behind Cotacachi and Hatuntaqui. It is the residence of landed proprietors who own sugar plantations or other farms in the neighborhood. Generally, however, their resi-

[1] "In the river Tauhando my hat swims along, and with its crown it tells me that my love is vanishing."

dence in Ibarra is of limited duration. As soon as they succeed in obtaining pecuniary independence, they prefer to transmigrate to Quito. The number of respectable families in Ibarra is therefore very small. A business of some importance in this neighborhood is the breeding of donkeys, for the purpose of sending them to Pasto and Popayan, where they always find a very profitable market. Sacks and ropes are manufactured to some extent from the fibre of the aloe. The elevation of Ibarra above the level of the sea is 7550 feet, and the climate very agreeable. It is not hot, and yet warmer than that of Quito.

The town has more churches and convents than the number of its inhabitants would seem to justify. All the public buildings were damaged by the earthquake of 1859. The Convent of La Merced was almost ruined. As the friars, however, pass their lives outdoors, none of them were hurt. The finest public building is the Church *De la Compañia*. From its terraced roof and steeples a very fine view may be had of the surrounding plain and villages. In one of the apartments of the church a most remarkable mummy is shown to visitors. It is a man in a sitting posture, greatly contracted, with his knees drawn up to his face, and the latter resting on his hands. His skin, and even his intestines, are perfectly preserved. He was found by a hunting party in a lonely, out-of-the-way place in the Cordillera. There are marks of wounds on his person, especially a hole in the back, through which the inner part of the body may be seen. The soil where he was found is limy, and the place probably one of those which are so admirably adapted to the desiccation of dead bodies.[1]

1 "A curious result of the extreme dryness of the atmosphere, charged with saline particles, has been observed in some of the more elevated regions

The women of Ibarra are not handsome. Those who are, emigrate to Quito as soon as they can. For the inhabitants of the interior, Quito is the great centre of attraction. They can hardly be persuaded that there can be any thing greater and finer in the world than Quito. "*Quito bonito*," is a proverb which may be heard all along the public highways. Another adage thus expresses the high opinion which the Serranos entertain of their capital: "*De Quito — al cielo; del cielo un agujerito para ver á Quito.*" ("From Quito — to heaven; in heaven a little aperture through which to look at Quito.") The most ardent desire of all young women in the provinces is to be able some day or other to go to Quito, which to their happy ignorance is the *ne plus ultra* of all human perfection.

The village of Carranqui, the birthplace of Atahuallpa, is about half a league from Ibarra. Its situation is higher and healthier than that of the latter, but its vegetable products are the same. In the gardens of both places I found figs, wild grapes, lemons, plantains, (these latter do not prosper much, as they require a hotter climate,) *limas*, tomatoes on trees, sour and sweet oranges, papayas, peaches, a kind of raspberries, aguacates, the dwarf cocoa-nut, *chirimoyas*, *nogales*, etc., etc. Inoculation is unknown in this country, nor are trees ever pruned.

of Peru. The pure drying winds have the effect of embalming dead bodies submitted to their influence. The ancient Peruvians appear to have occasionally availed themselves of the desiccating qualities of the air, by leaving their dead above ground instead of burying them. In the desert of Atacama there is a cemetery of this description, which was accidentally discovered by Dr. Reid, a late traveller in Peru. He found the dried bodies of 600 men, women, and children, all in a perfect state of preservation, and in a sitting posture, arranged in a semicircle, gazing, as it seemed, on vacancy. There they had sat for centuries. A jar of maize and a cooking utensil were found by the side of each." — From an article on Peru, published in the *London Quarterly*, January, 1863.

At Carranqui, Huaynacapac, the father of the last Inca Atahuallpa, is said to have held his court for many years. There he is said to have constructed a royal palace, forts, temples, and a convent for the virgins of the sun. Of all these edifices no vestige has remained. The parochial church of Carranqui is said to rest on the foundations of an ancient temple of the sun; but even this is doubtful. In their reckless search for gold the barbarous Spaniards left no stone upon the other. Their cupidity had been excited by what they had heard of the riches of the ancient kingdom of Quito. They came in the expectation to find the treasures of Atahuallpa, but they were disappointed. Either those treasures were fabulous, or they had been applied to swell the ransom of the captive Inca, or they had been hidden by the Indians before the arrival of their foreign enemies. This latter hypothesis has found most favor with Spanish historians, and it was generally believed in by the men of Benalcazar and Ampudia, who were the first to take possession of Quito. For this reason they pulled down the walls, and undermined the foundations of stately edifices; and not a stone was left at Quito and Carranqui to tell the tale of a destroyed civilization.

The only monuments in this neighborhood that escaped the fury of the conquerors, are the *tolas* or mounds. They were too many and too big to be opened; and probably those that were opened did not remunerate the trouble of excavation. The Indians of Quito and the neighborhood were not in the habit of burying their dead in subterranean graves. They placed them on the ground generally in a sitting posture, and mostly several of them together in a semicircle, and depositing their drinking vessels filled with chicha, their arms, jewels, and other ornaments at their sides, constructed a low wall of stones around them, which they covered with great quantities of earth and rocks, until the mound thus formed rose to the size of a little hill. Some of these hills are of astonishing dimensions. Narrow passages or channels were generally constructed, through which the dead could be supplied with chicha. The pots or vessels in the tolas were so placed as to correspond with the channels or air-holes leading to the surface. In an excavated tola at Carranqui, I saw vestiges of these channels, which betokened superior workmanship and a considerable degree of skill in masonry. They were well walled out, and their base most symmetrically designed. In many of the mounds that were lately opened, chicha was found in vessels at the side of the skeletons, and at the base of the channels through which it is generally believed that the Indians of the present day, actuated by a certain sense of piety, are still supplying their dead ancestors with their favorite beverage. Whether this is true or not, I am unable to say. It is but too probable that these channels should have become obstructed in the course of time. On the other hand, the Indians have lost their ancient traditions, and it is not likely that the poor, drunken brutes of the present day would waste their beloved chicha by pouring it into graves. Still it can hardly be believed that chicha should have been preserved in a mound for over three hundred years.

Several years ago, after the great gold discoveries in the graves of Cuenca had given a new impulse to excavating enterprise, a joint-stock company was formed at Ibarra for the purpose of opening the principal tolas of Carranqui. Two or three of them were excavated, but nothing of importance found. Heavy earrings of bronze were found on the shoulders of the dead. Earthen vessels, or pieces of the same, of a solid make, and of a blood-red color, were found in great abundance. But as no gold was discovered, the enterprise was abandoned. One of these tolas, which from time immemorial was known by its Quichua name of the "Tola of Gold," had attracted the attention of the company more than any other; but the proprietor asked eighty dollars for his permission to open it; a sum which the managers were unwilling to give. The vessels found in these Indian graves are greatly superior in workmanship, as well as in usefulness, to the crockery now manufactured in Ecuador.

Separated from the town of Ibarra by the river Tauhando, and a spur of the Cordillera which extends into the plain, is Lake Yaguarcocha, the waters of which are discharged into the river Tauhando. It is about one and a half miles in circumference, and its shores are covered with a vegetation of reeds called *totora*, of which, by tying them together in cables, a frail kind of *balsa* is constructed for purposes of navigation. The scenery along the banks is sad and melancholy, like its name. Yaguarcocha, in the Indian language, signifies "Sea of Blood." After the Peruvian Inca Huaynacapac had conquered the empire of the ancient Scyris of Quito, the Carranquis, one of its bravest nations, rebelled against the foreign yoke. It is said that while profound peace was reigning throughout the land, the Carranquis made a sudden night attack on the *Orejones*, the body-guard of the unsuspecting Inca, and after killing a great many of them, withdrew to their own province. But now the wrath of the conqueror was aroused. He followed them with his victorious army of veterans, defeated them in a frightful battle near the shores of the lake, and ordered the whole male population of the province to be killed. Their dead bodies were thrown into the lake, and so numerous were the victims, that their blood reddened its waters, and gave it the name which it has since retained, the "Sea of Blood." According to ancient traditions, the number of the slain varies from 40,000 to 80,000, which undoubtedly is an exaggeration.

A great number of tolas on the southwestern shore of the lake — the only side on which it is not hemmed in by mountains — are the surviving monuments of the great slaughter. In the rear of these tolas is a *pucará*, or Indian fort, consisting of a ditch, which, like a winding staircase (*caracol*), encircles, from below upwards, an isolated hill, commanding an interesting view of the lake and plain. This fort probably was the last refuge of the vanquished Carranquis.

## CHAPTER XV.

Trip to the Province of Imbabura concluded. — A Visit to the Valley of the River Chota. — The Heights of Alaburu. — The Mountain of Pialchan, with its Mysterious Cave. — Another Gold Legend. — Aërial Bridges. — Return to the Tropics. — Sugar Plantations and Negroes. — History of the Abolition of Slavery in Ecuador. — Landslips. — Mass Emigration and Disappearance of Indians. — The Strange Story of Pimampiro. — Geological Catastrophes. — Digging for Treasures. — The Village of Cacha swallowed up by an Earthquake. — Indian Graves. — Ancient Indian Crockery. — Guajara. — The Footpath to Peylon on the Coast. — The English Company. — Negro Dances. — Bomba and Alfandoque. — The Paramo Road to Quito. — Mojanda. — A Farewell to the Fairy Province of Imbabura. — Mountain Lakes. — Return to Quito.

My readers will now accompany me on an excursion to the valley of the Chota, which is the most important sugar-growing region of the province of Imbabura. Passing by Lake Yaguarcocha, with the Indian fort described in my last chapter to our left, we ascend a range of the Cordillera, which divides the plain of Ibarra from the low and sultry valley of the Chota. To ascend a high mountain on one side, and to descend it on the other, is the monotonous task of the traveller in the Andes. The point from which, after losing sight of the plains of Ibarra and Carranqui, we commence our dreary descent, is a group of miserable cottages called "Alaburu." They are constructed of reeds (*cariso*), plastered with mud, and thatched. The view which now presents itself, is desolate in the extreme. Whithersoever the eye may wander, the mountains are barren of vegetation, except a few crippled and miserable shrubs, which only add to the general gloom.

The muddy river far below, which with great precipitation hurries on over rocks and rubble, is hemmed in by sandy, arid mountains, and uninhabited deserts. Only occasionally the eye is relieved by fields of the yellow-green sugar-cane along the river banks, or on some of the protruding platforms of the mountains. From nine o'clock in the morning till about four or five in the afternoon, the sun sends down his scorching rays on the long sandy and dusty path which is now before us. The descent to the river occupies about an hour and a half, and there is not a hut on the road to give us shelter, not a tree to protect us for a moment from the parching sun. For this reason, it is always advisable to leave Ibarra very early in the morning, so as to reach the river before the heat sets in. Now and then the sand disappears under our feet, and we pass over plats of hardened earth without any vegetation. Not a blade of grass is to be seen for miles around. We feel as if the horrors of the desert were breaking upon us. After toiling down for about an hour, the scanty shrubs around us begin to rise into stunted trees, intermingled with all sorts of cacti; but it is not before we reach the valley itself that we meet with a useful and pleasing vegetation, conquered from the apparently unpromising soil by the industry of man.[1]

[1] The vegetation of the mountains lining the valley of the Chota, seems to be confined to four species. I have travelled through these deserts many a weary mile without finding any other plants except occasional groups of cacti. Those four species are: 1. The *Dodonea viscosa*, a shrub which the natives call "*mosquea.*" 2. The *Mimosa*, of which there are various species in the sultry valleys of the Andes, constituting diminutive trees, armed with spines. The natives call it "*espino.*" 3. The *Croton menthodorum*, a small shrub which is widely distributed on the sandy plains of San Antonio (to the north of Quito), Alchipichi, on the Guaillabamba, etc. Its popular name is *Chamano*. 4. An arborescent *Prosopis*, which the natives call "*guarango*," and which is used for dyeing purposes. The endless repetition of these four species is exceedingly displeasing. Their scanty foliage and

To the left of the road on our descent from Alaburu, is a mountain called "Pialchan," concerning which a queer story circulates among the common people. The mountain is said to contain a cave, and in the cave there is a giant of stone. Under the arm of that dread person, there is an entrance, or hole, which, however, opens only on Good Friday or other solemn occasions. Through this hole the lucky visitor passes into a second cave, in which there is a *calvario* (a representation of the crucifixion), and an immense treasure of gold and silver, of which, unfortunately, it is not permitted to take more than a measure found on the spot will hold. He who takes more cannot get out with his treasure. The opening under the giant's arm closes upon him, and after a few hours of anguish and despair, he falls into a swoon, to awake in the open air in another part of the inhospitable mountain. Many superstitious persons, attracted by this story, which they eagerly believed, explored the mountain in all directions, but without success. Some are said to have found the cave; but the giant, the *calvario*, and the treasure, remain undiscovered to this day.

The river Chota is exceedingly rapid. It is fordable at some places, but not after a rain in the mountains, when it rises immediately, and often inundates the haciendas on its banks, doing great damage. The bridge which we are now about to pass divides the valley into two parts, Chota Alto and Chota Bajo (upper and lower

scattered growth are insufficient to cover the sterile ground beneath them. The stunted trees soon wither, and cover themselves with floating garlands of *Barba de salvage*, to which I referred in a former chapter. In fact, the resemblance of the Chota valley to that of the Guaillabamba is striking. I may add here that the Chota (or *Mira*) and the Guaillabamba are the only rivers in Ecuador which break through the whole of the western Cordillera, carrying the snowy waters of Pichincha and Cayambi into the Pacific Ocean.

Chota). The bridge itself is a frail and trembling structure. It rests on two solid abutments of masonry, but it consists merely of logs stemmed against one another, and against the pillars below, into which the principal logs are inserted. These latter are covered with other logs, and over these staves are laid crosswise, and covered with a layer of gravel and sand. Not to concentrate too heavy a weight on such a dangerous contrivance, it is customary for the traveller to dismount and pass it on foot, leading his horse behind him. It is a thrilling sensation to walk high in the air over such a frail structure, trembling and shaking under your steps, with no balustrades at your sides, and the river beneath you, rushing on wildly as it were to death and destruction.[1] The river is spanned by several such bridges, and three or four *taravitas*, a kind of suspension or rope-bridge, which is an Indian invention. It consists of a number of cables twisted together, and fastened to poles driven into the ground. The passenger generally sits down in a basket and is drawn across.

Having passed the bridge over the Chota, we find a group of miserable huts, built of reeds, and inhabited by a few sickly looking people, mostly mulattoes and

[1] "At every step you meet with valleys, and in every valley torrents. The communication between the two banks is formed by bridges made of two trees, across which are thrown fascines covered with a slight layer of earth. This rude work trembles and seems ready to sink; there is no rail, and, by a singular coincidence, none of these bridges are more than four feet wide. If one of the rotten supports of these aërial bridges were to break under the horse's feet, the animal in its struggle would drag the rider into the abyss below, where he would perish on the pointed rocks. Yet such is the security arising from habit, that people pass over these frail bridges by night as well as by day, and without even feeling the least alarm at hearing the roaring of the waters below." — *Travels in the Republic of Colombia in the years* 1822 *and* 1823, by G. Mollien. Translated from the French.

negroes. They sell fruit, such as oranges, sugar and water-melons, lemons, *limas* (sweet lemons), pine-apples, plantains, *papayas* (pawpaws), etc. Dense avenues of aloes, *pencos*, and other cacti, are now before us — we are in a tropical country again. The broad leaves of the plantain-tree throw shade on our path; the orange glows among the dark leaves; the aguacate tree rises to a majestic height; the chirimoya looks temptingly down on the traveller. Swarms of mosquitoes, which the natives call *sancudos*, and sand-flies, try the extent of his patience, and his energies seem to fade away under the influence of an enervating sun. Another bridge similar to the one we just passed, leads us across the Chota Chiquito, an affluent of the great river. We found another group of huts on the other side, where we rested a few hours, and partook of refreshments. At the first bridge we passed, the road branches off to Tulcan, Pasto, and Popayan, and soon leads you out of the hot valley to the high table-lands again, and into districts much colder than Latacunga, Machachi, or Quito. The *Canton* of Tulcan is an agricultural and stock-raising country. Cheese is made in considerable quantities, and brought down into the low valleys for sale. But let us, for the present, continue our journey along the right bank of the Chota.

Our way leads us through a narrow and dense grove of *pencos* and gigantic cacti, interspersed with *mimosas* and *guarangos*, the protruding branches of which endanger our eyes and face. It would be the simplest and easiest task in the world to cut these branches away, and to make the road comfortably passable, but who should do it? Every body's business is nobody's business. The native is perfectly satisfied if he succeeds in dodging these obstructions and impediments without injury to his own person, and leaves those who come after him to get along as well as they can. I have often observed that many of the most dangerous places on steep declivities or descents to river banks, might be made passable by one man set to work for about two hours or half a day, at an expense of much less than a dollar ; but it is in the character of the race rather to risk their legs or necks than to trouble themselves about public works, from which no direct and immediate profit can be derived.

Emerging from the grove of cacti and spines, we discover that the valley has suddenly widened. On our right are the mountains, the sterility and baldness of which surpass any thing I ever saw ; but to our left opens another and lower plain, teeming with fertility and smiling with verdure. Here grows the sugar-cane in long and beautiful yellow-green fields, intersected by parks of orange and aguacate trees, *nogales* and willows ;[1] and through the broad plantain leaves peeps the coffee-tree, which in this part of the country is always raised under the protection afforded by the more rapid growth of the plantain. When the young tree has safely grown up, the plantains around it are cut down.

We stopped at a shed under which the negroes were engaged at a sugar mill. These mills are set in motion by a large wheel, propelled either by hydraulic or horse power.[2] The workmen employed are all negroes. The

[1] The *nogal* is a species of walnut-tree (*Juglans regia*). It is generally planted in clover fields, attains a considerable height, and presents a very fine appearance. In the plains of Tumbaco, Puembo, and Yaruqui, I saw a great many of them.

[2] " The hydraulic works of this country, principally for purposes of irrigation and the supply of towns, although not conducted with much skill,

Indians have entirely disappeared from the valley. The negroes, who have taken their places, are *concer tados*, like the Indian farm laborers of whom I spoke in the preceding chapter. They are slaves in fact, although not slaves in name. Their services are secured by a purchase of the debts which they owe. As long as they remain in debt, which state, thanks to the skillful management of their masters, almost always lasts till they discharge the great debt of nature, they must either work or go to prison. Like the Indians, they are ignorant of their legal rights. They are hardly ever able to pay their debts, which, on the contrary, continually increase, as their wages of one half real to one real are insufficient to satisfy their wants. When slavery was abolished in Ecuador, the owners of the negroes in the sugar districts immediately employed them to work for wages, and managing to get them into debt, secured their services as debtors. Thus it may almost be said that they profited, instead of losing by, the abolition of slavery. They pocketed the compensation which the law provided for the slave owners, and at the same time retained their slaves. It is true the blacks do not work so much now as when they were bondmen, nor can their masters beat them as unmercifully as they did before; but, on the other hand, it must be considered that it is much cheaper now to purchase a negro than it was then. Now, by paying a debt of fifty or seventy dollars which the poor

are really surprising from their extensiveness, considering the scanty population. In many places the water is conducted for miles, along the sides of precipitous and arid mountains, its channel frequently cut in the solid rock, for the purpose of fertilizing a single plantation, and consequently at the expense of its proprietor." — *Notes on Colombia, taken in the years* 1822–3, *by an Officer of the United States Army* The construction of such stupendous works, is considerably facilitated by the great cheapness of labor.

fellow owes to somebody, his services may be secured, while formerly it took, perhaps, ten times that amount to purchase a slave.

The introduction of negro slaves into the valley of the Chota was caused by a most remarkable event — a mass emigration of the Indians of the valley. In the year 1679 more than 11,000 Indians, tired of tyranny and oppression, left their habitations and took refuge in the inaccessible recesses of the eastern Cordillera. The village of Pimampiro, situated on the head-waters of the Chota, which until then was a thriving Indian settlement, was entirely abandoned by its population. There is a legend that the retiring Indians took the church bell, and some say even the curate, with them, and that the sounds of that bell are still heard occasionally in the fastnesses of the eastern Cordillera. What became of these emigrants has never been definitely ascertained. They may have retired to the tropical wilderness on the other side of the eastern range of the Andes, or they may have settled down in some intermediate valley, or on some out-of-the-way table-land. Numerous stories are afloat that some of their descendants emerged from their unknown retreat, and were seen on the road to Tusca or Tulcan in a state of absolute nakedness and barbarity, but with tools and weapons that bespoke their former Spanish connection. Whether these stories are true or not, I am of course unable to say. The general belief is that the emigrants did not go far, but settled down in some hidden valley a short distance from their ancient home To this belief the legend is to be ascribed that the sounds of their old church bell are still to be heard in the mountain passes in the rear of Pimampiro. The story has, no doubt, a romantic interest, reminding us of the lost tribes of Israel.[1]

In this connection it may not be out of place to give a short account of the abolition of slavery in Ecuador. It was effected gradually. It was initiated by the old republic of Colombia, of which Ecuador formed a part up to the year 1830. By a law of the 21st of July, 1821, it was provided that the children of slaves, born after its publication in the principal cities of the republic, should be free. They were to be maintained and educated by the owners of their mothers, in consideration of which these owners were entitled to the services of said children until they became eighteen years of age. In the mean time, however, the parents of such children could withdraw them from the custody of their masters, by paying them a reasonable compensation for the expenses incurred on their account. Provision was also made against the separation of slave-children from their parents. Slaves could not be sold out of the republic, nor exported for that purpose. The importation of slaves was likewise prohibited. Travellers were not allowed to introduce more than one slave as a body-servant, and if they failed to take him out of the country on their departure, he was to be free. Certain revenues were appropriated to the creation of an emancipation fund in each district, to be administered by provincial "*Juntas*," who were to superintend and direct the work of manumission. Out of this fund, so many slaves were to be redeemed every year, by compensation to the owners, as said fund would pay for ; the value of the slaves to be fixed by appraisement,

[1] See Villavicencio's *Geography of Ecuador*, page 221; also, Father Velasco's *History of the Kingdom of Quito*, vol. iii., book 2, § 2, sec. 12 and 13; Quito edition, page 45.

and the most industrious and honest of their number to be preferred. If there were no slaves in one district, the fund raised therein was to be applied to the same purpose in another.

These were the provisions of the Colombian law which, considering the importance of the subject, I have given in full. Aside from a certain bungling looseness with which almost all Spanish-American laws are drawn, it contains some very sensible regulations, and served to lay a solid foundation for the work of emancipation, since completed by the three republics which then constituted Colombia. It must be remarked, however, that as the war of independence and the frequent revolutions which followed it, continually kept the country in financial embarrassments, and compelled the government to seize whatever funds it could lay hands on, but little good resulted from the above mentioned appropriations to the cause of emancipation.

On the 25th of July, 1851, General José Maria Urbina, as "*Jefe Supremo*" (Supreme Chief) of Ecuador, issued a decree declaring, "That the few slaves who yet remain in bondage in this land of the free, are a contradiction of the republican institutions which we have achieved and adopted since 1820; an insult to religion, morality, and civilization, and a reproach to the Republic, its Legislators, and Governors." It then provided, that until Congress should appropriate the necessary funds to restore said slaves to freedom, the profits derived from the government monopoly of selling gunpowder should be applied for that purpose, and that as often as two hundred dollars were realized from said branch of the revenue, in any of the provinces, said sum should be applied to the redemption of the oldest slave therein, the age to be estimated by provincial Juntas who were intrusted with the execution of the decree. It was also made their business to prepare correct lists of the names, ages, and occupations of the slaves, and the names and residences of the masters in their respective provinces, and to transmit them to the central government. A supplemental decree regulating the manufacture and sale of gunpowder, so as to make the revenue derived therefrom more productive, was issued on the 21st of February, 1852. The prime mover and principal author of this decree, was President Urbina's Secretary of State, afterwards Ecuadorian minister resident in Washington, the late General Joseph Villamil, a native of Louisiana, of French and Spanish descent, his father having been a Spaniard and his mother a French lady. He emigrated to South America in 1810, and took an active part in her revolution against the mother country. In 1820 he was one of the leaders of the conspiracy which, by a very skillful movement, effected the overthrow of the Spanish power at Guayaquil, and thus destroyed the communication by sea (by land no communication was practicable) between the presidency of Quito and the viceroyalty of Peru; an event which greatly contributed to the subsequent liberation of Peru, Quito, and New Granada.

These decrees, however, being only provisional and insufficient, a law was enacted by the National Assembly in September, 1852, creating additional funds for emancipation purposes, and making it the duty of slaveholders to report the number, names, ages, occupation, etc., of their slaves to the authorities of their respective districts, who were to compile accurate lists from the information thus received. The slaves of such owners as should neglect to make said report within a specified time, were declared free without compensation to their masters. The slaves inscribed upon the official registers were to be appraised by two experts, one to be selected by the solicitor of the district, the other by the master; the municipality to appoint an umpire in cases of disagreement, and the appraisement not to exceed the price originally paid by the masters. Male slaves above the age of sixty-five, and female slaves over sixty years, as well as cripples, were declared free without indemnity to the masters. The latter, however, were obliged to provide for them during their natural lives, or as long as they might choose to remain with them. All slaves born after the publication of the Colombian law above referred to, were to be free without compensation to the owners; also the slaves imported in contravention of said statute. Every three months the funds appropriated for emancipation purposes, were to be applied to the redemption of slaves, beginning with the oldest in every district, the age to be ascertained by experts. On the 6th of March, 1854, slavery was to cease entirely, and if the emancipation funds should not suffice to indemnify all the owners, certificates were to be issued to them, to be redeemed afterwards, out of the proceeds of the revenues appropriated for these purposes. In most cases, however, the compensation stipulated by law, was paid only to special favorites of the government; while to all others, certificates were issued which, like all other certificates or bonds of the domestic debt of Ecuador, are doomed to eternal non-payment.

Thus was slavery abolished in Ecuador; and whatever just censure may be pronounced on the Spanish race in America in other respects, it must be admitted, that in doing justice and making reparation to humanity in the unfortunate negro race, it has set a prompt and early example to the Anglo-Saxons of the North. No sooner had the Spanish colonies declared their independence, than they took the necessary steps for putting an end to slavery; whereas we of the North allowed the evil to encroach upon us, until the Gordian knot could only be cut by the sword.

But let us continue our journey. For miles we now kept close to the river. The path sometimes became so narrow that it made the head swim to look into the yawning abyss below. At some places our road was hardly eighteen inches wide. At others, landslips, which are continually taking place on the brittle hill-side, had covered up the road completely, and sand and pebbles were giving way under our horses' feet, and hurled into the river below, as we hastily passed over the treacherous *débris*. Near the place where the Ambi joins the Chota, is the bridge of Santa Rosa, which had fallen in a short time before my arrival, and was then in process of reconstruction.

A short distance from the bridge a valley opens on the other side of the river, and discloses to our view the village of Salinas. This village is situated in an arid plain, which certainly would not have invited settlers, if it were not for the salt which is found there in great abundance. The soil for miles around Salinas contains salt. Even the water which the residents are compelled to drink is brackish. To extract the salt from the soil is the principal business of the inhabitants. It is done in a very simple and primitive manner. Mounds of earth are piled up around the village, and into these mounds a crude contrivance for distilling water is placed. The salt thus gained, which is known by the name of "*sal de Salinas*," is exported in great quantities to New Granada and Quito. In Quito, however, it is not used for culinary purposes. These mounds, by which the village is surrounded, and which almost conceal its houses from our view, give it the aspect of a town of the Orient, such as Bethlehem or Nazareth. To the west and north of Salinas, the valley is covered with sugar plantations, but on account of the higher elevation of that part of the country, the cane does not prosper so well as in the lower valley of the Chota, especially at Santa Lucia and Guajara.

Passing by the opposite valley of Salinas, or as it ought to be more properly called, the valley of the Ambi, the road leads us to the summit of a mountain around which the river takes a more northerly direction, and we see it before us for miles ahead, as it breaks through the Cordillera in its precipitous course to the Pacific. We are again surrounded by bald and sterile mountains on all sides, and of all shapes and heights. If the waves of a tempestuous ocean had suddenly been transformed into earth and remained stationary, they could not present a more grotesque and imposing appearance. In fact, we are now in the midst of an ocean of mountains, the silent monuments of the great geological revolutions of our globe. At last the Cordillera recedes on our right, and sugar, coffee, and cotton plantations, orchards, and clover fields, relieve the monotony of the desert through which we have passed. The sight of farm buildings is particularly pleasing after having travelled for miles without meeting with a human habitation. We now enter the parish de la Concepcion, to which the great haciendas of Guaquer, San Miguel, Santiaguillo, Cabuyal, Concepcion, La Loma, Chamanal, Santa Lucia, and others belong. Each of these haciendas is surrounded by groups of houses and huts, in which negroes, arrieros, and other farm laborers live, and which give them the appearance of a little village. La Concepcion, above all, with its plaza and parochial church, produces this impression. The soil is very fertile, although it needs much irrigation. The water of the river is useless for agricultural purposes, on account of the height and steepness of its banks. Springs and mountain streams and artificial aqueducts have to be resorted to. Some of the latter are very extensive. The frequent landslides and settling of ridges and hills often choke up springs, and otherwise interfere with agricultural progress. At places near ravines the soil cannot be relied upon with that certainty with which our own farmers would look upon a tract of land. In this connection I shall relate an incident which came under my own immediate observation.

The day I arrived in the valley of the lower Chota, I observed near Santiaguillo that from one of the curves of a receding mountain range, deep fissures and clefts ran down, which had furrowed the earth on both sides of the road, and across the same. These clefts, as I was informed by my guides, had opened recently. In one of them a donkey had perished a few days before my arrival. The water of the mountain streams which formerly passed over the ground to join the Chota, now lost itself in these fissures. A plantain *chacra* (small plantation), which we passed, was considered in imminent danger, because it was at the foot of a hill which the settling of the soil around it would certainly bring down. Several months before, another hill had come down in the same neighborhood. The governor of the province and his son had observed fire or burning gases at night, which seemed to issue from the soil. This phenomenon, however, is believed by the common people to indicate the presence of hidden treasures, and many persons had dug for them in various parts of the valley where the mysterious nocturnal fires had been seen. But the fissures which I saw, and which we had to pass, as they intersected the road continually, were the precursors of another catastrophe. A few nights after my arrival at the Governor's hacienda, our company, just before bed-time, were startled by a noise which resembled the report of a heavy gun. The supposition of an earthslip instantly struck our minds. We dispatched a man on horseback to the place where the crevices had opened, but he returned greatly frightened, and reported that dense clouds of dust had compelled him to retreat. Next day I went to the spot, and found that the hill had come down, burying the plantain *chacra*, and completely blocking up the road, so that the usual *cargas* of sugar and rum had to take another route for several days afterward, until the *débris* had been partially removed.

Such accidents are of common occurrence in the highlands of Ecuador. Sometimes they take place in consequence of earthquakes; sometimes they happen without them. Not only are earthslips frequent, but also the great mountains are said to change their shapes continually on account of the tumbling down of ridges or rocks, or the sinking in and disappearance of parts of the peaks. During such great geological revolutions, not only hills and lakes, but even villages, have disappeared. The unfortunate Indian village of Cacha, near Riobamba, was swallowed up by a revolution of the earth in 1640, like Korah, Dathan, and Abiram, in consequence of which five thousand Indians lost their lives and were never seen again. It is said that shortly before the catastrophe the curate had been called away from the village to administer the last sacraments to a dying Indian in the neighborhood, and that when he returned, the village and the lake near it were gone, and the curate could not even recognize the place where his house had been.

I established my head-quarters at Santiaguillo, an hacienda belonging to the then governor of the province, which is celebrated for the comparative salubrity of its climate. The mean temperature at midday was 83° Fahr. in the shade. Black mosquitoes and sand-flies were very vexatious in daytime, but only in the open air. In the houses there were none. The accommodations on haciendas in this part of the country are generally very poor. The owners are very friendly and hospitable, but their farm-houses are destitute of almost all the commodities of civilized life. The buildings are mostly dilapidated, either from natural decay or neglect, or in consequence of earthquakes. The construction of new buildings is a very slow work, continually interrupted by long intervals of inactivity, as I have already indicated. The furniture consists of a few common chairs, tables, bedsteads, benches, and perhaps sofas, in the style of the 17th or 18th century, from which they have generally descended to the present possessors. Such luxuries as wash-basins are but seldom to be found. The natives do not wash their faces in the country; they do it seldom enough in town. It must be borne in mind that the owners of haciendas do not live on them like the farmers of North America. They only visit them from time to time, and on such occasions, they "rough it" for a few days or weeks, rather than incur unnecessary expenses.

There is a chapel at Santiaguillo in which mass is

said every Sunday by the curate of the parish, whose residence is at La Concepcion, a great hacienda about half an hour's ride from Santiaguillo. Between the first and second parts of the mass, his worship made a speech to the congregation, in which he complained that some of them had buried their dead on the hacienda without paying the perquisites of the curate. He reminded them that the cemetery of the parish was at La Concepcion; but that for their accommodation he had allowed them to bury their dead at Santiaguillo, but that he had not consented that this should be done to his damage. If, therefore, they should continue to inter on the hacienda without paying his fees, he would revoke his permission, and compel them to take their dead to La Concepcion, however inconvenient this might prove to them. This was the only sermon preached. During transubstantiation the congregation, which chiefly consisted of negro farm laborers and their wives, sang *misericordia, Señor!* to the tune of one of their national airs. After the service the curate rode away to say mass in some other part of his dominions. Later in the day he returned to take part in the games of dice or cards, with which Spanish-Americans generally beguile their time when business or pleasure has taken them into the country.[1]

A great number of tolas of all sizes, chiefly in the neighborhood of Santiaguillo, denote that this valley

[1] "On going for a day's excursion from the capital, immediately on reaching the place of destination they hurry into a room, cards and dice are instantly produced, and the whole time until their departure for home in the evening, with the exception of the dinner hour, is sacrificed to this inveterate and pernicious habit of gambling, instead of diverting their mind and expanding their intellect by rational conversation, or remarks on surrounding objects or scenery." — *Journal of a Residence and Travels in Colombia during the Years* 1823–24, by Captain Charles Stuart Cochrane: London, 1825.

was formerly inhabited by Indian tribes, considerably advanced in some of the arts of civilization. The earthen vessels and crockery-ware found in these graves, are greatly superior in style and workmanship to those found in the tolas of Carranqui. The latter are of but one color — a brownish red. Those of Santiaguillo are of a light yellow color, most symmetrically embellished with red lines, triangles, and flourishes. In one of the graves I found several pieces of tasteful ornaments worked of shells, showing that the Indians of this valley must have been in communication with the sea-coast. In the smaller graves one skeleton is generally found, with a pair of bronze earrings, and one of the drinking vessels just described. I wanted to buy a pair of those earrings from a woman who, assisted by her children, had opened several of the smaller tolas; but she insisted that the Incas worked no metal but gold, and believing the earrings to be gold, would not sell them at the liberal price I had proposed to pay.

It is a poor compliment to the civilizing effect of Spanish rule, to observe that the ancient Indians used tasteful and handsome drinking vessels, and cooking utensils with legs to stand over the fire, while their "civilized" descendants have returned to the use of the calabash, and while even the cooking pots of their white superiors, on account of being pointed below, cannot stand over the fire without being supported by bricks or stones.

But the most remarkable antiquities I saw in this part of the country, were two forts, if such was their original destination, near the farm-house of Santiaguillo, and at a distance of about three or four squares from each other. They were both in the form of a regular circle, as regular as if a modern surveyor had laid it out. The first consisted of an outer earth-wall about ten or twelve feet high, and about three hundred paces in circumference on the inside, and of a second circular wall in the centre. The circumference of the latter was about one hundred paces on its outside. In the centre of the second circle there was an excavation resembling a well or cistern; which, however, may have been dug after the conquest by persons in search of hidden treasures. The second fort was built entirely after the same style, though of lesser dimensions. The inner wall, however, had recently been taken down and leveled by an individual who had hired the fort, temple, or tambo, or whatever it may have been, for the purpose of raising plantains within the inclosure afforded by the outer wall. The walls of both works were overgrown with green shrubs and arborescent plants, which pleasantly contrasted with the sterility of the surrounding country.

From Santiaguillo I went to the haciendas of La Loma, Chamanal, and Santa Lucia. The two latter are nearly opposite Guajara, which in former times was the great breeding-place for negro slaves. In the remotest parts of the country, such as Cuenca and Loja, Guajara negroes may be found. Guajara is on the left, Chamanal and Santa Lucia are on the right river bank. They are the last sugar-growing establishments in this direction. There are several stock-breeding haciendas beyond them; but after these the wilderness commences, penetrated only by the footpath to Peylon, on the coast. From Guajara, two journeys can be made on horseback in the direction of Peylon; then three journeys must be made on foot to a place called La

Tola, where the river commences to be navigable for canoes. The port of Peylon, and the road from the coast to Ibarra, are graphically described by Gerstaecker the German traveller, in his "Eighteen Months in South America." It would be a very easy and cheap task to construct a mule path from Guajara to La Tola. The distance from Ibarra to Peylon is but twenty-one leagues, about one third of the distance from Quito to Guayaquil. The present footpath presents less natural difficulties and obstacles than the footpath to Esmeraldas. Traders who take cheese and other inland productions to the coast, where they exchange them for gold-dust, travel over it continually. A good road from Ibarra to Peylon, even if it were only a mule path, would be of the most vital importance to the province of Imbabura, which it would raise to the rank of the first and wealthiest of the interior. And yet so great are the indolence and indifference of the Spanish race, that such a road, although continually talked of, has never been made, and will not be made for many years to come. In 1862, a company of land-owners of Imbabura, in concert with the English company of Peylon, proposed to build a road to that place from Ibarra, and applied to the President for the consent and support of the government. The latter was then wasting the scanty means of the government on a few miles of wagon-road in the direction of Guayaquil, an enterprise too gigantic ever to be accomplished by a poor country like Ecuador, without the aid of foreign capitalists. He had also commenced to construct a mule path to Esmeraldas; but he began the work before a thorough survey had been made. Unforeseen natural impediments presented themselves, and the work had to be abandoned. Prejudiced in favor of these two latter impracticable enterprises, the President received the propositions of the Imbabura company very ungraciously, and insisted on conditions so unreasonable and oppressive, that the company desisted from a further prosecution of their plan. One of the conditions was that the individual members of the association should hypothecate their lands to the government as security that the road should be finished. Other negotiations which had previously taken place between the English company and the Ecuadorian government were equally fruitless. The English company had been formed by certain holders of Ecuadorian bonds, who had agreed to take waste lands in satisfaction of their claims. Different tracts had been assigned to them on and near the Pacific coast, and on the headwaters of the Amazons on the eastern side of the Cordillera, but only of the Peylon lands has the company been able to obtain the necessary title deeds. The Ecuadorian government clings to these lands as if they were worth any thing in their present wild and unpopulated condition. The rulers of this country have not yet realized that a government does not need to be a land-owner, and that not in waste lands and deserts, but in a thriving and enterprising population, the strength and prosperity of a nation consist. But let us return to our subject.

Almost all the haciendas in Chota Bajo, formerly belonged to the Jesuits, until 1767, when they were confiscated and sold by the Spanish government. Sugar and rum are the principal productions of the valley. The rum is filled into hides. Two hides form a *Botija*, which contains one hundred and sixty bottles, and just makes up a mule load. The coffee which grows in the valley is excellent, but it is not planted in sufficient quantities.

While I was at Chamanal, the hospitable owner of the hacienda gave me the spectacle of a negro dance, which is called *bundi*, and is exceedingly interesting. The negroes of the hacienda, men, women, and children, assembled in the hall, bringing with them two characteristic musical instruments — the *bomba* and the *alfandoque*. The former is intended for a drum. It is a sort of barrel, over which a hide is spanned, and to beat which no drumsticks but the fingers or fists are used to make the singers keep time. The *alfandoque* is a hollow cane or reed, into which a quantity of buckshot, peas, or pebbles is put, whereupon the openings are closed with cotton or a bundle of rags. By shaking this queer instrument a noise is produced similar to that made in theatres to imitate the sound of falling rain. It is, however, shaken to the time of the songs, and chimes in not at all unpleasantly. But the main part of the orchestra consists of the voices of the women and children, accompanied by the voice of the player of the *alfandoque*. Clapping their hands continually, they sing a great variety of songs, to which the *bomba* and *alfandoque* keep time. In musical talent and taste, these negroes are infinitely superior to the Indians. Their melodies are neither so monotonous nor so lifeless as those of the aborigines. On the contrary, they are varied and fiery, and full of exciting vigor. Their dance is not the slow, measured step of the Indians, but is characterized by that wild sweeping and dashing, and the extravagant gesticulation peculiar to the Ethiopian. They dance various dances, some of which are irresistibly comic. In this they are of a higher inventive genius than the white and cholo rabble, who cannot advance beyond the slow and monotonous *alza que te han visto*. There was one figure which was particularly funny. It was a pantomimic representation of toros (bull-fights). The step was that of the *alza que te han visto*, although much quicker. The woman dancing attacks her male partner, whom she tries to butt, as if she were a bull. He, without falling out of time or losing the step, dodges her. This is continued for several minutes, when the parts are changed and the man attacks the woman, who in her turn dodges him. Woe to the partner who is not quick enough to avoid the butt; its force may fell him to the ground. The dance is generally accompanied by the vehement and comic gestures peculiar to the negro race. The partners keep on dancing without interruption, one pair at a time, until somebody else steps in to relieve them; but the change of performers does not interrupt the performance for a single moment, nor is there an intermission of the song. Even the fellow who beats the *bomba* never stops. When he is treated to a cup of rum, some one of the company presents it to his lips, and he swallows it while his hands continue to beat the drum. Perspiration pours down his face, but he has no time to wipe it off. With the agility of a monkey, he keeps on beating his *bomba* as long as there is a pair not too exhausted to keep up the dance. The male partner in a dance must keep on as long as the lady does, or until somebody steps in to relieve him. At Esmeraldas and other places on the coast, it would be considered an insult to withdraw from the dance without being relieved. The friends of the lady thus injured would be but too apt to resent the offense on the spot. Rum, as a matter of course, is not spared on such occasions, and the excitement and enthusiasm increase from hour to hour. The din caused by the shrill voices of the women and children, the drumming, and clapping of hands, and the noise of the *alfandoque*, together with the occasional exclamations of the dancers and by-standers, completely drowned the words of their song. I was unable to make out any of the verses, but my companions told me that the songs were composed by the negroes themselves, and in their own dialect. Like the negroes of the United States, the negroes of Spanish-America have a dialect and pronunciation of their own. The same guttural voices, and almost unintelligible pronunciation, the same queer gesticulation and shaking of the body, the same shrewd simplicity and good humor, the same love of fun and merry-making that characterize the negro in the rice swamps and cotton-fields of Georgia and South Carolina, distinguish his race on the banks of the Chota, at Guajara, and La Concepcion.

The wages paid to workmen in *trapiches* (sugar establishments), are one real a day; but the laborers are not entitled to the suit of clothes which is given to Indian farm laborers once a year. In other respects their situation and treatment are the same.

Insects such as beetles, cockroaches, mosquitoes, etc., abound in the valley. Snakes, too, are found, but not many, and it is generally believed that they are not poisonous. Chills and fevers are frequent, although I believe the valley is healthy, and that diseases are contracted only by exposure. The sterility and barrenness of the mountains continue as far as the eye can reach. It is not until you travel two or three days in the direction of Peylon that the forests commence. In the rear of the mountain range of Chamanal, is the

*Cordillera del Chiltason*, in which mines were formerly worked, of which vestiges are still to be found. But at present, mining seems to be abandoned all over Ecuador. Both capital and energy are wanting to carry it on.

From the valley of the Chota I returned to Ibarra and Otabalo. Having come from Quito by the *Camino Real* (the Guaillabamba road), I carried out my original intention to return by way of the paramo, although this latter road, when it rains, is one of the most terrible breaknecks in the country. It passes over the mountain and paramo of Mojanda, a wild and dreary scene. Otabalo lies at the foot of the mountain, and the ascent is steep and slow. Shrubs and bushes, and legions of wild-flowers surround you; an orchestra of birds pour forth a rich succession of sweet notes; at your feet expands a most interesting landscape: Lake San Pablo, separated by an isolated hill chain from the plains of Otabalo; Cotacachi, with Lake Cuicocha in its lap, and Mount Imbabura with its trachytic crown, give you a parting look of romantic sadness; the plains of Hatuntaqui and Ibarra in the distance, and mighty ranges of the Cordillera on all sides; — it is a view amply indemnifying you for the slowness and difficulty of the ascent; a view from which I tore myself with regret, because the melancholy thought crept over my soul that I should never see it again. I shall return to home and friends, and to the scenes of active life and enterprise; I shall leave for ever behind me this remarkable country in the stillness of its indolent decay, frowned upon by the grave majesty of its mountains; and the scenes through which I passed will be to me, in years to come, but the "memory of a departed dream." But it was a beautiful dream; and the hoary crowns of those giants of the Cordillera, the highland lakes and mountain streams, the Indian's humble hut and the crumbling temples of a bygone age, the long rows of aloes in the plains below, and the dreary grass of the paramo on high, will forever live in my recollection, although my foot shall no longer tread the virgin soil of this hidden land, and the voice of the arriero, scrambling up the craggy mountain passes, no longer strikes my ear. No scenery has ever made such a lasting and intense impression on my mind as the highlands of the Andes, and especially the province of Imbabura. I shall treasure it up as one of the fondest reminiscences of my life, and I shall give it a last lingering remembrance in the final hour of my dying day.

The view I have described is soon lost sight of as you enter the dreary region of the paramo, where almost no vegetation greets you except the high and dry grass which the natives call *paja* (straw). Numerous herds of cattle are found grazing in these elevated regions. The dreariness of the scene is enhanced by a queer-looking ghastly bird, which the Indians call "*uruquingui*," a species of hawk or buzzard, with a long, yellow-red bill. The bird does not seem to mind the approach of travellers. It stares at them until they can almost strike it with their whips, when it slowly prepares to fly away.

Crossing the heath near the summit of the mountain, Lake Mojanda is reached, the aspect of which strikes awe and almost terror to the soul. It forms one of the wildest, and at the same time one of the most melancholy views I beheld in Ecuador. A lake of an extension nearly equal to that of San Pablo, almost on the summit of a mountain, surrounded on three sides by bleak, perpendicular rocks, with only a dwarf vegetation on its shores and on the precipitous crags by which it is hemmed in; the atmosphere cold and chilling; the water clear and rippling; not a single human habitation, not even a solitary Indian hut, to be descried as far as the eye can reach — all is loneliness, wildness, and desert.

Passing the caldron in which the lake is situate, another smaller valley opens before us, with Little Mojanda in it. This latter hardly deserves the name of a lake; it having the appearance of a gloomy pond of stagnant water, surrounded by dreary hills overgrown with paramo grass. About half a league from the lake the descent of the mountain range commences. At its foot is the sandy plain of Malchingui, with the village of the same name. For miles around we see nothing but sandy plains, with sickly attempts at cultivation of peas, corn, and clover. The plain is suddenly interrupted by the deep defile through which the river Guaillabamba rushes on in the direction of the village of Perucho. It takes more than an hour to descend to the bridge. Before reaching the latter, a gently declining plain has to be passed, covered with fields of sugar-cane, cayenne-pepper, corn, and clover. This is the great hacienda of Alchipichi, noted for the benignity of its climate — warm without being hot, and producing tropical fruits without the tropical inconveniences of insects and fevers. The cane raised at Alchipichi cannot be compared to that of the Chota, but the proximity of Quito makes it very profitable.

The scenery and vegetation of the Guaillabamba, which we now pass, I have already described. After a tedious ascent on the other side, other sandy plains of a most melancholy character open before us. These are the plains of San Antonio and Pomasqui. At the latter place, in spite of the apparent aridity of the soil, clover for horses grows exceedingly well. After leaving Pomasqui, the aspect of the country begins to improve, until we reach the village of Cotocollao, about two leagues from the capital. Here green fields and smiling cultivation surround us again, and nothing seems to be wanting but an energetic population to apply the great contrivances of modern genius to a most promising soil, and the healthiest climate in the world.

## CHAPTER XVI.

### HISTORICAL REVIEW.

Indian Traditions. — Difficulties of Estimating Ancient Indian Civilization. — Scarcity of Materials. — Destruction of Indian Civilization by the Spaniards. — The Religious Element of the Conquest. — Fray Marcos de Niza. — Persecution of the Indian Writer Collahuaso. — The Old Quitu Nation. — Its Conquest by the Carans. — The Giants of Punta Santa Helena. — The Ancient Kings or Scyris of Quito. — Romantic Legend of Condorazo. — Invasion of the Peruvian Incas. — Cacha Duchicela, the last of the Scyris. — His Heroic Resistance against the Inca Huaynacapac. — Battle of Hatuntaqui. — Death of the last of the Scyris. — His Daughter Pacha. — Death of Huaynacapac. — War between his Sons, Huascar and Atahuallpa. — Battle of Quipaypan. — Defeat and Capture of Huascar. — Arrival of the Spaniards under Francisco Pizarro. — Capture and Execution of Atahuallpa. — Downfall of the Peruvian Empire. — Usurpation and Cruelty of Rumiñagui at Quito. — Benalcazar's Expedition to Quito. — Genius of Rumiñagui. — Battle of Tiocajas. — Evacuation and Destruction of Quito by Rumiñagui. — The Virgins of the Sun. — Horrid Cruelty of the Spaniards. — Execution of Rumiñagui. — Indian Slavery. — Encomiendas and Repartimientos. — Spanish Colonization. — The Blue Laws of Spanish America. — Protective Legislation. — Pedro de Puelles. — Revolution of the Colonists. — Gonzalo Pizarro. — Battle of Quito. — Death of the Viceroy. — Death of Gonzalo Pizarro. — Revolution and Execution of Hernandez Giron. — The Cause of the Indians Abandoned. — Plan for a Continuation of this History.

I HAVE already said that the Indians of Quito have lost their ancient traditions. While the Indians of Cuzco, and generally throughout the interior of Peru, delight in the remembrance of the great Empire of the Sun, and its many legends,[1] which they have pre-

[1] See Markham's *Cuzco and Lima;* also: *Travels in Peru and India*, by the same author; and Stephenson's *Twenty Years' Residence in South America.* The latter work is now out of print.

served in spite of the prohibitions of the colonial despotism of Spain, those of Quito have retained nothing beyond a general impression that there was a time once when they were the masters and sole inhabitants of the country. The precise period when they began to forget the traditions of their race, it is, of course, impossible to ascertain. In the seventeenth century, they were still preserved. In the record books of the Municipality of Quito, I found the description of a great celebration which began on the 26th of February, 1631, and lasted several days, in honor of the birth of Charles II., the news of which had then arrived. On that occasion, the inevitable bull-fights were varied by the addition of a grand Indian pantomime, representing the triumph of the Inca Huaynacapac over the Quijos, who had risen in rebellion against him. In the eighteenth century, frequent sublevations of Indians took place, which, though attributable to merely local causes, may have been promoted by the memory and proper understanding of their ancient independence, and the manner in which it was wrested from them. At present, however, no vestige of such knowledge remains. It is true they have dances and ceremonies which are evidently of heathenish origin, but the original signification of which they have forgotten.

It must forever be deplored, that among the Spanish conquerors there were no men of discernment and mental culture, who might have given us a clearer insight into the civilization and history of the Indians of those times. What little we know of the reign of Huaynacapac and his predecessors, and of the civil wars between his two sons, Huascar and Atahuallpa, is perhaps worse than hearsay. Garcilazo de la Vega, the principal and most favored authority on Peruvian antiquities and traditions, wrote his book from what, in after years, he remembered to have heard in his early youth from his mother, an Indian princess, and an old uncle, who was one of the royal family. He had left the land of his birth at the age of twenty, and not until after long years of an adventurous life, which must more or less have obliterated or confused his recollections, did he sit down to write his "*Comentarios Reales.*" He was prejudiced, by his very descent from the Cuzco line, against Atahuallpa and the Quito line; and in his mind the superstitions of the new faith were blended with the traditions of the old. The conquerors themselves were not even able to give a clear account of their own doings: how much less can their statements be relied on when they refer to a people with whose language, idiosyncrasies, opinions, and customs they were entirely unacquainted. With few exceptions, the Spanish conquerors were the dregs of ignorant and superstitious Spain. They were desperate men, who had nothing to lose and every thing to gain. What did they care for the intellectual condition and historical traditions of a race which they had come to enslave! To them, Indian civilization was an abominable idolatry, which they considered themselves bound not to study, but to extirpate. The principal, and in many cases the only, question which they put to the natives, was where they had hidden their gold. Their chief inquiry was for mines. These questions they enforced by a system of most cruel tortures, which the pen shrinks from recording. The Indians, on the other hand, were not likely to communicate to their tormentors what to the philosophic investigation of posterity would have been infinitely more interesting than apocryphal stories of buried treasures. Communicativeness is not a trait in the character of the Ecuadorian Indians. They hardly ever return a direct answer. They are noted for their ability to keep the secrets of their race. I was often struck by their propensity to evade the simplest and most insignificant questions; and it is not at all probable that those who, like Rumiñagui and his captains, endured the most cruel torments rather than disclose where their treasures were hidden, should have volunteered information to their conquerors on subjects which the latter cared but little to know. It is but too well known that the Indians shunned the society of the Spaniards, to whose presence in the country they owed all their misery and sufferings. This antipathy was but the natural consequence of the treatment which they had received. I frequently noticed that one may travel for miles with an Indian guide or companion, without his volunteering information on any subject. It cannot be wondered at, under these circumstances, that every thing relating to the Spanish conquest in America is involved in uncertainty. The opportunities to collect information, on subjects of incalculable interest for the history of human civilization, were thrown away by the ignorance, brutality, cupidity, and cruelty of the Spanish conquerors. It is true, there were some men among them who, restrained by the vows of holy orders, cared less for amassing riches than for the protection and conversion of the poor natives, and the acquisition of some knowledge concerning their customs, traditions, and form of government and society. Among those men Fray Marcos de Niza, who accompanied Benalcazar on his expedition to Quito, deserves to be honorably mentioned. From his writings, all the materials with reference to the antiquities of Quito, the history of the ancient Scyris, the conquest of their land by the Incas, and afterward by the Spaniards, are drawn. He is, in a measure, to Quito what Garcilazo de la Vega is to Cuzco. Unfortunately, I have been unable to procure a copy of his works. I even doubt whether they have ever been printed. Bravo Saravio,[1] who largely copied from them, availed himself of the original manuscripts. From this latter author, and Chieza de Leon, Father Velasco compiled his ancient history of Quito, to which I was frequently, although reluctantly, obliged to resort. But with all due deference to the goodness and humanity of Father Marcos de Niza, the question must suggest itself whether a Spanish monk of the sixteenth century was a proper person to collect, sift, and present those materials which are indispensable to what we now understand by studying and writing history. The Spanish monks who accompanied the conquerors were certainly not superior to the spirit of their age. They believed the miracles of their own church, and they also believed the miracles of which the Indian religions boasted. The former, in their opinion, were wrought by the saints and the Virgin; the latter by the Evil One. When they set themselves to study the civilization of the conquered races, they did not begin their task with the impartiality of one who sincerely seeks for truth, but they allowed themselves to be guided by two objects. The first was to trace the doings of the Devil in the history and religions of the pagan Indians; the second was to discover in the Indian traditions of the past and their then civilization, evidences of heavenly endeavors to impart to those benighted

[1] *Antiguidades Peruanas.*

nations some glimpses of the dogmas of the Church of Rome. A vague notion that two of the Apostles must have visited various parts of America haunted their minds.[1] The traces of Catholic rites were eagerly sought for in the religious ceremonies and edifices of the heathens; and when supposed resemblances were found, they were attributed either to the visit of the apostles St. Thomas and St. Bartholomew, or to the eagerness of Satan to copy the signs and rites of the church against which he eternally militates.[2] Relations in the language of the Indians, which the missionaries could have but imperfectly understood, or which they heard through the medium of unlettered and unreliable interpreters, were either misunderstood, or, as the wish is often father to the thought, consciously or unconsciously misinterpreted. Ancient prophecies of the victorious advent of foreign invaders, with long beards, were profusely discovered. The superstition of the converters fed on the superstition of the converted, instead of investigating the natural causes from which it arose. So strong was this tendency, that it infected not only the ecclesiastical, but also the lay historians of those times.[3] The belief in a continuous supernatural interference reigned supreme. Visions of saints, fighting against legions of demons, were seen in the air by the Spanish warriors during many a battle with the Indians. The thatched roof of the Spanish fort at Cuzco, which the Indians endeavored to set on

[1] Velasco, *Historia del Reino de Quito*, vol. i., lib. 4, § 6.

[2] See Herrera, dec. v., lib. iv., cap. 5; also, cap. 4. Garcilazo, *Historia General del Peru*, lib. i., cap. 30; also, Solorzano, *Politica Indiana*, part i., book i., ch. 7, and authors there quoted.

[3] As to the tendency of a change of religion to corrupt the early history of an uncivilized country, and to obscure and adulterate its ancient traditions, see Buckle's *History of Civilization in England*, vol. i., ch. vi., pp. 218–222 (American edition), and the examples there cited.

fire as often as they returned to the attack, would not burn because the Virgin stood on it putting out the flames.[1] St. James, the apostle, mounted on a splendid white steed, and armed with a sword of lightning, charged the Indians in person, killing and wounding them by hundreds.[2] The Holy Virgin frustrated the night attacks of the natives, by appearing in a circle of radiant light, and throwing dust in the eyes of the besiegers of Cuzco.[3] The lion and the tiger, let loose on Pedro de Candia at Tumbez, crouched before him in the dust, because he was armed with the holy cross.[4] The demons, who had held familiar converse with the Indians before the arrival of the Spaniards, were struck dumb as soon as mass was said in Peru; and only in the dead of night, and secretly, they dared to speak to the principal sorcerers in whose service they were.[5] Not the terror of fire-arms, so dreadful to the Indians, who believed the invaders to be masters of thunder and lightning; not the fearful havoc caused by those unknown four-legged monsters on which the conquerors dashed over the battle-fields, with a speed which their unfortunate adversaries could not comprehend; not the effect of iron and steel on the almost naked bodies of the helpless natives; not the superiority of civilization, military skill, and discipline, brought victory to the arms of Castile; but it was the direct interference of the Virgin, the Apostles, and saints.

The subsequent policy of the Spanish government, and its colonial officials, was not calculated to promote the study and preservation of Indian traditions. In the eighteenth century an Indian Cacique of Ibarra, Don

1 Garcilazo, *Hist. Gen. del Peru*, lib. ii., cap. 25.

2 *Ibid.* caps. 24 and 25.

3 *Ibid.*

4 *Ibid.* lib. i., caps. 11 and 12.

5 *Ibid.* lib. i., cap. 30. Gomara, *Hist. Gen.*, cap. 34.

Jacinto Collahuaso, wrote a book called the "Civil Wars of Huáscar and Atahuallpa," which is said to have contained many traditions that had escaped the attention of Fray Marcos de Niza. But the Corregidor of Ibarra, indignant at the presumption of an Indian to write a book, and on subjects which might prove dangerous to the tranquillity and submissiveness of the aborigines, confiscated and publicly burned the work, and imprisoned the author. Many years after this persecution, Collahuaso, encouraged by his confessor, a Dominican monk, re-wrote the most essential parts of his narrative, and a written copy of this reproduction came into the possession of Father Velasco, who was personally acquainted with the cacique. It does not seem to have been printed, and manuscript copies of it are no longer extant at Quito.

Considering all these circumstances, the extreme scarcity of the materials, the paucity of authentic and contemporaneous documents, and the ignorance of the Spanish conquerors, of whom many, like Pizarro and Almagro, could neither read nor write, while the more learned among them were influenced by the prejudices and superstitions to which I have referred, it is with feelings of great diffidence that I propose to give a brief review of the early history of Quito. Of the old *Quitu* nation which inhabited the highlands to the north and south of the present capital, nothing is known to tradition but the name of its last king, *Quitu*, after whom his subjects were probably called. His domains were invaded and conquered by the nation of the *Caras*, or *Carans*, who had come by sea in *balsas* (rafts) from parts unknown, and landing on the coast of Esmeraldas, followed the course of that river, ascending the western cordillera of the Andes, until they reached the table-lands of Pichincha.

According to ancient traditions, they were induced to leave their settlements on the coast by the arrival of a number of formidable giants, who had also come in balsas, nobody knew whence, and, landing at Punta Santa Elena, established themselves in the provinces of the *Carans*. When the Spaniards arrived in Peru, a tradition that a race of giants had come to the country many centuries before, was general.[1] By the ignorant, in many parts of Ecuador, this fable is believed to the present day. It is also adopted by Father Velasco, who makes a serious and elaborate attempt to prove its historical truth. These giants are said to have brought no women with them, and to have become so wicked that they were at last destroyed by fire from heaven. Certain ruins of a style entirely different from the architecture of the Incas, and wells sunk deep through rocks, discovered in the neighborhood of Punta Santa Elena, are attributed to their herculean efforts.[2] Bones of uncommon size, which have also been discovered there, and which, according

[1] Herrera, dec. iv., lib. ii., chap. 7. Zarate, *Hist. del Descubrimiento y Conquista del Peru;* Madrid, 1577, chap. v. Garcilazo de la Vega, *Comentarios Reales*, book ix., chap. 9. "At Punta Santa Elena, as well as at Manta, large bones have been met with. In a paper of mine, read at the Geological Society, on the fossil bones of the Mastodon in Chili, I have adverted to the bones found at the above places. Stephenson saw a grinder from this spot which weighed five pounds three ounces, the enamel spotted like the female tortoise-shell." — Bollaert, *Antiquarian, Ethnological, and other Researches in New Granada, Ecuador, Peru, and Chili;* London, 1860. Large fossil bones have also been, and are still being, found in the neighborhood of Riobamba, in the province of Chimborazo. The same story of a race of giants, who had infested the country long before the arrival of the Spaniards, was also current in Mexico. See Torquemada, *Monarquia Indiana*, vol. i., book i., chap. 13.

[2] Villavicencio says, in his *Geography of Ecuador*, that two leagues north of Monte Cristo, in the district of Manta, on the flat summit of a low mountain, is a circle of thirty stone seats, with arms, and that in all probability they were used on solemn occasions by the chiefs of *Cara*, ere they conquered Quito.

to Humboldt, are "enormous remains of unknown cetaceous animals," confirmed the common belief in this fabulous tradition; although it is evident that instead of the bones being attributable to giants, the giants must be attributed to the discovery of the bones. It was an easy way for the credulous and the unscientific to account for the existence of large fossils which they could not otherwise explain.[1] The giants in question are said to have been anthropophagi, each devouring about fifty victims a day, and so enormously tall they were, that common mortals only reached up to their knees. Whether the Carans were frightened from the coast by those apocryphal monsters, or whether they left because of its unhealthy climate, the fact seems to be that they easily reduced the Quitu nation, to which they were superior in the rudiments of civilization. The Carans are said to have constructed temples and other edifices, although their architecture was inferior to that of the Peruvian Incas. Father Velasco's statement, that they knew how to construct arches and vaulted roofs, seems to be without foundation, like so many assertions of the credulous Padre. They knew how to cut precious stones, of which the emerald[2] was held in greatest esteem; a

[1] In Europe, the discovery of such bones had given rise to similar legends. "The first application of the principles of comparative anatomy to the study of fossil bones, was the work of a Frenchman, the celebrated Daubenton. Hitherto, these bones had been the object of stupid wonder; some saying that they were rained from heaven, others saying that they were the gigantic limbs of the ancient patriarchs — men who were believed to be tall because they were known to be old. Such idle conceits were forever destroyed by Daubenton, in a memoir he published in 1762." — Buckle, *History of Civilization in England*, vol. i., p. 634 (American edition).

[2] "I was surprised not to see emeralds at Guayaquil, when at the conquest they were so abundantly found in Equador. This gem cannot have disappeared, but awaits intelligent searchers, particularly as we now know its geological position. Emeralds were obtained in considerable quantities from the river Tucamez; and the river Esmeraldas is said to be so

large emerald was the chief ornament in the crown of their king, or *Scyri*. Unacquainted with the Peruvian *guipus*,[1] they used to perpetuate the memory of important events by a significant juxtaposition of small pieces of wood, clay, and stones of various sizes, colors, and forms. These were kept in their temples, palaces, and tombs. How they buried their dead, piling up mounds of earth over their bodies, has already been explained. Their religion consisted in a worship of the sun and the moon, and their language is said to have been similar to the Peruvian Quichua. It is also said that they regulated their year by the solstices, and divided it into twelve months.[2] Their fortresses were square earthworks, entirely different from the *pucarás* of the Incas. Their principal arms were lances and clubs. They were very skillful in pottery, and wore large earrings of bronze. Some of these ornaments I saw as they were dug out of *tolas*, or graves, in the province of Imbabura.

These Caras, or Carans, established the dynasty of the Scyris at Quito, and extended their conquests

called from the ancient quarries of this stone. It is also mentioned that the name of Esmeraldas was given to this part of the country, seeing that it was so green with vegetation, by some of the conquerors who had been on the desert coast of Peru. Stephenson (vol. ii., p. 406) says he did not visit the mines, owing to the dread of the natives, who assured him that the place was enchanted, and guarded by a dragon which poured forth thunder and lightning. The locality of the emeralds may be arrived at by the river Bichile, the Alcalde of which gave Stephenson three emeralds, found in the sands at the mouth of that river. The mines were worked by the Jesuits." — Bollaert, *Antiquarian, Ethnol., and other Researches*. See, also, Herrera, dec. iv., lib. vii., cap. 9.

1 "The *guippus* was made of threads of different colors, which colors, the knots, and the distances between the knots and between the threads, afforded, first, a means of numeration, and afterward a species of hieroglyphic." — Helps, *Spanish Conquest in America*, vol. iii., p. 432 (American edition).

2 Velasco, *Hist. Antiq.*, b. i., § 2, p. 6.

to the north and south, until checked by the warlike nation of the Puruhás, who inhabited the present district of Riobamba. The eleventh Scyri, who had no male issue, gave his daughter Toa in marriage to Duchicela, son of Condorazo, the king of Puruhá, with whom he had agreed that in case either of the two reigning fathers-in-law should die, the young couple, superseding the surviving king, should succeed at once to the throne of the two countries, which were thenceforward to remain united. Condorazo, who, when he assented to this treaty had not anticipated the possibility of his surviving the Scyri, was so grieved by having to surrender the crown to his own son, that he retired into the fastnesses of a mountain, and was never heard of again. That mountain has ever since retained his name.

Duchicela was succeeded by his son Autachi, and the united kingdoms prospered and flourished, until in the reign of Hualcopo Duchicela, the thirteenth Scyri, the Peruvian Incas commenced to extend their conquests to the north. It is not within the scope of this book to review the traditions concerning the origin and history of the Incas. This has been done in many other works to which I must refer the reader.[1] It will suffice to say that about the middle of the fifteenth century the Inca Tupac Yupanqui, father of Huaynacapac, invaded the dominions of the Scyris, and after many bloody battles and sieges, conquered the kingdom of Puruhá and returned in triumph to Cuzco. Hual-

[1] Prescott, *History of the Conquest of Peru;* Markham, *Cuzco and Lima*, London, 1856; Helps, *Spanish Conquest in America;* Ulloa, *Voyage to America* (French and Spanish editions; in the English edition the history of the Incas has been omitted); M. C. Balboa, *History of Peru*, published in French by Ternaux Compans; Garcilazo de la Vega, *Comentarios Reales;* Lorente, *Historia Antigua del Peru*, Lima, 1860, etc., etc., etc.

copo survived his loss but a few years. He is said to have died of grief, and was succeeded by his son Cacha, the fifteenth and last of the Scyris.

Cacha Duchicela at once set out to recover his paternal dominions. Although of feeble health, he seems to have been a man of great energy and intrepidity. He fell upon the garrison which the Inca had left at Mocha, put it to the sword, and reoccupied the kingdom of Puruhá, where he was received with open arms. He even carried his banners further south, until checked by the Cañares, the inhabitants of what is now the district of Cuenca, who had voluntarily submitted to the Inca, and now detained the Scyri until Huaynacapac, the greatest of the Inca dynasty, came to their rescue. The latter first endeavored, by negotiations and promises, to induce the Scyri peaceably to yield to Peruvian sway. His offers, however, were indignantly rejected. The Inca now avoided a decisive action until he had succeeded in winning over secretly several of Cacha's principal generals. In the plain of Tiocajas, celebrated afterward for the battles between the Spaniards under Benalcazar, and the Indians under Rumiñagui, the two armies met at last. The result remained doubtful for some time, until the treason of his officers decided the day against Cacha Duchicela. The poor king, sick and grief-worn, but his spirit unbroken, was carried to Mocha, where he announced his determination to die in the defense of the place ; but, to his utter amazement, his generals advised him to accept the propositions which the Inca had not neglected to repeat, and to surrender to the invader, against whose forces, superior in arms, numbers, and discipline, resistance would be useless. The caciques of Cayambi, Otabalo, and Caranqui, alone remained true, and advised their master to dismiss his lukewarm servants, to evacuate Mocha, Llactacunga, and Quito, and to retire to the faithful north, where he could await the enemy in the great fortress of Hatuntaqui. Cacha acted upon their advice, and closely followed by the victor, withdrew to what is now the province of Imbabura. In the plain of Hatuntaqui he made his last stand. There the doom of the Caran dynasty was sealed. A terrible battle was fought, which lasted for several days. Victory seemed to incline to the side of the heroic Scyri, when pierced by a lance, he fell dead from his litter. Countless were the numbers of the slain, and to the present day a great many *tolas* commemorate the scene of the bloody slaughter.[1]

On the very field of battle the faithful Caranquis proclaimed Pacha, the daughter of the fallen king, as their Scyri. Huaynacapac now regulated his conduct by policy. He ordered the dead king to be buried with all the honors due to royalty, and made offers of marriage to young Pacha, by whom he was not refused. Whether under the Peruvian law he could marry a foreign princess, who was neither of the Inca family nor a Virgin of the Sun; or whether he, being the supreme law-giver, and indeed law itself, could do as he thought proper; or whether, as the partisans of the Cuzco line assert, he merely took her as a concubine, I shall not stop to examine. The issue of the mar-

1 Of the collateral male descendants of the Scyri dynasty, several acquired some celebrity afterward. Cachulima, a brother of the unfortunate Chalcuchima, who was burned by Pizarro, was one of the first native lords who welcomed the Spaniards under Benalcazar. He was baptized, receiving the name of Don Marcos Duchicela, and was allowed to retain his lands and vassals. The last of the race was Doña Maria Duchicela, of Riobamba, who died at Quito in the year 1700, enjoying the reputation of great piety. See Velasco, vol. ii., bk. 1, § 6.

riage was Atahuallpa, the last of the native rulers of Peru.

Huaynacapac immediately set himself to introduce Peruvian civilization in the conquered kingdom. He erected temples and royal palaces at Latacunga, Quito, Cayambi, and Caranqui; he built an admirable bridge (*rumichaca*), said to consist of a single block of stone, across the Angasmayu; and he constructed that wonderful road from Cuzco to the northern provinces of the empire, the few remnants of which excited the admiration of Humboldt and other travellers. Under him the Peruvian Empire reached its zenith, and its civilization that height beyond which it could hardly have passed. The form of the Inca government was an over-refined and centralized despotism, which left nothing to individual energy or enterprise. Every thing was regulated by law. From his birth to his death man's actions were circumscribed by inflexible rules, from which there was no escape. The subject had no free will, not even in the most insignificant concerns of daily or private life. What the father was, the son had to be. Every one had to remain within his sphere and caste. Not even individual property was known. Provision was made for every individual, and with that provision he had to be satisfied. He could not enlarge it, nor need he apprehend its being lessened. The Inca was the supreme ruler and the representative of the deity on earth. His commands were obeyed blindly; his will was law. He was served by an aristocracy of nobles and priests, who were maintained by the labor of the common people. He was both the head and the support of the complicated edifice which, without him, fell to pieces. The lives, the wills, and the energies of his subjects were in his hands, and he disposed of them at pleasure. Such a system had no vitality or strength in itself; it only existed by the credulity, veneration, and servility of the masses. The first vigorous blow from without, or a strong combination of unfavorable circumstances from within, must destroy it. It had to fall from its own weight, because it had suffocated in the people all those energies, capacities, and mental resources, which enable healthy nations to retrieve their misfortunes.

The battle of Hatuntaqui did not lead to an immediate pacification of the kingdom of Quito. The warlike Caranquis could not brook the foreign yoke, and after contracting alliances with the barbarous tribes of Pasto, they fell unexpectedly on the Inca's body-guard of *Orejones*, causing great slaughter among them. But their punishment was terrible. Huaynacapac followed them into their country, defeated them in a decisive battle on the shores of Lake Yaguarcocha, and ordered all the male adults of the province to be put to the sword without mercy. Thousands of the dead bodies were thrown into the lake, the waters of which were reddened with the blood of so many victims. Hence its name, "Yaguarcocha," which in Quichua means "sea of blood." On its western shore there are still many *tolas* (mounds), which are said to contain the remains of those who perished on that fearful occasion.[1]

As prudent and highly politic as the conduct of Huaynacapac is generally reputed to have been, so

[1] Herrera, dec. v., lib. 3, cap. 16. This author does not mention the Caranquis, but says that the war was sustained by the Otabalos, and a tribe which he calls Cuiyapipos; but from the situation of lake Yaguarcocha, which is in the ancient dominions of the Caranquis, I believe with Balboa and Velasco, that the Caranquis were the tribe that resisted the progress of the Inca until they were exterminated.

imprudent and impolitic was the division of the Empire which he made on his deathbed, bequeathing his paternal dominions to his first-born and undoubtedly legitimate son, Huascar, and to Atahuallpa the kingdom of Quito. He might have foreseen the evil consequences of such a partition.[1] His death took place about the year 1525. For five or seven years the brothers lived in peace;[2] each in the full enjoyment of his respective dominions. Into the probable causes of their subsequent quarrel it would be useless to enter. Some writers allege that it was brought about by a boundary question, involving the title to the province of Cañar. Atahuallpa's subsequent cruelty to the Cañares, who had sided with his brother, seems to favor this supposition. In the first battle, fought near the bridge of Tomebamba, Atahuallpa was signally defeated and taken prisoner; but in the night, while his brother's soldiers were reveling and rejoicing over their triumph, the captive, with an instrument of silver which a woman had secretly contrived to give him, opened a hole in the wall of his prison, through which he escaped and returned to Quito. There he told his people that while in prison his father, the Sun, had

[1] Herrera does not seem to believe in the last will of Huaynacapac, and considers Atahuallpa a usurper. But the weight of authority is against him. See Prescott, book iii., chap. 2, and authorities there quoted; also, Gomara, *Hist. Gen.* And above all, Garcilazo de la Vega, who, himself a scion and partisan of the Cuzco line, would certainly have preferred the charge of usurpation against Atahuallpa, had it been warranted by the facts. Garcilazo not only adopts the story of the division of the Empire, but also adds that Huascar, who had come to Quito at the command of his father, who desired to see him before his death, agreed to it, and promised to abide by it faithfully. — *Com. Real*, lib. ix., cap. 12. If the partition had not been the express will of their father, the brothers would not have lived in peace for five or seven years after the former's death, but their quarrels would have commenced immediately.

[2] Prescott says five. According to Jerez, *Conq. del Peru*, and Garcilazo, it was seven.

converted him into a snake to enable him to escape, promising him at the same time that he would give him a complete victory over his brother.[1] He soon found himself at the head of another army, commanded by his father's experienced generals, Chalcuchima, Quizquiz, and Rumiñagui; defeated Huascar's army at Ambato, and penetrating into the country of the Cañares, revenged himself on them in the same terrible manner in which his father, Huaynacapac, had punished the Caranquis. He then descended to the coast, but after a fruitless attempt to take the island of Puná, on which occasion he was wounded, he returned to the interior, and established his head-quarters at the baths of Cajamarca, while his generals after the battle of Quipaypan, in which Huascar was defeated and taken prisoner,[2] extended their conquests to Cuzco. Atahuallpa was now master of the whole Peruvian empire, and assumed the royal diadem of the Incas.

But his triumph was of short duration. The Spaniards, under Francisco Pizarro, had landed on the coast of Tumbez. Their arduous march across the Cordillera; their negotiations, while on the road, with the unsuspecting monarch; their arrival at Cajamarca; their treacherous invitation to Atahuallpa to visit Pizarro; their false pretenses of friendship and alliance; the unwariness with which the Inca fell into the snare; the unprovoked slaughter of thousands of unarmed Indians by the Spanish cavalry, and the capture of the

1 Gomara, cap. 116; Zarate, lib. i., cap. 12; Herrera, dec. v., lib. 3, cap. 17.

2 According to Herrera, dec. v., lib. ii., cap. 12, Huascar was taken after the capture of Atahuallpa by the Spaniards. Gomara says, "shortly before or after." But according to Prescott, book iii., chap. 2, and authorities there quoted, he was taken prisoner a few months before the landing of Pizarro.

confiding king; the cupidity of the conquerors, and the promise of Atahuallpa to buy his freedom by filling the room in which he was imprisoned, as high as his extended arms could reach, with gold; the expedition of Hernando Pizarro to Pachacamac, and the journey of Francisco's messengers to Cuzco; the immense treasures of the Peruvian empire, and the fulfillment of Atahuallpa's promise; the heinous breach of faith by the Spaniards, and the Inca's cruel execution; Pizarro's march to Cuzco, the burning of Chalcuchima, and the desecration of the tombs of the Incas: all these thrilling events are graphically described by the classic pen of Prescott, and it would be presumption on my part to attempt a repetition.

There is but one circumstance in the tragic fate of Atahuallpa calculated to lessen our sympathy for the victim. It is the murder of his brother Huascar. Father Velasco, who has undoubtedly followed the reasoning of Fray Marcos de Niza and Collahuaso, pretends that Huascar was put to death by Chalcuchima, without express orders from the Inca; that the general's instructions were to kill his prisoner in case an attempt should be made to liberate him; and fearing lest the Spaniards who kept Atahuallpa in prison might be induced to put Huascar on the throne, Chalcuchima committed the deed on his own responsibility. There is some probability in this plea, especially when we consider that Huascar, while being transported to a safer prison, was met by the Spaniards, Fernando de Soto and Pedro del Vasco, while on their way to Cuzco, and implored them to save him, promising them twice as much gold as Atahuallpa had undertaken to give. The two Spaniards, however, excused themselves with having no instructions to take charge of him, and passed on to Cuzco. It is very probable, therefore, that Chalcuchima apprehended danger to his master from such a promise, and considered it his duty to prevent, once and forever, an understanding between Huascar and Pizarro. On the other hand, when we consider the blind obedience of the most powerful nobles to the Inca, and the slavish awe in which they held him, it is difficult to believe that Chalcuchima should have ventured, without express orders from his sovereign, to kill the king's brother, whom he had been commanded to treat well.

The Peruvian Empire, shaken in its very foundations by the wars of Huascar and Atahuallpa, and without a people whose spirit and energy might have been roused by the emergency, fell to pieces after the death of its last ruler. The Yanaconas, a race of slaves who had occupied the lowest social position under the old system,[1] sided with the Spaniards, from whom they expected a favorable change of their situation. The Indian nobles, a herd without a shepherd, and divided by civil dissensions, did not know what to do, while those who resolved to resist the invaders could not forget the jealousies of the Quito and Cuzco lines, and other provincial considerations, which prevented them from making a united effort for the maintenance of their independence. The Curacas or caciques of the distant provinces who, upon seeing a handful of foreigners annihilate the dreaded representative of the Sun, had lost their veneration and awe for the Inca dynasty, returned to their original independence, endeavoring to set up governments for themselves in the districts over which they ruled. Of these chiefs, Rumiñagui, whose name I have already

[1] Herrera, dec. v., lib. 3, cap. 4.

mentioned, was the most talented, the most unscrupulous, and perhaps the most cruel. When Atahuallpa prepared himself to make that fatal visit to Pizarro, from which he never returned, he is said to have put Ruminagui on the guard before the city, to assist his master in case some unforeseen event should make it necessary.[1] Hearing the thunders of musketry, and learning the great slaughter of his countrymen, it was quite natural for the Indian chief, and the 5,000 men he commanded, to be seized by the general panic and seek safety in flight. At some distance from Cajamarca, he rallied his scattered forces, and without making an effort to save his lord, returned to Quito.

On learning of the death of the Inca, he conceived the plan of putting himself at the head of the ancient empire of the Scyris, which he thought himself able to defend against the insignificant number of the European invaders. To secure himself on the throne, he seems to have cultivated popularity with the army, and to have won over to his interests several influential members of the nobility. He also resolved to rid himself of all possible legitimate competitors. Availing himself of the opportunity which the funeral ceremonies in honor of the murdered Atahuallpa presented, he invited all the near and distant relatives of the latter to a great banquet, intoxicated them on their national beverage,[2] and pretending that by their cowardice and lukewarmness they had sacrificed his beloved king, put them to the sword without mercy. The principal victim was Atahuallpa's brother Illescas, of whose skin the usurper is said to have made a drum. He is also

[1] Wytfliet, *Descriptionis Ptolomaicæ Augmentum*, Duaci, 1607, page 81; Zarate, lib. ii., cap. 5.

[2] Gomara, cap. 125; Zarate, lib. ii., cap. 8; Garcilazo de la Vega, *Hist Gen.*, lib. ii., cap. 3.

said to have killed several of the wives and concubines of Atahuallpa, who were supposed to be with child; and to have appropriated to himself the Virgins of the Sun in the Quito convent, from whom none but the Inca would have been allowed to select a consort.[1] These and other unnecessary and revolting outrages would almost seem incredible; but why should we believe barbarous savages to be incapable of that spirit of fiendish cruelty which the Spaniards, who boasted of Christianity and civilization, were continually displaying? If Rumiñagui was a monster and a tyrant, he was fully equaled, if not surpassed, by the conquerors of Quito, to whom I must now introduce my readers.

Sebastian de Benalcazar[2] was a Spanish nobleman, who had come from Nicaragua, attracted by the fame of the riches of Peru. He seems to have been a man of some education, at least he knew how to read and to write, arts which were unknown to the famous Pizarro and Almagro. After rendering valuable services to Pizarro, the latter sent him to take charge of San Miguel, which was then the only port of entry in Peru, and consequently of the greatest importance. But Benalcazar's spirit would not brook mere garrison duty. His cupidity was excited by reports of the great riches of Quito. That place had not yet been occupied by the Spaniards. Huaynacapac had resided there for more than thirty years, and built stately palaces and temples, the treasures of which were supposed to equal those that had been found in the great city of Cuzco. The most alluring rumors were afloat. An immense quantity of gold was said to have been on

1 Velasco, vol. ii., lib. 4, § 1, sec. 8.

2 Herrera and Velasco spell his name Be*l*alcazar, which is wrong. I have seen his signature in one of the record books of the municipality of Quito. It shows a firm and somewhat practiced hand, and is very legible.

the way to Cajamarca, to be added to the ransom of Atahuallpa, when the news of his death reached the carriers, and induced them to take it back to Quito. That gold must still be intact. A splendid opportunity here offered to an enterprising and dashing captain like Benalcazar. At the same time, embassadors from the Cañares, the old enemies of the Quito tribes, arrived at his camp imploring his assistance against Rumiñagui, who was about to invade their province.[1] The temptation was too strong for Benalcazar; and without orders or permission from Pizarro, he left San Miguel at the head of about one hundred and fifty men, for Quito. His second in command was the monster Juan de Ampudia, whose memory deserves to be held up to eternal execration. His chaplain was the good Father Marcos de Niza, whom I have already mentioned.

If it had not been for his Indian allies, Benalcazar would perhaps never have returned from this expedition. He had to encounter the genius of a chief who was by nature a general. Rumiñagui was well aware that he fought not only for his race, but for his own life and ill-gotten possessions. He knew that the promises and assurances of the Spaniards could not be relied on, and consequently rejected the overtures of Benalcazar. His influence over his men, to judge from the statements of those writers who have given us detailed accounts of this expedition, must have been very great. They had supported his usurpation, and confided blindly in his leadership. He had skillfully overcome their dread of the Spanish fire-arms, and knowing the terrible advantage which the invaders derived from their horses, he provided against it. On all the roads and approaches by which the Spaniards could

[1] Zarate, lib. ii.. cap 9.

advance, he prepared snares and traps to entangle and destroy the horses. He dug deep holes and covered them with reeds and sand, which would break in under the weight of mounted men. He rammed sharp and pointed sticks into the sand of the plains, so as to line with them ditches skillfully hidden from the enemy's view, and when the Spaniards approached he placed his men behind those ditches, in order to allure the cavalry to certain destruction.[1] But, unfortunately, what the Spaniards would not have seen, their native allies discovered. The Cañares, who were always in the advance, preparing the way for the horses, enabled Benalcazar to avoid the most dangerous places. Herrera, who admits that the situation of the Spaniards was not only most critical, but even desperate, recognizes a miracle in the escape of the cavalry, which he ascribes to the direct interference of the Virgin Mary, who "on such occasions often appeared to the defenders of the true faith, conferring innumerable benefits on them, although by their deeds they might not have deserved such heavenly favors."[2]

Toward the latter part of the year 1533, Benalcazar descended into the plain of Tiocajas, where the Indians made a desperate resistance. For the first time since the arrival of Pizarro in Peru, a battle was fought which remained undecided. The Indians succeeded in killing and wounding several Spaniards, and in killing four horses, the heads of which were carried about in triumph, to show to the natives that those dreaded monsters were mortal like other creatures.[3]

1 Zarate, *ut supra*. Herrera, dec. v., lib. iv., cap. 12.

2 Dec. v., lib. iv., cap. 12.

3 The death of a horse was an immense loss to the Spaniards, considering the distance from which horses had to be brought, the cost of transportation, and the incalculable superiority which they gave the conquerors over the natives.

Ruminagui and his faithful partisan Zopozopangui, displayed the greatest valor, exposing themselves continually in the thickest of the fight, giving orders, and encouraging the wavering.

The accounts which contemporary writers have given of this campaign, are confused and contradictory. It seems, however, that several battles were fought; and that the Spaniards, although continually victorious, were reduced to a most deplorable condition. Several of them were killed, and a great many wounded; and the loss of horses weighed heavily upon them, as one mounted man was considered equal to a thousand Indians. Had it not been for an unforeseen event — a dreadful night-eruption of Cotopaxi, accompanied by an earthquake and a formidable rain of ashes — Benalcazar would have been compelled to fall back for provisions and reinforcements. But it was natural that such a phenomenon, which at such a juncture would have disheartened the ignorant and superstitious of many a civilized nation, should produce a fatal effect on the spirit and perseverance of the Indians. The invisible powers seemed to have declared against them. The elements were with those foreigners, who commanded the thunder and lightning, and rode on monsters which had never before been seen. In vain did the usurper endeavor to rally his men. The bands of discipline were severed; and with the disordered remnants of his army he fled to Quito. When Benalcazar looked over the battle-field on the following morning, the Indian army was gone.

The pious Herrera tells us, in this connection, of an oracle which had long before warned the Indians that if a certain volcano at Latacunga should once explode, foreigners from a distant land would invade and conquer the country. This oracle, he explains, was a prediction of Satan, "who although not omniscient like God, is well able to foresee the effects of certain causes which are known to him; and as he knew that the volcano would have to explode, and that the Spaniards would also find their way to Peru, it was easy for him to pass his calculation for a prophecy."[1]

On his arrival at Quito, Rumiñagui at once took the necessary measures to deprive the Spaniards of the great object of all their toils and hardships. Whatever treasures there were left, he sent out of the city; but where he hid them is a secret to the present day. It is possible that the treasures of Quito had already gone to swell the ransom of Atahuallpa; it is possible that the rumors of their immensity were fabrications or exaggerations; but it is also possible, and even highly probable, that the Indians sought to snatch from the greedy grasp of the Spaniards the idol, for the possession of which so many innocent lives had been sacrificed. It was the last but most telling revenge of the conquered. Until the present day, traditions of the great treasures hidden in the mountains by Rumiñagui, are eagerly repeated and believed at Quito, giving probability to the story of Valverde, to which I have referred in another chapter.

Another act of cruelty committed by Rumiñagui, whose valiant resistance seems to have inflamed the ancient writers against him, ought now to be recorded, although not strictly connected with the object of this narrative. He is said to have entered the convent of the Virgins of the Sun, and told them to be joyful as they would soon become acquainted with men with long beards, whom they might welcome as lovers. The poor,

[1] Dec. v., lib. v., cap. 1.

silly girls, not knowing what to answer, laughed, which so enraged their lord that he put them all to the sword.[1] Garcilazo de la Vega says that he ordered them to be buried alive.[2] Herrera, however, tells the story in a different manner.[3] According to him, Rumiñagui commanded them to leave Quito, where nothing but dishonor awaited them, and upon their refusing to obey, ordered their massacre. To me all these statements appear improbable ; and I am inclined to believe that, conscious of the impossibility of taking them along and maintaining them on his rapid and difficult marches over inhospitable mountains, he decreed their death to prevent them from falling into the hands of the licentious Spaniards.

Having removed the gold and killed the Virgins of the Sun, and thus placed two objects so eagerly coveted by the invaders beyond their reach, Rumiñagui set fire to the town, and evacuated it with all his troops and followers. It would be difficult to describe the rage, mortification, and despair of the Spaniards, on finding smoking ruins instead of the treasures which they had expected. The precious prize had slipped away from under their grasp, and thousands of innocent Indians were sacrificed to their disappointed cupidity. But of this hereafter.

It is an unmistakable proof of the genius of Rumiñagui, that notwithstanding the losses he had sustained, and the utter discouragement of his men after, as it were, the invisible powers had declared against them, he was again able to collect an army willing to be led by him to another desperate effort. Knowing that Benalcazar had sent out several detachments in differ-

[1] Velasco.
[2] *Hist. del Peru*, lib. ii., cap. 4.
[3] Dec. v., lib. vi., cap. 5.

ent directions to capture him, and that Quito was left almost without cavalry, and with very little infantry, he resolved on a night attack, in order to surprise and crush the little garrison. Reinforced by the tribes of Chillo (a beautiful valley to the east of Quito, from which it is separated by a low mountain range), and at the head of about fifteen thousand men, he attacked the fortifications which the Spaniards had hastily thrown up. But the old enemies of Quito, the Cañares, had again frustrated his plan by giving timely warning to the Spaniards, and Rumiñagui was repulsed with great slaughter.[1] His army was pursued and dispersed, and thus ended the last great effort to save the independence of the ancient kingdom of Quito.

It was followed by a series of barbarities so monstrous and shocking, as to eclipse even the bloody deeds of the Pizarros and Almagros. Learning from several of the Indians who were put to the rack, that the treasures had been taken to Cayambi, Benalcazar immediately proceeded to the north, with a division of his troops, but found only women and children, as the men had either fled, or were in the army under Rumiñagui. To set an example by which he hoped to compel the male inhabitants of other villages to return to their homes, he put these poor women and children to the sword.[2]

Only a few gold and silver vessels were found, just enough to gall and heighten the new disappointment of the Spaniards.

In the mean time Juan de Ampudia had succeeded in capturing Zopozopangui, the valiant aid of Rumiñagui. He was put to the rack, but revealing nothing concerning the treasures, he was executed.[3] Rumi-

1 Zarate; Gomara.

2 Herrera.

3 Herrera, dec. v., lib. vii., cap. 14.

ñagui, after a protracted defense in the mountains, was abandoned by his followers, who had become tired of the war, and betrayed by his own servants, he was taken by Benalcazar. His end was that of a hero. He showed no sign of weakness. No confession could be extorted from his silent lips; and after torturing him in vain, Benalcazar ordered him to be executed.[1]

Chambo, another Indian chief, was tortured and burned alive without divulging any thing.[2] Cozopangua, governor of Quito, Quimbalumba, governor of Chillo, Razorazo, Rima, and other nobles, shared the same fate.[3] Albis, another cacique, was tortured by having his feet burned at a slow fire, but revealed nothing.[4] Others, to obtain momentary relief, referred to

[1] Garcilazo de la Vega asserts, without any foundation, that Rumiñagui, after evacuating Quito, retired into the impenetrable fastnesses of the eastern Cordillera, and was never heard of again. Father Velasco, and other writers, repeat this statement. But Herrera, the royal historian who had free access to official documents and reports, gives the details of Rumiñagui's capture and execution. His statement is corroborated by the records of the Quito Municipality, which I examined with great care. I found an entry, dated June 25th, 1535, which recites that "the men under Pedro de Puelles had captured the principal nobles of these provinces, because it was supposed and believed that they would know of the gold and silver; these nobles were *Oruminabi*, Cozopangua, Quimbalumba, Razorazo, Rima, and others, their allies and friends; with whom every possible experiment was made and great trouble had in watching them and going with them to many places where the gold was supposed to be; but neither they nor any of them would tell; wherefore, *and for the crimes which they had committed*, they were executed, *so that now there are none left*." It will be seen that, in this document, the name *Oruminabi* is given. Herrera spells it *Yruminabi*. But evidently the same individual is meant, and the discrepancy will be explained by the fact that, in the beginning, as long as the conquerors were unacquainted with the Quichua language, all the Indian names were misspelled. Atahuallpa was frequently spelled Atabaliba, and Huaynacapac had been corrupted into Guayanacaba.

[2] From a relation of Fray Marcos de Niza, published by Las Casas in his *Historia de las Crueldades de los Españoles Conquistadores de America, o Brevisima Relacion de la Destruccion de las Indias Occidentales.* Works of Las Casas, published in Spanish by Dr. Juan Antonio Llorente, Paris, 1822, two volumes.

[3] *Quito Municipality Records.*

[4] Las Casas, *ut supra*, vol. i., 183.

certain localities; but when the Spaniards went there they found nothing, and the torturing of their victims was resumed. Every nook and corner of the province was searched, but only in the sepulchres[1] some little gold was found, which could not compensate the conquerors for the hardships they had undergone, and the perils they had braved. The common soldiers now vented their rage on the Indians they met on their fruitless expeditions. Hands, ears, and noses were cut off, without any provocation on the part of those poor creatures. Babes were snatched from the arms of their mothers and flung into the air. In the valley of Machachi, which was studded with Indian villages, a number of natives were driven into three houses, and the buildings set on fire. A little boy whom a priest, Ocaña, had rescued from the flames, was snatched from his hands by a soldier, and flung back into the fire. Countless houses and villages were burned by the enraged adventurers.[2] If, on the approach of the marauding Spaniards, the Indians remained at their homes, they were tortured to make them disclose deposits of gold, of which they knew nothing. If they fled, they were chased with bloodhounds.[3] These horrible animals, according to Palomino, were fed on the corpses of the victims. No faith was kept with the Indians. The caciques were invited to come to Quito by promises of safety and friendship; but when they made their appearance, and could not, or would not,

1 Velasco, vol. ii., lib. iv., § 6. Gomara, cap. 125. The latter author says, that they found enough gold in the tombs to defray the expenses of the expedition; a poor consolation for the greedy adventurers.

2 "Asimismo yo vi quemar tantas casas é pueblos que no sabria decir el numero seguro; eran muchos." — *Fray Niza.*

3 From a relation of Alonzo de Palomino, an eye-witness, quoted by Velasco, *ut supra.*

disclose the secret of the treasures, they were burned.[1] Burning seems to have been the favorite mode of putting Indians to death.[2]

During Benalcazar's absence at Riobamba, whither he had been compelled to go shortly after his entry into Quito, by the news of the arrival of a rival adventurer and interloper (Don Pedro de Alvarado, who was afterwards bought off by Pizarro and Almagro), the principal instigators of those cruelties were Juan de Ampudia, Benalcazar's lieutenant, and Alonzo Sanchez, his second in command. While they were ravaging the country, they made no provision for sowing and planting, but plundered the public granaries established by the Inca government.[3] The consequence of this improvidence was a great famine, from which the Indians suffered fearfully the year afterward.[4] It was only relieved by another cruelty, — the carrying away of thousands of Indians to accompany, as beasts of burden, the Spaniards on their discovering expeditions north and south. One of these expeditions, headed by Benalcazar in person, proceeded to Guayaquil, and of the four thousand Indians he took along, but a few returned to their homes.[5] Juan de Ampudia went north, also taking a great number of Indians with him. Many of them were carried along in chains.[6] He was followed by Benalcazar when he

1 "Yten vi que llamaban a los caciques é principales Indios que viniesen de paz seguramente é prometiendoles seguro; y en llegando, luego les quemaban." — Las Casas, vol. i., p. 185.

2 Helps' *Spanish Conquest in America.* This author supposes that the Spaniards, following the example of the Inquisition, selected this mode of putting Indians to death because they were pagans.

3 Las Casas, vol. i., p. 202.

4 *Quito Municipality Records*, July 26, 1535.

5 See chapter ii., page 32 of this work.

6 Las Casas, appendix to the work above mentioned.

undertook the conquest of Popayan. On this occasion he took about four thousand Indians with him, of whom but twenty returned to Quito.[1] Of those who remained, ten thousand were employed to rebuild the town.[2] It may be inferred from the preceding how they were treated. Some preferred suicide to the terrible tasks which they were compelled to perform.

Of the ancient buildings of Quito, no stone was left upon the other, and deep excavations were made under them to search for hidden treasures. Hence there is no vestige left at Quito of its former civilization; not a ruin, not a wall, not a stone to which the traditions of the past might cling. Where the palace of the Inca stood is now the Convent de la Merced,[3] and a potato-field occupies the place of the ancient Temple of the Sun.[4] Such, then, was the conduct of the defenders of the "true faith," and the special favorites of St. James and the Virgin Mary. I have abstained from making a single statement which I could not support by reliable authority.

On the 28th of August, 1534, the Spanish village of Quito was founded. The title of city, it received afterward. While in North America population always precedes the organization of municipalities, while with us there must be houses and settlers before officers are elected and ordinances enacted, in Spanish-America municipal organization always preceded population. When a site was deemed convenient for a settlement, a deed of foundation was executed, and a *cabildo*

1 From the relation of an eye-witness who accompanied Benalcazar on this expedition. Las Casas, vol. i., p. 204.

2 Velasco.

3 This fact appears from the *Municipality Records*.

4 On Mount Panecillo.

(municipality) instituted before buildings were erected. Whether the new settlement was to be a city or a village was not left to its future development, but prescribed by the military chieftain who ordered the settlement to be made. San Francisco de Quito was first intended for a village, while Santiago de Quito (Riobamba) was made a town. Yet, soon afterward, San Francisco had to be made a city, while Santiago was abandoned. Quito was named San Francisco in honor of the Marquis Francisco de Pizarro. Its ancient Indian name was *Quitu*.[1] The deed establishing the settlement is like all those documents, drawn up and acknowledged by a notary. It is executed by the "magnificent Señor Don Diego de Almagro, Marshal of His Majesty in the Kingdoms of New Castile, Lieutenant-Governor, and Lieutenant-Captain-General," etc., etc., in the name of the "most magnificent Señor Don Francisco de Piçarro, Governor Adelantado and Captain-General," etc., whose superior authority is most emphatically recognized. Among other things, it says "that the province of Quito, having been conquered and *pacified* by him (Almagro), in the name of His Majesty, and of the said Señor Gobernador, and it having pleased the Lord that most of the chiefs and Indians are now peaceful, and under the yoke and obedience of His Majesty; and in order to make them come truly to peace, and to convert them to our Holy Catholic Faith, *by the good example and teachings of the Spanish vassals of His Majesty*, who are to live in these parts, he founded in the name of His Majesty, the town of Quito," etc., etc. The document winds up with the characteristic declaration, that because the "magnificent Lord Almagro" said he did not know

[1] There are no "o's" or "e's" in the Quichua language.

how to write, Blas de Atiencia signed for him, and at his request.[1]

On the 6th of December, Sebastian Benalcazar, Lieutenant-Governor and Captain-General, ordered a list to be taken of those who wished to be considered permanent residents (*vecinos*) of Quito. This list contains but two hundred and five names, with Juan de Ampudia and Diego de Tapia as Alcaldes. The next and most important business of the conquerors, was to proceed to a division of the spoils, consisting of lands and Indians. These proceedings occupy a great deal of space in the old municipality records, as complaints were frequent, and petitions for increase or equalization of the repartimientos came in continually.

From the materials I have been able to collect, I conclude that the Indians at Quito were classified as follows by the conquerors: (1.) Indians *de paz* (of peace); (2.) Indians of war (*de guerra*); (3.) *Yanaconas;* and (4.) Nicaragua Indians. The latter had been brought to Quito by those adventurers who, like Benalcazar, had come from Nicaragua, attracted by the fame of the riches of Peru. The Yanaconas I have already mentioned. They had been slaves under the Incas, and as slaves they had passed into the hands of the Spaniards. Indians *de guerra* were prisoners of war, whom it was considered rightful to enslave. But to gratify their cupidity, the Spaniards made prisoners of Indians who had never fought nor even dreamed of resistance. The slightest provocation on the part of an Indian tribe, sufficed to declare war against them, and to reduce them to slavery. These Indians *de guerra* it was lawful to mark with the brand-

[1] Deed of foundation, dated August 28, 1534.

ing iron.[1] In Quito, however, the Spaniards do not seem to have long continued to call them *Indios de guerra*, but following the ancient custom of the country, called them Yanaconas also. The Indians *de paz* were apportioned among the conquerors in proportion to their rank, merit, and infantry- or cavalry-service (mounted men always being entitled to a larger share), so as to give to each settler a certain number of laborers corresponding to the quantity of his arable lands, mines, or other possessions. This proceeding of apportioning Indians among their new masters, was called "*repartimiento.*" It will have to be distinguished from the subsequent signification of the term, when it was made to express forced sales of a variety of articles which the Indians were compelled to buy at prices fixed by the sellers themselves, the *corregidors*. Of this I have already spoken.

From what we have seen, it will be clear that it made very little difference in point of fact, whether the Indians resisted or not. They were made slaves in either case, with the difference only that if they had resisted, they could be marked with the branding iron.

[1] "However, in 1528, if not before, a great step was taken which affected both slaves of ransom and slaves of war. This was that the government should be responsible for the branding of slaves, and that it should not be done by private persons. As this is a very important piece of legislation, and is briefly expressed, it may be given in full: 'By reason of the disorder in making slaves, and selling free Indians that are not slaves, it is commanded that whosoever shall possess Indians whom he asserts to be slaves, shall present them before the authorities *(la justicia)* in the place where the royal officers may be, and show the title or cause why these men are slaves; and the authorities approving, the slaves shall be inscribed by a scrivener *and branded with an iron which only the authorities shall keep, and no private person.* The Indian who is found to have been made a slave unjustly, let him be set at liberty, and notification made by the public crier.' This document was executed at Madrid on the 19th of September, 1528, and is signed by Cobos, the Secretary of State." Helps' *Spanish Conquest*, vol. iii., p. 120 and 121 (American edition).

To justify the enslaving of harmless and peaceable Indians, a fiction was resorted to. It was necessary to convert them to the Catholic faith. This, of course, the Spaniards had to do. A number of Indians were therefore allotted, or to adopt the term then in use, recommended (*encomendados*) to each principal conqueror, for the purpose of being instructed by him in the Catholic religion. In return for this infinite blessing, they had to repay their instructors with their labor and services. This is as short an explanation of the original character of the system of *encomiendas* in Peru, as the nature of the subject allows.[1] It varied in the different colonies according to circumstances too numerous to mention. The documents by which the Spanish Governors sometimes surrendered entire villages of freeborn Indians into perpetual slavery, were generally drawn up in the following form: "To you, A. B., I recommend by way of deposit —— Indians of the village of —— ; and I do authorize you to use them in your mines and on your farms, extracting gold, and availing yourself of their services, on condition that you take care to instruct them in the Christian doctrine and other things concerning our holy Catholic faith; because, thereby, I exonerate the conscience of His Majesty, the King our lord, and my own."[2]

The authority to employ those Indians in the mines and on the farms of their masters, was always made use of to the very letter. The condition, however, to instruct them in the doctrines of Christianity, was but poorly complied with. The *encomenderos* (so the conquerors to whom Indians had thus been assigned were called) worked their unfortunate Indians to death,

[1] Solorzano, *Politica Indiana*, vol. i., lib. iii., cap. 1, §§ 3 and 4.
[2] Las Casas.

without troubling themselves whether they learned any thing about Christianity or not.[1] Las Casas gives many instances of the recklessness of the Spaniards in this respect. He tells us of an *encomendero* who confiscated the golden idols which his Indians had, and afterward compelled them to buy copper idols from him, which he had seized in another village. "What could these Indians learn from the Spaniards?" exclaims the pious Las Casas, "the latter in many instances being ignorant of the ten commandments, and unable to recite the Credo. The Indians soon learn to content themselves with one wife, while the Spaniards often keep a dozen concubines. The Indians are humble and docile; they do not rob or kill; but the Spaniards are proud and vain, addicted to profane swearing, and rob and kill with inhuman cruelty."[2]

After this digression, which is equally applicable to the early history of most of the Spanish-American colonies, I must return to what exclusively belongs to the history of Quito. Having apportioned lands and Indians among themselves, the conquerors soon found it necessary to secure the possession and augment the number of their new slaves. Indians, who at the time of Benalcazar's arrival at Riobamba were residents of the province of Quito, were therefore declared to belong to the province, although they might have left it afterward, and they were commanded to return.[3] Pizarro was petitioned to send a branding iron to Quito, with which to mark slaves, "in order that the caciques and Indians who, in these provinces, had

1 Solorzano, *Politica Indiana*, vol. i., lib. iii., cap. 1, § 8.
2 *Ut supra*, vol. i., p. 269.
3 *Quito Municipality Records*, January 22, 1535.

given in their obedience to His Majesty the King, might better remain in the same and become afraid to revolt;"[1] and to send the rules and regulations for the branding of slaves.

An ordinance was passed prohibiting the exportation of Indians from the province without a license from the captain, under the penalty of ten *pesos* of gold,[2] or one hundred lashes in case of non-payment.[3] In the preamble to this ordinance, it was stated that many persons were in the habit of exporting their Indian slaves in chains, or with clogs (*cepos*) fastened to their feet, which, to the honor of the municipality be it said, was also prohibited.[4] Fugitive slave laws, too, were not wanting. An *Alguazil del Campo* was appointed[5] to catch runaways. His fees were as follows: For an Indian de repartimiento, four reals in gold; for a Yanacona, half a ducat; for a Nicaragua Indian, one peso, and for a negro, two pesos of gold. The negroes did not fail to come in for their share of legislation characteristic of the heroes of those times. A negro who should run away from his master was to suffer castration for the first offense, and to lose his life for the second.[6] An Indian woman who had connection with a negro, was to have her hair cut off and receive one hundred lashes, while the negro was to suffer castration.[7]

Side by side with these and other barbarous provis-

1 *Quito Municipality Records*, October 9, 1536.

2 One *peso* of gold must have been equivalent to at least an ounce of that metal.

3 *Municipality Records*, July 19, 1535.

4 *Ibid.*, vol. i., page 73.

5 May 22, 1538.

6 March 26, 1538.

7 " Que la India que se acostare con negro sea castigada con cien azotes junta á la picota, í trasquilada ó cortada del pelo, é qual negro se le corte el miembro genital é compañones." — January 26, 1551.

ions, we find that meddling spirit of legislation which interfered with every thing, regulated every thing, and left nothing to individual judgment, energy, or enterprise. As none of the English authors who have written on the Spanish conquest in America, has paid any attention to the social and domestic life of the conquerors, and the institutions they established after what they called "pacifying" the country, I shall try to present some of those enactments, which may, with great propriety, be called the blue laws of Spanish-America.[1]

Immediately after the foundation of Quito, the *Cabildo* commenced to regulate all the affairs of daily life. The charges of tavern-keepers were fixed by law, without any reference to the fluctuations in the market price of provisions.[2] Bakers were ordered to give thirty-five pounds of bread for one *peso* of gold, under penalty of ten *pesos*.[3] It was declared an offense to charge more for a *fanega* of wheat than two *pesos*, or one *peso* for the *fanega* of indian-corn. The shoemakers were commanded to make shoes at two *pesos* two *tomines* the pair, and boots at four *pesos*. In 1537, the prices of blacksmith work were regulated by law, and the transgressors threatened with heavy penalties.[4]

[1] In this connection I cannot refrain from acknowledging my great obligations to Dr Pablo Herrera, formerly Minister for Foreign Affairs, whose thorough knowledge of the antiquities of Quito, and the colonial history of Ecuador, as well as the amiable kindness with which he placed his manuscript notes, the result of long continued studies and profound researches, at my disposal, enabled me to find my way through the Municipality Records, which, without this clew, it would have cost me too much time and labor to examine. Dr. Herrera is the author of a very interesting work entitled *Ensayo sobre la Historia de la Literatura Ecuatoriana*, of which, however, but the first number has been published. It is to be hoped that the author will not withhold the other parts of the work from the public.

[2] Herrera, dec. v., lib. x., cap. 11.

[3] *Municipality Records.*

[4] *Ibid.*

It was declared unlawful [1] to leave the city without a permit or order from the Lieutenant-Governor; offenders to be fined fifty *pesos*. Persons who were out of Quito during the Christmas or Easter festivals, incurred a fine of ten *pesos*.[2] Under penalty of death and confiscation of property, it was ordained that nobody should barter or buy gold, silver, or pearls, from an Indian, except in presence of the royal *veedor* (superintendent), whose duty it was to see that the transaction was not against the will of the Indian, and that the king was not defrauded of his fifth.[3] This latter seems to have been the principal consideration, for the conquerors were certainly not overscrupulous with regard to the consent of the Indians. The sale and exportation of horses and mares was likewise prohibited,[4] under penalty of forfeiting the price obtained on such sale. It was declared that the exportation of horses might lead to troubles and insurrections among the Indians. The sale or barter of arms was also prohibited.

On the 16th of August, 1538, it appeared to the Cabildo that "since the arrival at Quito of a certain attorney, Bachiler Guevara (about a month before, more or less), many suits had been stirred up whereby, as there was no other attorney in the town, many persons might lose their legal rights." He was, therefore, "forbidden to exercise his profession, or to give advice or his opinion on any controversy or matter of litigation," under the penalty of one hundred *pesos* for the first offense, and a year's banishment from Quito for the second offense.[5] An individual who

1 *Municipality Records*, May 20, 1535. 2 *Ibid.* November 5, 1537.
3 *Ibid.* May 20, 1535. 4 *Ibid.* May 31, 1535.
5 "The world is so torn by differences of opinion that it is always very interesting, and somewhat delightful, to find any one subject on which

knew the art of smelting precious metals, was prohibited from leaving the town until another should have arrived competent to take his place.

After the ringing of the night-bell (*toque de la queda*) nobody was allowed to show himself in the streets.[1] If the transgressor should be found armed, his arms were to be taken from him and confiscated. If unarmed, he should for the first offense be put in the stocks (*en el cepo de los piés*) for three days; for the second offense for six days, and for the third he should be banished the city for four months. (Even as late as the commencement of this century, persons were liable to be arrested for showing themselves after the ringing of the night-bell in the streets of Quito.) Nobody was allowed to have himself carried about in a hammock by Indians, except in cases of sickness. Fine, ten pesos of gold.[2]

On the 22d of January, 1535, it was ordained that, considering the danger of conflagrations, on account of the many Indian *ranchos* (huts) within the city limits, every property-holder should, within eight days, destroy, or cause to be destroyed, all the *ranchos* on his lot or lots (*solares*), *under penalty of forfeiting for every offense the best Indian woman in his possession,*

there is singular unanimity. Now there was something wherein the Spanish conquerors and colonists universally agreed. Biscayan, Estremaduran, Andalusian, Castilian — men who had various points of difference, and numberless provincial jealousies — concurred in one request. As soon as any colony was in the least degree established in the New World, the colonists, almost in their first communication with their sovereign, were sure to entreat him to prevent lawyers from coming out to them." — Helps' *Spanish Conquest*, vol. iii., p. 24 (American edition). These petitions were at first complied with. — Villaroel, *Govierno Eclesiastico Pacificio y Union de los dos Cuchillos Pontifico y Regio*, vol. i., quest. xi., art. i., n. 3 and 4. Solorzano, *Politica Indiana*, vol. ii., lib. v., cap. 3, § 1.

[1] August 1, 1537.

[2] *Municipality Records*, March 8, 1538.

*whom the captain was thereupon to assign to whomsoever else he might think proper.*[1]

To judge from the wording of this ordinance, the early settlers must have lived in a state quite the contrary of celibacy. The existence of white women at Quito can hardly be traced to an earlier period than the year 1546, when the ancient historians mention the compassion of the women for the Viceroy, Blasco Nuñez Vela, on the day before he went out to fight Gonzalo Pizarro.

On the 8th of June, 1537, it appeared to the Cabildo that some persons, "and their servants and Indians," were in the habit of diverting the water-courses which furnished the town with water. It was therefore ordained that every person so offending should, if he were a Spaniard, be fined thirty pesos; if he were an Indian, *his nose was to be cut off.*[2] The height of kitchen walls was prescribed by law.[3] Nobody was allowed to visit farms or Indian *repartimientos* in the country, without a license from the Lieutenant-General.[4] A hammer was not to be sold for more than one peso, etc., etc.

Notwithstanding all these protective provisions, the first settlers of Quito remained poor, and poverty is their constant complaint until long after the final pacification of the country, following the civil wars. On the 25th June, 1535, the municipality enacted that, as the conquerors and first settlers of Quito had gotten very little in return for all their trouble, and that what they had obtained was divided among them, any treasures that might afterwards be discovered should belong to the actual inhabitants of Quito, with-

1 *Municipality Records*, March 8, 1558.
2 *Ibid.*
3 *Ibid.* January 3, 1537.
4 *Ibid.* November 5, 1537.

out a right of participation in those who had left the town to engage in other conquests. On the 9th October, 1536, when the Municipality requested Pizarro for the branding iron, they again referred to their poverty. On the 4th April, 1537, the Cabildo, in addressing the Lieutenant-Governor, referred to the small profits which the settlement had yielded; and the Lieutenant-Governor replied, that four years had passed without their having obtained gold, or other things of value. The idea that the title and right of possession to the treasures so eagerly coveted, were in the Indians, their legitimate owners, does not seem ever to have entered the minds of the conquerors.

When Benalcazar quitted Quito, to undertake the conquest of Popayan, he left Pedro de Puelles as Lieutenant-Governor in his place. This Puelles seems to have been a man after the heart of the Municipality. In their petition to Pizarro, to which I have already referred, they pray that he may be continued in his office, for "by executing the *suspicious* caciques, and *by the killing which he ordered to be done among the Ingas*, he has made the natives fear him, and they now hold him in great respect." [1] What a history of barbarity, injustice, and murder, these few lines contain! Men put to death on the mere suspicion of desiring to vindicate their natural rights! *Por la matanza que en los Ingas hizo hacer!* By the killing which he ordered to be done among the Indians, they learned to fear him, and now hold him in great respect! And that man must be retained as the first officer of a new city! That quality is expressly referred to in order to recommend him to his superior! These are the men who were to convert the heathens by their example, and to

[1] October 9, 1536.

teach civilization to the Children of the Sun! Let us drop the curtain on this horrible picture!

Benalcazar's successor in the government of Quito was Gonzalo Pizarro, the brother of Francisco, the discoverer, while Benalcazar, to his great dissatisfaction, was indemnified with the government of Popayan. Francisco Pizarro had undertaken the conquest of Peru in partnership with Diego de Almagro. They soon fell out, and made war on each other. Pizarro was cunning and treacherous; Almagro frank and unwary. The result was, that after they had, time and again, renewed and sealed their friendship with solemn oaths on the Eucharist, Pizarro captured and executed Almagro. He was, in his turn, assassinated by the friends of the latter, who proclaimed Almagro's son as their governor. This young man, however, was defeated, taken prisoner, and executed by the royal commissioner, Vaca de Castro; and peace would have been restored had it not been for the *ordenanzas reales*, a code of laws prescribed by the crown, for the government of the Indies and the protection and personal liberty of the Indians. And here we are struck by a remarkable phenomenon. The Spanish colonists, whose servile and abject loyalty to their king no act of tyranny could have shaken, rose in rebellion against him because he wanted the Indians to be free. They would not have struck for freedom, but they struck for slavery. They would not have risen *against* oppression, but they rose *for* it. They would not have lifted an arm to defend the rights of man, but they drew the sword for the privilege of trampling upon them. To an irresponsible despotism, to arbitrary taxation, and to the horrors of the Inquisition they submitted; but to laws declaring the Indians to be freemen, they would not submit. It was a revolution surpassed in iniquity only by the rebellion of those who, in our own age, have risen, not against a bad and despotic, but against a good and popular government, and not to defend or achieve liberty, but to preserve and perpetuate slavery.

Gonzalo Pizarro was proclaimed Protector of Peru, and placed at the head of the revolution. On the plain to the north of Quito, he met and defeated the scanty forces of the Viceroy, Blasco Nuñez Vela (January 18, 1546), who had come to enforce the *ordenanzas*. The Viceroy was slain, and Benalcazar, who alone of all the great chieftains had sided with him, not from motives of humanity and justice, but from motives of policy, was taken prisoner; but subsequently released by Pizarro, and allowed to return to his government. The court of Spain thought it best to yield. It would not have yielded a point of colonial liberty, but it yielded the point of colonial slavery. The priest La Gasca was sent out to pacify the country, and brought with him the repeal of the detested ordinances. Gonzalo Pizarro, who had now, but too late, conceived the plan of establishing the independence of Peru, and placing the crown on his own head, was defeated, taken prisoner, and executed (1548). He had lost almost all his supporters.[1] As soon as the point of Indian slavery in fact, though perhaps not in

[1] When every body deserted Gonzalo Pizarro, his friend at Quito, Pedro de Puelles, was about to do the same. But before he had time to carry out the plan he had formed, he was assassinated in his bed by Rodrigo de Salazar, another treacherous friend, who wanted to win the good opinion of La Gasca by showing great zeal in the king's cause. Under the pretext to invite Puelles to mass, he gained admission into his bedroom, and there murdered him, with the assistance of his fellow conspirators. For this meritorious deed the Cabildo elected him Lieutenant-Governor in place of his victim. The early history of Peru is written in blood; and it

name, was conceded, the colonists returned to their loyalty. Another effort was subsequently made by the crown to ameliorate the condition of the Indians, but it led to new convulsions and insurrections; and although Hernandez Giron, another revolutionary leader, was defeated and executed (1554), the cause of the natives was doomed. Laws, it is true, were continually enacted in their favor, but they were either not executed at all, or in a spirit of willful misconstruction which turned good into evil, and instead of relieving, added to the misery of the Indians. They were given up to a system of oppression, injustice, lawlessness, cruelty, and degradation which is almost without a parallel in the history of modern nations.

And here ends the first period of my history. I had collected the materials for a detailed review of Spanish colonial civilization, portions of which I have already written, because I intended to add it to this volume. I also intended to review the causes which led to the War of Independence, that war itself, the men and ideas it produced, and the bloody history of the republics which sprung from it. But I did not want to delay the publication of this volume unnecessarily. On the success with which it meets, my future labors will depend. If it is well received, I shall endeavor to carry out my original plan. If not, it will be an indication to me that either the public does not feel sufficient interest in Spanish-American subjects at this time, or that my manner of treating them has not proved satisfactory. I have done my best, however little it may

is remarkable that most of those who had heartlessly butchered the Indians, received their due by being murdered by their own accomplices in oppression and cruelty.

be. I have labored hard, and I am weak enough to confess that a failure would be a severe disappointment to me, leaving me no other compensation for years of patient research and study, but the cold comfort of the stoic: "*Non sibi res, sed se submittere rebus.*"

# APPENDIX.

## VALVERDE'S "GUIDE" TO THE INCA TREASURE BURIED IN THE LLANGANATI MOUNTAINS.

THE following is Mr. Spruce's translation of the "Derrotero" of Valverde, referred to in Chapter V. of this work. The introductory remark, or title (not in very choice Castilian), is that of the copyist.

(Guide or Route, which Valverde left in Spain, where death overtook him, having gone from the mountains of Llanganati, which he entered many times, and carried off a great quantity of gold; and the king commanded the corregidors of Tacunga and Ambato to search for the treasure: which order and guide are preserved in one of the offices of Tacunga.)

"Placed in the town of Pillaro, ask for the farm of Moya, and sleep (the first night) a good distance above it; and ask there for the mountain of Guapa, from whose top, if the day be fine, look to the east, so that thy back be towards the town of Ambato, and from thence thou shalt perceive the three Cerros Llanganati, in the form of a triangle, on whose declivity there is a lake, made by hand, into which the ancients threw the gold they had prepared for the ransom of the Inca when they heard of his death. From the same Cerro Guapa thou mayest see also the forest, and in it a clump of *Sangurimas* standing out of the said forest, and another clump which they call *Flechas* (arrows), and these clumps are the principal mark for the which thou shalt aim, leaving them a little on the left hand. Go forward from Guapa in the direction and with the signals indicated, and a good way ahead, having passed some cattle-farms, thou shalt come on a wide morass, over which thou must cross, and coming out on the other side thou shalt see on the left-hand, a short way off, a *jucál* on a hill-side, through which thou must pass. Having got through the *jucál*, thou wilt see two small lakes called "Los Anteojos" (the spectacles) from having between them a point of land like to a nose.

"From this place thou mayest again descry the Cerros Llanganati, the same as thou sawest them from the top of Guapa, and I warn thee to leave the said lakes on the left, and that in front of the point or "nose" there is a plain, which is the sleeping-place. There thou must leave thy horses, for they can go no further. Following now on foot in the same direction, thou shalt come on a great black lake, the which leave on thy left hand, and beyond it seek to descend along the hill-side in such a way that thou mayest reach a ravine, down which comes a waterfall: and here thou shalt find a bridge of three poles, or if it do not still exist thou shalt put another in the most convenient place and pass over it. And having gone on a little way in the forest, seek out the hut which served to sleep in, or the remains of it. Having passed the night there, go on thy way the following day through the forest in the same direction, till thou reach another deep dry ravine, across which thou must throw a bridge and pass over it slowly and cautiously, for the ravine is very deep; that is, if thou succeed not in finding the pass which exists. Go forward and look for the signs of another sleeping-place, which, I assure thee, thou canst not fail to see in the fragments of pottery and other marks, because the Indians are continually passing along there. Go on thy way, and thou shalt see a mountain which is all of *margasitas* (pyrites), the which leave on the left hand, and I warn thee that thou must go round it in this fashion [symbol]. On this side thou wilt find a *pajonál* (pasture) in a small plain which having crossed thou wilt come on a *cañon* between two hills, which is the way of the Inca. From thence as thou goest along thou shalt see the entrance of the *socabón* (tunnel), which is in the form of a church-porch. Having come through the cañon, and gone a good distance beyond, thou wilt perceive a cascade which descends from an offshoot of the Cerro Llanganati, and runs into a quaking bog on the right hand; and without passing the stream in the said bog there is much gold, so that putting in thy hand what thou shalt gather at the bottom is grains of gold. To ascend the mountain, leave the bog and go along to the right, and pass above the cascade, going round the offshoot of the mountain. And if by chance the mouth of the socabon be closed with certain herbs which they call "*salvaje*," remove them, and thou wilt find the entrance. And on the left-hand side of the mountain thou mayest see the '*Guayra*' (for thus the ancients called the furnace where they founded metals), which is nailed with golden nails. And to reach the third mountain, if thou canst not pass in front of the socabon, it is the same thing to pass behind it, for the water of the lake falls into it.

"If thou lose thyself in the forest, seek the river, follow it on the right bank; lower down take to the beach, and thou wilt reach the cañon in such sort that, although thou seek to pass it, thou wilt not find where; climb, therefore, the mountain on the right-hand, and in this manner thou canst by no means miss thy way."

The foreign words contained in the foregoing "Derrotero" are explained in the pamphlet of Mr. Spruce, to which I must refer the reader for particulars. Mr. Spruce also gives a description of the localities enumerated in the "Guide." His explanations and suggestions may prove of great value to some enterprising American who ventures to explore the fastnesses of the Llanganati mountains, in search of the treasure. The question is highly exciting, and ought to be solved.

www.ingramcontent.com/pod-product-compliance
Lightning Source LLC
LaVergne TN
LVHW020104110826
845151LV00001B/59

* 9 7 8 1 4 2 5 5 4 4 4 1 6 *